T[...]

John Short. Even [...]
possession of drug paraphernalia and stolen
credit cards, his arrogance showed through
in a defiantly smiling mug shot. Later, he attracted wife-to-be Candy Austin with his
cocky persona and macho posturing. His
dream of having it all eventually became his
nightmare—and his undoing.

THE COP

George Brejack. With an almost eerie sixth
sense, the bottomed out homicide detective
once could have picked a killer from a
crowd, or figured out where victims' bones
were buried. It was this talent, singleminded
dedication and lust for excitement that had
built his awesome reputation. Younger cops
had dismissed him as an old man whose great
day had passed. With the Candy Short
murder file in hand, George Brejack proved
them all wrong.

BURIED
MISTAKES

MICHAEL KAPLAN is a journalist based in
New York City. He has written for *GQ*, *Premiere*,
and *Interview*. This is his first book.

BURIED
MISTAKES

Michael Kaplan

AN ONYX BOOK

For my parents,
Stanley and Gladys Kaplan

ONYX
Published by the Penguin Group
Penguin Books USA Inc., 375 Hudson Street,
New York, New York 10014, U.S.A.
Penguin Books Ltd, 27 Wrights Lane,
London W8 5TZ, England
Penguin Books Australia Ltd, Ringwood,
Victoria, Australia
Penguin Books Canada Ltd, 10 Alcorn Avenue,
Toronto, Ontario, Canada M4V 3B2
Penguin Books (N.Z.) Ltd, 182–190 Wairau Road,
Auckland 10, New Zealand

Penguin Books Ltd, Registered Offices:
Harmondsworth, Middlesex, England

First published by Onyx, an imprint of New American Library,
a division of Penguin Books USA Inc.

First Printing, July, 1992
10 9 8 7 6 5 4 3 2 1

Copyright © Michael Kaplan and George Brejack, 1992
All rights reserved

ACKNOWLEDGMENTS

Buried Mistakes would have been virtually impossible to write without the participation of Lieutenant George J. Brejack. He provided otherwise unobtainable information and personal recollections. George's eye for memorable details and his frank point of view were both extraordinarily beneficial. As close to a co-author as a non-writer can get, George J. Brejack dedicates his involvement with this book to the memory of his mother, Christine Eckhart Brejack: "I pray for you quietly. I think of you often. I love you always."

Countless other people have been generous with their time, agreeing to be interviewed about various (often painful) aspects of the Candy Short case. While I am indebted to all of my sources, five people deserve a special thanks: Fred and Helen Austin, Steve Brizek, and Joe and Betty Frank. They all played key roles in the investigation of the murder as well as in the researching of this book.

My agent, Nick Ellison, was inspiring, available, and insightful. Kevin Mulroy, my editor, took a chance on a first-time author and helped shape the manuscript. During the first days of the project, Kenneth Petrie went out of his way to provide legal counseling. A trusted colleague and a good friend, Anne M. Russell offered invaluable advice when she line edited an early draft of *Buried Mistakes.* Steve Tager deserves a hearty slap on the back (not to mention the Peking duck dinner that I still owe him) for passing my book proposal on to Kevin Mulroy in the first place.

Without the aid of Passaic County's law enforcement agencies, this book would have been more difficult to write and less enlightening to read. Ronald S. Fava (the prosecutor of Passaic County) and Ed Englehardt (the sheriff of Passaic County) both lent their cooperation to this project. For that, I salute them.

Additional gratitude goes out to those who've offered various forms of support during the last three years. Thanks to Jane Cofer, Chuck Dean, Randi Kaplan, Ron Kaplan, Rose Kirschner, Dr. Glen Landesman, Kirby McCauley, Mary Nance-Tager, Steve Weil, and Dottie Wilson.

Words can not express my thanks to Melodie DeWitt. Watching this project progress from its earliest stages, she graciously endured the rough patches and offered encouragement all along the way. The value of her advice and unwavering faith (not to mention tolerance for late nights, early mornings, and lost weekends at the word processor) can not be overstated.

AUTHOR'S NOTE

Buried Mistakes is a work of nonfiction. The events depicted in this book are true. Although much of the dialogue is derived from personal interviews, police records, and court transcripts, in many instances it has been reconstructed based on interviews with relevant individuals. Additionally, some scenes have been dramatically recreated in order to portray most effectively the personalities of the people involved in this story and the atmosphere surrounding the events upon which this book is based. In several instances, portions of the criminal investigation have been combined or reconfigured to aid the narrative. The go-go dancer in chapter four is a composite character.

In order to preserve privacy, some names and identifying details have been changed. That is the case for all but the following people: the Austins, the Brejacks, Steve Brizek, Odessa Brown, the Capalbos, Pat Caserta, the Chamberlains, Mike Ferranti, the Fishmans, the Franks, Frank Graves, the Halberts, Clinton Hatchet, Judge Vincent E. Hull, Gail Hunter, Ernest Hutchinson, Everett Johnesee, Marty Kayne, Diane Lovejoy, Dr. Corrie May, the McCumbers, Jack Meurer, the Milanos, William Milne, John Nativo, Chuck Nolan, Bill Plant, Mary Anne Seegers, the Shorts, the Suarezes, Dr. William Van Vooren, and Gene Wilhowsky. Any similarity between fictitious names used and those of living persons is, of course, entirely coincidental.

PART ONE

June 22, 1981

CANDY

"I'll live to piss on your grave."
"And I'll haunt you from it for the rest of your life."
—A prophetic exchange between John and Candy Short

CHAPTER
1

A police car cruised through the darkened parking lot of Willowbrook Mall. Just two hours earlier, last-minute shoppers had battled for spaces and filled the stores. But now, at ten-thirty P.M., the shopping center was deserted. Driving from one end of the asphalt sprawl to the other, Patrolman Bill Plant kept an eye open for any kids or vagrants hanging around the empty mall. Plant made his way around a cluster of construction trailers, and had nearly completed his nightly route when he noticed a lone automobile parked in the middle of the lot.

The officer approached it cautiously and rolled to a stop near the driver's side. He turned on a spotlight and illuminated a gold Cutlass. The spot played over the vinyl interior, lighting it up like a sound stage. He saw no keys in the ignition, and assumed that a shopper's automobile had broken down earlier in the evening.

Judging from the coupons and baby photos scattered on the front seat, the vehicle probably belonged to a woman. Most likely, she or her husband would return the next morning to pick it up. Not bothering to write a report— this sort of thing happened all the time—he killed the light and proceeded on his rounds.

Later that evening, inside a home near the mall, the front doorbell rang. It was followed by the sound of loud, urgent knocking. In the upstairs bedroom Fred Austin awoke with a start, his eyes suddenly wide open. Lying alongside him, his wife Helen looked annoyed. She asked if their middle daughter, twenty-six-year-old Jeanne, had forgotten her keys. "I don't know," Fred replied, getting out of bed. "I don't know who the hell it could be at this hour."

Dressed in nothing but boxer shorts and a T-shirt, Fred made his way downstairs to the living room of the small Cape Cod cottage-style house in Belleville, New Jersey. Skinny and gray-haired, with a bulbous nose, bright blue eyes, and a slightly stooped walk, the fifty-six-year-old man bristled with annoyance. It was nearly eleven-thirty on the evening of Monday, June 22, 1981, and Fred routinely rose early for his job as an electrical sign repairman. He needed his rest and did not appreciate being prematurely roused from slumber. In case it happened to be Jeanne, he'd remind his daughter that if she's old enough to get married (her wedding was scheduled to take place later that year) she's old enough to remember her house keys.

But somebody other than Jeanne interrupted Fred Austin's sleep. He opened the door to find his youngest daughter's husband, twenty-eight-year-old John Short, facing him. Instead of his usual blue jeans and T-shirt, Short had on a freshly pressed sport shirt and black dress slacks. His longish brown hair neatly combed and his face freshly shaven, John looked like he was ready for a big date. His lean physique and angularly sculpted facial structure usually gave him a rakishly handsome look. Tonight, however, Short seemed agitated and worried. His overly confident demeanor appeared to have been drained and replaced by one of uncharacteristic concern.

More surprising than John's appearance was the fact that he had Jessica, his and Candy's two-year-old daughter, with him. Never mind that Candy and John lived in a garden apartment just up the block, his son-in-law's presence confused Fred. During the last few years he had become accustomed to a lot of John Short's odd behavior, but this late-night visit was a shock. If anything, John usually acted more removed and distant than most folks would consider normal. Tonight, however, John seemed to be unduly concerned about something.

"Where's Candy?" Short asked, inquiring after his wife. "She's not at home."

"We thought she went shopping with you," Fred said, stepping away from the door to let John into the house.

"No. I had a business meeting tonight. Candy left Jesse with Betty and Joe." He gestured next door, toward the home where Helen's cousins Betty and Joe Frank lived. "I just stopped there to pick her up, and they said Candy was at the Willowbrook Mall."

Helen came downstairs. Wearing a housecoat over her robe, the fifty-seven-year-old woman was trim and handsome, with tightly curled blond hair and a perpetually concerned manner. She reached over and took the baby away from John. Uneasy, but not yet upset about Candy, Helen figured that her daughter would come bounding into the house any minute now. She'd be smiling and bubbly, laughing about how she ran into an old friend and forgot to call to say that she'd be home late.

Beyond that, John's concern warmed Helen, who had never before seen him so worried about his wife. In a strange way, Helen was touched. She'd always had a soft spot for her son-in-law, feeling in her heart that someday he would come around and become the caring husband that Candy rightfully desired. Maybe, she figured, after the recent spate of arguing and a short-lived separation, things were finally working themselves out. Maybe John's concern indicated that the marriage was taking a positive turn.

Leaving the sleeping child, the three adults repaired to the kitchen. John insisted that he wanted to go out and search for Candy. Making eye contact with Fred, he continually expressed concern for his errant wife. Helen made a few telephone calls, checking in with Candy's friends and asking if they'd seen her. After getting no leads she tried Judy Halbert, Candy's best friend from high school.

Judy's mother answered the phone at about eleven-forty and hollered upstairs to her daughter, asking whether or not she had been with Candy. "I haven't seen her!" Judy yelled back, confident that it was nothing to worry about, that it would be just like Candy to lose track of the time.

As Helen hung up the phone, John jumped to his feet. "That's it," he said. "We should go to the mall and look for her." He turned toward Fred, apparently waiting for some kind of a response.

Finally Fred said what John wanted to hear: "Hang on a minute, and I'll come with you."

Fred went upstairs and put on a pair of chinos. While he wondered what had happened to his daughter, Fred reflected on how typical this was of John's behavior. He always asked for everybody else's help instead of doing things for himself. Why John couldn't go on his own to look for her made no sense. It only takes one man, after all, to find a car. If he's so goddamned concerned, why doesn't *he* take the drive out there and let the rest of the family sleep?

But Fred got his keys and wallet, swallowed hard, and held back his annoyance. In order to keep from getting Helen and Candy worked up he regularly avoided confrontations with his son-in-law, and this evening would be no exception. Heading back downstairs, Candy's father resigned himself to a late night.

The two men left the house and walked toward Fred's blue Chevrolet Nova. John's gray pickup truck and his parents' Pinto (which he was minding while they vacationed in Scotland) were both parked around the corner, near his and Candy's apartment. Helen closed the door behind them. As she seated herself at the kitchen table she suddenly felt a wave of nervousness wash over her. Hearing Fred backing his car out of the driveway confirmed the seriousness of the situation. While his wife worried, Fred rolled down the window and turned left on Passaic Avenue, heading in the direction of Route 3, a six-lane commercial highway that bisected Route 46 at the mall's entrance.

A few minutes later Helen heard a key in the door. She got up and walked toward the sound, picturing Candy in her mind's eye, as if she could summon her youngest daughter by sheer force of will.

"Hi, Mom." It was Jeanne. Helen registered a look of disappointment.

"What's wrong?" asked Jeanne, an attractive, petite woman with curly brown hair and an efficient demeanor.

"It's Candy. She's not home, and nobody seems to know where she is. Supposedly she went shopping, and Dad seems to think her car broke down. He and John just left to look for her."

"I'm sure she's okay," Jeanne said, playing down her concern in an effort to keep from alarming her mother any further.

A few minutes later Betty Frank stopped by. Short and thin, with neatly clipped gray hair and a pointy, beak-like nose, forty-year-old Betty was curious to see where Candy would turn out to have been. As the cousins talked, Jeanne quietly slipped down to the basement. There, out of her mother's earshot, she made phone calls to police departments and hospitals in neighboring towns, asking if any car accidents had been reported. None, they told her, that could have involved somebody matching her sister's description. After checking in with Tony Mancuso—Candy's high school sweetheart, who had recently spoken to her after months of being out of touch—and getting no news, she went back upstairs, where Betty and Helen sat on the couch.

"Maybe Candy took off," Betty hypothesized.

"Took off?" asked Helen, unsettled by this new wrinkle.

"You know, maybe she couldn't stand John anymore, and just left him."

A long silence followed as the three women considered the possibility, all of them agreeing that John was a lot to handle. Then Jeanne pointed out the improbability of such a scenario: "Candy would never leave without Jesse."

"That's true," Betty allowed, not bothering to mention how odd she found it that Candy had asked her to babysit in the first place. Except for a couple of instances in which Candy and John had attended friends' weddings, it was the first time she remembered Candy leaving Jesse with somebody else. On top of that, John rarely took his wife anywhere, least of all shopping. Earlier in the evening, Betty's husband Joe had suggested that perhaps the two of them were going to see a divorce lawyer. Considering the fragile state of their marriage, it was a perfectly plausible guess.

The women talked for a few more minutes before Betty got up to leave. She hugged Helen, asked her cousin to call as soon as word came through about Candy, and walked across the gravel yard to her home.

By the time Fred merged onto the highway, he and John had yet to exchange a single word. This was typical for the two men, neither of whom cared very much for the other. "My sons-in-law have to prove themselves to me," Fred often told his friends. "John's never done that."

At the moment, Fred was particularly ticked off. John had just spent Father's Day in his stuffy basement apartment, leaving Candy and Jesse to walk down the block without him and visit the Austins on their own. Things had been so stormy between the couple that John preferred to nap and watch television rather than spend the traditional family afternoon with his in-laws, wife, and daughter. Because he wouldn't give Candy enough money to buy a gift, she baked her father a peach pie for the occasion. John received nothing this year. Moping around the Austins' house that day, Candy seemed completely melancholy and preoccupied. Such behavior went against her nature, and Fred held his son-in-law responsible for Candy's dour state. Now, as they passed diners and shut-down outlet stores, Fred finally turned to John and told him, "Keep your eyes open for Candy's car. It's probably on the side of the road."

Nervously tapping his foot and squirming in his seat, John looked away. He stared uneasily at the rolling commercial scenery, resting his chin in the palm of his hand. The night was especially muggy, and two open windows did very little to cool the car off. Pools of sweat formed sticky patches on the back of John's shirt, and the vinyl seat turned tacky. Impatient for the Willowbrook Mall to become visible, John watched roadside establishments with the restlessness of someone sitting through the coming attractions before a long-anticipated feature film.

Approaching the shopping center, Fred Austin experienced a mounting sense of dread. Never one to panic easily—he often bragged about the cool head he had maintained during World War II—the worst-case scenarios that somebody else might have played out were far from his mind. Yet as he got closer to their final destination Fred couldn't help but think that something was wrong, that horrible news was sneaking up from behind.

Maybe John's increasing nervousness tipped him off, or maybe it had to do with the fact that this trip was progressing so differently from what he had anticipated. Ten minutes into the twenty-minute ride to the mall he came to a depressing realization: With every tick of the odometer, the chances of Candy's car being broken down on the shoulder became increasingly remote. When Fred reached Willowbrook he steered his Nova into the darkened parking lot, driving with the tentativeness of a city dweller turning down a forbiding country lane.

The lot sat in pitch darkness. Surrounded by trees and service roads, it didn't even receive the ambient glow of nearby houses. Just past midnight, the mall's parking area resembled a tight little valley, surrounded on all sides by dense mountains. There was nothing but the highway to offer illumination, and from where Fred now drove it beckoned like a glowing oasis. He turned on the high beams, but they did next to no good. "Can't make out a damned thing in here," he muttered more to himself than to John.

Choosing not to reply, John glumly stared out the window, glanced down at his shoes, fiddled with his wedding band—eager to do anything but look Fred in the eye. The old man proceeded about half a mile inside the parking lot, heading toward Ohrbach's department store, where Candy typically parked. One empty space followed the next one. With nothing better to do, and unwilling to go home without his daughter, Fred guided the car in random patterns around the lot.

Finally, when he reached the end of one pass where he was forced to turn left or right, John leaned over, grasped Fred Austin's forearm, and spoke in a tender voice. Fred had never heard that tone from his son-in-law, and the sudden gentility made his skin crawl. "Dad," John said, using the paternal moniker for the first time. "Turn around."

Fred did as he was told and made his way back along the path they had just taken. He passed Sears Roebuck and turned left to keep from exiting the mall. Then John jerked his head to the right, his nervous energy palpable, and shouted, "Stop! Stop the car!"

Slamming on the brakes, Fred initially thought John had spotted a stray animal in his path. He swiveled toward his son-in-law. John said, "I saw the car. It's back there."

Letting out a long sigh, Fred turned the Nova around again. He drove in the direction that John had suggested and continued for about three hundred and thirty feet. Suddenly Candy's car showed itself in the glow of his headlights. Pulling up perpendicular to her gold Cutlass, Fred Austin mumbled, "Great. Now where's my daughter?"

Before the car even came to a complete stop, John had popped the door open and scrambled from the vehicle. He hit the blacktop running, bolted for the Cutlass, and darted from one side of the vehicle to the other. Fred opened his door and gingerly stepped out. Perspiration covered most of his body, and this whole situation suddenly seemed very creepy. Neither man said very much, but they both knew that nothing here was as it should be. John shouted, "Candy's in here!" "Door's locked!" "Need something to break the glass with!"

That's the way the words came to Fred, in disconnected fragments, blips of sound that he barely discerned. Fred dutifully went to the trunk, where he had a hammer. He fished around, found it, and handed the tool to John, who then smashed the front window of the car. The breaking glass made a horrible sound in the silence of the parking lot. It reverberated in Fred's ears as he saw the passenger-side door open and the top of his daughter's corpse flop out. The lower portion of her body remained crumpled in a heap on the floor of the car, wrapped in a yellow blanket. Whoever had done this had pulled Candy's shirt and bra up to her neck, revealing two large breasts and pitifully exposing the woman.

The sight left Fred feeling as if he had been suckerpunched. He stared at the blood that spotted the floor. Broken window glass littered the area around Candy's torso. Change, eyeglasses, and a checkbook lay scattered on the floor mats. A seamlessly ugly bruise ringed Candy's neck in purple, and a gaping red hole smeared with blood marred the area below her left breast. "She's dead," John said, staring down at his wife's body. "Candy's dead."

Fred turned away, and asked God to make this a bad dream. It can't be true, he kept hoping, nobody deserves to die this way. Not in such an undignified manner.

Spontaneously cursing and praying and babbling, Fred suddenly felt very alone and very vulnerable. John kept moving. He circled the Cutlass and muttered to himself. The reactions of the two men were as different as their personalities—one hyperkinetic and adrenalized, the other standing frozen. Finally, after what seemed like a very long time but was probably less than a minute, Fred said, "I'm going to call the police." John circled around the death scene like a buzzard, rubbing his forehead with his right hand.

A few miles north of Willowbrook Mall, Barbara Capalbo couldn't sleep. She read, then watched television, but found it impossible to shake an image from earlier that evening. She hated thinking about it, but the memory proved impossible to block.

Barbara and her sister Joan had been shopping at the mall, needing to pick up swimsuits for an upcoming trip to the Jersey shore. They pulled into Willowbrook at about seven o'clock in the evening. Parking places were difficult to come by, so they circled from one end of the lot to the other. Sitting in the passenger seat, Barbara searched for an empty spot. "Maybe we should try the upper level," she told her sister. Joan turned the car around and drove past Ohrbach's, toward the parking annex.

She remembered passing a blue/silver car. The windows were down, and the couple inside seemed to be arguing violently. Angry shouts emanated from the open window. Dark-haired and taller than the woman alongside him, the man in the driver's seat repeatedly slammed his hand against the steering wheel and let out a vile string of curses: "Fucking . . . Bitch . . . Cunt . . ." The light-haired woman next to him cowered toward the window, like a dog that had been kicked too many times and was now prepared to receive the worst pummeling of its sorry life.

The two young women stared as Joan slowly passed the feuding couple. "That poor girl," Barbara said. "I don't know why anybody would put up with an animal like that. I don't care how good-looking he is or how much money he's got. She should tell him to get lost."

Joan turned around for a final peek and agreed with her sister. "Any man who treated me that way, even one time, he'd get his walking papers."

They finally found a space in the upper parking deck, did their shopping, and returned to the car an hour or so later, intending to leave the mall. Joan had just shifted into reverse when Barbara suggested, "Let's drive back toward Ohrbach's and see if that maniac is still out there. I want to make sure the girl's okay."

Cruising past the area where the fight had taken place, the Capalbo sisters saw no car. Joan figured that they had straightened things out and gone home. Barbara disagreed, but she knew there was nothing more they could do.

Barbara Capalbo went to bed, tightly closed her eyes, and tried to sleep.

At ten minutes past midnight the mobile police radio squawked out information about an aggravated assault at Willowbrook Mall. Detective Billy McCann and Detective Sergeant Andrew Webster—two beefy, dark-haired plainclothesmen in their late thirties—were cruising near Route 3 when they took the call. McCann affixed a Kojak light with its magnetized bottom to the roof of their sedan as Webster swung into the passing lane. Siren wailing, the unmarked automobile sped to the crime scene.

Law enforcement in Wayne usually entailed rousting drunks and collaring teenage vandals; murder barely existed in the area's upper-middle-class towns, and the call sounded as if it would be routine. Then, en route to Willowbrook, they heard something on the radio that made this incident exceptional: The dispatcher requested an ambulance at the crime scene.

By the time they got there at twelve-thirty, the area was already thick with official vehicles. Police light

bathed the night sky. An ambulance pulled up to the
gold Cutlass. Webster noticed a young man on his knees
cradling a dead woman's head in his hands. He saw an
older fellow looking dazed and confused, leaning against
the car's front grille and smoking. After a few minutes a
patrolman cleared the two civilians from the scene, then
Webster proceeded to give the vehicle a preliminary inspection, careful not to touch anything.

Resembling a punch-drunk boxer who doesn't realize
that the fight's over, Fred Austin was led to one police
car. John had already taken the backseat of another. As
he put physical distance between himself and Candy, the
older man's lips moved, but no words came out. Finally
he gestured toward his Nova. A young, earnest uniformed cop assured him that they'd come back for it.
Fred nodded as he stumbled away from the action's
epicenter.

Another police car pulled up and Sergeant Jack
Meurer stepped out. Black bags loaded with cameras and
rolls of film weighed down his left shoulder as he approached the crime scene. He took out the Mamiya 4″ x
5″ camera, aimed inside the Cutlass, and began shooting.
Each burst of flash illuminated a piece of the murder:
blood, glass, an open purse with coins, a wallet and a
checkbook dumped on the floor. After he had graphically
captured the victim, two medics placed Candy's body on
a stretcher and maneuvered her toward the ambulance.

On the floor of the car directly below where Candy
had been left, Meurer noticed a key ring attached to a
plastic tag in the shape of a T-shirt. Seriffed type that
ran around a bold number 10 read, YOU'RE ALWAYS A
10 WITH US—NEW JERSEY QUALITY HOMES. At the time,
none of the law enforcers recognized it as being the name
of John Short's contracting company. But the forensics
man photographed it anyway.

Using metal probes so as not to smear the fingerprints,
Meurer lifted the items, inspected them, and wrote an
inventory of the automobile's contents in his notebook.

Then he photographed the victim on the stretcher. Grimy smears marked her pants, telling Meurer that she had been dragged somewhere. He noted that these stains should be compared with the dirt in the adjacent woods. He photographed her neck, with the single ring of purple around it, then glanced down to the bloodied puncture in her abdomen. He surmised that it had been made with a screwdriver or an ice pick. Whoever killed her, Meurer figured, grabbed the woman's neck and didn't let go. The guy was like a fucking pit bull. He wanted to tear her throat apart from the outside.

After the final flash, the ambulance attendants placed Candy inside a body bag and zipped it shut. Wrapped like a sick gift and loaded into the ambulance, she'd be delivered to nearby Paterson General Hospital. Later, at the Passaic County Medical Examiner's Office, Dr. William Van Vooren would perform an autopsy and search for the precise cause of her death, hoping that it would lead to the killer.

Meurer was no medic, but his inspection of the scene told him a good deal. The woman did not appear to have been raped, and this had been no ordinary robbery. Candy's killer took the time to rummage through her purse, leaving the impression that he was either looking for something specific or simply wanted to make it resemble a holdup. In a world where people get knifed for fifty cents, robbers don't leave behind credit cards and checkbooks. Meurer surmised that the murderer had passionately hated his victim. In addition, he also guessed that the killer performed some kind of heavy labor that necessitated using his hands. Without the emotional and physical factors in his favor, he would never have been able to hold on to that one area of her neck for the two minutes that it takes to strangle a struggling, squirming person.

Things wound down at the crime scene. A flatbed tow truck pulled up, and attendants loaded the Cutlass. As patrolmen reinspected the area for further scraps of evidence, the truck's driver departed for the nearby New Jersey State Police barracks where crime scene technicians waited to examine the car for evidence. McCann looked around and realized there was nothing left for him and Webster to do there. "Might as well go back to the station," he said. "We'll see what the deal is with those two guys."

On the way to headquarters, the officers considered possible scenarios. They kept coming back to the same thing: Right off the bat, the husband seemed guilty. Something was fishy about the guy's attitude. John seemed unusually composed for somebody who just stumbled upon such an ugly, messy murder. Their next consideration, had either man voiced it, would most likely have been of a more practical nature. Solving a crime of this magnitude would leave an enduringly positive mark on any cop's record and very possibly lead to a promotion.

The Wayne police station was part of a modern municipal complex that also housed the town's public library, city hall, and courthouse. Before McCann and Webster walked across the manicured lawn and entered the detective bureau, Fred and John had already been sequestered in different rooms. At two-thirty in the morning they were each apprised of the situation. "Candy is dead," Webster and McCann told them separately. "From here on in her death is a police matter that's under full investigation. All persons, including you, are suspects."

Further shaken up by the finality of all this, Fred was escorted to a patrol room, briefly questioned, and told to wait. Too shocked to verbally provide any concrete information, he offered to do a sketch of the circuitous path John led him on in the mall's parking lot. It was a scribbled rendering that could hardly be called a map. He put down the pencil and thought of Helen.

"Can I make a call home to my wife?" Fred asked Detective McCann, who was charged with guarding him while Webster questioned John.

"No phone calls right now." Seeing the devastation in the man's face, McCann softened slightly, yet remained resolute. "Sorry about that, but it's department policy in this kind of case." He didn't have the heart to remind Fred that he was considered a possible suspect in his daughter's murder.

Just beginning to accept the reality of Candy's death, and concerned about what his wife would be thinking, Fred felt more distraught than he realized was possible. He couldn't have known that Helen and Jeanne were keeping an all-night vigil. Sporadically dozing off and frequently phoning local police departments, they asked the same question over and over again. "Have any accidents been reported?" Jeanne ceaselessly inquired, half hoping that it was only an accident and nothing worse. Helen tried in vain to get a handle on what had happened to her family, such a fragile unit that until several hours earlier had seemed so solidly anchored.

While Fred's requests for a phone call were continually rebuffed, John sat in a conference room at the opposite end of the wing. Detective Sergeant Andrew Webster punched a cassette machine's record button and began questioning the man across the table. John Short had not been arrested, and agreed to speak voluntarily. But Webster remained cognizant of Short's current status: Besides being the deceased's husband he was also a likely suspect.

For both Short and Webster the questioning was relatively uneventful, and the conversation shed little light. Webster continued to believe that Short had committed the crime, but Short offered nothing that would support such a suspicion. And neither person needed to spend the early-morning hours speaking to somebody he didn't like in order to learn so little.

Under questioning, John maintained an impressively high degree of composure. The man's wife had died, the police clearly viewed him as a suspect, but he acted as if this were a social call. If Webster knew anything about

John Short's past, however, the officer would have realized that up till now authority figures had intimidated him very little. As a teenager, Short was arrested for possession of drug paraphernalia and stolen credit cards. Through the entire arrest process, though, John had displayed a hubris that's evident in his mug shot. Told to turn toward the police photographer, John smiled. In his arrest photo he looked happier than most kids do when they're snapped for graduation portraits.

Imagining that he'd get nowhere with a line of questioning about the relationship between John and Candy, Webster started out softly, asking Short to summarize how he'd spent the evening on which Candy was murdered. John lit a Marlboro Light and began talking. "I got home from work at about five and played with the baby until dinnertime, which was about five forty-five. We finished eating at six-fifteen, then I laid down in the bedroom for a while and read. Candy came in and we fooled around a little bit. At six-thirty she got changed and left with the baby. She was going shopping for dance tights, and our neighbor down the block, Candy's cousin, had agreed to watch Jesse. Then I went into the kitchen, had some dessert, got changed, and stopped at the deli for cigarettes before driving to West Orange. I was scheduled to meet with a man named David Jones and give him an estimate on some exterior home repairs. I got lost on my way up there and arrived a half hour late. The meeting lasted until about eleven-ten. I got home twenty minutes later and noticed that Candy wasn't around."

Webster walked Short through the rest of the evening, having him describe the car ride to the mall and the discovery of his wife's body. "Upon smashing the passenger side window and opening that door," he asked, "what did you first discover?"

"My wife's arm. I saw an arm sticking out from under the blanket."

"After opening the door, did you notice anything in particular that drew your attention to her?"

"Her face, it was black-and-blue. Her breasts were exposed."

"Do you know of any particular person who may have wanted to cause harm to your wife?"

"No."

With that last answer, the interview ended. At quarter to six in the morning everybody was exhausted and eager to leave the station house. McCann drove Fred and John to the mall so they could retrieve the Nova. Candy's car had already been towed away as evidence, and maintenance men had scrubbed the area clean of debris. Early-morning shoppers found no hint of what had taken place the previous night.

Without comment, Fred and John got into the car and drove back to Belleville. Just like the trip to the mall, the ride home was silent. Uncommunicative under the best of circumstances, in this case neither man had anything to say. Fred drove slow and steady, maintaining a speed of fifty-five miles per hour in the center lane. Occasionally he glanced into the rearview mirror. An unmarked sedan with Webster and McCann in the front seat followed close behind.

CHAPTER
2

Betty Frank's alarm clock went off at six o'clock on the morning of June 23rd. Clumsily feeling around the back of the clock, she punched a button to make it stop buzzing and turned on the radio. After waking up Joe, Betty went downstairs and loaded the Mr. Coffee. She dressed quickly, eager to run next door and make sure that Candy had gotten home safely.

As she stepped outside, Betty heard cars approaching around the corner. They came to a stop in the gravelly area sandwiched between her house and the Austin place. "Oh my god," she said, holding a hand to her lips.

She saw John and Fred sluggishly climb out of the Nova. Fred looked terrible, exhausted and washed out. A man resigned to an awful fate, he focused on the ground as he exited the car, avoiding any sights that would remind him of Candy. Eyes rimmed in black, hair sticking out in several directions, Fred's all-night ordeal seemed to have instantly aged him. John walked with a dejected gait, a hangdog expression marking his face. The two plainclothesmen, Webster and McCann, were all grim business. Fred Austin's younger brother, Harry, brought up the rear, driving in his own car.

A policeman in nearby Nutley, he was the person that Fred chose to contact when the Wayne police finally broke down and allowed him a single telephone call.

Big and gruff and short-tempered, fifty-two-year-old Harry Austin instantly wanted to get involved in the investigation.

Betty approached him and noticed that the man looked emotionally shattered. As a patrolman he routinely witnessed all kinds of ugly situations, but this was different; this was family. He couldn't understand why somebody would kill his niece, such a lovely girl who had never hurt anyone. Then he looked over at John, and a rush of fury suddenly surged inside him. Harry struggled to keep from grabbing the guy by the collar and beating the truth out of him. Twenty-four years of police work had left Fred's brother with a good deal of cop's intuition, and from the moment he met John three years ago he had instinctively believed that Candy's love interest was no good.

Concerning this particular incident, Harry felt certain that John knew more than he admitted. But he silently acknowledged that raising the point with Fred and his sister-in-law would result in unnecessary and unwelcome tension. Putting himself in the place of Webster and McCann, he also came to realize that outside interference would only serve to muddle things.

Betty turned to him and reluctantly asked, "Was there some kind of an accident, Harry? Is Candy all right?"

Harry turned away from Betty. He averted his eyes from hers so as to avoid seeing the hurt that would surely be there. "They found her in the car," he said. "She was murdered."

Retreating back toward her own house, Betty's head throbbed and her knees felt like Silly Putty. She had prepared herself for something horrible, but this was far worse—so much more gruesome than what she had anticipated. As Betty broke the news to her husband and three children, a small fracas was about to erupt on the walkway leading up to the Austins' home.

Upon seeing the group of men approaching, Jeanne opened the front door and bolted outside. She demanded to know what had happened to her sister. Overbearing and intense during times of stress, she called on all of her lawyerly jargon and hurled it at the cops; she worked for an attorney, and her legal vocabulary was extensive. Taken aback by the young woman's aggressive stance, Webster and McCann tried to calm her, unsuccessfully assuring Jeanne that things were as under control as could be expected.

While Helen remained in the house, crying and holding the motherless baby Jesse in her arms, Jeanne assumed the role that she would maintain throughout the investigation. She became the family's mouthpiece and primary representative. Exercising her knack for getting what she wanted, Jeanne requested all the details of the death and wanted to know precisely how the investigation would proceed. Besides working for an attorney, the middle Austin girl had a strong, outgoing, and take-charge personality, making her the only member of a basically reserved family who'd be suited for the task.

As the two cops explained what would happen over the next couple of days—many pacifying generalities about scouring the area for witnesses, finding anybody who might have had a grudge against Candy, figuring out the exact cause of her death—John walked toward the house like a zombie. He headed straight for Helen, took the woman in his arms, and bawled onto her shoulder. "My baby!" he cried out, loud and shrill. "They took my baby away from me!"

Ironically, John's behavior served Helen well for the time being. A woman with a motherly instinct, Helen needed somebody to protect and coddle. It allowed the reality of what had happened to sink in slowly, and John became the child who was needy for her comforting. While Fred made funeral arrangements and Jeanne held a swell of reporters at bay, John sat on the couch and grasped his mother-in-law's hand. He kept Jesse cradled in his lap like a kitten and rocked the crying baby until she fell asleep. "I saw her wedding ring," he lied. "It was turned around so that the muggers couldn't get at it."

John worked as an independent building contractor, and the three or four men he employed typically congregated on the gravelly drive near the Austins' home each morning. Taking the five-minute drive down the hill from his apartment to their house, John usually met the guys and they piled into a truck or two, then drove off to whatever project they were working on. When Dan Solowe, the most punctual of the laborers, showed up that morning, John couldn't bring himself to face the man. He remained on the couch, crying without tears and refusing to let go of Helen's hand.

True to form, Jeanne took it upon herself to break the news. Walking out the back door, Jeanne strolled through the yard where she and Candy had played as little girls. Suddenly everything in her field of vision resonated with memories of the dead sibling, and Jeanne began to fully understand that she'd never see Candy alive again. "My sister was murdered," she told John's employee in a strangely matter-of-fact way, slowly hearing the acknowledgment from her own mouth for the very first time. Jeanne shielded her eyes from the early morning sun and saw Dan continuing to stand there, so unresponsive that she wasn't sure whether or not he heard her. "There's been a death in the family, and John's not working today," Jeanne repeated.

Inside the house Helen suggested to John that he call his parents and notify them of the tragedy. "I can't do that," he told his mother-in-law. "They're in Scotland right now, touring somewhere through the countryside, and I have no way of reaching them."

The response left Helen feeling particularly sorry for John. It saddened her that he had such a distant relationship with his folks, and this drove the point home: Even in his great time of need, John could not rely on his mother and father for emotional support. John usually attributed the breakdown of the family fabric to his pursuit of carpentry instead of college. "My father and I never really got along after I decided to work rather than attend school," he'd say, neglecting to mention that the relationship with his stern, Scots old man began to deteriorate long before then. It was one thing, Helen believed, that attracted John to Candy in the first place. Marrying her had provided him with a ready-made family. However, while he craved familial closeness, he also found it impossible to express his emotions like a true member of the household.

That, too, inevitably elicited pity from Helen. She often saw John as a confused, mixed-up man who hid his most basic feelings behind a blustery exterior. Even when he unapologetically arrived late for family functions, or publicly belittled Candy, or refused to move the family out of their dreary basement apartment and into a private home (he was, after all, a building contractor, and had access to many suitable properties), Helen mothered this angry young man who never knew how to drop his guard.

John handed the baby over to her and went into the kitchen to pour himself a cup of coffee. Friends and relatives already filled the house, forcing him to wade through a crowd of people who blocked the doorway and acknowledged him in only the most cursory way.

Belleville was the kind of town where neighbors pulled together during times of crisis, and the news of Candy's death traveled quickly. These old friends of the Austins, many of whom had heard about John but never actually met him, now hoped to help Fred and Helen through their hour of need. They arrived one by one, carrying flowers and platters of food, filling the house with items that would have been a delight on any other day. Today, however, all the goods only served to remind Fred and Helen that their daughter was dead.

When Judy Halbert's parents, Gloria and Chick, arrived, Fred hugged Gloria and practically burst into tears as he said, "Candy's face was so blown up and swollen, there's nothing they can do to bring it down. We have to have a closed casket."

Confident that the Austins were in good hands with so many people there to comfort them, Betty prepared to go home. She took the day off from her job as a teacher's aide, but happened to have a few chores to do around the house. "Do you want me to take Jesse?" Betty asked Helen, anticipating that things would be easier without the little girl underfoot.

"No." Helen held the child tightly and added, "She's my baby now."

As the day progressed, John's behavior became increasingly perplexing. The extreme outward displays of emotion seemed odd to those who knew him. Typically private about his feelings, John now appeared to be a single exposed nerve.

Loudly whining and carrying on, he spouted crackpot theories as to who had killed his wife. "The niggers did it," he told Harry at one moment. Then he confided to Fred that an upstairs neighbor of his didn't get along well with Candy. "If I find out that that son of a bitch murdered my wife, I'll take care of the guy myself," he vowed.

In the early afternoon he cornered Joe Frank in the kitchen and described his attempts to give mouth-to-mouth resuscitation to Candy. Fred overheard the conversation and felt like coldcocking his son-in-law. He didn't remember John doing anything of the sort. But fearing that he'd get Helen aggravated, Fred declined to verbally or physically intervene. Becoming increasingly melodramatic, the grieving widower painted an aural picture of his lifesaving heroics. "I looked into her face and she had her eyes open," John recounted. "One pupil was fixed, and the other eye had a glimmer."

From the couple of years that thirty-three-year-old Joe had spent working as a medical technician, he knew that these pre-death symptoms might be apparent in someone who had just suffered a stroke—but a bad heart had not killed Candy. "Well, maybe the lighting made it look that way," said the thin, reddish-haired man who usually got a kick out of John's tall tales and enjoyed encouraging them. This time, however, he attempted to gracefully bow out of the conversation while simultaneously placating a person who was obviously fabricating a story. "You never know," Joe added, nervously rubbing his mustache. "A lot of things could give you that impression."

John's display embarrassed Fred and created an air of uneasiness throughout the room. It sealed Harry's opinion of John: guilty as charged. In the policeman's mind there was no question about who had committed the murder. But this was not the right time to broach the subject with Fred. Instead, Harry made an offer that was both more subtle and more effective than finger-pointing.

"Rather than burying Candy in her own plot, why don't we put her alongside my ex-wife?" Harry gently suggested to his brother. Having remarried, Harry had decided he'd rather be buried alongside his current wife, and that left the second half of a double plot available at the small, bucolic Vincent Methodist Cemetery in Nutley.

Agreeable to nearly any suggestion, Fred said that would be fine. As Harry made the necessary telephone calls, he remained mum about his true reasons for wanting Candy to join his wife. But he later voiced them to Joe Frank: "Good. Now that murderous bastard can't be buried next to Candy. He won't have the satisfaction of torturing her for an eternity."

With the exception of Harry, members of the Austin family found it impossible not to feel some sympathy for John Short. Everybody mourns in his own fashion, the reasoning went, and if John is a little ostentatious with his grief, well, so be it. The Austins were basically simple, good, God-fearing people. They understood the importance of supporting kin in difficult times, and couldn't fathom the possibility that John's emotions would be anything less than genuine.

Viewing this as a pressure-inducing situation for everybody, and acknowledging John's standing as a member of the family (never mind that it was only through wedlock), they instinctively stood by him. Even if John had not been the ideal husband, and his marriage to Candy had brought more grief than happiness, here he was, standing alongside Fred and Helen mourning the death of their offspring. Besides, the grieving parents loved Jesse, and John was definitely the link to their granddaughter.

People who didn't know John so well found his brand of grieving to be a bit histrionic. "What the hell is his problem?" an aunt of Candy's wondered, as John paraded from one end of the kitchen to the other, crying about the death of Candy and braying over being left all alone.

Finally Harry suggested that John go down to the spare bedroom in the basement and get a little rest. Ostensibly it would be an opportunity for John to catch up on much-needed sleep. In reality, however, Harry had noticed how John's caterwauling was grating on his brother's nerves, and he knew that mild-mannered Fred would never issue a word of complaint.

Physically and emotionally drained, John lay down on the bed in the basement. One week later, from this very room, he placed a call to Dan Solowe, the construction man that Jeanne had sent home a few hours earlier. Dan answered the phone, and John asked him for a favor. "I want you to meet me at my apartment and give me a hand with cleaning the place out. I'm getting rid of Candy's stuff. I don't want any of it around."

Eager to avoid upsetting Short, Solowe acquiesced to the seemingly odd request. He later expressed surprise at John's noticeable lack of emotion as Candy's belongings were tossed into a nearby dumpster.

Detective Andrew Webster was keyed up to be working on his first murder after fourteen years in law enforcement. Operating on adrenaline in place of sleep, the large, imposing forty-four-year-old man began the first of several virtual around-the-clock shifts. A day after the murder at 8:30 A.M. he stopped at the Willowbrook Mall and questioned the manager of Sears Roebuck, the store near where Candy's car was found. Attempts to turn up a witness proved futile, and a short meeting at the office of David Jones, the prospective client that Short met with on the night of the murder, confirmed John's story.

Jones, a successful real-estate developer, agreed to be interviewed on the matter, but his responses were brief and hardly enlightening. He answered Andrew Webster's questions, yet avoided discussing any more than he had to. The only useful revelation stemmed from his acknowledgment that John Short had shuffled around the time of their meeting. "My office received a call at approximately five that day from John Short," Jones remembered. "I wasn't there at the time, and called him back approximately forty-five minutes later. John asked if he could change the appointment to another day, perhaps Tuesday night. He indicated that he had something to do, and that perhaps the weather conditions would prevent him from looking at the outside of the house. I asked that he make it some time that evening, and he agreed to be there between eight-thirty and nine."

While this information alone did nothing to pin the murder on John Short, the fact that he had wanted to reschedule the meeting indicated that Short had had other plans for the evening. Even so, the fact that Jones remembered nothing unusual about John's behavior weakened the case that McCann and Webster endeavored to build. Nevertheless, John Short seemed to be the only suspect who made sense. Hoping that somebody from the family could solidify that theory, Billy McCann called Jeanne to arrange an interview.

Because things were hectic at her home she agreed to meet the policemen at her Uncle Harry's place at seven-thirty that evening. Despite being understandably shaken up, Jeanne arrived there with the desire to dig deeply into her memory for any facts that could aid the investigation. However, like the other family members, she kept John and Candy's marital problems to herself. Beyond wanting to avoid implicating an innocent man, she believed that the couple's personal differences were their business. Dredging them up would be disrespectful to the memory of her dead sister. Besides, Jeanne rationalized, what did the marriage have to do with the murder? She let on that Candy rarely left Jesse alone, and acknowledged that her sister had been scheduled to be in a dance recital, yet added that Candy had mentioned nothing about needing to go to the mall in order to buy a pair of silver tights.

Striving to get at possible suspects who might have held some kind of a long-term grudge against Candy, McCann asked, "During that day, did Candy mention anything to you about old friends?"

"Yes," Jeanne remembered, "she mentioned Tony Mancuso, her boyfriend from high school. He had just gotten his own apartment in West Orange [coincidentally, the same town that Jones lived in]."

"Did Candy mention that she had intentions of contacting Tony?"

Jeanne said no, yet McCann made a mental note to pursue the Mancuso angle. For now, however, he decided to give it a rest, and switched over to a more general tack of questioning. "In your own words, Jeanne, will you tell me what type of woman Candy was?"

"She was a loving mother, close to her parents, and a loving wife. Candy enjoyed life. She was punctual and was good to people. Candy had no enemies and she respected everybody. She just lived for the baby and John."

Following the interview, the detectives proceeded to the Belle Maid Delicatessen, the small grocery store where John claimed to have stopped for cigarettes before going on to Jones's house. The woman who worked the cash register that evening could not say for sure whether or not she had seen John, and a canvas of the nearby complex of garden apartments where the couple lived produced similar, non-confirming reports.

By the time McCann returned to the police station, Dr. William Van Vooren had determined that the cause of Candy Short's death was asphyxiation due to manual strangulation. A potentially more illuminating message also awaited him. This one was from Barbara Capalbo, a woman who read about the murder in the newspaper that morning and claimed to have seen a violent incident in the shopping mall's parking lot. When questioned, however, she described the car as being bluish silver rather than gold. The detectives dismissed her as an unreliable witness.

Johnesee's Funeral Home was an impressive, solid-looking three-story building. Located on a congested main drag in Nutley—one of the towns that bordered Belleville—it was a brick structure with shiny white columns lined up along the front. A neatly manicured lawn served as a buffer against passing traffic. In an effort to make it resemble something other than the typical, clinically modern funeral home, the architects had tried to imbue it with a classic sense of timelessness.

During the two-day wake, which began a day after the killing, the casket was closed as Fred had predicted. Even those who had known Candy only in the most tangential way paid their respects; friends and relatives filed in and out of the downstairs room where the murdered woman's body rested. The days came and went in a blur for the Austins, all of them too absorbed in their own emotions to pay very much attention to the behavior of anybody else.

Over the course of the two days, many of John's friends dropped by as well. Guys from high school, people who knew him through work, a few couples that he and Candy were friends with, all filed in and out of John-

esee's. John spotted them and his behavior swung errati-
cally, guided by the depth of each person's relationship
with Candy. His psyche seemed to be the emotional
equivalent of a drunk behind the wheel of a skidding car
on ice.

When it suited John he sat with the immediate family.
He held Helen's hand and sobbed softly to himself, yet
never exactly cried. To those on the outside, John
seemed to be struggling for dignity in a very difficult
situation. If they had watched him long enough, however, they would have seen quite a transformation whenever he spotted one of his drinking buddies.

Still devastated by the death, Helen failed to notice
John's frequent forays downstairs to the smoking room.
There he sparked up one Marlboro Light after the other
and changed dramatically. It was as if he slipped out of
some mourner's shroud and back into a jester's costume.
Holding court for a few of the guys he knew, Short maintained a steady stream of patter and small talk, all the
while keeping an eye out for pretty girls.

Upon spotting his boyhood friends Steve Gottlieb and
Louie Derringer, both of whom were also in the construction business, Short ran up and greeted them with
a party host's exuberance. "Long time no see!" John
cried jubilantly. He wrapped an arm around the back of
Gottlieb's neck, drawing his friend close, and whispered
something in his ear. The two of them remained momentarily huddled together before breaking apart to the
sound of their raucous laughter.

Then, just as suddenly as John had turned jovial, he
broke up and appeared on the verge of tears. Turning to
Gottlieb and Derringer he wailed, "I loved her! I loved
this woman! I never cheated on her or anything!"

While John emoted, Derringer confided to Gottlieb,
"Now you know John's *really* bullshitting. I remember
him calling me at three in the morning after he screwed
some hooker in a hotel room. He locked his keys in the
car and I had to help him break in."

Nodding politely, but uncomfortable with the way this situation appeared to be unfolding, Steve stood silently for a moment before catching his wife's reproachful glance. Finally he turned to John and said, "Look, man, I'm broken up over this thing with Candy. I'm so sorry for you."

"Yeah," Short replied, with a shocking dismissive wave of his hand. "What are you gonna do?"

The widower took a couple of deep drags off his cigarette, then snuffed it out and headed back upstairs. Suddenly as solemn as a saint, he slid into his seat alongside Helen, where her hand was open and waiting for him to grasp it.

Others, less preoccupied by grief, found themselves doubting John's sincerity. Candy's aunt and uncle, Harry and Geri Austin, watched in horror when John exited the funeral home crying, but suddenly, after catching up to his friends outside, burst into gleeful laughter as he shared some inside joke with them. Then a few minutes later, when John met Candy's aunt and uncle at their car for a ride back to Belleville, his knees buckled and he collapsed onto the lip of grass that abutted the curb.

"He didn't faint," Harry muttered to himself, kneeling down and speaking to John from an intimate angle. "If you don't get your ass up, we're leaving you here."

Without a word, John rose to his feet and climbed into the car.

The burial took place three days after Candy's murder. Mourners filled the chapel to standing-room capacity, and town marshals were called in to direct traffic. A trio of uninvited law enforcers mingled among the guests. Billy McCann, Andrew Webster, and Howard Blakey (a thirty-eight-year-old investigator from the Passaic County Prosecutor's Office, who was assigned to the case) tried to mix in as mourners, but with their anxious faces, roving eyes, and jumpy behavior they looked about as natural as uptight narcs in a crack house. The three cops scribbled down notes and kept their eyes open for anybody who might be able to supply information. McCann fruitlessly searched for one person in particular, then he spotted Joe Frank.

The policeman hustled over to Joe and cuffed him on the back of the neck. It was intended to be a friendly greeting but came out as more of a slap. "What is it?" Joe asked, jumping back.

"Where is he?" McCann wanted to know.

"Where is who?"

"The boyfriend."

"The boyfriend?" For a few seconds Joe Frank couldn't figure out whom McCann was referring to. Then he spotted Candy's old high school sweetheart. "Oh. You mean Tony Mancuso. That's him over there, the guy with the beard."

He pointed toward a group of people in their early to mid-twenties, members of Candy's crowd from high school, and McCann headed over there in a flash. Dressed in a black sport jacket and white dress shirt, twenty-four-year-old Tony looked trim and handsome, affecting an artistically hip demeanor. An aspiring actor, he played at being the local bohemian.

"Tony," the policeman said, extending one hand in friendship and the other one holding a business card. "My name is Detective McCann, and I'm investigating the murder of Candy Short. I'd like you to come over to the Wayne police station and tell me anything you know that might assist us in our investigation."

Taking the card, Tony agreed to go there after the funeral. They settled on a time and McCann disappeared, slipping back into the crowd of Candy's friends and relatives, continuing his awkward search for anyone who might have something to tell him.

Silence followed McCann's departure. Then a guy piped up, "Hey, Tony, I think you're Dick Tracy's number-one suspect."

The joker's delivery fell flat, and Tony didn't laugh at

all. He got a funny vibe from McCann. It seemed that the officer wanted to see Tony for more than the little bits of background information he might be able to offer about Candy's high school years. He tried to put the patently absurd notion of himself as a murder suspect out of his mind, and struggled to think about Candy and the fine times they had shared. She had been a good kid, and Tony wanted to pay his last respects without distraction. But now he couldn't stop thinking about the way McCann had looked at him, as if he were waiting for Tony to blink.

The Candy Short funeral proved to be a prodigious event for McCann. Not only did he make contact with Mancuso, but he also scheduled a meeting with Betty and Joe Frank for later on that day. McCann stood at the back of the chapel during the service, and waited on the sidelines as the pallbearers loaded Candy's coffin into a silver-colored hearse.

Although they were well-meaning cops in all the basic ways—they had patience, knew the mechanics of solving crimes, wanted to do good for the public, and believed wholeheartedly in the importance of maintaining law and order—McCann and everybody else involved in the investigation lacked the skills that one develops by working murders on a regular basis. They didn't really know how to finesse a point rather than force it; the master sleuth's artistry eluded them.

Like most people who rise to comfortable levels of professional mediocrity, they couldn't find the self-analysis that would have told them how unsuited they really were to be working on a crime of this caliber. Had any of them possessed a special gift for investigation, he would have taken over the case and pieced it together independently of the others. Nobody took on that task.

The long funeral procession snaked down the street and proceeded to the cemetery. Once the last taillight in the line slipped from sight, Billy McCann went to work. He walked into the funeral home, found the funeral director's modest, sparsely furnished office, and introduced himself to Everett Johnesee, a tall, heavyset, middle-aged man. McCann wanted to interview the funeral director while the morning's events were still fresh in his mind.

"I'm trying to find a motive for this murder," the detective said. He seemed to announce this more for his own benefit than for Johnesee's. "I wonder if you have any thoughts on the matter."

"The deceased had no life insurance," Johnesee acknowledged. "But John said that he had some money in the bank. That's how he'll be paying for the funeral."

"Was there anything unusual about this particular funeral service?"

"Just that there were so many people here." The funeral director fidgeted with a paper clip, careful to avoid giving away any information that it would have been indiscreet to share. He had built a twenty-six-year career by maintaining client confidentiality, and he wasn't going to let some overly anxious cop destroy that now.

"Did you notice anything unusual about the husband's behavior?"

"Well . . ." He debated whether or not to reveal what he thought. Ultimately, considering the suspicious circumstances surrounding Candy's death, Johnesee decided that prudence might not be the best course. "Yes. His behavior was very odd. There was something false about John Short's grief. I've never seen somebody act the way he acted: simultaneously stingy over the burial and obviously in a state of mourning when his in-laws were around. Then every few minutes he'd run down to the smoking room and joke with his friends. Detective McCann, there was something terribly strange about his behavior. At various times his grief seemed forced, not at all genuine, and purely for the benefit of the people around him."

Elated by this information, McCann proceeded to the Wayne Police Department and prepared for his meeting with Tony. By now the husband stood out as the only person who could have committed the murder, yet intuition could not always be trusted. McCann would continue questioning and accusing. Beyond simply covering himself if his hunch was wrong, it also served as a good technique for winning cooperation from potential sources who might lead him to the killer.

At three-thirty that afternoon, when Tony, accompanied by his girlfriend Bonnie Nichols, arrived at Wayne police headquarters, the polygraph machine was already out. Tony volunteered to take the test. Thirty minutes later, after he indisputably passed, McCann felt secure that Tony wasn't the killer. Never letting this on, he continued to question the visibly nervous man for the record. The tactic proved effective, as Mancuso willingly told the policeman everything he could about Candy.

"How do you know Candy?" McCann asked, remembering what Jeanne Austin told him about Candy's recent conversation with the former boyfriend.

"We used to date. Back in high school, Candy was my girlfriend. I took her to the prom. We went steady for about two years. Then, in twelfth grade, we broke up but still remained friends."

"When was the last time you spoke to Candy?"

"She called me about a week ago and seemed pretty upset. Things weren't going so well with John. A while back Candy thought she was pregnant, and John wanted her to have an abortion. She told me that he said he couldn't afford another child, but she wanted to keep the baby. It turned out that she wasn't pregnant, so it wasn't much of an issue anyway."

"Do you remember anything else about the conversation?" McCann asked.

"Yeah. Last week, she told me, John stayed out all night and didn't come home. He claimed that he had a business meeting, but Candy didn't believe him. According to Candy, John had also been drinking a hell of a lot more than usual and he seemed very irritable."

This revelation solidified McCann's theory, as Short's carousing and drinking gave him more of a motive. He thanked Tony and ended the the interview session.

"Was that all right?" Tony asked, practically begging to be told that he wasn't considered a suspect in the murder of Candy Short.

"You did fine," McCann said, thumping the young man on the back and walking him to the door of the station house.

Out in the parking lot, when they were too far away for McCann to hear them, Bonnie asked Tony if he had told the cops everything. He nodded. "You told them that Candy called you?" she asked. He nodded again.

What Tony chose to keep from both his girlfriend and the cop was something which he felt might have been at the root of Candy's call. Tony wondered whether or not his high school sweetheart had telephoned with the hope of rekindling their relationship. However, that inkling remained secret for several reasons: He had so little interest in getting involved with a married woman that there would have been no chance of anything developing; he could not divine what relevance it would have to the case; and, most important, there was no way of ascertaining that hopes of an amorous liaison motivated the call in the first place.

They got into Tony's car and drove out of the parking lot. A little while later, at about six-thirty, Betty and Joe Frank pulled in. Physically and emotionally drained from the funeral, they entered the police station arm-in-arm, looking as if they were the ones who had just lost a daughter. Betty simply told the police what happened on the night of the murder. She had nothing else to add.

That's why McCann tried something a little bit different with Joe. "I'm going . . . to ask you some questions, and I want you . . . to answer each one . . . very quickly." The policeman spoke in a slow, laconic tone, explaining the simple procedure as if it were complex.

The tenor of his voice relaxed Joe to the point that he

jumped back when McCann shouted in his face, "Did you kill Candy Short?"

"No!" Joe shot back.

"Did Fred kill her?"

"No!" he replied with even more conviction.

"What about John?"

Joe Frank hesitated. He felt as if somebody had lifted up a giant curtain and unveiled a previously hidden philosophy, a new way of thinking that he had never before considered. Joe looked back at Billy McCann, his eyes reflecting a combination of worry and shock. "I don't know," he told the police officer. "I'll tell you, I really can't say for sure one way or the other."

CHAPTER
3

Drive through Belleville, and you feel the town closing in on you. It's a claustrophobic place, with limited tolerance for those who don't conform to the community's staunchly blue collar way of life. The small two-story houses (locally referred to as "Capes"), lined up one after the other with their tiny backyards, cluttered front porches, and homey interiors, serve as physical testimony to the mind-sets of their owners. Adhering to solid family values, they hold fast to a lifestyle that has as much to do with the 1950s as today. The town has seen little change in the last thirty or forty years, and most of the Bellevillers like it that way.

Suburban and tired-looking, it's the sort of place that might have thrived once but has now settled into a faded, frumpy middle age. Stores that had been there for decades line Belleville's main streets and competed for business with newer, neon-lit mini malls. Closed-down factories loomed in the smokeless distance, relics from another era. Where farms and barns had once stood are squatty houses lined up in uniform rows along most blocks.

Fred's great-grandfather had been one of the area's earliest residents back in the mid-nineteenth century. Three generations later, Fred, an electrician by trade, helped build a house right next door to the one he grew up in; Betty and Joe eventually moved into his parents' home and he raised his own family in the new place.

An old cap-and-ball rifle, which had once belonged to Fred's grandfather and dated back to the Civil War, hung above the fireplace in his living room. The heirloom went well with the other pieces of Americana that filled the Austins' home, but it served as more than simple ornamentation. The firearm also represented Fred's yearning for days that he would never know, those simpler times when men solved problems face-to-face and didn't need cops and lawyers and courts for settling differences. In his life, as far as he could control it, Fred maintained the lost values of trust and friendship and believed in those closest to him—whether through blood or wedlock.

A former Navy man, Fred enjoyed reminiscing, and he would enthusiastically recount salty tales from his days at sea. Anybody who smiled at a particularly ribald anecdote would be asked, "How come you're grinnin' like a skunk eatin' shit?" This rarely failed to get a second rise out of the listener and annoy Helen. Hearing that phrase, she would remind Fred that he no longer lived on a battleship and should refrain from speaking as if he did. A strict Episcopalian, Helen prayed each Sunday and successfully encouraged the girls to do the same. While his wife made cakes for church bake sales and socialized with the other parishioners, Fred had to be dragged to services. He didn't care much for religion, but placed a heavy stake in morality and often said that a man was only as good as his word.

Personal and local pride run deep in Belleville, and high school rivalries between neighboring towns regularly result in brawls at varsity football games. But those very people who bang heads as kids frequently marry somebody from nearby and become instantly related to their former rivals. Family supersedes everything else in this town, and among relatives few favors are refused. The bond of marriage, and the trust that comes with it, remains an important factor for people who cling to old-world values even as they eat fast food and speed-shop at the local mall. Surnames change, old grudges mend, new ones form, and life goes on. That's the way it has been since 1849, when settlers first arrived in Belleville.

Candice Carol Austin entered that cozy world on April 25, 1957. An extended family of cousins, aunts, and grandparents coddled this youngest of three girls. Her older sisters, Cindy and Jeanne, included Candy in their games of jacks and pushed the baby around in a stroller when they played house. At an early age Candy developed a flighty confidence and a happy-go-lucky attitude that followed her through life. Helen called her youngest daughter the "little comedian," and laughed louder than anyone when the confident six-year-old told jokes at the dinner table. Even in her crib Candy rarely cried. As a girl and as a woman, complaining did not suit her.

While Candy lacked the physical presence of Jeanne— three years older, Jeanne was blessed with an angular face and a naturally thin physique—the younger girl's ungainly features, a tendency to chub up, and her four-foot, ten-inch frame hardly impeded her popularity. A smart, good-natured, even-tempered girl, she made a lot of friends.

By the time she began attending high school, Candy had fallen in with a group of kids who were very much like herself: good students with the potential to be their families' first college graduates. They didn't fit in with the school's most athletic or popular cliques, but they were all well-behaved, well-meaning kids. For the most part they stayed out of trouble and spent their evenings hanging out on New Street, a well-lit block crowded with the Cape-style homes that were ubiquitous in Belleville. Occasionally they drank beer, but they managed to stay away from pot and the other drugs that had become increasingly popular among area teenagers.

Unlike Jeanne, who was a varsity cheerleader and traveled in the company of the football team's most desired players, Candy found boys intimidating. This stemmed from her early physical maturity. Although she often joked, "When God handed out breasts he gave me Jeanne's as well as my own," Candy felt her overly developed body weighing her down; she didn't want cleavage, she wanted to be like everybody else. Eager to camouflage,

Candy wore loose-fitting garments that deemphasized her chest and draped her torso with a tentlike effect. Additionally, she did what she could to put off intimate involvement. It was almost as if she viewed her breasts as some deep secret that should not be revealed.

More than any of the other boys in her crowd, Tony Mancuso wanted to be privy to those secrets. But his attraction to her went beyond the surface. She offered Tony a level of emotional support that seemed unavailable elsewhere. A mixed-up young man, Tony was torn between devotion to his family's mores and a desire to pursue his own dreams.

Fancying himself something of an actor, he performed in the school's annual dramatic productions and harbored a desire to live among his fellow thespians in New York City. His parents wanted to hear nothing of those dreams, and continually told him that he should finish high school, get a job, and find a nice woman to marry. They viewed Tony's goals as being of the least attainable sort. Candy, on the other hand, could sit all day and listen to Tony describing his optimal future.

The prototypical "nice girl," Candy cared more about others than she did about herself. That appealed to Tony. His high hopes and modest talents charmed her, and the two of them became an item. They attended the junior prom together and Tony gave Candy a ring. It wasn't an engagement ring or anything, just an exact duplicate of a crucifix that Tony wore on his own right ring finger. She enjoyed opening her left hand, exposing the band of silver, and prodding people to wonder where she'd gotten it. Smiling and milking the moment, Candy would drop her head back and finally acknowledge, "My boyfriend gave it to me."

After Tony, Candy's closest friend was Judy Halbert, an ebulliently attractive girl with ringlets of dark brown hair and a good sense of humor. Their parents socialized, and the two girls began playing together before they knew how to walk. Despite the level of intimacy that they achieved over the years, Judy never understood Candy's reluctance to reveal private details from her life. While their other friends discussed and recounted adolescent sexual adventures, Candy silently listened. Even after her relationship with Tony had ended nobody knew the cause of their breakup. As outgoing as she appeared to be, Candy maintained a private side to which few people ever gained access.

Because the Austins were such accommodating folks, their house became a meeting place for Candy and her friends. The kids hung out upstairs and watched television, lying together on Candy's bed or sprawling on the floor. At ten o'clock Helen made baloney sandwiches and the gang came down for a late-night snack before heading home. They sat at the table and sipped from glasses of Pepsi. Occasionally Fred snuck out a couple of Budweisers for the boys.

Candy grew up in a manner that's become increasingly rare in the United States. Idyllic memories marked her childhood. Major family flare-ups and emotional setbacks, which are so common in the lives of other girls, seemed conspicuously absent from Candy's own adolescent years. The Austins rarely raised their voices, and would be hard pressed to remember a time when they had punished their daughters. Even on the odd occasions when money became tight, it hardly affected Candy. By all outward appearances she had everything she needed—her hair was always freshly permed, clothing stylish and neatly pressed, makeup subtle and flattering—and managed to compensate for her less than perfect looks. All of this care paid off when Candy's senior classmates nominated her for the yearbook's Best Dressed award, in 1975.

During that same year, however, things began to go sour with Tony. Though trouble had been brewing for months, it came to a head when the two of them went away on a school-sponsored trip. They arranged a switch that landed them in a single room together, and Tony made sexual advances.

She didn't respond, so he interpreted her silence as a green light to proceed. But each time he tried to get past the elastic band of Candy's panties, she squirmed away. "Come on!" Tony pleaded in frustration. Lying alongside her, he said, "We've been going out for a long time. You know I love you."

Candy refused.

"We've done everything else," Tony persisted. "Why not this?"

She remained resolute, and Tony finally turned away from her to spend a restless night sleeping with his back to his girlfriend. Following that spurning, Tony ended the relationship. Upset, but not so upset that she'd sacrifice her virginity, Candy requested an explanation. Instead Tony gave her a sexual ultimatum. Candy didn't like it, but she tried to understand, and the two of them agreed to remain friends.

After graduating from high school—her entry in *Monad*, the Belleville yearbook, reads: "Likes smiling . . . dislikes pushy people over 4' 11" . . . plans to continue education and just live a good life"—Candy surprised Judy and a few others by not enrolling in college. Pushed by her parents, she wound up at Berkeley secretarial school and did poorly, as she could muster no enthusiasm for the stenography and shorthand classes. She wound up behind the counter at the Towne Deli, a small grocery store just up the block from her house. Soon after taking the job and saving a little bit of extra money, Candy made a decision that surprised nobody: She decided to enlist the services of a plastic surgeon.

Candy hoped that getting a breast reduction would allow her to feel more emotionally and physically comfortable. The operation was simple, and Candy left the hospital in a day. A ropy red scar from the incision ran along the undersides of both breasts, and Candy viewed that as the procedure's one drawback. But she only needed to look in the mirror and see her improved proportions in order to know that her goal had been realized.

After the scars had faded, Candy's personality drastically changed. Her body had been transformed from something embarrassing into something admirable, and showing it off suddenly exhilarated her. With a new sense of confidence, she flirted with men and felt comfortable around them. A few of her old friends believed that she had become a little *too* comfortable, as the number of her intimacies rapidly rose from zero. Candy became obsessed with disco music—all the rage in 1975—and established herself as a fixture at many of the clubs in northern New Jersey. Accompanied by friends from work, Candy dressed in the overblown fashions of the day and boogied seductively.

Her new look and attitude attracted men on the dance floors. Candy became surprisingly promiscuous, dating a lot of different guys and sleeping with many of them. Even Tony received the opportunity to make up for lost time. While behavior like Candy's routinely raised few eyebrows during that pre-AIDS era of sexual liberation, nobody had expected her to become so loose; it upset the few close friends who were privy to this change in Candy's lifestyle. Nevertheless, they refrained from commenting to her face, and remained as outwardly supportive as possible. Beyond simply opting not to meddle, Candy's friends also were occupied with their own affairs. Many of the kids that she had once hung around with were now dating the people they would eventually marry. Others were attending college, and had brand-new lives outside of their home town. Candy's antics held little interest on all but the most gossipy, superficial level.

During this time of her sexual awakening, a trim, good-looking, twenty-three-year-old man began shopping at the Towne Deli. Candy noticed him stopping by on a regular basis to buy cigarettes and lunch meat and TV dinners, and she sensed a mutual attraction. Even when he stood still and silent, the man emitted a cocky, undeniably dangerous quality that appealed to her. And Candy's newly perfected skills as a flirt were not wasted on this customer. Something in her smile, something in the way she spoke, tipped him off. He always returned the smile and met Candy's eyes in a way that made her feel she was the most wanted woman in the world.

On one of his visits to the store, after Candy tallied the cost of the goods and bagged them, he asked, "What are you doing after work tomorrow night?"

Candy allowed that she had no plans. The man asked her to dinner, and she gladly accepted. Later that day Candy phoned her good friend Judy. "I met this great guy," she said. "He comes into the store all the time and I really like him."

"Is he handsome?"

"Gorgeous. And so nice."

"What's his name?"

Candy hesitated, giggled, and said, "You know, I don't remember."

The next night he picked Candy up at her house and introduced himself to Fred Austin. The man shook hands with his date's father and said, "Hi. My name is John."

At the same time that Candy was employing surgery to make herself more attractive, John Short was making another woman's life miserable. His marriage to Donna Olson—a thin, attractive woman with long, chestnut-colored hair, who had met Short in 1971 when they were both twenty—had deteriorated into a blur of violent beatings. During their first year of dating John managed to balance his outbursts of physical abuse with overwhelming amounts of care and affection. He sent flowers, took her on dates, spent time with Mr. and Mrs. Olson—and it all seemed like enough.

Even so, Donna's mother Shirley begged her daughter not to marry the man. The wife of an alcoholic herself, she recognized something evil in John. "Please don't make a mistake," she told Donna one evening over dinner.

"Can't you see that there's something wrong with him? He loses a game of Monopoly and dumps the board on the floor and threatens to kill everybody in the room. It's like he has a brain tumor or something, his temper's so bad. How's he going to be when there are real problems?"

"You don't know John," Donna insisted. "You're only looking at his bad side. Sometimes he can be so nice, so loving, and so caring."

Shirley remained unaware of the relatively minor beatings that had already become an ongoing part of the relationship. Administering physical abuse gave John a certain amount of control and leverage over his women. As long as he kept them beaten down and insecure, he could get away with even the vilest behavior on a day-to-day basis. John was the worst sort of bully, insidious in that he not only preyed on people weaker than himself, but also managed to convince them that he was a terrific guy.

In the middle-class neighborhood where John had grown up—just a few miles south of Belleville—he was known as a helpful boy, willing to aid family friends with repairs or odd jobs around the house. Through his last year of high school, John regularly attended the Methodist church where his mother, a small-framed, blond-haired woman named Adele, taught religious classes every Sunday. She had a cheerful, friendly presence and was the polar opposite of her husband James.

A Scottish immigrant, James Short ran the modest household with an iron fist and was known for his stern, implacable demeanor. At his behest the Short home was kept immaculate, with every item in its proper place and nary a trace of dust anywhere. Not surprisingly, his son's appearance was expected to be equally flawless. Through grade school John was forced to wear his hair shorter than seemed fashionable at the time, and he dressed with a neat formality that his father imposed upon him. Unlike many of his friends, John's visible rebelliousness remained limited. For the most part, he listened to his well-meaning parents and did his best to please them—persevering as an intelligent model student until his last few years of high school.

As the only child in a middle-class family—both parents held full-time jobs (James as a foreman and Adele as a figure clerk)—John was perpetually spoiled in a financial way that clashed with the strict emotional discipline. Much of the money earned by the Shorts—who were not especially wealthy people—went to their son. They showered him with gifts but kept John emotionally bankrupt. His father (who rarely initiated conversation, even under the best of circumstances) maintained a distant relationship, but Mrs. Short compensated by over-protecting the boy. At her behest he received a brand-new car at the age of seventeen, a sixty-five-thousand-dollar truck a few years later, and after that enough money to continually bail out of faltering business ventures.

Watched over by a black nanny named Odessa Brown, young John Short became accustomed to getting his own way, and developed a slyly manipulative style at a young age. For all that he was given, however, John's social and emotional growth remained horribly stunted. John beat up anybody he could get away with hitting, punching open-fisted like a girl but choosing his targets judiciously enough to avoid retaliation. Even in church, there were spates of trouble that hinted at extremely violent tendencies. Friends remember a pushing incident that ended with John's inexplicably kicking another boy in the kidneys and bringing the teenager to tears.

Possibly because of the strict discipline at home, John eventually found himself over-expressing his independence on the outside. By his sixteenth birthday he fell in with a rough group of black and Hispanic kids and gradually drifted away from his local friends. However, long after he began running with the faster crowd, John's parents remained unaware of what he was up to. The many years he had spent avoiding communication with James and Adele made it easy for John to continue concealing his life from them. They assumed that nothing in their son's world had changed.

They were hardly alone in viewing John as a slightly rambunctious innocent. Neighbors remembered him as the young man who would help put up a Christmas tree if somebody's husband was out of town. Gene Wilhowsky, John's counselor at the YMCA day camp, will always think of him as a handy teenager who voluntarily plowed every driveway on the block when it snowed. Years later, when the Wilhowsky's house required extensive carpentry work, John drove sixty miles to get there and did the job for free.

To those who saw John at his best, he was a prince of a fellow. But there definitely was a dark side to the Jekyll-and-Hyde persona that had begun taking shape at a young age. A high school girlfriend became one of his first female victims. Back in 1970, Short, his pal Steve Gottlieb, and their dates were parked on a guard-railed precipice of Garret Mountain in nearby West Paterson, New Jersey. High above Route 46—a highway that leads to Willowbrook Mall—it provided a picturesque spot for high school Romeos and their girlfriends.

On any warm night you could drive past there and see cars pulled up to the mountain's edge. Doors locked, windows steamed, the vehicles were filled with teenagers kissing and touching and exploring. The local police knew this as well as anybody, and they made frequent tours of the area. On the night that Short and his friends were parked there, a patrolman pulled up alongside the car. He tapped on the window with the butt of his flashlight, and the couples jumped.

"All right," he told them. "Get out of the car."

John had been sharing a pint of bourbon with his girlfriend in the backseat, so he slid it from sight as the four of them complied with the officer's request. The cop gave a cursory inspection of the vehicle, more concerned about drugs than liquor, and satisfied himself that the teenagers were clean. "I want you to leave this area right now," he told them, slowly backing away. "I'm returning in a few minutes, and if you're still here there's going to be trouble."

Once the cop had gotten into his car and disappeared from sight, John blew up like a cherry bomb. "You fucking bitch!" he shouted at his girlfriend for no apparent reason.

Seemingly accustomed to these outbursts, she retreated and covered her face, but it was too late. John lunged at her with his arms flailing. Horrified, Gottlieb's date exhorted him to pull Short off of the girl. He managed to break up the fight, but the incident remained in Steve's memory, flashing like an amber warning signal. From then on, he knew that turning his back on John Short might not be a great idea.

As Helen Austin would later note, John never developed a strong relationship with his parents, and as a young adult he found himself rudderless in a world where the family typically serves as an anchor. Desperate for reassurance and emotional bolstering, John Short grew to be a loudmouthed braggart, exaggerating his skills as a mechanic and boasting about his abilities as a cocksman. He drank more, drove faster, and broke laws with a recklessness that overwhelmed Gottlieb and the other guys in their circle.

In his late teens John spent a brief period dabbling with intravenous drugs and dealing in stolen credit cards. After being nabbed and quickly released by the police— a secret he managed to keep from even his closest allies—the illegal adventure ended. The pattern, however, remained in place: Showing off paid off. The attention imbued John with a false sense of emotional control over those around him.

He evolved into a heavy drinker and pot-smoker. His temper grew increasingly quick and explosive, yet Short could just as easily slip back into his giving, generous mode. He felt a growing need to prove his wealth, even if it kept him financially bankrupt. Picking up tabs wherever he drank, and tipping lavishly, John preferred the atmosphere of a dark go-go bar to practically any other place.

Considering that John's jobs—which went from pumping gas to driving the sixty-five-thousand-dollar truck to doing construction work—never produced enough money to satisfy his dream of reversing the downward mobility that plagued him, he felt the frustration of constantly mounting debt and physically vented his anger. If things didn't go perfectly on a construction job, Short threw tools at his assistants. He stormed around work sites and threatened everybody within earshot.

One man who entered into an ill-fated construction project with Short still shudders when he remembers the experience. Never mind that the easygoing fellow had been swindled out of thousands of dollars, he backed away from the partnership with the very real fear that Short would bring violence upon him or his family. As the investor learned, John's lifestyle stretched so far beyond his means that money always seemed to be in limited supply. In this instance, he funded his extravangances by grossly padding expenses. How else could he have afforded to continually treat his friends to food and drink? Even among the gas station attendants, who earned about the same as Short did, he frequently insisted on buying shots and beers and burgers at a nearby bar.

They'd leave the tavern tipsy and well fed, patting Short on the back and bolstering his ego. Like taking drugs, spending big excited him. After one of those boozy lunches, with John feeling particularly brazen, Donna Olson pulled up to a pump.

Twenty years old, just like John, she asked him to fill her tank with unleaded. He chatted her up, suggested that she come back next time she needed gas, and grabbed his crotch as she pulled away. John walked back into the gas station to an encouraging audience of co-workers. "When she comes back," he pledged, "I'll fuck her."

Nobody actually believed this, but they played along. The next time Donna came in for gas John did not make good on his promise, though he took a big step in that direction: He got her to agree to go out with him on a date. Six months later, in 1973, the two of them were married in a religious ceremony. They moved into the second-story apartment of a two-family house in John's hometown of Bloomfield. But within the first year, their blessed union deteriorated into a nightmare.

The beatings intensified. They fought over the most mundane things—what Donna made for dinner, why John spent so much on his friends and so little on her, his refusal to visit her parents on a regular basis—and Donna found herself walking on eggshells, living in continual fear of saying something that would enrage John. She had good reason to be nervous. In the course of one argument he nearly broke her arm, and another time he grabbed a fistful of Donna's hair and threw her against the wall.

Adding to the chaos, their high-strung Italian-American landlady invariably responded to the racket. "What are you two, crazy?" she screamed. Banging on the door, the woman demanded that they let her in. John often greeted her at the apartment's entrance, brandishing the very belt with which he had just beaten his wife, and menacingly advised the woman, a mother in her early fifties, to go back downstairs and tend to her own affairs.

"Why do you stay with him?" the landlady often asked Donna, attempting to comfort the clearly distraught girl.

Donna never responded. She'd turn away, embarrassed, unable to give herself an answer to that question, much less somebody else.

After seeing bruises on his daughter's arm, Eddie Olson, Donna's elderly father, did what any conscientious parent would do: He told John to keep his hands off Donna. All concerned were at the Olson home when Eddie made the request, and John blew up.

"What the fuck business is it of yours?" he wanted to know. Glaring at his wife, he added, "And what trouble-maker told you all that bullshit?"

"Nobody had to tell me," Olson responded. "I see the bruises."

He gestured toward the black-and-blue marks on his daughter's arms. John began to formulate a response, then decided to settle the matter another way. He charged at the fifty-year-old man. "You better learn to mind your own business," John said. He cuffed Olson on the side of the head, smacking him with the hard, lower part of his palm. The two men tumbled to the floor and rolled around on the carpet.

"Leave him alone!" Donna cried. "Get off of my father!"

Her mother tried to break it up and got shoved out of the way. Luckily for Olson they grappled past a coffee table, where a half-smoked cigarette rested in the ash-tray. Eddie reached for the tray, then grabbed the ciga-rette instead and ground it out in John's face. Skin singed, the younger man released his grip. He jumped to his feet and held his hand to the burnt area.

Much to her parents' surprise and chagrin, Donna re-mained married to John. The more he beat and abused her, the more tightly she clung to the relationship, her self-esteem deteriorating to the point that she couldn't imagine herself fit for a less brutal man. Breaking women down, and ultimately controlling them through fear and intimidation, was the key to John Short's success as a bully. He instinctively chose weak, insecure victims who found his hard-edged nature appealing—Donna grew up with an alcoholic father, and had a strong need for au-thority—then turned that very quality against them. At first finding comfort in Short's physically imposing blus-ter, his victims eventually cowered under it.

During the last phase of the relationship with Donna, the two of them were scuffling at the head of the stair-case outside of their second-floor apartment when John kicked his wife from behind and sent her tumbling. At the bottom of the flight she picked herself up slowly, made certain that no bones were broken, and staggered out the door. Icy cold winter winds enveloped her as she walked the streets of Bloomfield without shoes or a coat. A group of high school kids jeered her from behind. "She thinks this is Florida!" one girl said. A boy yelled, "Goddamned crazy low-life, she doesn't even know where she is!"

Donna ignored the taunts and kept walking, preferring this form of humiliation to that which she faced at home. Her friend Alice Cooke lived a few blocks away, and Donna's plan was to wait there until John cooled off. Crying as she walked, the battered woman struggled to gain her composure when a gray pickup truck slowed down alongside her. John sat in the driver's seat, looking as if nothing untoward had happened. He came to a stop and called her name. Donna turned toward him.

"Where're you going?" John asked.

"Alice's house."

"Come on in. I'll give you a ride."

"No, it's okay. I'll walk."

"That's ridiculous. It's freezing outside. Let me give you a lift to Alice's."

Donna thought about it for a moment, felt a chill cut through her light blouse, and agreed. She climbed onto the front seat and shut the door. John silently proceeded in the direction of her friend's house. Then he hit the brakes, looked at Donna, and said, "I'm not taking you there." He turned the car around and appeared to get aggravated all over again. "Why the fuck should I take you to Alice's house? I'm taking you home. That's where you belong."

It wasn't until 1975, following a series of particularly brutal beatings, that she began to realize John could seriously injure her. While he had never actually threatened Donna with death, clearly it was only a matter of time before things would get dangerously violent.

During the three years of marriage, Donna went from being an upbeat teenager to a victimized woman. The soft edges of her personality became battle scarred and developed a hardened, self-protecting armor. For several years after the marriage's dissolution, Donna found it difficult to trust men and feared that John would come back to find her, liable to do God knows what in order to seek out some violent form of retribution.

She filed for divorce proceedings in 1976 and John Short grudgingly moved out of their home. He transported his clothing to a small garden apartment on Joralemon Street in Belleville, and furnished the place with a few mismatched odds and ends. Soon after settling in there he began shopping at the Towne Deli and caught the eye of the busty blonde behind the cash register.

John and Candy met in 1976 and dated for two years. By then he had started his own contracting business and was struggling to turn a reasonable profit as he disentangled himself from Donna. Candy asked John for information about that first marriage and he shrugged, simply stating that it hadn't worked out, as if there were inexplicable reasons for those things. If the evasiveness initially bothered Candy, she grew fond enough of John to overlook it.

Her interest in him was partly spurred on by the nature of Belleville, where unattached girls in their twenties got odd looks from the locals who wondered why they were still single. Quickly approaching that age, Candy was increasingly eager to walk down the aisle. As the relationship with John progressed, he seemed to be her likeliest prospect. Hearing her friends discussing bright futures with children and husbands, Candy pursued marriage the way other people her age worked at earning college degrees.

When Candy discussed her dream future she described herself living in a nice but modest home, maybe a place that John would build for her. There'd be lots of kids, lots of pets, lots of friends. Candy would be a wonderful wife and John would be a great provider. A simple girl with reasonable expectations, she desired nothing more than the life that her mother had. For Candy, that would have been everything a girl could want.

Nevertheless, several family members failed to see John as suitable husband material. Betty Frank, Fred Austin, and Geri Austin all had negative impressions of him; yet they chose to keep those opinions to themselves. After all, they simply wanted Candy to be with somebody who made her happy. And more than anything else, John seemed to do that.

Only four years older than her, he already had a life's worth of experience behind him, though that ranked among the things that she liked. As different as he was from Candy's high school friends, this older, sometimes cold and distant man brought her a kind of contentment that she had never known before. He favored grand, showy gestures over day-to-day kindness. By sending lavish bouquets of flowers—"Just because I love you," he routinely said, when asked what the occasion was—John created an illusion of romantically pampering Candy.

One afternoon Candy sat at Betty's dinette table and discussed the relationship she had with John. "He's so nice to me," she told her older cousin (who really functioned as more of an aunt), sounding like the narrator of a fairy tale. "We have so much fun when we're together. John told me that one day we'll get married and he'll build a great big house for me."

Divorced once herself, Betty knew all about the promises that men make and refrained from commenting about John's. She considered warning Candy about unconditionally taking John at his word, then decided against it and broached a safer topic. "What are your plans for the weekend?"

"We're going to the shore," Candy said. "John's friend has a houseboat moored down there and we sleep on it. It's so cozy."

"You be careful," Betty told her.

She hoped that Candy understood the double entendre in her warning. Later that day, Betty told Joe about their cousin's romantic nights at sea, adding, "If Candy keeps spending weekends on that boat with John she's going to get herself in trouble."

Though Candy told her friends and relatives nothing but nice things about John, anybody could see that he came with problems. To begin with, John never felt comfortable about doing things as a couple, particularly when other people were involved. Socially awkward, he avoided situations in which he wasn't the center of attention. This included most gatherings with Candy's friends. As a result, Candy spent decreasing amounts of time within the circle of people that she had known since her evenings on New Street. More and more, she came to rely on John to fill expanding chunks of her life, a task that he couldn't possibly have been up for.

Looking for excuses, he dismissed Candy's friends as college snobs—even though a lot of them had chosen not to continue their educations—and avoided them at all costs. It upset Helen to see her daughter pulling back from that crowd, so she took John aside and asked him what the problem was.

"They make me uncomfortable," he insisted, looking down at his feet and feeling sorry for himself. "They're all in school and stuff, and they don't seem to like me."

"Candy says they like you fine," Helen told him. "You just need to give them a chance."

"Maybe."

John did give them a chance. He attended a party with Candy, Judy Halbert, and Judy's boyfriend (who eventually became her husband) Richie Chamberlain. More accustomed to the seedy environs of go-go bars, he found himself with nothing to say to this group of relatively straightlaced kids.

Hardly elitist Ivy Leaguers, they still possessed far more polish and class than John did. Unable to shine as the center of attention, he sat in a corner, sulking, smoking, and drinking. That night, as John drove home, he asked Candy to do him a favor and not drag him to any more of these parties. Candy avoided pressing the point. She didn't want to risk ruining the relationship, and held tightly to her dream of domestic bliss.

Several months later, during the third quarter of 1978, unforeseeable events turned that dream to reality with a suddenness that every girl dreads. Helen was the first to find out.

"Mom," Candy said, "I have something to tell you."

"What is it?"

Candy began crying, then broke down and blurted it out: "I'm having a baby."

In a household as religious as the Austins', abortion wasn't even an issue. So Helen raised the only question on her mind: "Does John know?"

"Yes. And he promised to marry me if I'm pregnant."

In a funny way, this made the pregnancy good news for Candy. She wanted to get married, and having the baby would simply speed up the process. Helen hugged her daughter. Then she too cried. The tears were bittersweet. She was glad to see Candy getting married, yet hated the thought that an otherwise wonderful occasion would be marred by the circumstances surrounding it.

Now Candy had to tell her dad. Fred always maintained an even temper and never hit the girls, so breaking the news to him was less daunting than it might have been in some households. She walked downstairs to his basement workshop, sobbing as softly as she could so that her father wouldn't hear her.

"Daddy, I need to talk to you," she said.

"Okay. Let's talk." Fred loosened the vice containing a wooden Donald Duck toy that he was carving for one of the neighborhood kids. Then he looked at Candy and saw her red eyes and flared nostrils, and noticed that her lips were quivering. Now his voice brimmed with concern. "What's the matter?"

"Nothing's *the matter*." She took a deep breath and

said the next sentence as if it were a single word. "I'm going to have a baby."

Fred got up and hugged his daughter. She cried onto his flannel-shirted shoulder, and between the sobs managed to tell her father, "John said he'll marry me, and everything's going to be fine."

"I know it is." Fred patted her back and did his best to console Candy. Remembering a friend's sister who had been beaten with a strap when she told her father the same thing, Fred reminded himself to stay calm, to be supportive. He held Candy tighter and repeated, "I know it is."

Pure optimism, combined with a teenager's naiveté, allowed Candy to block out the downside of her predicament. Now, with the relative approval of her parents, she saw a rose-colored future awaiting her beyond the forced marriage. Considering the way Helen and Fred had raised her, Candy had no reason to believe that her union with John would be any different than that of her parents. She joked about Mrs. Short being an apt name for somebody under five feet tall, and even discussed wedding plans. Nobody dared mention that the wedding needed to be within the next month, unless she wanted to walk down the aisle in a white maternity outfit.

Before proposing marriage for the second time, though, John had some unfinished business to resolve in Bloomfield. As Candy and her parents awaited his arrival, he paid a visit to Mary Milano.

Not especially pleased to see her former tenant, Mary stood behind a screen door and suspiciously asked John what he wanted. "I'm just coming here to let you know that I'm going to be marrying a lady named Candy Austin," Short began. "Her parents have friends who live on this block, people that you know."

John gestured toward a home a couple of doors away, and when Mary said nothing he asked her for a favor. "Well, in case they say anything about me, I would just appreciate it if you could keep from mentioning any of the, uh, things that went on here with Donna and I."

Mary Milano shot him a strange look. She was flabbergasted by the request, but willing to honor it. "What you do is your business," she testily told him. "I don't say a word about you to anybody. I just don't want to hear that my name's coming out of your mouth."

Assuring her that it wouldn't, John hastily retreated back to his pickup truck. Relief saturated his soul as he made the short drive to Belleville. Aware that Candy would be seeing her gynecologist that afternoon, John planned on stopping at the Austins' home before heading up the hill to his own apartment. What seemed like a positive resolution of his past might have accounted for John's good spirits as he greeted his future wife and in-laws.

Smiling and agreeing to live up to his promise of matrimony, he turned to Fred and explained, "I do this differently than most people. With me the baby comes first, then the marriage, then the engagement ring. Next year we'll go steady."

Candy started giggling and wrapped her arms around John's neck, pulling him close for a hug. From the corner of his eye, John could see that Fred found no humor in the joke. He looked at the man with a half grin and asked, "Do you want to put a bullet through me?"

Unable to believe the gall of this boor, who'd just impregnated his youngest daughter and now had the poor sense to joke about it, Fred fought back an urge to say yes. Instead he swallowed the word like a wad of bile, turned away from John and replied, "Just take good care of her and the baby."

CHAPTER
4

A dark tweed couch, a big battleship-gray desk, and a tiny dining room table comprised the bulk of John and Candy's furniture. One wooden, homemade end table filled out a side of the living room, and a TV/stereo setup rested on boards supported by bricks across from the couch. A small hallway led to a cramped room crowded with a bed, file cabinet, dresser, and crib. The domicile offered the newlyweds nothing in the way of privacy or comfort.

With only a month to prepare for their life together, Candy had to move into John's basement apartment. She hated those small, dark rooms, the low ceilings, and the tiny windows that looked out on people's feet. Conveniently, Helen and Betty lived close enough that Candy could easily spend the afternoons visiting them. She used any excuse to escape the apartment, which became the subject of an ongoing argument during that first year of marriage.

"We need to move," Candy insisted soon after Jesse's birth in the spring of 1979. "There'll be no room here when the baby starts growing up."

"Not now," John said. "I don't have the money. I can't afford it. Once we get caught up, I'll build you a house. A really great house that will be made especially for us. If I move I'm going to move into my own place, a place that *I build*."

"Please tell me that it will be soon, John."

69

"Yeah, it'll be soon. Just as soon as we can afford it."

John walked out of the apartment and to his car. He drove to The Red Shingle, a nearby go-go bar where the barmaids and dancers knew him by face if not by name. A long barn of a place, it was loaded with mirrors that reflected the flashing lights as well as the dancers' barely clad bodies. Standing on a rectangular platform encased by the bar, they wore G-strings and sequined bras that enhanced their breasts. Their asses all but exposed, the women jiggled seductively for this room full of customers.

Despite the endless string of dance numbers from the jukebox and the festive array of flashing colored lights, The Red Shingle remained dreary below its garish surface. Many lone men occupied the stools, sipping beers and cocktails, in search of refuge or escape. The girls on stage, with their phony smiles and vacant eyes, had their own agenda. Between sets they mingled with the patrons, though each dancer's interest in any single man waned when his tip well ran dry.

Deep down John must have known that, but apparently he didn't care. Sitting at the bar, sipping beer, watching the girls dance—this was the life John desired. The glow of swirling disco lights, the beat of the music, the smile of a well-built bikinied woman, all gave off a sense of excitement that Candy could never provide. She had gained a good thirty pounds since they'd begun dating, and as her hips and thighs blew up like fleshy balloons John's interest in her diminished.

From the outset, John resented being the sole breadwinner in the household. For him, marriage was something that cut a wide swath through his paycheck and infringed on his free time. At least when he and Donna were together, she had continued working. But Candy stayed home with the baby. The pressure to earn enough money to support them grated on John's nerves. He grew parsimonious, reserving as much cash as possible for himself and his own activities. The way John saw it, it was important to be generous with his employees and clients. Anything less would make him appear unsuccessful. True or not, this was what he told Candy when she requested more money for herself and the baby.

"If you need a few dollars," he snapped, "ask me for it and you'll get it. But you can't expect me to just give you a big chunk of money at the beginning of each week."

"That's the way everybody else does it," she complained. "It's called a household allowance."

"We're not everybody else."

So began a routine that would last throughout the marriage. Every day or two Candy and Jessica got into the gold Cutlass and drove to wherever John happened to be. They got out of the car, and Candy asked her husband for money. Sometimes he slipped her several bills, other times he didn't. The experience humiliated Candy, but it proved to be the only way she could put groceries on the table. John refused to properly fund the household, and he would accept no alternative plan.

To supplement her husband's meager funding, Candy babysat for a dollar-fifty per hour, but she still found her lifestyle to be sorely compromised. John refused to buy decent clothing for her or Jessica, and friends who knew Candy from before the marriage were shocked to see the way she now dressed. Not only had Candy bloated up from the pregnancy and found it increasingly difficult to stay away from sweets, but the once stylish girl who earned a nomination for Best Dressed in her high school class was now slovenly.

Her clothing looked old and frumpy. Unable to afford the permanents that suited her so well, Candy kept her hair chopped short and wore it like an unflattering crown. She told people that it was more convenient. But they knew better. One afternoon Candy got together with a few of her old friends. They hadn't seen each other since the wedding, and agreed to meet for coffee and cake. As the afternoon passed, Candy announced that she had to leave in order to be home in time to cook John's dinner. Candy drove back to the apartment in Belleville, and the conversation continued without her.

"Married life has really changed her," one of the women sadly remarked, sipping from her cup of coffee. "Candy seems so worn down and bummed out."

"She's probably tired," Judy Halbert replied, leaping to her friend's defense. "You know how babies are. They keep you up all night."

"No," the other one insisted, "it's more than that. Candy didn't even look like herself. Remember when we were in school? How often did you see Candy dressed like that? With her shirt untucked, her hair a mess, those horrible stretch pants?" The woman waited a moment, then answered her own question. "You never saw her looking like that. I just hope that John is taking care of her and the baby."

Judy felt sorry for her friend and continued to defend her. "Well, you don't know how it is when you get married and have a kid right away. Money gets tight. Sometimes you have to make sacrifices. I guess that's what Candy is doing right now."

Unlike his wife, John refused to compromise his style of living. He stayed out more than ever and came home from work increasingly tired—often because he had spent the afternoon drinking. On those occasions, when John wanted to sleep in the late afternoon or early evening, Candy and Jesse went down the block to Fred and Helen's place and spent a few hours there. Candy watched TV, ate popcorn, and laughed with her father. She reveled in these visits. They allowed a brief return to more pleasant times, far from the cramped apartment and domineering husband. While Fred and Helen enjoyed seeing Candy and their infant granddaughter, the visits left them concerned about the state of the marriage.

"Don't worry," Candy insisted. "Everything's fine. John is just tired, that's all." She looked down at Jessica and cooed, "He works so hard to support mommy and his baby, doesn't he?"

Helen and Fred reserved comment. They strived to be good parents and avoided meddling in their daughters' personal affairs. Yet they couldn't completely repress the resentment they felt toward John, particularly on those nights when Candy, even as she expressed a desire for a more stable home life, had to come over there with the baby so that John could be alone. Within a few months this emerged as a pattern. Jessica and Candy were always together; John stayed in the apartment and relaxed after work, sometimes sending his wife to buy hot dogs from a nearby grill or out for a six-pack of beer. Exhibiting startling obedience, she complied with his demands.

John and Candy rarely entertained. Early in the marriage, however, he made an effort to help his wife maintain her friendship with Judy. Just like the storybook couple that Candy longed to be a part of, they invited Judy and her boyfriend Richie Chamberlain over on a Saturday night. John surprised everybody by being animated and forthcoming. Maintaining a generous flow of Black Tower wine, he told Judy and Richie about the house he'd be building for his family.

"My Tara," Candy said, beaming as she referred to the mansion in *Gone with the Wind*. "John says it's going to have four bedrooms and a great big yard for Jesse to play in."

"Here, let me show you what it'll look like," John said. He pulled a blueprint from the bedroom file cabinet and unfurled the plan for their guests.

While Judy and Richie knew nothing about architecture or contracting, it looked impressive and they nodded approvingly. If the conversation was a bit one-sided and focused on a topic about which they were completely ignorant, Judy didn't care. She would indulge John for as long as it made her friend happy. That night he put on the kind of show that sparked Candy to love him in the first place: taking control, remaining in charge, seeming to mesmerize guests with an assured charm that Candy herself never possessed.

Then the telephone rang. John answered it and began speaking to his boyhood friend Steve Gottlieb. Not bothering to mention that he and Candy had company, John engaged in a fifteen-minute conversation that ended with him tuning the radio to an oldies station broadcasting a rock 'n' roll trivia contest. Suddenly forgetting about Judy and Richie, John left the plans for the house on the table and started in on the kind of frivolous telephone conversation that most people have when they're alone and bored. He and Steve rattled off names of vintage rock 'n' rollers as Candy did her best to make this all seem natural.

Nobody in the room found it to be even remotely natural.

Nevertheless, Candy happily dealt with that side of John. Unlike a lot of wives, she accepted her husband unconditionally and tried to love his faults as well as his virtues. When John wanted a cup of coffee he made a pouring motion with his hand, and Candy jumped up to fill his mug. She always cooked dinners that John liked, reserving those dishes that only she enjoyed for the nights on which he came home late.

Every few months, however, John committed some transgression that brought Candy to the breaking point. He might have stayed out all night every night for a full week, or screamed and yelled at her for no apparent reason, or maybe simply refused to have anything to do with Candy's family. But when John sensed that Candy had truly reached the end of her rope, he would buy her something: a pair of costume earrings, an appliance for the kitchen, maybe a shirt. The inexpensive gifts allowed John to temporarily slip out of trouble. In a relationship as dismal as John and Candy's, any show of kindness was perceived as a major gesture.

"Where's your Christmas tree?" It was December of 1980 when Helen looked around the living room of the small apartment, certain that it had to be somewhere within the room. Then she realized that it wasn't, and her stomach did a sad little somersault. Helen placed a tin of wreath-shaped cookies on the kitchen table and looked at Candy.

Embarrassed, Candy tried to smile, tried to make it seem like no big deal. "John's been so busy lately. You know, we just haven't had time to go get a tree this year."

"Well, you and I are going out right now to buy one. You can't have Christmas without a Christmas tree."

Helen wanted to believe that John's hectic schedule prevented his family from celebrating the holiday in a reasonably traditional manner. She couldn't bring herself to face the reality that her daughter had married a man so cheap, so uncaring, that he wouldn't spring for a tree and the gifts to put around it. And reflecting on John's supposedly busy work schedule naturally led Helen to wonder where all of the hard-earned money went; clearly it wasn't being spent on supporting her daughter.

Eager to enjoy the afternoon, though, she kept her concerns to herself as they drove to Willowbrook Mall. Besides, the strings of holiday lights and the crowds of shoppers eager to spend money gave Helen's spirits a lift. Pulling into the lot, Candy steered the Cutlass toward Ohrbach's, the department store that anchored the shopping center. Helen looked at her beautiful granddaughter, admired the likeness that she bore to Candy, and found it difficult to display rancor toward the man who had fathered her.

At that very moment, John downed a shot of Jack Daniels. He chased it with a swig of beer and stared at the girl on the stage. She rotated her pelvis to the rowdy beat of a song by The Cars and paid particular attention to a group of regulars that consisted of Short and a few cronies—several employees and a client. They were in the midst of an extended lunch break, putting off their inevitable return to work. As the woman teased, Short turned to the man who employed him and asked, "How'd you like to get some of that?"

"You shittin' me?" he replied. "I'd give my left nut to

have that broad's tongue on the right one." He finished his beer and Short motioned to the bar maid for a fresh round.

Aspiring to some macho ideal that they discovered in the glossy pages of *Hustler* magazine, Short and his friends were products of their time. They all made less money than their fathers and couldn't ever have afforded the houses that they grew up in. It filled them with a mounting cynicism and an unsatisfied hunger from an era that had promised its children everything and delivered nothing. A go-go bar's solace and the sport fucking that occasionally came with it were the best they could hope for. There, amidst the flashing lights playing off of flat-bellied dancers in sequined G-strings and push-up bras, they could see themselves as high rollers. Making eye contact with the girls, operating with an impossible case that doesn't exist in the outside world, they enjoyed a sense of warmth and belonging that could not be found in less seedy environments.

A tall brunette with legs that went on forever and a slightly doughy face finished her set. She wrapped a blazer around her shoulders and began circling the bar. The hem of the jacket came to the tops of her thighs and she wore it open so that her cleavage remained visible. When she neared Short, he nodded his head in acknowledgment and struck up a conversation. The woman knew John as a habitué of the bar, and when he asked if she wanted to slip off to his client's office for a few minutes in private she readily agreed.

Short's friends continued nursing their drinks as he and the dancer escaped for their quick tryst. By the time lunch ended, she was back onstage and Short had returned to work. He spent the remainder of the afternoon overseeing his crew and suggested returning to the bar at five o'clock for a few post-work brews. Everybody, including Short's client, thought it was a fine idea.

As evening turned into night, it became clear that they would be there for a while. The camaraderie was too strong, the girls too pretty, and the drinks too potent for anybody to contemplate an early departure. The fellows who were married called their wives throughout the course of their reverie, making excuses as to why they'd be home later and later. John, on the other hand, firmly believed that calling your wife made you look pussy-whipped. "When I get there is when I get there," he told Candy if she tried pinning him down to a time. "You know I hate wearing watches and letting clocks rule my life."

John taught her to expect the unexpected, so she wasn't surprised to see him walking into their apartment at eleven that night. Candy ran up to her husband and kissed him on the lips. She felt John tense up, as if her mouth were the last thing that he wanted there. Then she backed away from him a little bit and pointed to his desk. "Look what Mom bought for us today."

The miniature Christmas tree sat atop a pile of construction contracts and forms, giving it the look of a bulky paper weight. The tree was tiny by most people's standards, but just having one in the house filled Candy with happiness.

"Yeah," John said, actually feeling good himself, momentarily experiencing the honest warmth that you don't get from a go-go dancer's hired attention. "This looks really great. It reminds me that Christmas is nearly here."

"Now we just need the gifts to put around it," she hinted.

"As soon as I get a little bit of time we'll go Christmas shopping," John promised, as his wife put a steak in the oven for him and cut out a chunk of freshly baked brownie for herself.

True to his word, John shopped for presents when he found the time that year. Unfortunately, it wasn't until Christmas eve. As a result he stumbled into the Austins' Christmas dinner late and awkward, his arms clutching bags of freshly purchased, unwrapped presents. "John!"

Helen said, secretly relieved that he'd showed up at all. "We're so glad you're here." Fred didn't say anything. He simply shook John's hand and burned up a little bit inside, while doing a good job of camouflaging it from everybody else.

The next day when gifts were exchanged Candy received something special from John: the engagement ring that she should have gotten two years ago. Candy put it on, and the diamond caught the light in just the right way. It suddenly made her and everybody else around the Austins' Christmas tree forget all of John's foibles. Candy cried tears of joy. She hugged her husband and ran to the kitchen to telephone Judy Halbert.

"I got it!" she told Judy, barely able to catch her breath. "John bought me the ring!"

"Oh, I'm so happy for you," Judy said, as she checked herself in the mirror. Judy saw the reflection of her own engagement ring and felt a tinge of selfishness, grateful that Richie did things the right way. "I bet it's just beautiful."

"It's so nice. I love him so much, Judy."

Sitting alongside Helen in the other room, holding Jesse in his lap, John beamed. For once the Austin family appeared to be completely pleased with him, and he savored the rare moment.

Most other times an underlying tension followed him into situations, and that particularly rankled Fred. He came to see John as somebody who could not be counted on for his help—whether it was a small errand that he agreed to run, or a major home improvement that he'd offered to help with—and in Fred's eyes a man like that could not be trusted to deal with life's bigger issues either.

Ironically, considering his stormy relationship with the rest of the family, John had immediately hit it off with Candy's cousins next door. Joe Frank, a naturally easygoing man, worked as a hospital attendant at the nearby Essex County Geriatrics Center. Like John, he enjoyed sitting in the backyard and drinking beer after work. While Joe, with his soft features and compliant personality, lacked John's swagger, the two men became drinking buddies by default. Brews in hand, they whiled away post-work evenings together. On Saturday nights they teamed up with their wives, always managing to find something inexpensive to do. The two couples generally watched TV, played board games, and drank.

On those evenings, Betty and Joe saw John's domineering presence emerge. "Trot out to the liquor store," he told Candy when the refrigerator ran low on beer.

"Why don't you get up and go yourself?" Betty asked, trying to defend her cousin.

"That's Candy's job around here." John leaned back and smiled, remaining calm. "I work all week, and she takes care of the groceries."

"John thinks he's the king of this castle," Candy said, rolling her eyes and struggling to make the episode resemble a running joke. Then she put on her coat, found the keys to her Cutlass, and waited for John to hand her some money.

Feeling sorry for Candy, Betty reached for her own coat and offered to go along. "We'll leave the men alone," she said, in an effort to alleviate Candy's embarrassment.

Betty and Joe heard John brag about being the best contractor in the county, and saw him turn sullen at family affairs. When Fred and Helen celebrated their thirtieth wedding anniversary with a Sunday afternoon party, John barely said a word to anybody before heading for the bedroom and sleeping through the day. As he disappeared Fred muttered, "Good riddance. Everything'll be more enjoyable without him around anyway." He arrived late at one Thanksgiving dinner, then touched none of the turkey, claiming not to be hungry because he had already eaten.

But when John offered to take Betty and Joe along with him and Candy to some New Year's Eve parties in

1980, they had reason to believe that it would be an entertaining night. John had been invited to several of his clients' celebrations in some of the area's most upscale communities.

The two couples—all dressed in their best clothing, John looking particularly dapper in a suede sport jacket—piled into the gold Cutlass. In the front seat, eighteen-month-old Jessica sat on Candy's lap. "We're taking you to Grandma Short," Candy told the little girl, who sputtered baby talk and napped for most of the ride. "You're going to stay there tonight while Mommy and Daddy go out."

Once they arrived at James and Adele Short's home, however, Jessica cried loudly and ceaselessly. Not only was she unaccustomed to being without Candy, but she hardly knew these grandparents and refused to be left alone in a strange house with them. John's relationship with his parents was so strained and distant that they rarely spent time together, and he visited them only in a pinch. As a result his little girl knew next to nothing about her paternal grandparents, and this did not seem destined to be the night on which they'd get acquainted. Each time Candy put her down and got ready to leave, Jessica wailed uncontrollably. Finally everybody agreed that bringing her along would be the simplest solution.

"Shit," John muttered to himself as they approached the car. "You can't bring a baby out on New Year's Eve."

Candy considered telling him that if he hadn't been too stingy to hire a babysitter, bringing her along wouldn't have been necessary. But she held back and cheerfully said, "Oh, it won't be so bad." Then, looking down at the baby, she added, "Jesse's going out for her first New Year's Eve party."

Silence marred the trip to the earliest bash. John's mood turned sullen, and he infected everybody else with the dour vibe. Once they'd arrived at their destination, John got out of the car and brusquely led the group inside. Upon seeing his host, he went through another transformation; it was as if a heavy drop cloth had been lifted from his body. John greeted the man with a warm handshake, didn't bother introducing his wife or cousins, and left Candy, Jesse, Betty, and Joe to fend for themselves as he made his way to the bar.

Standing awkwardly among the revelers, they looked out of place. Besides not knowing anybody and being too far out of their element to mingle, they were saddled with the baby. In a room full of unencumbered adults, Candy felt foolish. Her husband's refusal to look out for her compounded Candy's unease. Watching other couples—attentive men bringing drinks to their wives, drawing them into conversations, introducing them around as a matter of course—left Candy miserable. True to character, though, she never said a word about her unhappiness to Betty and Joe. Whether she was embarrassed or simply trying to make the best of a bad situation, Candy emitted an air of indifference.

"This is unbelievable," Betty whispered to her husband. She looked around at the people and couldn't remember ever having been such an outsider at a social event. "I feel like a jerk here. Maybe we can get John to leave and go on to the next party."

Eventually, after John had tired of bragging and talking into the faces of guests at this gathering, they departed. At the next stop, though, it was more of the same. The word *networking* had not yet been coined, but that's what John would have called it. He considered the evening good for business, a business that was finally growing at an impressive rate. Whether or not it pleased the people with him—indeed, his wife and members of her family—was far from John's mind as he all but strapped on a smile and bullied his way to the bar at the next party on his New Year's Eve itinerary.

When the clock struck midnight, ushering in 1981, Candy stood alone. Smooching, toasting couples surrounded her, and strains of "Auld Lang Syne" blasted through her brain. She couldn't have known to what extent this night's misery would be a harbinger of the coming six months.

Geri Austin reached into her pocketbook and handed Candy six one-dollar bills. It was her fee for four hours of babysitting. "I really appreciate your paying me today instead of waiting for the end of the week," Candy said. "There's hardly any food in the house, and I have to pick something up for dinner."

Jessica reclined in the baby carriage and smiled at her mother, who placed the money in her wallet. In the course of doing it Candy's shirt sleeve hitched up, exposing something that caught her Aunt Geri's eye. "What happened?" she asked, pointing to the purple welt on Candy's forearm.

"Oh," Candy said, smiling crookedly, "I banged my arm. You know how clumsy I am."

"Really. How'd you manage that? I mean, it's an awkward spot. I've never banged my forearm like that."

Candy didn't say anything. She packed away the disposable diapers that she had brought along for Jessica and tried to make a hasty exit, but Geri persisted. "Candy, did John do that to you?"

Candy stopped in mid-motion, stunned. "How do you know?" she asked her aunt.

Rather than answering that question and forcing Candy to recognize just how obvious the bruises were, Geri asked how it had happened. "He has such a bad temper," Candy said, her head down, holding back the tears that often accompany intense confessions. "We fight over tiny things, things that wouldn't get somebody else upset. If dinner isn't exactly the way John wants it, if I bug him about going to visit Mom and Dad, if Jesse starts crying when he wants to sleep, John yells and screams. Sometimes he pushes me and hits me. That's why I don't mind spending so many evenings with my parents, Aunt Geri. Beyond a certain point, I just can't take it."

"If you have those kinds of problems with John you should speak to Harry," she said, referring to her policeman husband. "If anybody will know how to handle John, it'll be him."

Candy nodded, realizing that she would never bring Harry into it. She asked Geri not to mention the bruises to anybody, unable to admit that she still loved John in spite of the beatings. Like many battered women, Candy isolated the behavior from its source and continued to believe that if she could just find the right formula, the brutality would cease.

"It's not always bad," Candy explained to Geri as she carried Jesse out the door. "You've got to know that John can be a very sweet man."

"I don't know about that," her aunt responded, "but you can't let him go on treating you so badly."

As Candy maneuvered her daughter into the car and rumbled away from the house, Geri couldn't lose the mental image of that lurid purple circle on her niece's forearm.

While nobody else acknowledged the marks, most anybody close to Candy found it impossible to keep from recognizing her marriage's fragile state. During a telephone conversation with Judy, Candy mentioned that their sex life—which John once prided himself on—had diminished to nearly nothing. John stayed out later and later, spending increasing amounts of time after work at the go-go bars. When he was outside of the house with Candy, John became remarkably sullen. Within the apartment's walls, his outbursts escalated.

One evening in January of 1981, following a long discussion about the usual problems—John's drinking, his refusal to properly support Candy and Jesse, a lack of devotion to the family—John flared up. "You want attention?" he asked. "Here, I'll give you attention." He picked up the high-impact plastic walker that Candy had purchased for Jessica and heaved it at his wife. She scrambled out of the way and the heavy toy crashed against the wall. It hit the floor in two pieces.

Candy began crying, her body crumpling in a heap to the linoleum floor. "I can't believe you did that!" she wailed at John. "You broke Jesse's walker! Now you owe her a new one!"

"I don't owe nobody shit," John said, his voice rich with menace but his body suddenly drained of the frustration that this marriage filled him with. It was as if by breaking the walker he had smashed some emotional lock that kept him pinned down in an impossible situation. "You want a new walker? You go to the store and buy one."

Candy knew what would be coming next, and chose not to stick around for the physical altercations that often followed these verbal fights. She scooped Jesse out of her crib and ran with the baby from the apartment. Hustling down Joralemon Street to her parents' place on Passaic Avenue, she kept looking back to see if John was trailing her. But she needn't have worried. He remained in the apartment to pop the top on a fresh beer and let the anger melt away. Candy opened the unlocked door of her childhood home and walked inside to find Fred and Helen sitting on the couch. Her mother worked the thread in and out of a needlepoint pattern, and Fred stared at the television. What a change! No yelling, no screaming, everything so peaceful. The realization was obvious: Life is supposed to be this way.

"Is John tired again?" Helen asked, absently looking up from the eagle and liberty bell that slowly took shape.

Candy meant to say yes. Then she wanted to say no. In the end neither word passed her lips. She began crying instead. "We had a big fight, Mom. I don't know if I'm ever going back to him. I can't take all the changes he goes through. Sometimes he's so nice, but other times he can be so moody and mean. It's just too much for me."

"Tonight you and Jesse can stay here," Helen said, hugging her daughter and trying to comfort her. "You think about it. Maybe you and John can work things out."

"Whatever you decide to do, you know we're behind you," Fred told Candy, not so sure that the situation was resolvable.

Candy and the baby spent the next week with her parents. Being away from John, and living without the yelling and screaming and tension that came with him, had a soothing effect. Yet it also left her blue. She missed her husband. After three days Candy spoke to him on the telephone, then he sent flowers and dropped off a new walker for Jesse. At the week's end he came over for dinner, looking handsome and acting relaxed. Candy and John had a long talk. Seven days alone had mellowed both of them. The anger was gone from John's voice and Candy aired no complaints. His tone soft and rational, John once again seemed the smart, caring, confident man who had shopped at the Towne Deli.

"We'll work things out," he insisted to Candy. His promises served as a panacea, calming her and making it impossible not to remember the good times they had before all the problems began. They agreed to give the relationship another shot.

But John's vow to turn things around quickly proved worthless, and the marriage resumed its downward slide. During the first few months of 1981 the relationship became as bad as it had ever been. Now John desperately wanted out of the marriage—though, as before, he sought to avoid the alimony and child-support payments that would come with leaving his wife to raise their daughter on her own. Then Candy mentioned that she believed she was once again pregnant.

"Get an abortion," John told her.

"I can't do that," Candy responded, her Christianity more important to her than appeasing John.

"Well, we can't afford another child."

"Let's see, John. Maybe my period is late. Maybe I'm not pregnant at all."

"Well if you are, we can't keep the child," he insisted, walking away.

As usual John got the last word, and Candy avoided raising the subject again. A couple of weeks later John saw a Tampax wrapper in the bathroom trash basket. He stared at the paper the way a miner gratefully eyes a hunk of gold in a dry-bed of rock.

By the time of Candy's twenty-fourth birthday on April 25, 1981, she stopped expecting very much from John, and had reached the gloomy conclusion that her life was as good as it would get. Yet the thought of divorce left Candy petrified. She didn't want to be alone; Jesse needed a father, and Candy needed a husband. The marriage, she believed, should be salvaged at any cost. Considering that many of her friends were already married or on the brink of it, a newly single Candy would have nobody to disco with, even if those flashy times had not already passed her by.

She experienced a mild sort of gratitude on that Saturday morning when John sipped his breakfast coffee and slid his MasterCard across the table to Candy. "Here," he said. "Buy yourself something for your birthday."

"Thank you," Candy said, numb to the more personalized modes of gift-giving. "I'll call Judy and see if she wants to go shopping with me."

"Sounds good," John said, getting up from the table. "I've got a few errands to run today, and I need to pick up some supplies for a job we're doing in Jones's building."

"Don't forget to be home early. Your parents are coming to my parents' place, and we're all going to have birthday cake."

"Uh-huh," John replied, slamming the door behind him and not bothering to say good-bye or wish his wife a happy birthday.

That afternoon Candy, Jesse, and Judy shopped at the Willowbrook Mall. After trying on a few different styles of pants, Candy settled on a pair of blue jeans that looked attractive and successfully concealed her stomach. On the way back Candy suggested to Judy, "Since it's my birthday, why don't you come over and have dinner with us?"

"Okay," Judy said. "But I'm supposed to go out with Richie tonight, so I can't eat too late."

"That's no problem. We're eating early so that we can meet John's folks at my parents' house for birthday cake."

Even though they saw each other infrequently, Candy and Judy found it easy to pick up their friendship where it had left off, losing very little intimacy in the process. Judy talked about her upcoming wedding, and Candy mentioned her recent brush with pregnancy. They reminisced a little bit, Judy marveled at how much Jesse had grown since Christmas, and Candy avoided discussing anything that would give away the unraveling state of her marriage.

Back at the garden apartment, Judy sat on the couch and watched her friend prepare dinner. "Since it's my birthday, I'm treating myself to roasted chicken," she said. "It's my favorite dish, but I never get to eat it because John hates chicken."

"But he's going to eat it tonight?" asked a disbelieving Judy.

"No." Candy reached into the refrigerator and pulled out a cellophane-wrapped chunk of red meat. "I'm going to make this for John just as soon as he comes home, which should be any minute. Since chicken takes longer to cook than steak, the timing should be perfect." Candy smiled, then joked in a crackly Julia Child voice, "Here in the Short household, culinary excellence is a way of life."

An hour later the chicken had finished cooking, but John had yet to arrive. Candy reduced the heat to keep it warm and started making phone calls. She finally reached him at a friend's gas station. Annoyed that she called him there, John said that he'd be leaving in a little while. A half hour later, at six-thirty, Candy and Judy ate dinner without him. When the meal was finished Judy had to leave, and still there was no sign of John.

"Well, I hope you have a happy birthday," Judy said, careful not to mention John and risk upsetting Candy.

"I will have a happy birthday, if that husband of mine ever comes home."

Fifteen minutes after Judy had departed, Helen called on the telephone. "When are you and John coming by?" she wanted to know.

"As soon as John gets home."

"He's not *home*? His parents have been sitting here for twenty minutes already. Where is he?"

"At the gas station, Mom. He told me he'll be back in a little while. I don't know what you expect me to do. You know how John's been lately."

"Well," Helen said tersely, "I'm just calling to tell you that the Shorts are here and that as soon as John gets back, you, him, and Jesse should come over."

Candy hung up the telephone and waited for her husband. She cut herself a jumbo-size rectangle of brownie, resigned to the reality that this year's birthday would not be a happy one.

CHAPTER
5

Summer weather arrived early in 1981, and the prematurely warm afternoons brought a giddy air to Joralemon Street. But John and Candy were too embroiled in their joyless existence to notice flowers blooming and trees growing thick with green leaves. Two-year-old Jessica learned to walk and spoke her first words, though her parents barely communicated. They neglected to put their winter clothing into storage and didn't bother making weekend plans for the summer. John simply turned up the air conditioning and griped about the electric bills. As had become the custom, Betty and Joe frequently dropped by to enjoy a cool respite from the fans that spun ceaselessly in their house, recirculating warm air but doing nothing to truly cool the place off.

Standing in the kitchen with Betty, Candy looked sad, dejected, and confused. Despite Betty's experience in dealing with the soured marriage that had preceded her union with Joe, Candy refrained from asking for advice. Maybe she feared that word would get back to her parents, maybe she didn't want Betty to know the extent of her problems. Whatever the case, Candy did her best to maintain a screen of indifference about her difficulties with John.

The two women brought bottles of beer and bowls of potato chips to their husbands in the living room. Sitting alongside Joe, John spoke loud and fast, aiming his remarks in the face of Candy's cousin. "When I'm on a job, I'm the boss," he said. "You do what I say or you work for somebody else. This little jerkoff of an apprentice carpenter—" He cut himself off, turned toward Candy and Betty, then said, "I'm telling him about the job we're working on in Newark." He turned back to Joe and continued, "The guy thought he had a better way of putting on a door. Shit. I showed him how to do it, he didn't want to listen, I finally told him, 'My way or highway.' He got the point, he did it the way I wanted him to, and it worked just fine."

On that note John got up and went to the bathroom. Candy rolled her eyes at Betty but didn't dare say a word. The commode was situated close enough to the living room that every sound carried there, and Candy didn't want to gct John riled. Lately it took very little. Betty sensed this and retreated to a neutral topic. "So, how's the dancing going?" she asked, referring to the tap dance classes that Candy had enrolled in at the beginning of the year.

"Really great. We're getting ready for our big recital at the end of the month."

"That's so exciting. Are you going to have a special costume?"

"Just silver tights. Anything heavier than that would weigh us down."

The toilet flushed and John reentered the living room. He walked past his desk, which occupied the far corner, and fished around on it, searching for a blueprint that Joe wanted to see. Papers and books and magazines were piled high in the center of the tabletop. Among the collection was the new issue of *Hustler* magazine. John grabbed the sex publication instead of the blueprint, which he couldn't find anyway.

Trying to get a rise from his guests, he opened the magazine to its centerfold and revealed June's *Hustler* Honey. "Hey, Joe," he called out, "how do you like her?"

Sensing Betty's disapproval, Joe said nothing. He simply looked at the beautifully built woman and raised his eyebrows in acknowledgment. Had John put the magazine down and forgotten about it, the incident would have passed without comment. But he always took things a step further than seemed reasonable. "This is what my next wife is going to look like," John added.

"What next wife?" Candy asked, trying to sound more coy than peeved. "You're married to me."

"I mean after I divorce you."

She reacted as if John had taken a prod and jabbed it into an open sore. "Divorce me, John, and Jesse and I will take you for every cent you have," she vowed. "You'll be paying alimony for the rest of your life."

Betty and Joe sat on the couch, taken aback by the sudden outburst. This was a side of the marriage that they had suspected but never witnessed. What had begun as a tasteless joke seemed to be escalating into something more sinister. Behind the seemingly harmless quips were sharp barbs that stung. As the comments grew in severity, it became increasingly clear that this conversation represented more than the standard tiff between a couple. Candy must have known that her last rejoinder would set John off, that the possibility of perpetually supporting his wife and daughter in absentia would upset him more than any other threat she could have made.

Appearing to be on the verge of attacking her, John turned to Candy, and, without the slightest bit of irony, he said, "I'll live to piss on your fucking grave."

"And I'll haunt you from it for the rest of your life," Candy responded, in the singsong tone of a taunting schoolgirl.

Before John could reply, Jesse started crying. Grateful for an excuse to stop arguing, Candy tended to the baby. Betty and Joe felt extremely uncomfortable. They struggled to relax and make small talk, but clearly it was forced. Neither one said anything about it, but they now both realized that the marriage had frayed beyond mend-ing. Joe already knew about John's regular forays to the go-go bars, and Candy kept Betty apprised of his late nights and unpredictable schedule. Prior to this fight, however, neither one of them had realized how much hate and resentment had built up between the couple. Joe later characterized the argument as a safety valve, a way of blowing off steam to postpone the inevitable final explosion. Still, Betty saw no real danger. "What's the worst that could happen?" she mused. "Maybe they'll get divorced?"

Betty, however, could never have known Candy's deep-seated aversion to being alone, to admitting that she had failed to make the marriage work out. Even as the relationship and the institution that it was inextricably bound up with collapsed all around her, Candy still held tightly to a clichéd notion of what marriage should be. She continued to daydream about a future with white picket fences and puppy dogs, and a loving husband who brought her flowers when he came home from work.

Long after John had stopped unraveling the blueprint for visitors, Candy still mooned over the dreamhouse that she called Tara. Even as John demanded that she have a baby aborted, Candy saw a big family of kids filling up the house that her husband had promised her. Candy pathetically clung to the fantasy, fearing that if she let go she'd have no other form of support, nothing else to keep her on her feet. Only the hope of a promising future kept Candy going from one day to the next. Without that, she might as well have been dead.

John maintained fantasies of another sort. Sitting in the bars, numbing his brain with Jack Daniels, he exposed himself to a world of implied sexual and financial freedom—something he hadn't known for years.

On the seventeenth floor of 17 Academy Street in Newark, New Jersey, in a room filled with computers, John thought about a draft beer, a shot of bourbon, and a hamburger. He snuck a glance at a digital clock on somebody's desk, saw the time closing in on 12:30 P.M., and read the date as June 15, 1981. He struggled to make a piece of Sheetrock fit into a 7' x 4' slot of window insulation. The idea was to cover the window glass, preventing condensation from leaking into the room and hampering the computers' software.

It was a routine job, but in his rush to get it done Short became careless. He pressed his thin lips together and attempted to force the sheet into place. "Son of a bitch," he grunted, stepping back from the layer of insulation. Maneuvering himself to get a fresh angle on the job, he brushed a few strands of stringy brown hair out of his face and kicked at the material, as if the Sheetrock could be made malleable by sheer force.

He cursed again, louder this time, and smashed an open palm against the sheet, putting on a hot-headed show for his two helpers, Dennis King and Dan Solowe. This was nothing out of the ordinary. King and Solowe, two guys in their early twenties who were reasonably skilled laborers, had already witnessed many tantrums; they'd watched John fling hammers at inept employees, and had learned to expect their boss to react first and ask questions later. Yet they also acknowledged his habit of swinging from nasty to nice and back again. Glancing over at them, Short managed a halfhearted smile and said, "Life's too short for this shit, especially on a Monday. Let's break for lunch."

Dutifully, the two men put down their tools and followed John to the elevator. The ride down was a quiet one, their T-shirts and soiled Levi's looking shabby next to the pin-striped suits worn by a group of men who shared the car with them. Stepping off of the elevator, Short and his workers discussed the progress they were making on the job upstairs. The small talk continued as they went out through the building's double doors onto Academy Street, a modern commercial strip that contrasted with the urban squalor surrounding it.

A Marlboro Light already in his mouth, Short cupped

his hands against a warm breeze and ignited a match as they headed down to The Coach Light go-go bar. Standing in the shadow of a skyscraper that housed the Prudential insurance company's state headquarters, it attracted an afternoon crowd of blue-collar laborers. A relatively peaceful clientele, they mingled easily with the insurance firm's middle-management personnel, who also lunched there.

Beyond the long wooden bar that ran the length of the lounge, they saw Will Lambert, Lester Firth, and a few other regulars gathered around the pool table. Elbowing through a crowd at the bar, Short ordered a round of drinks and met Solowe and King near the pool area, where Lambert was setting up for what could be a game-winning shot. His double chin padded his neck as he applied a soft, smooth touch, nudging the cue ball toward the eight. It dropped into the corner pocket, and good-natured Lester Firth skulked off in a defeat.

Lambert took a long draw from his beer, then nodded at Short and asked, "You want to be my next victim?"

"You want to buy me a drink?" Short playfully shot back, draining his mug of beer and continuing to nurse a shot glass filled with Jack Daniels. He dropped a quarter into the pool table and began racking the balls, as the thirty-year-old Lambert proceeded to the back end of the bar.

While trying to flag down the bartender, Lambert found himself face-to-chest with Diane Lovejoy. Wearing lacy white panties and a matching bra, both of which she'd recently purchased from the Sears Roebuck catalogue, Diane stood on a five-foot by five-foot platform, just twelve inches above the ground, bumping and grinding to an old Rolling Stones song on the jukebox. The twenty-six-year-old woman had long blond hair and a thin frame that was topped by full, round breasts, which the mail-order lingerie barely contained.

She smiled at Lambert, a stocky, good-natured man with light brown hair and a physique that recently started going to flab. He grinned back, one eye focused on the errant barkeep. "A guy could die of thirst trying to get a drink in this place," he told her, holding up the pair of empty mugs.

"Don't die on me, honey," she drawled, shaking her breasts to the beat. "It'd cause an awful scene."

Short racked the balls on the pool table, but the game was no longer on his mind. Initially catching a glimpse of the dancer from the corner of his eye, he now stared, unable to shift his attention away from Diane. When Lambert returned with the drinks, he teased Short about appearing to be hypnotized by the well-built dancer.

"She is one stacked bitch," John said, reaching for a pool cue. "I'd like to see if she's as hot in bed as she is on stage."

"So what's stopping you?" Lambert asked, breaking the triangular pack of balls and landing a solid in the side pocket. At first glance, John and Will appeared to be unlikely friends. Short was stridently blue-collar, a hell-raiser with a knack for consistently going one step too far. He had a taste for hard liquor, soft drugs, and large-breasted women. Will, on the other hand, was low key and a diligent manager in the accounting department of a Newark-based shipping corporation. He graduated from Rutgers University, wore a suit to the office, worked hard, and kept his staff of bean counters under a tight but friendly rein.

The two men had met when Lambert expressed an interest in buying a house that Short had constructed. Soon after the deal was completed they began palling around together; and when Short mentioned that he was having trouble getting work, Lambert offered to help him out. He passed the contractor's name on to the people at his company, who eventually hired Short for a couple of small jobs, including the computer-room insulation assignment.

Things went well enough that other companies along Academy Street began throwing contracting work his way. As a result, he found himself spending a good deal of down-time at The Coach Light. Cheap and friendly, with an owner who was more than likely to match customers drink for drink and dancers who "accidentally" let their breasts pop free from their tops, it was Short's kind of place. But for all of The Coach Light's congeniality, its dancers tended to be what John categorized as "dogs." Diane Lovejoy, however, as anybody there could attest, was clearly not in that class.

After losing his game of pool and finishing a hamburger, John Short expounded on that very fact. "I'm gonna ask her out," he told a half-dozen guys crammed around a small square table, his voice revealing elements of bravado and a desire to be dared. "What do you think of that? Think that broad'd go out with me?"

"Shut up, shut up," Lambert said, elbowing Short in the ribs. "I think she's coming over here."

"She's coming over here?"

The sentence was barely out of Short's mouth before Diane toddled to the table, beaming down at the men gathered there. Looking at Lambert, the only one she'd actually met, Diane now wore a wraparound that pretty much covered her bra-and-panties ensemble. She asked, "Can I join you fellows?"

"Sure," Lambert said, moving over and grabbing a chair from the adjacent table. "What are you drinking?"

"J.D. and Coke," she said, settling onto the seat as he scuttled off to the bar.

"Cocktail of southern nobility," Short managed to get out, cribbing a line he'd heard in some movie. He held up his own glass of bourbon, seemed about to say something important, and took a sip of the liquor instead.

Each man at the table introduced himself, and Diane explained that she recently relocated to the area and hoped to be dancing at The Coach Light on a regular basis. This was followed by a round of double entendres and semi-dirty jokes—"Don't worry," one guy said. "If your outfit falls off, I'll be there to cover you"—that amused Diane without offending her. She ordinarily avoided socializing with customers, but Lambert and his group seemed reasonably civilized and Diane was needy for friendship, so she decided to make an exception.

After a few minutes the men became immersed in a heated discussion about the coming season's Giants football team. Diane listened quietly, occasionally allowing herself to be led into the conversation by Lambert, but most of the talk went over her head. Ruminating over what seemed to be a matter of great importance, John Short said very little. Slouched in his chair, he sipped at his drink and stole occasional glances at the blonde next to him.

Her twenty-minute break began winding down, and he could hold out no longer. With everybody else's attention diverted by sports talk, Short leaned over and softly told Diane, "I got a hundred dollars in my wallet that says you'd like to spend the night with me."

Slightly startled, she looked at him and contemplated the desperate bid. Then she smiled sympathetically. "Now, why would a handsome guy like you have to pay for somebody like me?"

Her eyes approvingly took in his physical form: angular face, high cheekbones, smooth complexion, thin physique. Break time was over. She sashayed off, deposited a handful of quarters into the jukebox, and retreated to the little platform at the end of the bar. It was just as well, anyway, as lunch had already stretched into two hours and the guys needed to get back to work. As they prepared to leave, however, John announced that he'd be staying and told Solowe and King to take the afternoon off.

On his own, he found a fine vantage point at the far end of the bar and ordered a beer and a shot. No man could have denied Diane's seductiveness, and anybody attracted to her in this environment would doubtlessly try to imagine what the dancer looked like naked. They'd be wondering if her nipples were wide and light-colored, the delicate shade of shell pink common to true blondes. By all indications, John Short was no different from the typical go-go bar habitué; apparently, he was smitten by Diane Lovejoy.

"Early day today?" the bartender asked John, sliding across a shot on the house.

"You betcha." John dropped his head back and downed it in a single swallow. "What's with that new girl?"

"She just moved up here from Florida. I think she's working her way through music school or some shit. She sure is pretty, though."

John wanted to know more about Diane, but it would have been awkward to pursue the issue. Like most of the crowd from Academy Street, Short was not above a lunchtime quickie with one of the bar girls, but Diane represented something different. He fantasized about them sharing a vague future together. It was ridiculous, he had to have known that, but he couldn't think of her in any other way.

Diane's voice interrupted his pleasant musings. "Penny for your thoughts," she said from behind the bar, squirting herself a diet Coke from the soda gun.

"I've got a lot on my mind," Short said, silently remembering his financial problems.

"I know what you mean," Diane replied. "I've been going through some hard times of my own."

"Like what?" John sensed a crack in her sexual armor.

"Mostly learning to deal with the death of my husband." Looking into her glass of soda, Diane reached for the bottle of Jack Daniels. She spiked her drink and refilled John's shot glass. "Brett, he was my husband, died two years ago. We were jogging on the beach and he had a heart attack. Passed away right before my eyes."

John lightly pressed for details, and Diane explained that they were on holiday in the Bahamas when it happened. "The worst vacation of my life," she added.

"I can sympathize with you." John slowly shook his head, stalling as he formulated a lie designed to elicit sympathy. "I'm going through a similar thing myself. Six months ago my wife was mugged and murdered in the parking lot of a shopping mall. They never even caught the bastard who did it."

"That's horrible!" Diane explained. Cutting through the pity—*so lonely that he'd pay to sleep with me*—Diane sensed a common link that suddenly turned John into a man she could empathize with. "Do you have any children?"

"Just Jessica. She recently turned two years old. I don't see her as much as I'd like to, though, since she's moved in with her grandparents."

After two years of suffering the loss in relative silence, Diane was thrilled to find somebody who could understand her sadness, a man who could relate to the extreme sort of isolation that comes with the sudden passing of a spouse. Attracted to John from the start, Diane now felt an interest that went beyond the physical. In John Short, Diane saw a man who could make her feel important again, the way Brett had done. Surprised by his lack of emotion—Short recited the details of his wife's murder as if they were items on a shopping list—she assumed that he had not yet come to terms with the death. Her father, after all, was a psychiatrist, and she knew all about those things. Before long John would have to confront the reality of it. It would be painful, but she wouldn't mind being there to help him along.

They talked for a few more minutes before agreeing to meet at six that evening, when Diane's workday would end. "I've got a few errands to run anyway," John said, paying his bar tab. She returned to the small stage and John walked out the door, shielding his eyes from the mid-afternoon glare on Academy Street.

Will Lambert's office was overly elaborate. Outfitted with a wood-burning fireplace, wet bar, Italian-designed fixtures, and a tasteful chandelier, the place would have better suited a movie mogul. Indeed, its previous occupant had been a Warner Bros. executive, back when the entertainment conglomerate had maintained a division in Newark. Due to an odd contractual clause, the pricey fixtures had been left intact, and Lambert lucked into the swankiest office a middle manager could hope for.

Nicknamed the Pussy Palace, its amenities impressed the Coach Light girls and Lambert took full advantage of that fact. When other people on the floor saw his door shut, they learned to view it as a sign that he had company of the non-business variety. With no female employees in the vicinity, and few higher-ups around, his indiscretions were easily overlooked.

Minutes after leaving Diane at the bar Short was helping himself to Lambert's private stock, pouring a generous shot of Jack Daniels. Sipping at the drink, and fidgety with anticipation, he sat on the couch and waited for his friend to finish a phone conversation. Lambert hung up, raked a hand through his thick hair, and knew the answer before he asked the question: "Any luck with Diane?"

"Plenty of luck," Short said, hoisting the glass in an imaginary toast. "I'm supposed to meet her after work."

"Smooth move, buddy." Lambert held out his hand for a high-five; Short stood up and complied.

"The only thing is, I need to borrow your credit card, the one that gets billed to the office. I figure I'll take her to Howard Johnson's and pay you back when the invoice comes."

"What's the matter, don't you have any money?"

"Well, to tell you the truth, I have a hundred bucks . . ." Short's voice trailed off, and he fiddled with a bottle on the bar before admitting, "But it looks like I'm going to have to give the money to her."

"You're *paying* her for sex?" Lambert asked incredulously. Not waiting for a nod, he reached into his wallet and fished out a Carte Blanche card. Short reached for the plastic, took it, and slipped it into the pocket of his flannel shirt.

"Thanks a lot, Lamb," he said, patting him on the shoulder. "You're a real buddy."

"Yeah," Lambert replied. "I hope you get your money's worth." As John Short's form disappeared from the Pussy Palace, Will Lambert softly mused, "The poor son of a bitch, now he's paying for it."

Back at The Coach Light, Short sat at the bar and drank two more glasses of Jack Daniels while he watched Diane dance. At the set's completion she changed into her street clothes—a silver wraparound dress, black body stocking, and black pumps—and sat down next to him. "Did you miss me?" she asked, signaling the bartender for a fresh drink.

"I've been thinking about you all day," John truthfully said, his eyes cruising the length of her body.

"You're a real cutie, John. Do you know that?"

He absorbed the praise, smiled charmingly, and said, "You're not too shabby yourself." Reaching behind Diane, John rested his left arm on the back of her stool. She swayed toward him and placed a hand on his thigh. Any attraction that John felt for Diane was more than mutual. She found his lanky build and kindly, laid-back demeanor to be extremely appealing. If Diane needed an emotional clincher, it was the tragedy of his wife's murder. As much as Diane Lovejoy wanted a man to love, she also wanted one to nurture.

Two drinks later, they were out the door. Walking arm-in-arm, they buzzed with the heady combination of alcohol and sexual anticipation.

"My car's right here," John said, stopping at a gold-colored Cutlass. "Why don't we take it? We'll get yours later."

Diane climbed into the passenger seat, not bothering to question where they'd be going.

"Are you into dance, John?" she asked, sounding a little skeptical.

"What makes you think that?" he wondered, merging

the car onto the highway that led to the nearby Howard Johnson's.

"The bumper stickers on the back of your car: 'I'd Rather Be Dancing' and 'Capezio.' "

"Candy, ah, my wife, had put them there. She loved dancing."

"Oh, I'm sorry. Sometimes I say the stupidest things."

"Don't worry about it. You didn't do no harm."

Appreciating John's easy way, Diane curled up on the front seat and leaned against him, neither of them saying very much until they reached the motel.

John checked them in, using Lambert's credit card, and they made out like high school kids on the elevator ride up to their floor. Once behind closed doors, the two of them undressed with a passionate urgency. Diane climbed on top of John, kissed her way to his crotch and took him in her mouth. Drunk and anxious, on this night John was hardly the stud that he once had been.

After orgasming during foreplay, he couldn't apologize enough. Surprisingly, Diane didn't mind; she did not view this as a one-night stand, and was willing to give their sexual rhythm a chance to develop. "Don't worry about it," she assured John, secure in his arms, enjoying the sensation of him running his fingers through her hair. "I liked it just fine. I liked it because I like you."

They talked throughout the night, discussing their dreams and hopes for the future. Diane revealed her ambition to be a classical violinist, and confirmed that she was dancing to earn tuition for music school. John told her that he had big plans for the contracting business. He wouldn't always be working on small-scale interior jobs. "Jesus Christ," he said, more to himself than to Diane. "I wish I'd met you five years ago. Before my life got complicated."

"Do you want to talk about it, John? Do you want to talk about Candy?"

"No. I'd rather discuss the future."

*   *   *

Late-night phone calls became routine for Candy Short. The way another wife might put her kids to sleep, watch some TV, and prepare her husband's bag lunch for the next day while the eleven o'clock news rumbled in the background, she would reach for the telephone and try to track down John. But she was forbidden to call him at The Coach Light, and in the end he invariably came home—albeit sometimes at four in the morning—so, she convinced herself, maybe there really was nothing to worry about. Still, Candy had to admit, John's increasing absences made her anxious.

Sooner or later the late-night carousing would have to stop. Candy knew that. But she also knew that she would never be able to directly confront her husband about it. He'd start screaming and yelling and throwing things around the house. Then he'd hit her and storm out the door. She would end up alone anyway. So what was the use?

Candy tried to look attractive for John, but she had a tendency to be a little overweight, and after the baby's birth it became impossible to drop the extra pounds. Candy checked on Jessica, who slept soundly, looking so peaceful in her crib. On her way back to the small apartment's living room, she cut a slice of brownie and placed it on a paper plate.

Grabbing the phone directory with her free hand, Candy walked to the couch, sat down, and picked up the telephone's receiver. She pressed the seven digits that would connect her with the Lambert home.

Francis Lambert picked up on the third ring, sounding annoyed at getting a call after eleven.

"Hi, Francis, this is Candy Short." Silence on the other end of the line. "I'm sorry for calling you so late, but I'm wondering if Will might know where John is."

"Hang on, Candy. Let me see." She came back a few seconds later and reported that he didn't know where John was. "I'm just happy he's home tonight," Francis said in a confidential tone. "You've got to understand that I'm having trouble keeping track of my own husband."

Candy told her that she understood. She thanked her for checking and apologized for calling so late, then agreed that the two families should get together sometime. As if fearing that a light sleeper alongside her could be easily awakened, Candy gently returned the receiver to its cradle. Stretched out on the couch, waiting like a sentry for John to come home, she wanted to sleep but couldn't make herself stop crying. When she finally did doze off, the TV was still on.

John slept fitfully that night, unable to get comfortable and plagued by his sub-par sexual performance. Rather than imagining this to be a symptom of guilt, Diane Lovejoy viewed it as an indication of John's sensitivity. Their encounter was so meaningful that he couldn't even sleep.

That morning they showered together, soaping each other down and pledging their love. As he dressed, John suddenly realized he had neglected to give Diane her money. "I know you may not want it, but I really think you should take it," he said, counting out one hundred dollars.

"Forget it." Diane was a little insulted by the offer, and also aware that it would distance Short from the potential relationship, reducing what had transpired that night into little more than a business deal. "Don't you remember me saying that a guy like you shouldn't have to pay women for sex?"

"Look, what if I give you the money as something that you can use for your schooling? Believe me, it would make me feel good to help you out."

Put that way, she found the offer more palatable. Never mind that it amounted to the same thing. Diane took the money.

Since she didn't have to be at The Coach Light until ten o'clock, and had more than an hour to kill, Diane agreed to join John for breakfast. They parked near 17 Academy Street and proceeded to Lambert's office, the place where John usually ate when he worked in the building.

"Ready for some breakfast, Lamb?" Short jovially asked, as he and Diane strolled inside. They held each other close, and John paraded the dancer around as if she were a trophy.

The three of them talked a little bit before ordering bacon-and-egg sandwiches; then John dispatched Diane to Lester Firth's office. Once she walked out of earshot, Short allowed a giant smile to break across his face. "No doubt about it, she gave me the best blow job I've ever had," he bragged.

"You're quite a stud, John," Lambert said, his voice a meld of envy and disgust at the thought of his friend paying for such services. Like a lovesick eighth-grader, Short trotted off to Firth's office and brought Diane back for breakfast.

When they were done eating, John walked Diane to the elevator, leaving Lambert and Firth alone. "That wild motherfucker," Firth marveled. "You know what he told Diane? He told her that his wife is dead."

"He told her *what*?"

"That his wife was murdered in a shopping mall. When we were sitting in my office, Diane was telling me what a great guy John is, how lucky she feels to have met him. Then she says that it's a shame about his wife getting murdered."

"What did you say?"

"I didn't *know* what to say," Firth laughed. "So I just played along."

"Well," Lambert said as Firth began to walk out, "it's true."

"What's true?"

"John Short is definitely crazy."

A few minutes later Short strolled back to Lambert's office, looking as if he had just gotten the luckiest break of his life. Will, however, was in no mood for a re-hashing of the previous night's events. "What the hell are you doing, telling that broad that your wife is dead?" he demanded to know.

"You've got to picture this," Short said coolly, sprawled on the couch, shifting into a raconteur mode. "She's behind the bar, her tits are practically in my face, and she's telling me about her past. She tells me that her husband dropped dead of a heart attack while jogging on the beach. Can you imagine a broad like that having a husband who gets a heart attack *jogging*? C'mon, give me a break. So I did her one better. I out-bullshitted the bullshitter."

"You better hire a bodyguard for your wife," Lambert advised, only half joking. "Anything happens to her, and you're in deep shit."

"Get out of here." Short waved his hand dismissively. "Nothing's going to happen to Candy."

The following Thursday, on June 18th, Diane sat alongside John in the front seat of his truck. His voice shook, and he couldn't keep himself from nervously bobbing his right leg up and down. But that's what Diane did to him; she completely enchanted John with her firm body and large breasts. He loved the way she smiled and couldn't get over his luck at having finally fallen in with a dancer. Women like Diane had always cavorted through John's fantasies as he sat at bars and sipped Jack Daniels. From what John told Diane, he seemed eager to work things out with her, get away from Candy. Never mind that if he divorced his wife she would do her best to bankrupt him.

John reached over and put his arms around Diane. They kissed, and he ran his fingers along her breasts. The Howard Johnson's beckoned on the other side of the highway, and returning there, getting her back in bed, would seem like the obvious thing to do. But even John Short, a man with limited respect for fidelity, realized some limitations and acknowledged the importance of keeping the late nights to a minimum.

"Uhm, I want to show you something," he said to Diane. John reached into his back pocket and pulled out a wallet. He opened it to a snapshot of Jesse. The recent photograph depicted a cute and smiling two-year-old with big blue eyes and a head of wavy blond hair. Outwardly ignoring the strong resemblance between his daughter and wife, he passed it to the go-go dancer. "This is my little girl."

"She's beautiful, John, really cute."

"I want you to meet her. I know that you two will get along."

"Okay. I'd like that a lot."

"I know," John said, as if he had just stumbled upon an idea. "Next weekend, a week from this Saturday, the three of us can get together. My parents have a place in the Hamptons [which was not true, although James and Adele Short did own a house in the New Jersey shore town of Ocean Grove] and you, me, and Jesse can go out there."

"That sounds nice." Diane flicked her tongue in and out of John's mouth and wondered whether or not they would soon repair to HoJo's. Then John stole a glance at her watch and saw that it was nearly seven o'clock.

"I'd love to take you back to the motel again. But I've got to get home." John hesitated and nearly choked on his words as he added, "Jesse's, you know, waiting for me."

They kissed in an intricately syncopated way, their tongues dancing around and sliding off each other, before Diane got out of the car. Exiting, Diane handed John an envelope with a card in it. "Happy Father's Day," she said, looking forward to their weekend with Jesse.

On the way back to Belleville John stopped at a liquor store for a six-pack, sprang for Heineken, and opened one of the bottles as he merged back onto the highway. By the time he pulled into the gravel drive, it had turned dusky outside. As usual, Joe Frank sat in his backyard with a cold can of Miller in hand.

"You still drinking that nigger shit?" John shouted, by way of a greeting. He took a long pull from the green bottle and made his way toward Joe.

"Long time no see," Joe said, his voice sounding slightly remote.

"You know how it is, Joe. I've been real busy working on a project."

"I hear that you've been a bad boy, John."

Both men swigged from their beers, and John couldn't help but smile.

"Oh, yeah. What'd you hear?"

"Candy says that you stayed out all night."

"I *was* out all night, but I had a business meeting."

"You can bullshit Candy, but you can't bullshit me. Come on, John, where were you? I'm not going to tell your wife."

In all likelihood, Joe would probably not tell Candy. A more realistic concern was that the story might leak to Betty, who would tell Helen, and then there'd be no telling what could happen. But as much as it would have been smart to remain discreet, John's macho pride and natural desire to brag got the better of him. He couldn't help but reveal all to an eager listener.

"To tell you the truth," John began, "I spent the night with a go-go dancer, a broad named Diane. Beautiful girl." He cupped his hands over his chest and continued, "She's got tits bigger than your head, and gave me the best blow job I've ever had."

Joe found himself somewhat intrigued by John. What man didn't secretly wish he had the moxie to stay out all night, and then come home and brag about it to his wife's cousin? Most guys would happily trade some other quality for a touch of John's machismo, even as they hated him for being so rotten to his wife. And that was the catch for Joe. Overriding any curiosity he had about John's exploits was the pity he had for Candy. Nobody, he thought, least of all his cousin, should have to put up with a guy like this.

"You'd better be careful," Joe warned. "Candy's really upset."

John didn't say anything, though the remark visibly soured him. He took another sip from his beer and sullenly stared into the distance.

At that very moment, Candy needed to talk. But she wanted to speak with somebody far enough removed from her life to react candidly to the current circumstances. Candy was scared. She didn't like the way John had been acting lately. He drank too much, stayed out too late, blew up at the slightest provocation, and showed a mounting disregard for the welfare of her and Jesse.

First she tried phoning Tony Mancuso, thinking that he could give her a male's point of view on the subject. On his way out the door when the phone rang, Tony could talk only for a few minutes. In the course of the conversation, Candy explained that things were not going well with John. She suggested that they get together sometime, and Tony vaguely agreed before cutting the call short. "I'd love to talk, but I really have to run," he begged off, ignoring the uncharacteristic neediness in her voice.

A few seconds after the conversation with Tony had terminated, the telephone rang. Candy picked up the receiver and was pleased to hear Judy's voice on the line. The two friends had spoken for a few minutes, with Candy doing her best to sound congenial, when the operator broke in. She announced an emergency call for Judy and suggested that they hang up; both women complied. The caller turned out to be Judy's cousin, who needed to firm up the evening's dinner plans and didn't feel like waiting for the line to clear. At the time, of course, Judy could not have known that she was turning from the urgent to the trivial.

Years later, what Judy most clearly remembered about the call were her friend's final words: "I have to talk to you about something important." She never found out exactly what that was.

CHAPTER
6

On Monday morning, June 29, 1981, a full week after the murder, Detective Lieutenant Jim Wilson and Detective Billy McCann pulled up alongside the Austins' home in an unmarked sedan. Helen came to the door but, still shaken from the recent events, she was in no condition to speak with them. Protectively, John joined his mother-in-law at the front of the house. Considerably more composed, he not only agreed to meet with the policemen but also allowed them to inspect his apartment. The three men strolled up Passaic Avenue and turned right on Joralemon Street. As they neared the complex, John retold his story. This time, however, he included information about Diane Lovejoy, claiming to know only her first name.

Leading the way to the door, Short's demeanor was restrained but hardly relaxed. "Look wherever you want," John offered, as he unlocked his apartment for the officers and sniffed at the stale odor that escaped.

They proceeded to the bedroom and began inspecting it for clues that Candy might have left behind. Noncommittally, John shrugged. "Maybe you'll find something in here that'll help you with your investigation."

He opened the closed dresser drawers for them, standing by as they looked through his closets and explored what had once been a home. The cops ignored a bag of marijuana and a cache of porn films—"We're not interested in that stuff," one of them later told the suspect—before noticing the cardboard top of a plastic package resting on the dresser. It read "GB-46, silver, small. 100% nylon, $3.50 pr." This grabbed Wilson's attention.

"Do you know what came in here?" he asked Short.

"Maybe they were silver shoes or slippers." John's face gave nothing away, remaining inscrutable as he sat on the edge of the bed.

Wilson remembered Short telling him that he and Candy laundered their clothing at Fred and Helen's place. "Why don't you call down to the Austins," he suggested to McCann. "See if there are any silver tights in the wash over there."

Given John's claim that Candy had gone to the mall to buy silver tights, the discovery that she already had a new pair could cast fresh doubt on his version of what had taken place one week earlier, on the night that Candy was murdered. Coupled with the limited information they already had pointing to John as the primary suspect, this could represent a break in the investigation. When Jeanne had been reached on the phone, she agreed to go through the dirty clothing, while the two detectives continued on their tour of the house, taking copious notes all the while.

They paid particular attention to a set of arrows mounted near John's desk—McCann noted that one had a broken tip; taking the victim's bleeding into account, he wanted to return with a search warrant and confiscate the potential murder weapon—and dried red splotches on the wall of the dining area. When Jeanne called to announce that she had indeed found a pair of silver tights in the laundry, the two detectives realized that they'd have no trouble obtaining a warrant. On their official search they would find out the source of those red markings. Even though this visit seemed to end on neutral note, it was precisely the sort of thing that caused John's ulcer to act up. Churning and stabbing, it felt as if it would cut through his stomach lining.

A day later the officers returned to the apartment, warrant in hand and chemist in tow. As John stood behind them looking smug, arms folded over his chest, the chemist inspected small patches of red on the wall. McCann and Wilson watched anxiously from the sidelines as their man hoped to match these samples with the victim's blood. They both felt quite optimistic about the tests yielding positive identification, linking John Short to the murder of his wife. But the chemist had no need to scrape for samples, and the two law enforcers were sorely disappointed: The so-called blood stains proved to be spots of tomato sauce, probably flicked onto the wall by Jesse as she ate her Spaghetti-O's.

Incidents like this one, coupled with the Austins' insistence that John had not committed the murder and that the police should stop harrassing him, sapped their enthusiasm. Their efforts were further hampered by Allen Brooks, the cautious assistant prosecutor. He had a reputation for refusing to proceed on all but the strongest cases. From the way the material had been presented— unorganized, and piecemeal—this investigation hardly qualified. Judging from the facts with which the officers furnished him, convicting John Short of the murder looked to Brooks like a longshot. After refusing to request a grand jury hearing, he advised the investigative team either to secure more concrete evidence or else pursue other angles in their search for the person who had murdered Candy Short.

Despite all of the interviews that had been conducted with many of John and Candy's relatives, acquaintances, and friends, the detectives still lacked the findings that would connect John to his wife's death. The closest they came to that was an anonymous phone call: "John Short committed the murder at Willowbrook," the caller said. "He was married once before, and was a son of a bitch to his first wife, Donna Olson. He tried to kill her."

The caller then hung up. Wilson and McCann tracked down Donna, interviewed her, and walked away with only the vaguest of allegations: John was antisocial, he had a bad temper, and she ended the marriage because she had outgrown him. Whether it was to protect herself from John's potential retribution or the result of lingering shame, Donna played down her ex-husband's violence and insisted that he never tried to kill her.

Frustrated by successive dead ends, the cops soon found themselves entertaining even the most implausible scenarios, welcoming all phone calls that came their way. It was under these circumstances that Billy McCann took a call from Sylvia Jenson and hoped for the best. Street traffic from outside the phone booth rattled behind her wavering, singsong voice, and this conversation seemed unlikely to lead anywhere. Nevertheless, McCann's training told him to find out what Short's mentally disturbed neighbor had on her mind. Cops call it grasping at straws, anybody else would call it wasting time.

A few minutes into the conversation it became clear that her reason for phoning was to announce the discovery of evidence. Yesterday she reported finding a piece of Candy's jewelry, which turned out to be a cheap, gold-colored chain that could have belonged to anybody. Today, another item had turned up. "I was asleep," she said, "and when I sleep I get messages. Please don't think I'm crazy."

"I don't," McCann replied.

"It's just that I'm with God. I love him a lot. Anyway, the dream told me to look in the dirt by the grass, so I went to it and found something on the ledge near there. . . . But I don't want to say what it is."

"You have to." McCann attempted to squeeze the information from her, working the disturbed girl as if she were an invaluable witness.

Eventually, though, he tired of her religious talk and spacy meanderings.

"Okay, so what did you find by the ledge?" the detective wanted to know.

"I found men's underwear."

"Men's underwear?"

"Uh-huh."

"Very good. Is it still there, or do you have it?"

"I have it in a plastic bag."

"Sylvia," McCann said, expressing enthusiasm that this discovery could not have legitimately warranted, "you're a doll."

She hesitated, giggled, then made another admission: "It's full of poop."

"Okay."

"Does it mean anything?"

"It could mean very much, yes."

Incidents such as this one created a general consensus that the team of police officers had gotten in over their heads. McCann, Webster, and their boss Jim Wilson were inexperienced murder investigators. They had spent many hours amassing reams of evidence, but they lacked the experience to properly catalogue their findings and turn them into incriminating leads.

The one person who should have been capable of pulling the troops together and directing them was the investigator from the Passaic County Prosecutor's Office, for presumably he would be a seasoned pro. Unfortunately the man assigned to this case, Howard Blakey, had been with the office for only two years; previous to that he counted welfare investigations as his primary experience. All of this added up to a situation in which the forces and fates seemed to conspire against the murder being solved, although you'd never know this from John's apparent efforts to deflect guilt away from himself.

Following the funeral, John jury-rigged a makeshift bedroom in the basement of the Austins' home, and left his in-laws with the impression that he'd be sleeping down there only for a few days. But after Helen asked John when he planned on moving back to the apartment—secretly dreading the thought of giving Jessica up to someone who couldn't possibly care for her—he replied in an emotionally shaky voice, sounding on the verge of a breakdown. "Mom, I can't go back to that apartment. There are too many memories."

"You stay down here for as long as you need to," she suggested, believing that John's edginess had been brought on by the sudden death of his wife combined with the incessant hounding from the police.

Considering the way they treat him, she told Fred, it's no wonder he jumps every time the telephone rings. Finding it impossible to see John as anything but a second victim of the murder, she wished they would leave him alone and let him get on with his life.

The other man in the Austin home allowed no time for self-pity. Operating on grief-fueled adrenaline, Fred immersed himself in work. He regularly logged overtime at the electrical repair shop, and he became scarce during the day. Helen hid all photos of Candy and tried to erase the painful memories. When her daughter's name inadvertently came up, Helen held her hand to her mouth and excused herself. At her mother's urging Jeanne went on planning her wedding. She continued working at the law firm, and did her best to monitor the police department's progress. John took to oversleeping and staying out late, maintaining a shadowy presence around the Austin home.

At eight o'clock each morning, when her son-in-law's workers gathered in the gravel driveway, Helen would step outside with glasses of iced tea for them. She'd suggest that they relax and wait for John, then scurry back inside to rouse her perpetually hung over house guest from slumber.

Eventually John dressed and groggily walked out to the backyard, cup of coffee in hand. Betty and Joe waved to him from behind the kitchen window as they watched John and his laborers take off for work. They wouldn't see John again until late that evening, when he usually returned home drunk and sullen, retiring to his basement room after a night of ogling go-go dancers.

❖ ✦ ✳

Will Lambert couldn't have been surprised when Jim Wilson and Billy McCann finally caught up with him at four-fifteen on the afternoon of July 2nd—two-and-a-half weeks after he first heard John's lie about Candy's premature death and ten days after the actual murder. After all, Short used his credit card at Howard Johnson's, and many people knew that the two of them frequented The Coach Light together. Lambert liked to talk, and should have been a natural source of information for McCann and Wilson. Despite any allegiance he felt for his friend John Short, Lambert was a born blabbermouth. When the detectives walked into his posh office in Newark, he asked them to take a seat.

He confirmed what they already knew about Short, and admitted loaning him the credit card. Then the conversation took a strange turn. Suddenly they asked Lambert a series of personal questions, inquiring as to whether or not anybody could confirm where he had been on the night of the murder. As if they had blindly accepted assistant prosecutor Brooks's dictum to find other suspects, the two cops looked for killer's eyes in every source they interviewed.

"I was out of town that night," Lambert said, suddenly as nervous as somebody who truly needed an alibi. He reached into his desk and pulled out a handful of receipts that had been drawn up on June 22nd. "I've already been reimbursed for the trip, so you can take these as evidence."

Neither cop accepted the pile of credit card chits. Instead they let their eyes roam around the office. McCann's stopped on a pair of dirty Converse sneakers.

"How'd your shoes get so muddy, Will?" McCann pointed to the Cons in the corner.

Lambert began to explain that he'd been doing some field work a couple of weeks ago, and saved them as a souvenir. Then he stopped, suddenly realizing exactly what the cops were getting at. "Look, I don't know what you two are trying to accuse me of, but that mud is not from the woods around the Willowbrook Mall."

"Nobody's trying to accuse you of anything," Wilson said, attempting to calm Will down. But it was too late, for the mild-mannered man already had blown up at them.

"I think I've had enough of this conversation! If you want to interview me, come back here with some kind of a warrant or whatever, and you can talk to my lawyer! He's right upstairs!" Simultaneously miffed and appalled, he sputtered, "Why don't you go speak to Diane Lovejoy? John told *her* that Candy was dead in the first place."

"He told her *what*?" asked McCann.

"A week before Candy died, John told Diane that his wife had been murdered."

"This is Diane the go-go dancer?" the detective continued, now speaking in a surprised tone. "The one that John had been screwing around with?"

"Yeah," said Lambert, showing the cops to the door. "You can find her in the bar across Academy Street."

Three and a half hours later Wilson and McCann entered The Coach Light. Though they were plain clothesmen, the two detectives might as well have had badges pinned to their lapels; every head in the place turned as they asked for Diane Lovejoy. Like Lambert, Diane had known it would be only a matter of time before the police materialized. Enough people had heard John's tall tale about Candy that it would eventually filter down to the authorities. Wearing a loose-fitting dress over the white underwear that she danced in, Diane briefly spoke to the officers. She confirmed what Lambert had just told them and arranged to talk further at the Wayne police headquarters.

Later that evening, Diane showed up there at ten-fifteen and received congenial treatment from Wilson and McCann. They ordered sandwiches and sodas from a nearby diner, and the interview began on a positive note. But when she couldn't confirm for them that John definitely had killed his wife, the conversational tone shifted.

"Let's have a look at your date book," Wilson suggested. "I want to see where you were on the evening that Candy was killed."

Diane handed them the book and watched the policemen flip through pages filled with her oversized, deliberate handwriting. When they came to June 22nd, the day of the murder, the page was blank. McCann inspected it, leaned forward, and asked Diane, "Where were you on June 22nd?"

"The 22nd," she repeated, more to herself than to the cops. "Oh, I didn't dance that night. I spent the day at the shore."

"Who'd you go there with?"

"I went by myself. I needed to relax. See, I had twisted my ankle dancing and wanted to take the day off so that it could heal a little bit. It was sunny out, so I figured I'd spend the day on the beach."

"You can't prove that you were at the shore, though, can you?"

"Of course I can . . ." Diane's voice momentarily trailed off as she tried to get a mental grip on what was going on. ". . . prove it. That's why I didn't work on the twenty-second."

A picture slowly took shape in her mind. They were considering her as a suspect in the murder. And why shouldn't they? After all, she was involved with John Short, she obviously found him attractive and would have liked to see more of a relationship develop. But John's wife had stood in the way. And on the day of the murder she couldn't account for herself. So of course, she would be a suspect.

Wilson and McCann slipped into their amateurish version of the good-cop/bad-cop routine. Playing the heavy, McCann laid into the go-go dancer. "We've got a few people lined up as suspects in this case, and right now you're one of them. I'll tell you, Diane, you better start giving us some reasons to believe you didn't do it, or else you're looking pretty good as an accessory to the murder of Candy Short."

Unable to believe what she had walked into, and not realizing how easy it would be to simply pick up and leave, Diane began crying. McCann continued to hector her, insisting that she knew more than she was telling, that holding back the truth would lead to nothing but trouble. "I'm telling you everything I know!" Diane whimpered. "Believe it or not, I slept with John only that one time. *I never even met Candy.*"

McCann slammed his fist against the table, stood up, and announced that he needed a glass of water. He exited the room and left Diane alone with Jim Wilson, the fatherly good cop, the one she could supposedly talk to and trust. That's when he made the pitch which had necessitated this charade. "There is a way you could help us," he told Candy. "And if you do this one thing for us, I'm sure I could get McCann off your back."

He handed Diane a tissue. She blew her nose, wiped her eyes, and asked Wilson what he had in mind.

"Maybe you could get together with John one more time."

"Yeah . . ." she said, willing to hear the rest, but imagining that there'd be more to it than simply getting together. "And do what?"

"You just do what you did last time. Take him back to the motel room and talk to him, find out his opinion on what happened to Candy. Maybe he knows who killed her and for some reason he's not telling us."

Wilson softened his face so that he would appear to be on her side, so that he wouldn't look as much like a cop trying to coerce a go-go dancer into entering a wired room and trapping a customer in order to guarantee her own freedom.

Diane didn't even have to consider the offer. "Forget it," she said. "There's no way I could do that to somebody. You've got to realize that I have feelings for John. And I can tell you right now that I don't believe he killed Candy. I don't know who did it, but it wasn't John."

McCann returned to the interrogation room and the two cops took one last shot at double-teaming her, but it was no use. Diane refused to cooperate and didn't allow them to intimidate her into lying. The implied threats and bullying and piercing stares would not break her. In fact, at four-fifteen the next morning, six hours after she'd arrived at the Wayne police station, Diane left there believing more strongly than ever that John Short was innocent. If they would wrongly accuse her of the murder, then why wouldn't they do the same thing to John? She also felt fresh resolution on a second point: After receiving such shabby treatment at the hands of the Wayne police, she would avoid cooperating with them in the future.

Fearful of what he might hear on the airwaves, John stopped playing the radio in his truck. It was bad enough that people were telling him they'd heard he'd been arrested and convicted of his wife's murder. He couldn't stand the thought of hearing it himself. Somebody had spent the summer and early fall leaking word to the local stations that John had been implicated in the fatal strangulation of Candy. While he couldn't pinpoint the source of the leak, John had a good idea of where it had come from. He called Billy McCann in hopes of plugging it up.

Billy's jaunty telephone demeanor contrasted sharply with John's nerve-wracked style. If he wasn't guilty, the investigation had certainly made him act like a guilty man, and many people familiar with Short's hair-trigger temper viewed him as the killer. The McCann conversation started with a little bit of small talk, both men trying to sniff the other one out, before the detective finally asked after John's contracting business.

"Are you back to work?"

"What work?" John replied with a self-pitying laugh.

"I don't have any work anymore. My jobs are all going down the tubes."

"What do you mean?" McCann wanted to know, his curiosity piqued.

"Well, they just say, 'Oh, we heard on the radio that you were in jail, so we got somebody else to do the job.' "

"I'd try to go after those radio guys if I were you," McCann suggested, baiting him, then added that he and the other cops kept the investigation completely confidential.

"Well, we're trying to find out who it is, but you know how those rumors go around. One person hears this, he mentions it to somebody who adds something else, and before you know it they have me lined up as the killer."

Although McCann seemed indifferent to John's plight, the Austins were concerned enough to make up for a whole department of unsympathetic cops. Their desire to squelch the rumors intensified once the household phone began ringing on a regular basis. Friends and relatives called to announce that they had heard on the radio about John's arrest. Jeanne contacted a couple of the local stations in an effort to find exactly when these news reports had been broadcast, but she had no luck in turning up leads.

Despite all of this bad publicity, however, John still attracted women. Days after Candy's burial he began dating again, rationalizing his frequent late nights by telling the Austins that he needed to get out a little bit in order to clear his head.

Within a month of the murder, Lambert offered to fix John up on a blind date with Judy Reiger. Gail Hunter, a secretary at David Jones's company, had first proposed the set-up to Lambert. Considering that Gail and Judy were sisters, John obviously did a good job of refuting those radio reports. While one would have thought he'd have a hard time buying a cocktail anywhere in New Jersey without being pointed out and ridiculed, Short never lacked for female company. Judy, a skittishly hard-edged, twenty-two-year-old woman with a druggy history, just happened to be the one that he truly fell for.

Fittingly, John and Judy met at The Coach Light on one of Diane's nights off, and the two of them instantly got along. The fact that John had a child made him particularly appealing to Judy. Recently divorced herself, she hated dating guys who couldn't understand her need to get home to her two-year-old son. As the evening wore on Will Lambert and Gail Hunter both went their separate ways, leaving Short alone with Judy. The two of them spent the remainder of the night barhopping, and John wound up sleeping at her place.

Through the summer of 1981 he developed the routine of staying overnight at Judy's apartment and meeting his construction crew in the Austins' gravel driveway the next morning. As this pattern took hold, Candy's family members discussed John's behavior among themselves, but they never confronted John directly. Only Jeanne had the nerve to challenge him as to his true feelings. "The way you're treating my parents is a disgrace," she told John. "Staying out all night and sleeping God knows where, while expecting them to cook and clean up after you."

John listened, not saying a word. Then he turned away and told Jeanne that he had to start living his own life. He had to get out of the emotional cocoon that Candy's death had built around him.

Unlike the other family members, Jeanne believed that John was pulling off the worst sort of charade. It was an intimate deception, perpetrated against people who lived by a code of ethics that prevented them from questioning the intentions of a loved one—which John had inevitably become, particularly in the heart of Helen Austin. She and Fred couldn't truly conceive of him as having had a hand in Candy's murder, and any dissatisfaction they felt did nothing to raise their suspicions.

Diane Lovejoy shared that belief in John's innocence. On July 9th, seventeen days after the murder, she saw

Lambert at The Coach Light and did something few women in her profession considered doing. "I have some money for John," she said, handing him an envelope. "I'm returning the hundred dollars he gave me on the night we slept together. I think John needs it more than I do."

On a couple of occasions Lambert tried to give the envelope to his friend, but Short refused to take it. "That bitch is nothing but trouble," he insisted, citing the fact that she turned his lie about Candy's death into public knowledge. "I'm trying to get my life together, and at this point the less I have to do with her the better."

In late July the two men got together for a drink, and Lambert had the envelope in his pocket. "John, you should take this money," he urged, once again proffering Diane's offering. This time Short grabbed it, and a few days later he claimed to have thrown it away unopened.

While Lambert wanted to maintain his friendship with John, he found himself becoming increasingly distant. His wife, with whom his relationship had grown shaky, insisted that John Short stay away from their house. Fearful of him, she mandated that he not come over for any reason. One August evening, over post-work beers and go-go girls, Lambert passed this information on to his friend. Short blew up, and appeared ready to have a physical confrontation about it.

"I don't like the way you've been acting lately!" John complained. "What? Do you think that I killed Candy?"

"John, only you know for sure. I really don't know. If you did it, you'll live with it. If you didn't do it, don't worry about it. But when you tell me you got lost for one and a half hours between your house and Jones's place in West Orange, I have to wonder about that. I have to figure that there are a lot of phone booths where you can stop and make a call." After a few awkward seconds of silence Lambert added, "You want to meet for a drink, John, that's fine. We'll go to a bar. I'm still your friend. But I want you to know that if anything ever happens to my wife, you're the first guy I'll go after."

Following their brutally honest conversation, John and Will saw less and less of each other. But Lambert frequently thought about his friend. Possessing a new view of Short, he experienced pangs of guilt as he wondered whether setting John up with Judy Reiger had been such a great idea after all.

But the time to reverse the act had passed. Just like Candy and Donna before her, Judy fell under John's spell. She adored him, liked the way he related to her baby son, and looked forward to spending more time with Jessica. They also shared a taste for soft drugs, particularly marijuana, which the couple regularly smoked. While high, they talked about moving in together and merging their lives. Of course that hinged on whether or not the kids would get along. In October, only four months after Candy's murder, John and Judy decided to find out. He brought Jessica to a birthday party that Judy's child also attended.

Toward the Austins, John remained cryptic about his relationship with Judy. Eventually, he was staying with her four or five nights each week, expecting Helen to care for Jesse and appease his workers until he returned home on weekday mornings. Because she felt sorry for John and dreaded losing her granddaughter, Helen grudgingly did as he requested. Most mornings his employees waited in the gravel drive until John pulled up in his truck. He honked the horn, jauntily called them over, and quickly departed.

With Judy fulfilling the role of girlfriend and the Austins playing babysitter, John had it both ways. He caroused as actively as he pleased, with no repercussions from Judy. As tight as money had become for him—with jobs continually drying up—John still lived fairly well. Rent was no longer an issue, and Helen or Judy cooked most of his meals. His parents, understandably sympathizing with their son's plight, and believing his constant pleas of innocence, subsidized John, and he suddenly found himself financially flush.

But his potential role in the murder still brought with it numerous problems. Even though the Wayne police began running out of steam after only a month of active investigation, they maintained an impression of advancement well into the fall. This produced no leads, but the mystery of how they were progressing inadvertently drove John mad, for months after the murder investigation had all but dried up. "The police are trying to turn me into a fall guy," he told anybody who would listen. "They're trying to make me confess to Candy's murder, they're questioning my friends, they're leaking information to the radio stations."

Internally, John deteriorated. His ulcer raged, he became plagued with a bad case of shingles, and his nerves seemed completely shot. He constantly questioned people's allegiances and developed a finely tuned paranoia. He correctly recognized his fall into further disfavor with Fred Austin and did what he could to avoid Candy's father. Judy became an emotional and sexual crutch. For the same indecipherable reasons that so many other women had welcomed John into their lives, she too turned herself over to him.

While the Austins slowly learned of Judy's existence, they never actually met her until an unseasonably cold early-winter evening. That's when John found himself in the uncomfortable position of having to come back to the house for a change of clothing while she remained outside in his truck.

Helen stood at the front door and saw the girl in the passenger seat. Wearing a T-shirt and lacking a jacket, she was underdressed for the chilly night. Partly out of a perverse need to know what sort of woman had replaced Candy, partly out of a motherly curiosity to see who her granddaughter's father spent so much time with, Helen needlessly asked who was waiting for him.

"Oh, that's Judy," John nonchalantly replied, "the woman I've been dating."

"For goodness' sake," Helen said, her voice laden with concern. "Why don't you invite her in? She'll freeze to death out there."

"Judy!" John shouted from the doorway, not wanting to step outside himself without some kind of a coat. "Come on in here."

Resembling a throwback to the early 1960s, the hardened young woman with long, stringy hair gingerly stepped across the gravel and entered the house that John's first wife had grown up in. The situation became increasingly awkward as Helen and Fred disdainfully checked her out. They suspected that they were looking at the woman who might eventually raise their granddaughter, and the prospect of losing Jesse to her left them heartbroken. With Jeanne married, Jessica had become the centerpiece of their existence. They exercised what control they could, not letting John take Jessica to Judy's house overnight, but it became increasingly obvious that the little girl would serve as a wedge for John Short to continually get his way.

John retrieved a handful of clean clothing, then kissed Helen and the baby good-bye. Eager to escape, Judy led the way back to the truck and gladly climbed inside, not even minding the inoperable heater. Standing by the window, Helen held Jessica in her arms as she watched the couple take their seats in the vehicle. She stayed at the window, looking out into the dark night, for a few minutes after John's taillights had disappeared.

CHAPTER
7

Candy's grave remained bare for too long. In a cemetery filled with jagged rows of tombstones, many of which dated back to the nineteenth century, her plot could be recognized only as a dirt patch. An old oak tree shaded the spot in summer, but by late fall dead leaves had mulched up around the area. Sharp winds cut across from an adjacent park, blowing over a baseball diamond and through a backstop. It added an eerie sense of isolation to Candy's final resting place.

When family members came to visit the grave and saw its shabby condition, they each died a little bit themselves. Other visitors, particularly those unfamiliar with the situation, laid down flowers and silently wondered what had happened to the tombstone.

Providing the stone was an obligation that fell to John Short. Not surprisingly, he put off making the purchase for as long as possible. Ever since the day of the funeral he had been promising to take care of it in a timely manner, but he still managed to skirt around the issue whenever it came up. Never an especially caring man when Candy was alive, he became downright hardhearted after her death. First he lied, maintaining that the funeral director, Everett Johnesee, had told him there was a six-month wait for a tombstone. When Johnesee refuted that claim, Short came up with another excuse: He wanted to construct something special for

Candy. Rather than the standard slab of granite, his wife's grave would be marked with a handcrafted tribute.

While it may have been galling to remember John's unfulfilled promises to build Candy a house and to realize that now her Tara would exist only in memory, the Austins took John at his word. In spite of recent events, Helen still championed his innocence, and the rest of the family members followed suit, outwardly doing their best to give John the benefit of the doubt.

The grieving widower's mourning period reached an abrupt end when Judy Reiger became a part of his life, and Helen accepted the unexpected recovery. Suddenly John no longer moped around the house, but acted instead as if Candy had never existed. Ironically, this was very much in line with Helen's technique for handling the situation. All physical traces of her daughter had been removed from sight, and Jesse now occupied the room that had once been Candy's. To her credit, Helen avoided living in a past that had been irrevocably altered for the worse.

At her mother's urging, Jeanne went on with her wedding as planned, struggling to keep the event from resembling another wake. John attended the affair with Jesse, and had the good sense to leave Judy Reiger at home. Suspicions that John might have killed Candy circulated through the family grapevine, and those outside of his immediate circle greeted him coolly at the reception. Moody and on edge, John sat by himself, watching couples dancing and looking eager to be somewhere else, anywhere but there.

Another wedding took place that year, when Judy Halbert married Richie Chamberlain. Along with Jesse and the Austins, John attended that wedding as well. There, however, he made a better showing, and was received with the sort of sympathy that his situation would ordinarily warrant.

During the reception, John approached Judy and handed her an envelope. "Here's a little something from me and Jesse," he said. "I know that Candy would have wanted you to have this."

Judy closed her eyes tight to keep tears from ruining her mascara and staining her veil. Suddenly she found herself overwhelmed with memories of her best friend. Damming her emotions, Judy wished with all her might that Candy would be there when she opened her eyes. But when she regained her composure, John remained the solitary figure in front of her; Candy was nowhere in sight. Judy hugged the man whom she had once considered a potential killer, and she believed him when he said, "We all miss Candy so much."

Considering the emotional upheaval she'd just undergone, Judy felt compelled to find out exactly what was in the envelope. She turned so nobody could see and opened it to discover one hundred dollars in cash and a heartfelt card. It was signed "Love, John and Jesse." Judy stared at the familial signature with the mother's name missing and could no longer keep her emotions in check. She cried tears of pity, tears of joy, tears that had been building up since Richie proposed and Candy died. Happy for herself, she felt sorry for Candy and Jesse. She missed her friend, and hated thinking that Jesse would grow up without her. Right now, though, she felt sorriest for John—this good natured, misunderstood man who found himself not only widowed but also accused of causing his wife's death.

"That poor guy," Judy sobbed to a friend. "He's been through so much. It must be so hard on him." She placed the card and cash in with her other gifts and struggled to stop crying. Judy took uncertain steps in John's direction and hugged him again, feeling closer to the man than she had ever thought possible.

Nothing could have revealed so clearly John's Jekyll-and-Hyde personality as this ability to elicit such different responses at two basically similar events. When he wanted pity and attention, he adroitly managed to attract it. For some reason he found it important that Judy should believe in his innocence, yet the feelings of Candy's relatives hardly mattered at all. Maybe it was because they had already made up their minds about John, and he sensed it.

While Fred and Helen tried to rebuild their lives, get over their daughter's death, and resume the routine that preceded it, other family members wondered what had happened to the search for Candy's killer. For all intents and purposes the Wayne police appeared to have dropped the case at the summer's end. McCann and Webster rarely phoned, only briefly interviewed Helen, and spoke to Fred no more than a couple of times. Even Geri Austin, the woman for whom Candy had babysat each day, was never called in for a sit-down. Nevertheless, Fred and Helen were grateful for the modicum of stability that returned to the domestic surfaces of their lives. Helen stopped breaking down for no apparent reason, and she took a part-time job as a bookkeeper. John's jumpiness sporadically abated, and Jesse no longer cried each night for her mommy.

However, Helen had a fresh problem to contend with: It had become glaringly obvious that Jessica would soon have a new mother. The little girl got along well with Judy Reiger's son, and it seemed inevitable that John would eventually marry Judy. Once that happened, Fred and Helen's involvement with their granddaughter would taper off. They wondered just how long John would wait before committing himself to the other woman. Helen hoped that it would be a respectable period of time, at least a year or two, although she had no reason to expect such civilized behavior from her son-in-law.

While the death of Candy had become a taboo topic of discussion among her immediate family, other relatives privately developed hypotheses as to what had happened. Strangely, they not only honored Helen's wishes by refraining from broaching the topic with her and Fred but also avoided it between themselves. Betty and Joe, for example, obsessively rehashed the murder and shared

ideas on who the killer could have been, as did Harry
and Geri. Yet Betty and Geri rarely talked about it.
Largely due to this code of selective silence, theories that
might have contributed to solving the case never went
beyond the closed doors of the Cape-style homes on the
quiet suburban streets in and around Belleville.

Sitting at the breakfast nook, waiting to go on duty,
Harry discussed with Geri the motives that could have
led to Candy's death. "I wouldn't be surprised if this
was all planned out," Harry suggested to his wife. "John
became involved with [Judy Reiger] awfully fast."

Geri poured her husband some coffee, topped off her
own cup, and commented that the manner in which the
Wayne police had handled the investigation was a crime
in itself. "They don't seem to know what they're doing,"
she said. "The killer's right under their noses, and they
can't bring him in."

Harry ate his breakfast in silence. A uniformed cop in
Nutley, he had no right to interfere with the work that
Webster, McCann, Blakey, and Wilson were doing, yet
he felt that they had not investigated the murder properly. It frustrated him to sit on the sidelines and watch
these other guys botching an investigation that he had a
personal stake in.

"Lazy police work," commented Harry, typically a
man of few words. He turned to Geri and shook his head
in disgust. "It kills me that I can't do a damned thing
about it. Can you imagine a cop from outside of Wayne
trying to get involved in that investigation? Forget about
it."

"Do you think the Wayne police will ever talk to us,
Harry?"

"To us? They spoke to Fred only twice, and one time
was on the night that Candy was killed. They barely even
interviewed Helen. I'm telling you, the whole thing is a
disgrace."

Harry finished breakfast and put on his blue hat. He
checked himself in the hallway mirror, then headed out

to the car. It would be another day of tending to small-town altercations as the murder of his niece continued to go unsolved.

While the table talk at Fred and Helen's place tended to be more genteel, Fred couldn't get Candy's death out of his mind. On most nights he relived it in his dreams. In the hazy way that past events nocturnally replay, he saw himself driving through the parking lot with John. Nothing was visible in front of him, then all of a sudden they came upon the dead and beaten body of his daughter. He routinely broke from slumber, sweating in the middle of the night, jumping up like a war veteran dreaming of mortar attacks. Or else he heard the sound of John smashing the Cutlass's window glass. The crash turned into a long wail, as Fred jerked his body from the mattress to see the sun rising and hear his alarm clock buzzing.

Day and night, the trip to Willowbrook haunted Fred Austin. As he distanced himself from the event, it seemed increasingly odd. The lot had been so dark that Fred couldn't figure out how John came across the car. He hadn't been able to see more than a couple of feet in front of him, yet John recognized Candy's Cutlass from the other side of the parking lot. He considered discussing this with Helen, but knew it would only upset her. Given the opportunity, Fred would have told the whole story to anyone who wanted to hear it. This time, he promised himself, there'd be no ineptly drawn maps or emotional outbrusts. Straight and clear, he would explain what had happened in the parking lot of Willowbrook Mall, and make it clear that John had to have known where the car was, that the son of a bitch had killed his daughter. Fred would have told the police everything, if only they had inquired.

Across the gravel drive, Betty and Joe kept in close contact with Billy McCann, frequently calling the detective on the telephone and monitoring the progress of the case. The two of them viewed McCann as a good man and an efficient cop. Their dealings with him seemed to show that he was progressing with the investigation, though the law enforcer explained that all developments remained confidential.

"Anytime you have something you want to discuss with me, feel free to call," McCann amiably told Joe. "You know we're always here for you."

So when John offered to take Joe to lunch at The Coach Light, Candy's cousin couldn't resist the urge to play Junior G-Man. He checked in with McCann for advice, and McCann suggested that Joe should accept the offer, and keep an eye open for any odd behavior on John's part.

Four months after Candy's murder, the two men drove in John's pickup truck to David Jones's building on Academy Street. Short gave a tour of the job site, then they walked across the street to the bar.

"Hello!" John called to the manager as they entered. He threw a dollar at one of the dancers and led Joe to a seat at the end of the bar, where they would have the best vantage point. John seemed unusually sullen that afternoon, and said nothing even remotely incriminating.

Already convinced that John had committed the murder, Joe sat tense and ready to pounce. He had one pocket filled with change, and was prepared to call McCann at the first sign of guilt. Joe hoped that John would get drunk and reveal some critical information about Candy's murder. "One slip," he had told Betty that morning, "and I'll drop a dime on that sucker's ass so quickly . . ."

Joe never got the chance. As soon as they finished eating lunch John paid the check, then turned to Joe and impatiently said, "The least you could do is leave the fucking tip."

His mood had suddenly shifted from reasonably friendly to recognizably hostile for no discernible reason, and he wanted to leave the bar as quickly as possible. Perhaps John sensed some apprehension or nervousness in Joe's actions, and it made him suspicious. Or perhaps it was something minor. Maybe Diane was around and John simply wanted to avoid her.

Despite the fact that nothing interesting transpired, Joe touched base with Billy McCann. "Don't worry about it," the cop assured him. "We're working some interesting angles on this end."

"Really?" Joe asked, enthused. "What's going on?"

"Like I said before, I can't tell you just yet. But something's going to happen very soon. I think there's going to be a break that will split this case wide open."

Joe continued pressing for details, but Billy McCann remained mum.

The secrecy aside, Joe Frank felt good as he hung up the telephone. From what McCann had told him, the Wayne police were on the ball. No doubt everything was under control.

John hunched over the thick board of wood and worked Fred Austin's saw back and forth. Despite the brisk fall weather, he had brought the tools and wood outside so as not to make a mess of the basement workroom next to where he slept. Grating sounds filtered over to the window of Betty and Joe's eat-in kitchen, as the couple enjoyed a Saturday morning breakfast of bacon and eggs. They looked up from their meal and glanced across the gravel driveway, into the Austins' backyard. "I wonder what John's up to now," Betty mused, as much to Joe as to herself.

Joe put his food aside, grabbed a couple of Millers, and headed through the back door to find out. "Building a house, John?" he joked.

Short looked up from his work, accepted the beer, and didn't smile. "I'm making a cross for Candy's grave," he said. "This is going to be beautiful."

John worked at a slow and methodical pace, playing to the audience after Helen and Fred and Betty joined Joe in the yard. All of them watched John sand and saw and hammer, trying to imagine what he would do with the seemingly simple pieces of lumber. Whenever they asked him, John—in a style not unlike that of Billy McCann—cryptically replied, "You'll see."

Knowing him as a skilled carpenter who certainly had the ability to build something beautiful and moving in memory of his dead wife, John's relatives had high expectations. They eagerly watched him at work, talked among themselves, and occasionally offered to help—only to be rebuffed.

That afternoon was burnished with a somberness, as they silently relived Candy's life and death and burial. It turned into a day of reflection and memory, with each person recalling Candy in the light that best suited them. No longer the unfeeling heathen who had been marked as a killer, John himself sporadically broke down and began crying. After a couple of hours he put the work aside, hugged Helen, and returned to his room in the house, leaving behind a yard littered with half-constructed carpentry.

The family sat around awkwardly, nobody knowing what to say. Then John returned and resumed his work. He dragged it out till dusk, so that at the end of the day there were several pieces of wood, none of them attached or painted. He took a short nap, went out that evening, and returned the next morning to complete his monument to Candy.

Finally they realized what the finished piece would look like, and what they saw took them aback. With each smash of the hammer that came down on the nails holding together the grave marker, it seemed that Candy was being murdered for a second time. What John had spent two days meticulously crafting turned out to be a simple cross, the sort of thing that a child would make from picket fence slats and prop above a dead pet's grave. It made John's feelings for Candy abundantly clear.

"It's nice, John." That's what Fred told his son-in-law. He really didn't know what to say, for he didn't have the nerve to tell John exactly what he was thinking: "You cheap, lying son of a bitch." He managed to push that phrase out of his mind, and grudgingly told John that they would have the cross planted at the cemetery within the next couple of days.

John whitewashed the wood and painted along a beam in boxy black letters: CANDICE CAROL AUSTIN SHORT— DAUGHTER, WIFE, MOTHER—1957 TO 1981. By the time he had finished, Helen, Fred, Joe, and Betty were standing on the gravel drive between their houses, all of them on the verge of tears. They reflected on a lot of things that afternoon: the death of Candy, the coldness of John, the uncertain future that loomed ahead for Jesse. Soon after he put the tools away and placed the cross in the basement, however, the family members regained their composure and went their separate ways.

Later that week, Fred and Helen visited the tiny cemetery. The caretaker's kids whacked a volleyball back and forth over a low net on a grassy area that bordered the burial sites. They looked on curiously as the Austins stood in the newly turned dirt and stared at a crudely rendered cross. Helen placed a bunch of flowers at the foot of the grave and Fred silently apologized to Candy, acknowledging that this was an improper way for her life to be remembered.

As he glanced around the cemetery at all of the granite tombstones, he pitied his daughter, well aware that a heavy snow could knock down John's homemade cross. Helen dipped her head toward the burial site, communed with Candy, then shakily looked up and began to sob. The couple, appearing older than their fifty-something years, held one another and solemnly climbed into the blue Nova that would take them home.

A few days later, Judy Chamberlain made her weekly pilgrimage to Candy's grave. Ironically, she saw more of her friend now than she had during the last years of Candy's life, but Judy felt compelled to continually pay her respects. She had gotten used to the absence of a tombstone, and made it a point to spruce up the area with freshly cut flowers. Today she had a few roses.

When Judy pulled her car up to the grave she saw the cross, and her stomach turned. "Who would put *this* here?" she wondered, thinking for a moment that it must have been a cruel prank. Hoping to lend dignity to the grave site, she placed a fresh batch of flowers at the spot where the cross penetrated the dirt. Judy used her hands to clean up some dried branches as she swallowed a scream of frustration.

Betty opened the front door of the Austins' home late in the day on November 1st. She propped it ajar with one hand and held Jesse with the other. "Helen!" she called out, stepping into the entranceway. Nobody answered. Odd, she thought, considering how close it was to dinnertime. Figuring that her cousin might still be working, was out back, or simply hadn't heard her, Betty walked in anyway.

Passing through the dining room she saw John sitting at the table. "I have Jesse for you," she said, handing the little girl to her father. John looked up listlessly and accepted the baby, but he didn't say a word to Betty.

She couldn't help noticing his sorrowful appearance. John hadn't looked this bad since the morning after the murder. He drummed his fingers on the table and rocked his leg, as if a calf muscle were spasming. All the color seemed to have drained from his face. "Are you all right?" Betty asked warily.

"Those goddamned cops!" John mumbled, banging a fist on the table. "They're trying to make trouble for me."

"What now?"

"They're calling me in for questioning."

"Just tell them the truth," Betty said, although she was not so sure that frankness would really be in John's best interest at this point. "As long as you're honest, nothing will happen to you."

"You don't know those guys. They can twist evidence so that anybody can be made to look guilty of anything. I think they found skin under Candy's fingernails, and they're going to try to prove it's mine." John held his face in his hands, as if he wanted to hide his head from the world. "There's a good chance that they'll make a positive identification."

John's fear confounded Betty. "What would your skin be doing under her fingernails?"

"Before Candy went to the mall we were fooling around—you know, in bed—and she got excited and dug her nails into my back."

Betty wondered what kind of fooling around would have compelled Candy to so violently claw at John's back, but she put on a sympathetic face. "You just have to explain everything to them. Don't worry so much, John. I'm sure it will all get straightened out." Wondering how long it would take for the mystery of Candy's death to be resolved—the murder, after all, had taken place nearly five months ago—she reached for the little girl and said, "Here, let me put Jesse to bed."

Betty carried the baby up to her crib, silently resolving not to bring her back to the house unless she knew that Helen would be around. Besides questioning the sense of leaving Jesse in John's care, Betty herself dreaded being alone with him. Hence, a couple of days later, when John asked her to accompany him back to his old apartment, she refused.

"Come on," John said. "It'll only take a few minutes. I just need a hand moving some things."

"No," Betty insisted. "Let's wait till Joe gets home, then the three of us will go there together."

"What's the matter, Betty?" John taunted. "Are you afraid of me?"

"No," she lied. "I just want to wait here until Joe returns from work. I'm sure he'll be happy to come along with us."

John didn't want to wait, and Betty never heard him

raise the issue again. After those two incidents, however, she and Joe made it a point to limit their dealings with John Short. It wasn't so much that they actually *feared* him—in fact, despite what they would later claim, one has to question just how seriously they took their speculations that he might be Candy's killer—but his presence did carry a dark undertone along with it. Increasingly, John seemed desperate and unpredictable. You never knew in what way his infamous temper might manifest itself. At best, John was an unpleasant person to spend time with. When things turned tense, it simply was easiest to avoid him.

On the morning of November 4th, John Short received the call that he dreaded. It was the day of Fred and Helen's anniversary, and John tried using that as an excuse to avoid going to the Wayne police station. But McCann and Webster would hear none of it. They were under strict orders from Jim Wilson to bring him in that night.

Word had it that at the week's end, Wilson would be leaving for a vacation, and that he wanted to see this case wrapped up before he departed. This was in spite of the fact that they lacked any new information to threaten Short with, and had to realize that his limited cooperation was wearing thin. As per Wilson, it had to be this night.

"We have some jewelry here that we need you to identify," Short was told.

"Tonight's the only night that you can meet with me?" he asked into the telephone. "That must be some goddamned important piece of jewelry."

Despite his suspicion that the cops had more in mind than they were letting on, Short—who never bothered to contact an attorney—agreed to speak with the detectives. He showed up at the station house at the appointed time of seven-thirty, dressed in a denim jacket and sport shirt, with his hair slicked back and a cigarette dangling from between his lips. Surprisingly relaxed, though a bit guarded, John Short entered the interrogation room resembling anything but a guilty man.

"This has to be quick," he distractedly told the three cops—Webster, McCann, and Wilson—who had assembled to question him. "The Austins are celebrating their anniversary tonight, and they're waiting for me."

"I'm sure Mr. and Mrs. Austin will understand that you came down here to work on the case," McCann assured him.

"No," John said. "They're going to be upset when they hear about it."

Like respectful adversaries, the cops and their suspect began to jovially banter back and forth. Short settled into a chair at the head of the table, and a video camera focused on his face. Somebody jokingly asked John if he knew why they call black people "Negroids."

"Why?" John replied.

"Because it rhymes with hemorrhoids, and they're both a pain in the ass."

"Gotta respect them. You gotta have respect for niggers," John solemnly told him.

A few minutes after John's arrival the detectives settled into place, the camera began rolling, and somebody read the suspect his rights. He never questioned why the simple identification of jewelry should require such an involved procedure, but went along with it voluntarily. Perhaps he believed that this final cooperation with the Wayne police would get them off of his back once and for all. More likely, John had no idea what he was opening himself up to by being there, or how intense the questioning would be.

At the start John seemed drowsy and distant. His eyes hovered at half-mast and he answered questions in a sluggish tone, dropping hard consonants with a thud. Slouching in his chair, he resembled nothing so much as a school kid brought into the principal's office to be questioned about a prank with which he had some minor involvement.

When the cops produced the gold chain that Sylvia Jenson had found, and asked John if it belonged to him or Candy, suggesting that the piece of costume jewelry could have been used to strangle her, he burst out laughing. "Who the hell would wear something like that? It looks tacky."

Obviously, John was saying, it belonged to neither of them. As the police tried to impress upon him the importance of cooperating, Short remained cool. He lit another cigarette, looked down at his feet, didn't bother taking off his jacket. He planned on staying for only a few minutes and reminded his interrogators of that.

From the people facing John, there was an audible urgency to the questioning. Everybody must have realized that this could be their last chance to get a confession from him. They tried to prime John by commenting on the investigation's growing momentum, mentioning that they had discovered somebody who could disprove John's proclaimed ignorance of the area surrounding Stone Drive (where John had his meeting on the night of Candy's murder), and reiterating their dissatisfaction with his limited cooperation thus far. After getting into a long-winded discussion about the color of Candy's glasses—John set the pace by claiming not to remember—the cops moved on to another seemingly innocuous topic.

McCann offered the suspect a Ziploc bag with a key ring in it. On the ring was a white plastic tag that read YOU'RE A 10 WITH US—NEW JERSEY QUALITY HOMES. It had been discovered beneath Candy's body. Without emotion, John picked up the bag and inspected it. He yawned, slouched further down in his chair, and acknowledged that those were indeed his dead wife's keys.

"This is the fob that was always on her key ring?" Webster asked, referring to the T-shirt-shaped tag.

"Always?" John lazily replied. "Yeah. I used to get a

lot of junk in the mail, and Candy would take it and use it. You know, one breaks and she'd stick another one on."

They went back and forth on this point until John convinced the cops that these keys had belonged to Candy. The importance of this matter rested in the fact that if these were John's keys that obviously placed him at the crime scene. How else could they have wound up underneath the body of his wife? But John held fast to his initial response that they were Candy's, and that he had his own set of keys.

Grudgingly, the cops accepted this and went on to the next point. They engaged John in a detailed discussion about his encounter with Diane Lovejoy. He insisted that it had been nothing but a one-night stand. Eager to find a motive for John to have killed his wife, the cops pressed the point. They recounted what the go-go dancer had told them about John's desire to spend a weekend with her and Jesse.

"What?" John replied, appearing ruffled for the first time. "I never said nothin' like that at all."

With John remaining tight-lipped, the time had come for McCann to begin playing hardball. He unveiled the scenario that he suspected: "Now, number one fact. On the weekend of the 20th and 21st, did you ask her to go down to your parents' place at the shore?"

"No," John maintained. "No plans to go anywhere with her. Maybe I told her, 'I'll see you again when you're dancing down here,' but that was it."

They volleyed information back and forth, with John continually returning their serves no matter how hard and slicing they came. It was an interesting contest of wills, but one in which nothing seemed likely to break John Short. He remembered very little about the days surrounding the murder and steadfastly denied committing it. Better interrogation advice could not have been furnished by the finest criminal lawyer: Deny everything, and what you can't deny, claim to have forgotten. The detectives asked John to use common sense—bringing up the fact that copping a plea would result in less jail time than if he had to be arrested—then played on his conscience by attempting to employ Jesse as a tool of coercion.

"What's your daughter going to think a few years from now when we finally accumulate enough evidence against you, and she has to see her father being led away in handcuffs?" McCann wanted to know. "By then she'll be a lot more aware of what's going on."

"I'm never going to leave my little girl," John maintained. "Somewhere along the line, you guys made a mistake. You're crazy if you think that I killed Candy."

Trying to reason with him, the three cops continued to tell John that they didn't believe he was as forgetful as he claimed, and they continually used his liaison with Diane Lovejoy as a reason for him to have killed his wife. That he lied to her about Candy already being murdered, they contended, proved that John had entertained the plan of killing Candy before he did it. Stubborn and cold, John barely reacted to any of this, dismissing all of their theories and continually claiming a loss of memory for any details.

Finally Webster could take it no longer. Nose to nose with John Short, he exploded in the suspect's face. "You're full of shit!" he bellowed. "You're full of shit! Let me tell you your life story!"

"This is really getting out of hand!" John screamed back. Voice shrill, eyes wide open for the first time all night, he covered his face and struggled for composure. "You guys are going fucking nuts. I don't know what that crazy broad from The Coach Light told you, for Christ's sakes."

"Crazy broad from The Coach Light, John? Crazy broad from The Coach Light?" McCann jumped in. "Let's get it together here. You're insulting my intelligence. I don't say you [committed the murder] premeditated. No way. You panicked, John. You panicked. You made a mistake that night."

"You're crazy," Short said. "My only mistake was in agreeing to come here tonight."

Webster calmed down, and debated with John about how long it had taken to get from his home to David Jones's place on Stone Drive. John continually maintained that anybody could get lost on West Orange's dark, winding roads, and the cops told him that they had made the trip themselves several times. They questioned his conveniently selective memory and kept punching away at the fact that Short would have had enough time to go with his wife to the mall (as Betty thought he had; "She's a liar," Short recounted), kill Candy, drive away in his parents' Pinto (remember, the automobile had been left in his care while they vacationed in Scotland), and still make it to his meeting at Jones's house with time to spare.

They mentioned how odd it seemed that John had tried to get out of his business meeting with Jones because of a hurricane warning, yet had no qualms about Candy driving herself to Willowbrook. John claimed that he hadn't wanted to work on that particular Jones project at all, and the weather excuse became an easy way to get out of it. The cops—veering from good guy to bad guy to the fatherly tone of Jim Wilson—kept telling Short they didn't believe him and begging their suspect to tell the truth, to confess for every good and bad reason imaginable.

None of these gambits visibly affected John Short. While at some moments his voice became screechy as he buried his face in his hands, John generally maintained an impressive degree of composure under fire, repeatedly fending off their accusations. Ironically, the one question that nobody asked out loud was, Why would an innocent man subject himself to this kind of scrutiny?

An hour after he had sat down, John finally stood up. For a moment he looked ready to leave. Then he took off his jacket, lit another cigarette, and resumed his seat. They rehashed the Diane Lovejoy mess—paying particular attention to what John had prematurely told her about Candy's murder—and queried him as to another recent liaison that he and Dan Solowe had with a couple of go-go dancers. John's response? "I don't remember."

Wilson adopted a scolding tone as he said, "John, you want to remember just the things you want to remember. And everything else you're trying to block out of your head."

In an effort to rekindle John's recollections, Webster sorted through a folder of evidence. He came up with what he was searching for and slid a photo across the table. John recoiled. "No, I'm not looking," he said, shaking his head, turning away from the post-mortem image of his dead wife. "You guys are trying to shock me with that shit."

"No," McCann reasoned. "There's no shock, John. It's pure fact. You've seen it before. You were there."

"I saw it that night, and I've been trying my damnedest to forget it, my friend."

"Right. Because you know exactly how it happened, John Short."

"I'm sorry you believe that."

"John, Christ almighty, *you* turn things around for us. *You* be the builder, man. *You* show us something different."

"You don't think if I could I would?"

"You can't."

Double- and triple-teamed, John still held up under their interrogation, chain-smoking, sweating, swabbing his forehead with a paper towel. Occasionally he yelled back at them, but for the most part seemed resigned to his ordeal and resolute to tough it out. The cops frequently changed tacks, sailing off on totally unrelated subjects. They tried to trip John up and break him down from behind, but he never fell for any of it. For nearly four hours they asked him the same questions over and over again, rephrasing them, changing the order, altering the emphasis. John kept coming back with the same answers: I don't remember, I didn't commit the murder, you should look for other suspects. Interestingly, his responses jibed reasonably well with what assistant prosecutor Allen Brooks had thought—i.e., that the evidence failed to support Short as a viable suspect—after reading the Wayne Police Department's findings.

Getting nowhere, they felt compelled to employ a threat that clearly amounted to a last-ditch effort. "I'm going to be very frank with you," McCann said, his voice calm and rational. "We've held off from doing something that our superiors told us to do, because we're trying to be decent to you. They want us to get in touch with your parents."

More than any of the other verbal blows, that one cut closest to his heart.

"Don't do that," John pleaded. "I won't let them talk to you. They're in Scotland and—"

"You cannot say you won't let them talk to us," Webster butted in. "I'm sure we would learn something from them. No matter who we speak to, we learn a little bit."

"You go ahead and call them and bring them up here. But if my mother winds up in the hospital with a nervous condition, you try to sleep peacefully."

Believing that John might turn around if it meant sparing his parents, McCann painted an insanely rosy picture of what life would be like after he had confessed. "They're going to put you in a minimum-security place, John. Did you ever live on a farm? It would be like a vacation. You'll be cutting grass, and they'll pay you for doing it, too."

"Are they going to let me see my daughter?" John asked, in a soft voice that made it difficult to tell whether he was considering confessing or simply killing time.

"They're going to let you see your daughter, sure they are. We're in a humane society nowadays."

Something in McCann's tone must have put John off,

because he suddenly retreated back to his defensive cover: "In the meantime you're trying to get me to take a fall so that I'll lose everything that me and Candy ever worked for. I'll never see my daughter again."

The cops even tried putting themselves in John's situation. They got chummy and intimate with him, claiming to be his friends, to be looking out for his best interests. McCann admitted to roughing up his own wife on occasion: "I grabbed her by the neck and choked her because I didn't want her to go to a wedding." The officer gestured so that his hand hovered a few inches from the floor. "I lifted my wife by her neck so she was *this* high off the ground."

"That's crazy," Short said.

"He can get pretty pissed off, *and he works here*," Webster allowed. "We all can get aggravated. You can, too."

"Not like that."

"But you know the little thing called temporary insanity? You've heard of that?"

"Oh, Jesus Christ," replied John, bemused by the level to which this conversation had sunk. "Are you trying to imply that I was temporarily insane that night?"

"Then tell us you knew what you were doing."

John laughed wildly.

Throughout the questioning, Jim Wilson maintained a low profile. He participated in the proceedings primarily when a fatherly voice of reason seemed likely to turn Short around. Now, with the session about ready to wind down, he stepped up his participation. Speaking in the studied tone of an evangelist, Wilson tried tapping into John's conscience.

"This outburst went further than you ever wanted it to," he began. "And you know it, John. Don't face that long time. I don't know what words will convince you that we're trying to do you a favor."

"So, you are offering me the choice of either saying,

'Yes, I did it,' or waiting for you to come up with some worse stuff and haul me away."

"That's the whole point. If we wait, you'll be facing life. And you have to realize that we have an unlimited amount of time before we have to come and pick you up. And when we do come we don't have to be gentlemen anymore. You know, it might be Santa Claus knocking at your door, and he might have a badge under his red coat."

"Yeah, I know. You take me and beat the shit out of me."

"No, no. They're not going to beat you up. They're not going to lay a hand on you at any time."

John fished in his jacket pocket for a silver cigarette lighter. He flicked it open and ignited a fresh Marlboro Light. Wilson used this lull in the conversation to revert back to his priestly demeanor. "John," he said. "Save yourself some more time. Get it over with tonight. You'll find us to be the best friends in hell that you will ever have. We'll go to bat for you. At this point we'll go to bat for you. I'm going to leave this room. I'm going to come back in about five minutes, and I'll want to know what you've decided to do."

"I'm sorry, Lieutenant," John said in a small, solemn voice. He didn't give Wilson the opportunity to step out as he'd offered. "I can't do what you're asking me to do."

"Why can't you, John?"

"Because it's not right."

They once again threatened to call in his parents, begged John to plead guilty and accept a reduced sentence, and finally asked him to take a polygraph test.

"What good would it do?" John calmly wanted to know. "You guys are totally convinced that I did it anyway."

"John?" Wilson said in his thickly cushioned tone.

"I gotta go home," John replied, standing up.

"Listen to me, John. All we need is for you to say, 'Look guys, enough is enough. I did it.' "

John issued no response. He simply put on his jacket. As he buttoned it closed, McCann mentioned John's well-documented temper. "A shrink in court is going to testify that Mr. Short does have a history of being overly emotional. He has stepped over that fine line before."

"And that makes me the murderer?"

"That doesn't make you the murderer. But it establishes a pattern of your capability. And we're trying to tell you here that you didn't mean to choke her. You rapped her a good shot or two, but you didn't mean to kill her."

As McCann spoke, John made his way to the door and stopped there.

"I'm going home."

"Wait. One thing, John. Can you tell me honestly and emphatically that you did not murder your wife?"

"That's the point I've been trying to make all along."

"Do you want to take a polygraph?" McCann asked hopefully. "You'd have no objections to taking a polygraph?"

"You want me to take a polygraph *now*, after—"

"Not now, I want to set up an appointment with you."

"And if I pass it will you leave me alone?"

"If you pass it, of course, to a degree."

"I'm going home now." John walked out of the room to the front door of the police station. The cops called after him—"You're making a mistake, buddy." "Let me give you a date for the polygraph." "Do you want to think about it a day or two?"—but John Short never looked back.

In the station house, one cop laughed. "Haw!" he chortled. "Did you see John *crawling* to his car?" But that was the last time they would see him. John managed to outfox the police officers. They knew he had committed the murder, yet failed to put together a case that would convict him. As the door closed behind John Short, it also slammed shut on the Wayne police department's investigation.

CHAPTER
8

John Short's parents bailed him out again. As life with the Austins grew increasingly tense, James and Adele Short agreed to let John and Judy Reiger occupy their vacation home in Ocean Grove, a small town along the southern New Jersey shoreline. In December of 1981, when he revealed his plan to Fred and Helen, it was met with a combination of relief and sorrow. While it saddened them to give up Jesse, the Austins would not miss her father.

Constantly running in and out of the house, spending nights with Judy, shuttling Jesse back and forth as if she were a piece of furniture instead of an astute, intelligent, surprisingly well-adjusted two-and-a-half-year-old girl, John did nothing to help the Austins adapt to life without Candy. If anything, his constant hyperactive motion kept the family continually off-balance and on edge. Despite their early efforts to help John in any way they could, Fred and Helen eventually found themselves wondering how much longer he would abuse their hospitality.

When he mapped out his plan for them, they heard what they halfway expected. The primary wrinkle was Jesse. She had become a fourth daughter to Helen, who experienced a mother's feelings of possessiveness when John explained that he wanted to take Jesse with him.

"Are you and Judy getting married?" Helen asked, concerned about the welfare of her granddaughter.

"Maybe," John replied, becoming antsy as he anticipated her next question. "I want to take things kind of slowly, at least at the beginning. But the one thing I do know is that I want Jesse to be with me."

"You and Judy are equipped to take care of her?" Helen queried skeptically.

John nodded. "Judy already has a son of her own, and he and Jesse get along great. It will be a ready-made family."

John promised that Fred and Helen could see their granddaughter as often as they pleased. He explained that it was nothing personal, but he simply had to get his life in order. Moving with Judy into the shore house—*A house very much like the one that Candy had hoped for*—represented a new lease on life for John. It gave him an opportunity to get away from all the bad luck and bad memories. He would move his contracting business down there and try to attract jobs from the locals. These would be people who knew nothing about him beyond the impressive references from clients up north; none of them would have heard false radio reports about John Short's imprisonment.

"We wish you the best of luck, John," Helen said, unsure of what else she could tell him, and suddenly fearful that saying the wrong thing might jeopardize her access to Jesse.

"Remember to take good care of the little girl," Fred grudgingly offered, shaking John's hand.

A few Saturdays later, during the early part of 1982, John packed his belongings into a bunch of cardboard boxes. He took some of the furniture from the apartment on Joralemon Street, but left most of it behind. John wanted a fresh start, with no bad karma. He and a buddy loaded the pickup truck, solemnly marching in and out of the Austins' house.

Then John turned the ignition and drove away from Passaic Avenue, making a clean getaway. The police had questioned him but never attempted to arrest him, and apparently they had nothing on him. Once he picked up Judy and throttled down the Garden State Parkway, heading south, heading toward a new life, John must have felt like a card shark who broke the bank.

The smoke-spewing industrial landscape of North Jersey turned pastoral as the pickup proceeded along the Parkway. The New York radio stations gave way to broadcasts from Philadelphia. For the first time in many months, John was able to enjoy the radio without fearing that his name would be announced.

The Wayne police could not have been surprised by John's decision to leave the area. Sensing that he might move, they attempted to bring him in for another round of questioning. This time, however, it didn't work. John hired a lawyer, and under the advice of counsel he refused to answer any questions without an indictment warrant.

Having lost the cooperation of their star suspect, the Wayne police coasted on the last puffs of energy that propelled them through the investigation. They conducted no more personal interviews, and proceeded in only the most detached way. As a last-ditch effort, soon after John left Joralemon Street, the state police lab compared fingerprints found on Candy's Cutlass to those of Tony Mancuso's. They came up negative. They also attempted to match the prints with those of Richard Glazer, a transvestite suspected of an assault near the mall. No luck with that either.

These were the final entries made by the Wayne Police Department in its investigation of the Candy Short murder.

Without Jesse around, the Austin house seemed empty. Fred and Helen did what they could to keep themselves occupied, to not think so much about their daughter's death and their granddaughter's absence.

Watching them from across the gravel drive, Betty

found herself impressed by her cousins' desire to keep moving, to remain socially active. She mentioned this to Joe, and he agreed. Sitting in the living room, sucking on a Miller, Joe responded, "They're regular social butterflies."

Fred routinely came home from work, pulled the Nova into the driveway, and headed straight for the shower. Cleaned up, he changed into a sport jacket and slacks and took Helen out to dinner, to a movie, to an event at the church, or for a visit with friends. They had to keep busy. It was as if slowing down would force them to think long and hard about the events of the last year. Remaining active kept them from dwelling on the negative.

But then something would happen that resurrected thoughts of Candy. Suddenly, John and Jesse and the murder would come crashing through their defensive barriers. Every time they passed a gold Cutlass it triggered images of Candy in Helen's head. Fred lived with it on a daily basis, suffering in silence as he mentally played out the Willowbrook scenario as if it were a repeating loop of horror film.

The dead woman lived on in the minds of others as well. On Saturday mornings when her kids watched cartoons, Betty regularly flashed on Candy's face. Over coffee with Joe, she heard *Scooby Doo* playing on the TV set in the living room and sadly recalled, "Candy said that she couldn't wait until Jesse got old enough to watch kiddy shows. That way Candy would be able to watch with her. It would give her a good excuse for liking cartoons."

Across town, in the apartment that she and her husband Richie had moved into, Judy Halbert Chamberlain stood on a chair and touched up a kitchen cabinet with paint. She learned to deal with her friend's death, and now made only sporadic visits to the grave site. On this particular day her thoughts were wandering as she brushed the wood with color. The radio played softly in the background, and pleasant memories coursed through her mind. She and Richie had recently discussed having children, and the thought of a family filled Judy with joy.

One rock song melded into another, each tune as anonymous as cars on a freeway. Finally the DJ played a selection that she knew. Judy didn't recognize the first few bars of the intro, but then she realized it was the Loggins and Messina song "Your Mama Don't Dance and Your Daddy Don't Rock 'n' Roll," a silly novelty rocker from her high school years. Suddenly Judy realized why the song sounded so familiar. *It was Candy's favorite.*

She became a bit dizzy and stepped off of the chair. Sitting on the floor, Judy thought about her departed friend. After singing along with the chorus, she pulled her knees in close to her body, put her head down, and began to cry.

One person who was relieved to see John Short with a new woman was Francis Lambert. Now that he appeared to have settled down, she agreed to have John, Judy, and their two kids over to the house. As long as he's not alone, she reasoned, John Short can't be too much trouble. Glad to renew ties with his old friend, Will Lambert called down to John in South Jersey and extended an invitation.

Even though it was a little cool outside, Lambert decided to barbecue. He laid out a nice spread of hamburgers, hot dogs, and London broil. Naturally, the refrigerator was stocked with cold beer and his liquor supply included a full bottle of Jack Daniels. John and Will imbibed liberally, and it almost felt like old times. Instead of go-go dancers, though, they watched their women and kids and tried to be on reasonably good behavior.

Early in the afternoon, Judy became restless. "John," she nagged, "we should get going soon."

"Not yet," Short insisted. "I want to check out the pool table downstairs."

The men repaired to the basement and enjoyed a friendly game of Eight Ball. Short sipped from his glass of bourbon and complained. "Fuckin' broads," he said. "They drive you crazy."

"Tell me about it," Lambert agreed. He recounted an argument he had with his wife over frequent nights at The Coach Light. It resulted in an ultimatum: Either stay away from the dancers, or our marriage is over. Will accepted the former option. "I haven't been back there since. It just stopped being worth the aggravation."

Short said nothing. He began setting up a shot when Judy's head poked out from the middle of the staircase. "John, the babies are really getting overtired."

"Will you give me a goddamned break!" Short shouted at her. "I only get to see this guy once in a while."

She retreated back upstairs, then reappeared a few seconds later, just after Lambert left the basement to get fresh drinks from the kitchen. Alone, she told John that she wanted to go home. Short suddenly blew up, calling Judy a bitch and insisting that they wouldn't leave until he was good and ready.

By the time Lambert returned, John was brandishing his pool cue at a menacing angle. Judy cowered away from him on the other side of the felt. Lambert placed the drinking glasses down and shook his head. Remembering John's temper, he tried to maintain his composure in order to diffuse the situation. "All right," he said, taking the stick from Short's hand. "If you want to fight, that's fine. But you do it outside. I don't need to have you down here wrecking my pool table."

Embarrassed, the couple followed their host upstairs. The bickering continued for a few more minutes until John finally agreed to leave. After the two of them had strapped Jesse into the front seat and pulled away in Judy's car, Will Lambert turned to his wife and said, "Some guys never change."

During the spring of 1982 John returned to Belleville with Judy in tow. Betty and Joe had not seen him since the day before he moved to Ocean Grove. Short parked

Judy's car in the gravel drive and carried the baby over to Candy's childhood home. Thrilled to be spending the day with their granddaughter, Fred and Helen took the little girl in their arms.

Judy stood back, unable to ignore the situation's inherent awkwardness, and waited impatiently for John to finish up with the Austins. "We're going over to Betty and Joe's," he finally told Helen. "I promised that we'd visit them."

Once they made it next door John shook Joe's hand, gave Betty a hug, and enjoyed their warm welcome more than he had anticipated. After a few minutes of catching up, Judy reached into her pocketbook and pulled out an empty beer mug. "I brought a glass, but I don't have anything to put in it," she bluntly told Betty.

John found this to be hilarious, though it left the hosting couple annoyed. Nevertheless, Betty went to the kitchen and Judy followed. John settled down on the couch, and Joe found it impossible to hold back his curiosity any longer. "Is that your mountain man costume?" he asked, referring to the heavy growth of beard that now covered John's face.

"You know," John said, relishing the attention, "I figured I'd try out a new look."

The women entered the living room just as John was responding, and Betty asked, "What made you decide to grow it?"

She handed John a can of beer, and he answered her honestly. "I didn't want anybody who knew me from up here to recognize me down in Ocean Grove. We're trying to start over again, and I didn't want people asking me a bunch of questions about what happened with Candy."

Judy sipped from her mug as Betty and Joe exchanged discreet glances. Now neither one of them could look John in the eye without remembering Candy and wondering about the exact nature of her death. That, both of them believed, was how it would be as long as they knew John Short.

PART TWO

August 15, 1987

RUN TO GROUND

"I'm never off-duty."
—Investigator George Brejack

CHAPTER
9

A daughter's death scars the memory. Late at night, alone in the dark, questions are silently raised about how her passing could have been prevented. But the answers remain elusive; the inexplicable must be accepted if the living are to get on with their own existence. Fred and Helen Austin grudgingly learned to deal with realities that they could not change.

Six years after Candy's murder, a semblance of conformity had returned to the house on Passaic Avenue. Helen still refused to display photographs of her youngest daughter, but she tried to compensate with framed snapshots of Jesse. Now a bubbly nine-year-old, the girl resembled Candy with her button nose, pinched-in face, and tiny frame. Intelligent and independent, she was well liked in school and appeared to have adjusted well to the tragic circumstances surrounding her mother's death.

Over the last year Helen and Fred had both retired from their jobs. The middle-aged couple suddenly found themselves with more time on their hands than they knew what to do with. Like many people who are unexpectedly confronted by expansive leisure, encroaching age, and limited funds, they spent many hours watching television and doing busy work around the house. Helen contented herself with baking, and Fred whiled away days at a time in his basement workshop.

The TV room served as a gallery for Fred's handiwork,

with his whimsical dog- and cat-carvings mounted above the window frames. Staying busy kept his mind away from Candy and that night in the parking lot of Willowbrook Mall. If he wasn't turning a piece of wood into some kind of toy or wall hanging, he was working on restoring a few of the old neon Budweiser beer signs and bar-top carousels that friends had given him. Fred reglued the Clydesdales' necks to their torsos and left only the slightest trace of a crack. Sometimes, if he thought about it for too long, Fred found himself wishing that human breakage could be so easily repaired.

On weekends, when the weather permitted, the Austins enjoyed long drives through the country. Though Belleville hardly qualifies as a rural community, it takes only a couple of hours driving west on Route 80 for the suburban developments to give way to charming small towns where cows graze in roadside fields. Besides a change of scenery, the trips offered Fred and Helen a break from the home that remained filled with memories.

Ironically, the events surrounding Candy's death seemed to have been all but forgotten. Over the years, the incident came up less and less frequently. The Wayne police had apparently given up on solving the crime only six months after it had occurred, and the Austins failed to see what good it could do to continually recount the tragedy. Nothing could be done about it anyway, so why harp on nightmarish memories? The only physical reminder of their daughter was Jesse, whom Fred and Helen saw as often as John would allow. Every few weeks she spent a couple of days with the Austins, who did what all grandparents are supposed to do: They spoiled her silly.

Believing that Jesse always looked a bit dirty after John dropped her off, Helen routinely treated her granddaughter to a long and luxurious bubble bath, then dressed her up for shopping. When she returned to the Short home in Ocean Grove, Jesse invariably had a new shirt or dress or pair of jeans. Perhaps the gifts helped to alleviate some of Helen's misplaced feelings of guilt.

Each time the little girl went back to her father, Helen became upset over the situation. Deep in her heart she feared that John and Judy were unfit to take care of their three children (one of his, one of hers, and a son that Judy recently had given birth to), but she didn't dare mention it. She couldn't risk angering John, and thereby jeopardizing her access to Jesse. Expert at manipulating his former in-laws, John used the little girl for leverage, subtly hinting that things must be done his way if the visits were to continue.

The Austins seemed content to live this way, accepting the blinders and restrictions and controls that had been placed on them. Then, in August of 1987, a call came from Jeanne that threatened to destroy the years of readjustment, to shake things up like the plastic snow in those clear little globes filled with water and winter scenes. If mishandled, the fragile globe, which the Austins' life had come to resemble, could drop and shatter. Cracked glass would splinter off in all directions, spinning through the air and littering an emotionally jagged landscape.

A few minutes into the telephone conversation—despite Jeanne's efforts to postpone an inevitable revelation—mother's intuition told Helen that her middle daughter was holding something back. Rather than pressing the point, though, Helen waited until Jeanne got to the matter that prompted this call in the first place.

"John [Suarez, her husband] and I were contacted last week by an investigator from the Major Crimes Unit of the Passaic County Prosecutor's Office," Jeanne finally said.

"Is everything all right?" With Candy's murder always lingering in her mind, any mention of the police alarmed Helen.

"I guess so. But this man . . ." Jeanne looked at the business card that had been left with her. "George Brejack, he wants to reinvestigate Candy's murder."

Silence initially met Jeanne from the other end of the line. "I thought it was over. Those men from Wayne told us that it was unsolvable," Helen said after a few seconds, unable to bring herself to use the word *murder*. "Oh, Jeanne, I don't know if I can go through all of that again. Your father and I are getting older, his health isn't what it used to be. I'm just not sure whether or not I want to deal with the police right now."

Jeanne couldn't have agreed more, and her husband John Suarez had told Brejack as much, insisting that the investigator had no right to make the family relive the murder. Considering what had gone on with the Wayne Police Department, one could understand their reluctance to get involved again. After all, who was George Brejack? The cops had failed to build a case at the time of the killing, how was he supposed to patch one together six years after the fact?

Brejack's blustery confidence in his ability to bring about this delayed justice caused him to look foolhardy rather than competent. And while the idea of finding out who had killed her sister intrigued Jeanne, she clearly shared her husband's desire to maintain the family's hard-won stability.

Jeanne and her mother discussed the matter for a few minutes, with Helen saying that she wasn't sure she wanted anything to do with a new investigation.

Sympathizing, Jeanne replied, "I don't know, Mom, he's an awfully persistent man. And legally, we can't stop him. I just hope he doesn't put too much pressure on you and Dad."

"We won't let him," Helen said with stern defiance.

"Well," Jeanne sighed, "now you know what's going on. You're prepared for him."

Helen glumly thanked her daughter and hung up.

On August 25, 1987, the call came from Brejack. He was polite but unrelenting, emphasizing the importance of meeting with her and Fred. They scheduled a get-together for the following week. George would drop by the house on Passaic Avenue for an hour or so before dinner. After completing the conversation, Helen sat down and wished she had the power to prevent that day from ever arriving.

A cluster of ancient-looking crackheads loitered in the doorway of Eva's Soup Kitchen. From around the corner, they had a view of the former church office that now housed the Major Crimes Unit in downtown Paterson, New Jersey. The neighborhood had once been a thriving shopping district, but, like many inner cities, through the 1960s, and '70s it began a downhill slide and never recovered. Today it's replete with overpriced discount stores, former mansions converted to slummy boardinghouses, and throngs of drug dealers.

One of the skinny addicts allowed himself to stop day-dreaming about torched glass pipes and powdery white rocks. He eyeballed the burly, suited figure with the mustache and thinning tufts of light-brown hair. At six feet three inches, two hundred and seventy pounds, with a classically large Eastern European build and huge hands, he cut a memorably imposing figure. "Fuckin' Brejack," the crackhead croaked to the law-enforcer's back. "You coming out here to bust me again?"

The man in the suit stopped abruptly, jerked his head around, and stared into the crowd. Nobody said a word. Forty-seven-year-old George Brejack, who had been decorated as one of the city's most dogged criminal investigators, continued walking, feeling good to be back on the street. Six years away from law enforcement had given him enough perspective to recognize it as his true calling.

Freshly appointed as an investigator with the prosecutor's office, he climbed into his silver-colored Volvo coupe and navigated it through Paterson's decrepit downtown area. He tuned the radio to WPAT, the local easy-listening station, and mulled over what would be his first case in so many years.

Recalling the procedure he had followed during his days as a city cop, Brejack first sifted through the basic facts: A guy's wife is murdered, the Wayne police do a half-assed investigation, they suspect the husband but can't get a confession. A few months later they stop leaning on him, he moves to South Jersey with some bimbo, and, *boom*, the case is over. The murder might as well have never happened from the way this guy is living.

The investigator had spent the previous weekend at the Swinging Bridge campground in the Catskill Mountains. He owned a trailer-home there and kept it planted on a plot of land leased by the year. While his girlfriend Lisa Clarke—a serious young woman who worked as an accountant and had a propensity for sulking—hiked and swam and enjoyed the warm July weather, Brejack hunkered down with his work.

Lisa floated downstream in a rubber inner tube, as her boyfriend sat on a lawn chair beneath a shade tree. He batted away mosquitoes and looked through the incomplete files on Candy Short. Twenty years younger than he, Lisa could have been George's daughter, and that age difference had something to do with their mutual attraction.

She told Brejack that she had grown up in a broken home and he speculated that she craved the stability that came with dating a cop who was old enough to be her father. George found her relative youthfulness appealing in both physical and emotional terms. Ordinarily, he lavished Lisa with both kinds of attention. This weekend, however, she noticed that he seemed preoccupied, more concerned with the satchel full of files and police reports than he was with her. She paddled alone in the Mongaup River and assumed that his one-track interest in this case would eventually derail; Lisa Clarke would soon regain her status as George Brejack's primary obsession.

At the moment, though, Brejack's only interest in women concerned a dead blonde who had been strangled and abandoned on the floor of her car. He absorbed the information about Candy as if it were a novel—even though half the plot seemed to be missing. Former Passaic County Investigator Howard Blakey had left the case files behind after being transferred to a job with the State Attorney General's Office, and their condition was such that he must have assumed they would never again see the light of day. Even though a good deal of the information apparently had been mislaid, and the police reports were sketchy at best, Brejack believed that this case still could be pieced together.

But before he attempted anything, Brejack wanted to get the family members involved. Ultimately, they would provide him with information that an investigator working so long after the fact rarely has access to. Brejack needed them to not only stand behind the investigation, but to truly want the mystery behind Candy's death cleared up. Such participation is more difficult to obtain than it sounds. While most people long to see the murder of a loved one avenged, few are willing to endure the day-to-day psychological ravages that come with it.

Brejack would constantly solicit a family's input and ask for painful recollections that seemed of little use. But even the tiniest elements contained important nuggets of truth. Brejack likened circumstantial evidence cases—inherently the most difficult to prosecute, for the lack of eyewitnesses—to lengths of chain: By itself, no one link is important, but without it the chain breaks. Resistance from the Austins would not prevent Brejack from taking the case on—he had already emotionally committed himself to doing so—but it would certainly weaken his chain.

That's why Brejack questioned a Wayne policeman whose tenure dated back to the time of the murder. He wanted to know which of the Austins would be likely to lend the highest degree of support. The cop suggested that Brejack first contact Jeanne. Being the strongest member of the family, the reasoning went, she'd find the reactivation of the investigation most appealing. Thus Jeanne Austin Suarez became the first link in Brejack's chain.

However, his initial meeting with her and her husband John on the evening of August 18th hardly marked an auspicious beginning.

A corporate sales manager, John Suarez was a feisty little barrel of a man. He wore his salt-and-pepper hair feathered back, and he had a full, handsome Mediterranean face that effused confidence. He and Jeanne lived on one side of a large two-family house (his mother occupied the other half) and didn't try to conceal the fact that they were well-off. The couple traded in their car each year for a new one, and they enjoyed flashy vacations. They lived with all the trappings of first-generation affluence.

As befits a macho patriarch, Suarez welcomed nobody who threatened his standing within the household. During the course of Brejack's twenty- or thirty-minute visit, Suarez smiled condescendingly and treated the investigator like some corporate flunky who had wandered into his office with a dumb idea.

"I'm going to solve this murder, and I know that," Brejack confidently said, undaunted by Suarez's arrogant undercurrent. "But I need you people to help me."

Jeanne welcomed the offer. She felt swindled by John Short, believing that he had conned the Austins and stolen something irreplaceable from them. She wanted to put the grief-filled past behind her, but she knew it would be impossible to do that until the murky circumstances around her sister's death had been cleared up. "We try to go on with our lives, but we'll never fully recover from what happened," she confessed to Brejack.

Again he expressed confidence in his ability to solve the case, and she silently answered him with an expression of disbelief. John simply laughed. It was a braying put-down designed to keep this intruder in his place. Brejack didn't mind somebody challenging him, questioning his abilities, but he could not stand being the butt of a joke. Something inside him exploded.

"Don't you *ever* laugh at me!" he warned John, his

voice rising as he unsuccessfully struggled to keep his anger in check. "This isn't some big game to me. I'm going to catch the guy who killed Candy and do my damnedest to see him put behind bars."

The Suarez incident plagued George all weekend. Amid the peaceful surroundings of his Catskill camp, he continually replayed and reworked the brief confrontation. Even now, as he drove through Paterson to the Austins' house on the afternoon of September 1st, Brejack's ears burned with the sound of Suarez's mocking laughter. He struggled to concentrate on the facts and attune his mind so that every helpful piece of information, no matter how obscure or seemingly irrelevant, would register. After his long absence from law enforcement Brejack felt a little rusty at reading people, and he could not take the risk of operating with any of his sensors in remission. Particularly if he hoped to regain his reputation.

During his glory days in Paterson, Brejack had earned the moniker "psychic cop." He became famous for his ability to crack seemingly unsolvable cases, to pick a killer from a crowd, and figure out where dead men's bones were buried. Today, though, after six years away from law enforcement, Brejack didn't know whether that intuitive ability remained intact. Solving this case would provide positive proof for Brejack and the others at the prosecutor's office that he still had what it took to crack the most puzzling crimes. Blowing it, however, would offer proof of a less appealing nature.

In his desire for redemption, to prove that his abilities had not atrophied, Brejack strove to avoid negative thoughts. He maintained an unwavering faith in himself and his ability to screen out distracting responses. In the instance of the Short murder—Brejack's first shot at solving an old crime, and the only case he'd ever worked on outside of Paterson's crime-riddled slums, where ordinary procedures don't necessarily apply—he needed to ignore the negative feedback and concentrate instead on the desired end result.

This strategy ran through Brejack's mind as he strolled up the walkway that led to the Austins' home. He thought positively, and keyed in on coming up with a solution. The couple nervously greeted their visitor and ushered him into the house. Helen already had a pot of coffee on the dining room table. She and Fred sat down on either side of Brejack as he mapped out his plan.

While he talked, Brejack scrutinized the house. He sympathized with this couple, whose lives had been savaged by a senseless murder. Brejack couldn't help but think he was sitting alongside the sort of people to whom these things are not supposed to happen. They were a nice, middle-class couple that worked hard and did everything society expected of them. Brejack took in the simple living room furniture, the frilly curtains hung over the windows, the needlepoint framed on the walls, and he pitied the Austins for having to receive him under these circumstances.

"It was such a long time ago," Helen said in an almost apologetic tone. "We really don't remember very much. You have to understand that it was an extremely trying period for all of us."

Brejack responded as if he hadn't heard a word she just said: "Have you thought of anything at *all* since the night of the murder, something that might help me in the investigation?"

Helen shook her head no and Fred stared off into space, his eyes seemingly focused on some invisible object in the living room. Nevertheless, Brejack felt plagued by the notion that the silent, rail-thin, gray-haired man had something important on his mind.

"I have a few theories on what might have happened," Brejack offered. "And I plan on working this case very closely with the two of you. I'll be in contact on a regular basis. I'm sure that there will be a lot of questions as I go along, and I'm reaching out to you people for support."

"We'll help you in any way we can," Helen said noncommitally. "Of course we want to see whoever hurt Candy arrested."

Brejack wasn't so sure. Their attitude—or Helen's at any rate, for Fred barely spoke a word—seemed even less receptive than Jeanne's. The lack of enthusiasm led Brejack to believe that the Austins simply couldn't bring themselves to live through the murder once again. Or just as likely, they didn't really want to know whether John killed Candy. Any time he mentioned John in connection with the crime, Helen rose to her son-in-law's defense.

"The Wayne police have already put John through so much," she said. "He's taking good care of Jesse, and we hope that you'll leave him alone."

Brejack let this sink in. Then he laid his meaty right hand on the table, palm down, so that the Austins could see an intrusively large, solid-gold PBA ring resting above the knuckle on his middle finger. Partly to gauge their reactions, partly because he felt obliged to tell them, the investigator said, "You two seem like beautiful people, and I hate the thought of putting you through this, but you have to understand the importance of arresting and convicting whoever committed the crime. Besides bringing peace of mind to the both of you—and I guarantee that it ultimately will—it'll get a dangerous guy off of the streets."

Helen considered saying something, but suddenly she looked ready to break down. Regaining her composure, she listened to what Brejack had to say. "You work on an investigation like this, and you never know what you're going to find. I've been in law enforcement for nearly twenty-five years. During that time I've seen a lot of crazy things. There's no telling who might have committed the murder. It could have been a friend of Candy's, maybe somebody she grew up with. Who knows? Even John could have been the killer."

This last bit of information provoked Helen. She slammed a hand down on the table and pointed an index finger at Brejack. "I will not have you sit there and tell me that John Short murdered our daughter!" Helen said sharply. "He lived and mourned with us for six months after Candy's death. I don't think he'd be able to do that if he killed her. You leave John Short alone."

Surprised by the outburst, the investigator shrugged and said softly, "Who knows? Stranger things have happened."

Neither Fred nor Helen responded.

Helen's protectiveness toward her son-in-law perplexed Brejack. At that time, he couldn't have understood the complexities that Jesse brought into the situation. Helen found the notion that her granddaughter's father could have committed the murder to be patently unacceptable. Her response laid down a clear boundary line between her and the investigator.

Rather than getting worked up, however, Brejack explained that all potential suspects would have to be questioned. As he tried to reassure the woman that nobody would needlessly harass John Short, Brejack decided that he would need to learn more about Short. Anybody who's cunning enough to sway the victim's own mother, he thought, has got to be pretty talented. Brejack wanted to lock eyes with the son-in-law and see how good he really was.

After spending half an hour with the Austins, leaving them shaken up and wishing that George Brejack had never entered their lives, he got into the Volvo and made his way back to the prosecutor's office. As he drove Brejack replayed that meeting in his mind, and he kept coming back to Fred.

While it certainly wasn't the first time he'd seen a wife overshadowing her mate, there was something odd about Fred's behavior; he seemed to lack the ability to articulate even the simplest thought. It was as if by opening his mouth and speaking he would unwittingly reveal some deep secret. Because the man had barely said a word, and because he had the greatest promise as a source of information—it was he, after all, who discovered the body—Fred was the person who most intrigued Brejack.

That night, as he and Lisa prepared for bed, Brejack mentally digested Fred's role in all of this. He slipped under the covers alongside his girlfriend but knew it would be impossible to fall asleep immediately.

He closed his eyes and thought about Fred Austin. Brejack's body needed rest, but the fatigue felt good. Just as a runner welcomes shin splints after months of being sedentary, he happily greeted this insomnia that comes with working a case.

Lisa began dozing off when George said, "I've got a good vibe about this murder. I'm going to solve it. It'll put me back on top."

She murmured acknowledgment, half hearing his words through a veil of sleep. As she dreamed alongside him, Brejack's mind cranked out bits of information and shuffled them around, switching possible scenarios and subjects like the colored blocks on a Rubik's Cube. His mind moving slowly at first, he set up the strategy that he hoped would see him through to the conclusion of this investigation.

When Brejack woke up at five the next morning, he felt rejuvenated by just a few hours of deep sleep. He padded around the small, low-ceilinged apartment with its clunky wooden furniture, National Rifle Association prints framed in the living room, and the antlers of an eight-point buck hanging over the doorway that led to the kitchen. Brejack made himself a pot of coffee, while events from the previous night continued to dominate his thoughts. He still felt a deep urge to pump Fred for additional information.

Later that morning, in the eight-foot by ten-foot room that he worked out of at the prosecutor's office, Brejack dialed the Austins' number. "Please, Freddie, pick up the phone," he whispered, having already decided that if he heard Helen's voice he would hang up. Asking for Fred would arouse all kinds of suspicion. Brejack believed that the man's ability to help with the investigation had already been hampered by his wife's incessant proclamations of John's innocence; he certainly didn't want to exacerbate the situation.

On the third ring somebody lifted the receiver from its cradle. "Hello?" It was a man's voice. Brejack rolled into action.

"Hi. Is this Fred Austin?"

"Who's this?"

"It's George Brejack, Fred, the investigator from the Passaic County Prosecutor's Office. It was nice meeting you and your wife. The two of you told me some interesting things as far as the case goes. But I'm wondering if you and I can meet alone sometime."

"All right."

"How about tomorrow morning? I'll meet you at the Tick Tock diner for breakfast."

They settled on a time and agreed to hook up in the diner's parking lot.

Fred had gotten rid of the Nova and drove a station wagon these days, so the next morning Brejack kept his eyes open for the large car with its metal roof rack. As promised, his little Volvo was idling in a spot that looked out on the highway. When Fred pulled up alongside it, Brejack waved in greeting and popped the button on the front passenger door. Fred shut off the ignition, climbed out of his car, and gingerly slid in alongside the investigator.

Brejack looked into Austin's bright blue eyes and spoke in a voice that sounded very small as it came from the mouth of such a big man. "Freddie," he said, "you've got something to tell me. What is it?"

If Fred Austin could have jumped further away from Brejack, he would have. This mind-reading display had spooked him, and left him with fresh respect for the lawman's instincts. Shocked by his eerie intuition, Fred told

George exactly what had long been on his mind. "I'm not saying that John was involved in anything," Fred began slowly, staring across the highway, watching cars approach from above the hill and zoom past him, leaving invisible trails of exhaust. "But he had to know where the car was parked."

"What do you mean?" Brejack asked, intrigued.

"That night at the mall, Investigator Brejack—"

"Call me George."

"George. That night at the mall it was pitch-black, so dark that I couldn't see more than a couple of feet in front of me. But John spotted Candy's car from the other side of the parking lot." He contemplated this for a moment, then backpedaled and fabricated an out for his granddaughter's father. "Like I'm saying, I don't want to accuse John of doing anything, but that night was very strange. I believe that John knew exactly where Candy's car was parked."

Brejack absorbed the information, eager to know more but not yet drawing any real conclusions from this. Then he suggested that they head into the diner. A former truck stop, the Tick Tock was an oversized, glossy, slicked-up place that appealed to suburbanites who wanted to dine out without paying the high tariff of a full-fledged restaurant. The only remnant from the diner's old days was a clock on its roof and a neon sign that read EAT HEAVY. Because it was mid-morning, with most patrons already having finished their meals and gone on to work, George and Fred had the place pretty much to themselves. They chose a table near the window and ordered a couple of specials from the breakfast menu.

After the waitress walked away, Fred turned over his paper place mat and pulled a pencil from his shirt pocket. "I want to draw a map for you," he told Brejack, and proceeded to sketch a series of squiggles and lines that zigged and zagged around the clean surface. "See, we were all the way back here," Fred maintained. He drew a small dot, then dragged a line across the white sheet.

"How could John have seen the car at the other end of the parking lot?"

George nodded, though he still failed to grasp the importance of what Fred was telling him. As the two men ate breakfast, Brejack proceeded with a more general line of questioning. Fred rehashed the evening at the Willowbrook Mall. He described John smashing the front passenger side window of the Cutlass and sighed deeply, as if it were all he could do to hold back the tears. "I see my daughter's dead body every day and every night. I will never get over what happened to her."

After allowing a moment or two of respectful silence, Brejack wondered where the car was.

"As far as I know the Wayne police still have it," Fred responded with a shrug. "John told me that the police had called him and asked if he wanted to come for the car. He said he didn't want it. He told the cops that they could junk it for all he cared."

"Are you close with John right now?"

"Well, we spend a good deal of time with our granddaughter Jesse, but John doesn't come up and see us all that often. When we invite him and Judy and Jesse up for dinner or whatever they're usually late, or else they don't bother showing up at all."

"Besides that, is there anything odd about John's behavior?"

"Since the crime, whenever I'm with John he talks about things that don't make sense. He'll go off on these long tangents about his business that I really can't understand. I'll just sit there, looking at him, not saying a word, and he'll keep right on talking."

"Have you ever played cards or board games with John?" Brejack wanted to know, realizing that the question sounded out of place but hoping that it would lead to information about the suspect's personality.

Fred nodded in the affirmative.

"What happens when he loses?"

"Oh, John gets very upset. He'll start yelling and try

to ruin the good time for everybody else. At least he does that for a few minutes, then I'll look at him and he'll simmer down. The thing with John is that he's one of these guys who really hates to lose."

Nice, Brejack thought to himself, giving away nothing through his facial gestures. *Exactly what I would have figured.*

In order to make sure that he understood precisely what had happened that night at Willowbrook, Brejack repeated a few questions to Fred, concentrating on who had suggested going to the mall and looking for Candy in the first place. "John suggested it," Austin confirmed. "He came into the house and told me that we should go to the Willowbrook Mall." Fred shook his head and lit a post-meal cigarette, then reiterated in frustration, "I don't know how he saw Candy's car. It was on the other side of the parking lot. *I couldn't see it.* It was like he knew that the car was there or something."

By the time they finished breakfast Brejack's curiosity about the mall had been piqued. He wanted to see for himself how events had transpired that night. After all, the investigator silently reasoned, so many years later distances can play tricks on you. They can expand and contract in your mind without your even knowing it.

"I want to find out exactly what you and John saw," Brejack said as they exited the restaurant. "I want to go with you to Willowbrook Mall one afternoon, and you can explain precisely what happened on June 22nd."

The two men were about to shake hands and go their separate ways when George remembered Helen's hesitancy about dealing with him and her reluctance to implicate John as the murderer. He settled on a way to win a few brownie points with Helen while proving that her son-in-law was worth considering as a suspect. "And Fred," he said. "When we go I want you to bring Helen along. There are no secrets in this investigation."

Fred, experiencing the light-headed relief that comes with confession, agreed to do that. Each man got into his own car and drove off.

CHAPTER
10

Several weeks after his breakfast with Fred Austin, Brejack arranged to meet him and Helen at Willowbrook Mall. The investigator had been working this case on and off for more than a month, and a clear picture of exactly what had happened and the ways to prove it had not yet come together.

But he was getting there. Even as an otherwise full case load prevented him from spending all his time on this investigation, Brejack had a lot of loose facts—or, as he liked to call them, unconnected links—rattling around. By following seemingly incongruous leads, the investigator hoped to uncover the facts that would result in an airtight case.

On an Indian summer afternoon, Brejack and the Austins convened in front of Sears Roebuck. Pulling up alongside Fred's station wagon, George saw Helen sitting in the passenger seat and smiled at her. She grudgingly acknowledged him.

During times of stress Helen pressed her lips together, creating an exaggeratedly forbidding facade. On this particular afternoon her lips looked about ready to bleed from the pressure being exerted by her teeth. Fred waved an amiable hello and Brejack joined the couple in their car.

"Let's get out on the highway," he told Fred. "I want you to show me the exact route that you took with John Short."

As they pulled out of the mall, Brejack asked them about Jesse, found out how John was doing, and inquired after Fred's health.

While this small talk had no bearing on the case, Brejack believed that the conversation would help forge some kind of a relationship with the Austins. Hopefully communicating with Helen while offering her a taste of what had gone on that night in the shopping mall would force her to see things Brejack's way.

Fred retraced the drive that he had taken with John Short. Reliving the discovery of his daughter's body, he remembered precisely where each turn had been made. As he notated landmarks on this guided tour, Brejack could not have calculated the horrors reenacting themselves behind Fred's eyes. He accelerated along the path, describing the pitch-black lot, revealing that John had called him "Dad" for the first time that night, and shedding fresh light on the information first revealed at the Tick Tock. It solidified Brejack's belief that John Short had to have known where the Cutlass was. How else could he have identified Candy's car from a distance of three hundred and thirty-three feet?

As they drove back into the mall's main parking lot, Brejack turned to Fred and gently suggested, "I'd like you to come down to my office next week and make a formal statement."

The man agreed. And whether they liked it or not, Fred and Helen Austin were once again involved in the investigation of their daughter's murder. Judging by what had just transpired, Helen had to believe that John Short ranked as the primary suspect. This time, however, she understood the reasons for those suspicions. While she hated the thought of Brejack hounding Jesse's father, Helen now kept those feelings private. After today, she would never again leap so blindly to the defense of her son-in-law. While she still remained one of John's staunchest advocates, seeds of doubt had been sown by

Fred's retelling of the night he had discovered their dead daughter.

The Austins headed home, and Brejack made the short trip from the mall to the Wayne police station. Navigating back roads that ran away from the highway, he drove past the lushly landscaped, high-priced houses that made Wayne the county's wealthiest town. Set a good distance from the street, each home was occupied by people who felt insulated from evil. While most of them had little in common with plain, blue-collar folk like the Austins, they shared an innocence that went beyond class distinctions. Most white suburbanites believed that murder couldn't touch them, that their well-bred daughters would never know killers, much less marry them. Brejack, of course, knew differently. Now Helen did as well.

In the Wayne police parking lot, the silver Volvo occupied a visitor's spot. George kept the motor running as he sat for a moment and gathered his thoughts. He scribbled a few jottings onto a pad, recollecting the hour he had just spent with the Austins and drawing his own map of what Fred had shown him. The more he considered the case, the more difficult he found it to understand what had gone wrong with the investigation mounted by the Wayne police. They had the killer in their hands, but couldn't get an indictment warrant? It made no sense.

Brejack marveled at the amateurism that permeated their handling of the case as he laid the groundwork for his own investigation. Before going inside he printed two more entries in his notebook—*Helen coming around* and *Must visit John Short*—then prepared for the worst. After locking up his car, Brejack proceeded to the back entrance of Wayne's detective bureau.

The door opened into a long rectangular room furnished with metal desks and filing cabinets. The place had about as much character as a Holiday Inn, and was a carbon copy of all the other municipal offices he'd ever walked through. Bare, institutional gray walls, broken up only by the occasional bulletin board, dominated the dreary facility. Desks cluttered the space, and a coffee maker rested on a table at the far end. Brejack preferred to work in environments imbued with a more personal feel—his own office was already laden with mementos, awards, photographs, and gag plaques—but the state of Wayne's files concerned him more than the design sensibility of the town's police force.

More complete than what Blakey had left behind, these records were still an indecipherable mess. Pages turned up in no logical order, some reports were typed, others had been scribbled on sheets of legal paper, and quite a few seemed to be missing. Tired of having to search through all of it in order to find, say, Webster's transcript of his interview with John Short, Brejack resigned himself to the tedium of reorganizing. In the course of doing that, he familiarized himself with the original investigation and eventually knew where to find whatever material he needed in the future. Meticulous to the point of obsession, Brejack could work no other way.

He became a frequent, though unwelcome, presence at the detective bureau. Brejack got the feeling that the lower-ranking cops hated seeing an outsider in a suit scrutinizing the results of their investigation and trying to make them look bad. But he didn't care, especially since the town's detective lieutenant, deputy chief, and chief all were cooperating. Whenever necessary he showed up in Wayne and went to work, using their sketchy materials as a launch pad. "Polishing dog shit into gold," is how one of Brejack's colleagues would later characterize this investigative alchemy.

Any information Brejack wanted on the Wayne effort had to come from these files, since the original detectives would provide only the most limited help and encouragement. Six years after they gave up on the Candy Short murder, things had changed considerably: Webster had gone from plainclothes detective to patrol sergeant; Jim

Wilson, now a uniformed patrol captain, was nearing retirement with full benefits; Billy McCann, Wayne's point man in the case, had died of a heart attack. Ironically, he suffered the coronary while painting parking lines in the lot of the Willowbrook Mall.

Soon after taking on the murder, Brejack wanted to know about the records' inconsistencies and the unsavvy police work that had been the hallmark of the initial investigation. A shrug of ignorance greeted most of his queries. "That was Billy McCann's responsibility," came the standard reply. "He never completed his reports, and he's the only one who could answer that."

While the information did nothing to help Brejack's campaign, it told him that he was proceeding correctly. Had these cops not feared him as somebody who might solve the case and make them look bad, they would have eagerly cooperated with a fellow officer.

Finally, after responsibility for yet another incomplete report was directed toward the dead man, Brejack blew up at Webster: "You guys are pouring so much shit on Billy McCann he should have been buried with a funnel sticking out of his asshole!"

Comments like that one contributed significantly to the friction between Brejack and the Wayne detectives. Sitting at a table, going through the materials, he routinely heard them whispering about how the crime was unsolvable. Six years after the murder, they insisted, no jury would find John Short guilty.

"You watch," Brejack said, looking up from his work. "I'm going to get that son of a bitch convicted."

This rarely failed to bring smiles of condescension from anyone within earshot. One person not smiling at all was Andrew Webster. Of all those who had worked the case, only he remained on the force with a full career in law enforcement ahead of him. If Brejack succeeded, the patrol sergeant would look incompetent and the incident would trail him for years. Brejack saw that accounting for Webster's desire to dampen enthusiasm within the Wayne Police Department.

During one of the many verbal jousts that George invariably found himself getting suckered into, a cop practically taunted, "Look, Brejack, this isn't one of those smoking gun murders that you were so good at solving down in Paterson. It's not a case of niggers shooting niggers."

The comment raised Brejack's hackles, as it not only called into question his ability to work outside of a ghetto but also intimated that his success there had been somehow illegitimate. It was the last thing he needed to hear after a few frustrating hours with the files. He knew that if this kept up somebody would get hit, and picking a fight in a room full of hostile police officers invariably leads to more trouble than Brejack felt like courting.

Concerned that Wayne's bad vibes would adversely affect his ability to work the case, the investigator requested permission to remove the records from the station so that he could refer to them in the relative peace of the Passaic County Prosecutor's Office. The request went unanswered until Brejack showed up a couple of days later with a subpoena. Now nothing could be done to prevent him from transferring the files.

When the two boxes of badly organized materials were delivered to his office, Brejack took another small step toward solving the murder of Candy Short.

A videotape labeled "John Short's Interview" was jammed up against the side of one box. Wondering what secrets resided within that reel, Brejack inserted it into the office's videocassette player and sat back to watch. After a brief shot of John and Candy's apartment, he saw a rocket ship blasting off. Brejack fast-forwarded to more of the Joralemon Street domicile, which segued into a troop of Brownies getting a tour of the Wayne police station. Before the interrogation itself even came on, Brejack stopped the tape and put it away. He wondered how a department of policemen could be so unorganized that they would tape TV programs and a childrens' tour of the station onto a piece of documentation that stood to provide so many clues.

Rather than building on the Wayne detectives' existing work, Brejack used their files and reports as maps and reference guides for tracking down potential witnesses. With so much of the paperwork incomplete or nonexistent, he feared that following the initial investigation too closely would lead him astray. On one of his morning visits with Passaic County Deputy Chief John Nativo, Brejack complained about the problem.

"I look at this stuff and it doesn't even make sense to me," the investigator said, sipping black coffee as he watched for a reaction from the bald, heavyset man on the other side of the desk. Nativo took a deep drag from his ever-present cigarette and waited to hear more. "I'm going to start from scratch," Brejack continued. "Do all the research myself. Fuck those guys in Wayne."

"Whatever it takes, George." Nativo coughed, with a phlegmy-sounding smoker's hack. "I know you'll do it." More than anybody in the prosecutor's office, he believed in Brejack and felt convinced that the investigator still had it in him to solve the big crimes.

Colleagues from Paterson, they had met in a cemetery back when the two of them were moonlighting as hearse drivers for competing funeral homes. Over the years fifty-eight-year-old Nativo had become a mentor of Brejack's; they worked on enough cases together for Nativo to recognize the investigator's talent and tenacity. "You remember that in the end the only thing that matters is results," he said. "Just do your old-fashioned police work, keep pounding the streets. The information's out there. You just have to find it."

As Brejack got up to leave, his supervisor quickly reminded him not to forget about his other cases. Besides working on the Short murder, Brejack had nearly a dozen active crimes that he had to investigate.

Nativo thought about what he had just told Brejack,

then felt compelled to add one other point. "Remember the challenge of the Short case: You not only have to arrest John, but he must be convicted of first-degree murder." Nativo hacked violently, and the squat, heavyset man's ruddy cheeks looked about ready to explode. Brejack respectfully waited for the coughing fit to subside. "That cocksucker gets convicted of manslaughter and he walks. The statute of limitations is already up on everything but murder. And you know as well as I do that circumstantial evidence rarely leads to a murder conviction."

Interrupting his boss, Brejack began to explain the strength of the case he'd be mounting against Short, but Nativo had other points to make. "The evidence has got to be so strong that a jury can say, 'This man intentionally killed his wife. He wanted her dead.' Otherwise we're just wasting a lot of time and money. Six or seven years later it's a tough thing to do. But I have faith in you, George. You're like me; you operate the old-fashioned way. You get results."

Brejack considered the advice, then realized that even his good friend Nativo could not understand everything that hinged on a conviction. Upon arriving at the prosecutor's office, Brejack encountered the kind of derision that scares off less determined men. Many of his new colleagues believed that anybody who spent six years away from law enforcement should stay away.

Behind Brejack's back they ridiculed him, badmouthing this loner who was once again trying his hand at meting out justice. They viewed him as an old man whose great day had passed, and snickered at his desire to reenter the pantheon of supercop. Brejack hoped that solving a case like this one would silence them. It would force them to acknowledge that he had returned and was operating at full capacity.

By the time Brejack earnestly embarked on the Candy Short murder, the trees outside his office had begun shedding their leaves. Crack addicts hunched their shoulders against the cold, and fall scents managed to permeate the polluted air of downtown Paterson. It was Brejack's favorite season. He regretted that he'd have no time for deer hunting this year, but he intended to break this case before the weather turned warm again.

Working the telephone, Brejack scheduled a round of interviews with several of the people who seemed closest to Candy. He remembered the icy reception he received from Helen and braced himself for more of the same, even as he vowed to prevent any of it from sapping his spirit.

Upon realizing that Betty and Joe Frank lived next door to the Austins, he decided to begin by interviewing them. His hope was that they were close enough to Candy to supply relevant information, but not so close that discussing the murder would be difficult for them. Later, once he finished with their cousins, Brejack would also pop in on Helen and Fred.

When he entered the Franks' house, they received the investigator with more warmth than any of the other family members had. But Betty and Joe harbored their own doubts about Brejack's ability to do all that he promised. Nevertheless, both of them wanted to see Candy's death avenged. They would do what they could to help him. Trying to be friendly, Betty poured George a glass of iced tea and Joe showed off a baseball signed by the 1928 Yankees. It was prominently displayed in their living room.

"Our family heirloom," Betty said proudly.

Brejack, an ardent fan of the New York Giants before they had moved to San Francisco, delicately handled the ball. At the same time he scoped out the living room, which reminded him structurally of the one across the gravel drive. "Freddie grew up here," Betty told George, struggling through the small talk and eager to hear what the investigator had to say. "This property has been in our family for over one hundred years."

Brejack nodded and sipped his iced tea. Then he explained what he intended to do. He offered Betty and Joe the same laundry list of promises and credentials that he had recited for the Austins.

"Here we go again," Joe Frank said through pursed lips, speaking softly enough so that Brejack did not hear him. He distinctly remembered the previous investigation, which resulted in vanquished hopes and a hard letdown. This guy, he figured, would bring more of the same.

Then, as their conversation turned to the murder, Betty and Joe saw something different in Brejack. He showed that he cared about the case in a way that went beyond the purely professional. He seemed to have a legitimate concern for what they had to say, as if he wanted the information for his personal use rather than in a coldly official capacity. This loosened the couple up, and encouraged them to discuss the last several years of their life.

After explaining, for what seemed like the umpteenth time, the events that had led to the discovery of Candy's body—and jibing with her original telling of the story— Betty admitted something that she couldn't bring herself to acknowledge six years earlier. "They were not happily married," she told the investigator resignedly. "Candy and Jesse did without a lot of things, while John was free to do as he pleased and buy whatever he wanted."

If Brejack had trouble understanding the full importance of Fred Austin's parking lot revelation, what Betty was telling him needed no further elucidation. The marriage was rockier than information culled during the previous investigation had made it appear. Remaining calm and scribbling on his police pad, Brejack wondered aloud whether they had had any fights prior to the night of the murder.

"A few weeks before the crime they had a big argument," Betty remembered, recounting the "I'll piss on your grave" incident. "John was very demanding. He was a quick-tempered, macho guy. He'd get very bossy with Candy."

"Yeah," Joe said, gesturing toward the backyard that they shared with the Austins. "One time we were out back, and John made her take a fifteen-minute drive so that she could get him a hot dog from the Red Chimney."

"Did he seem remorseful after Candy's death?" Brejack wanted to know.

"Remorseful?" Betty chuckled sardonically. "A few months after her funeral [actually only a few *weeks* after his wife was buried, though John managed to hide it] he already had a new girlfriend. John actually made a pass at *me*."

Joe scowled sourly. Brejack looked at Betty with an expression of concern and interest. His tired-looking eyes, with the baggy flaps of skin around them, urged her to continue. "He put his hand on my leg and told me, 'If there's anything I can ever do for you, just let me know.' It reached the point where I felt very uncomfortable around him."

They discussed the Wayne police department's investigation, and Betty got riled up. "For some reason," she said, "John refused to take a lie detector test. He never came right out and told them, 'I didn't kill Candy.' Instead he skirted around the issue, avoiding Webster and McCann whenever possible."

Satisfied with what they had told him, and not wanting to push too hard on a first visit, Brejack began wrapping up by asking Betty if there was anything else she wanted to add. Betty nodded. "Whenever Candy went shopping she took Jesse with her. My cousin was the type of mother who rarely left her daughter with somebody else. That one thing always bugged me: I could never figure out why she didn't take Jesse with her that night."

Brejack thanked the couple for their hospitality and stood up to leave. They walked him to the front door and each shook the investigator's hand. Brejack turned his back to them, and Betty added, "I'm glad the case is being reactivated. I was very close to Candy. The person responsible for her death should be punished."

Walking away from the house, Brejack realized that he had scored a victory. Somebody had finally welcomed his involvement; never mind that he had anticipated a warm reception from all of Candy's relatives. While Joe had seemed a little prickly at first the guy eventually came around, and Brejack believed they both would prove to be vital founts of information. Feeling confident, he strolled next door and popped in on the Austins. They surprised him by also seeming to welcome the visit.

Buoyed by good spirits, Brejack drove back to the Passaic County Prosecutor's Office and spent the early evening hours processing the information he had received from Betty and Joe. What they told him supported his hunch that the marriage had been a mess. The idea of John as a frustrated and abusive husband also matched the killer's profile. Now that he was getting positive feedback, Brejack knew that taking this case on had been the right thing to do, even if it looked like some of the investigating would have to be conducted on his own time.

During this most recent visit with Fred and Helen, Brejack uncovered another potential source of information about Candy: Geri Austin. Not only had the victim spent several days each week babysitting for her aunt's son, but Geri's husband Harry happened to be an ex-cop. No doubt he would have some ideas about the killing. Or at least he would have, had it not been for a recent stroke; it left fifty-eight-year-old Harry near total paralysis. Nevertheless, on the afternoon of September 29th, Geri clearly recalled Harry's feelings about the case.

A good-natured, devoted family woman, Candy's thirty-nine-year-old aunt had nothing but scorn for the Wayne police. Brejack, however, made every effort to remain discreet, and avoided appearing to agree with her. He sensed her pleasure in seeing the case revived, and explained that the most useful memories would be those that directly pertained to the marriage and murder.

"What did you think of John?" Brejack asked, after Geri informed him that she had known Candy for twenty years, from the day she'd married Fred's brother.

"My husband and I both disliked him," Geri said. "We avoided him, we didn't trust him, and we believed that he took advantage of Candy, who was a very nice but very lonely girl."

"How did she and John get along?"

"They argued a lot while they dated, and after the marriage John abused her on a regular basis. It was the sort of treatment that few women would tolerate."

Geri recounted the afternoon on which she noticed the ugly bruises dotting Candy's arm, then gestured toward Harry, who now sat still and silent in his wheelchair. Brejack looked at the paralyzed man and would have loved to hear his take on the whole thing. Knowing that his wish could never be fulfilled, he settled for Geri's presentation of Harry's hypotheses. "After the murder," she said, "Harry forbade me to be alone with John. We both suspected that he had killed Candy, and figured we needed to take special precautions where he was concerned. For instance, when we went on vacation, Harry used to leave his guns with Fred Austin. But after the murder, once John moved into the house with him and Helen, Fred refused to take the guns. He didn't trust having firearms around the house as long as John could gain access to them."

A grimace played across Geri's face as she shook her head and added, "Helen often bought gifts for Candy and Jesse and gave them to John so that he could present them. He was so moody, and a terribly sore loser, yet Helen defended John all the time."

Silence followed that statement, and Brejack silently wondered what Helen could tell him about John's behavior. As if reading his mind, Geri explained, "Helen knows a lot about what went on with John and Candy, but she'll never tell anyone. She's very closemouthed."

Brejack left Geri Austin's home and spent the remainder of the day at his office. He typed up a report and used an innate filtering system that allowed him to instinctively sift out useless information. Brejack was back in the business of building cases, and he believed that this would be his best one yet. While good fortune remained on his side he wanted to try his luck with Judy Halbert Chamberlain, Candy's best friend from high school. Like the others, Judy expressed puzzlement about why he would be attempting to solve the case now, so many years after the murder, but she agreed to meet with Brejack anyway.

Her husband Richie was at work on the morning of October 6th, when the investigator paid a visit to the second-story apartment inhabited by the couple and their young son. Toys lay on the living room floor and a framed poster of Miss Piggy hung above the couch. A friendly woman with a desire to help solve the mystery, Judy offered nothing new, though she did corroborate all of the background information on John and Candy.

While Brejack felt let down by her inability to provide any fresh details, he had a feeling that she would come in handy later on. There's no telling what a longtime friend of a murdered woman will recall when she least expects it. He handed Judy his business card and told her, "Keep thinking about Candy. Anything at all that you figure I might be interested in—even if it doesn't seem important—please give me a call. You never know when a trivial detail can lead to a big break."

She agreed to do that, and Brejack believed her. Plenty of potential sources say they'll phone a cop back, then never bother making the call. But that didn't seem like Judy's style.

Cruising back to the prosecutor's office, he heard WPAT playing a Muzak version of "Yesterday" and pictured a chain in his mind. It looked small, but the links were solid. Each source contributed a tiny bit of information that Brejack would need in order to solve the case.

He stopped at a red light and looked across the street to a hardware store. Brejack pulled over and walked inside. The length of chain he purchased that afternoon would serve as a talisman throughout the investigation. The fat, silver links reminded him of every element's importance and the necessity of using each one to its fullest potential.

Across the street from Cedar Lawn cemetery stood St. Brendan's Church, a modern building on Crooks Avenue. The two-lane street ran through the eastern tip of Paterson—one of the city's few remaining safe neighborhoods—and curved down into neighboring Clifton. Brejack enjoyed many early-evening strolls through the cemetery, and he spent most every Sunday morning in church.

St. Brendan's bells rang loud enough for him to hear them in his second-story apartment, never letting George forget the importance of maintaining faith in the Lord and himself. The bells gently roused Brejack at five o'clock each morning, and within the hour he was invariably drinking black coffee, reading the newspaper, and toasting a muffin. On this particular day he scanned the first section of the Sunday *Herald News*, Passaic County's paper of record. The local daily's reporters had always treated Brejack well, and he checked to see if any of his acquaintances had bylines.

More than most lawmen, Brejack courted the media. He tipped off certain reporters so that they could be at crime scenes as the events unfolded. Good press, he believed, kept citizens aware of what the enforcers they employed were up to. And just as important, it fed Brejack's considerable ego, which required constant nourishment. Viewing attention as part of the payoff for his hard work, Brejack had managed to build a thick scrapbook of news clippings. His face had even graced page one of

The New York Times after he helped bust a kidnapping ring.

His cozy relationship with the journalists frequently initiated razzing from his colleagues, who viewed him as a glory-seeking publicity hound, but Brejack didn't care. "Fuck 'em," was his typical response. "The assholes are jealous. If they worked as hard as I do they'd get their pictures in the paper, too."

As Brejack dug into the color comics, Lisa sleepily made her way out of bed and into the bathroom. She showered, got dressed, and joined her boyfriend for a cup of coffee. She found him fascinating and unique, even if his behavior often seemed incomprehensible. Now, for instance, watching him operate in law enforcement for the first time, she couldn't grasp exactly why he got so keyed up every day. Nothing really seemed to be happening with the Short murder, yet each evening George came home from work tightly wound and intense, his mood as predictable as a roll of the dice.

"I've got the vibe on John Short," he told Lisa this morning, starting her day with a subject that she was, at best, only mildly interested in. "Every day I get closer to building a case against him."

"You'd better get dressed, George," she said.

Freshly showered and shaved, he wore nothing but a bathrobe. Brejack got up and walked toward the bedroom.

"I know he did it!" he called over his shoulder. "No way it can be anyone else. Now it's just a matter of amassing enough evidence so that a grand jury will believe me."

Lisa said nothing. She checked her watch and waited for George to get ready for church. After a few minutes he emerged from the room, resembling a race track dandy in a plaid sport jacket and navy blue slacks, his tufts of hair tamed into submission. The bottom stub of a fat gold watch peaked out from below his shirt cuff, and Brejack announced that he was ready to leave. Even though it would have been a short walk to St. Brendan's the couple typically drove, as their Sunday morning routine always concluded with breakfast at the home of George's seventy-four-year-old mother.

Sitting in the pew, Brejack made sure that his pant leg didn't hitch up to reveal the ankle holster that held his off-duty weapon, a Smith & Wesson snub-nosed revolver. George spent his first few minutes saying the Rosary, then knelt down during all of the service's appropriate moments. But he felt fidgety, as if something inside him needed to escape. Only during the sermon, when Brejack allowed his mind to wander around the periphery of the case, did he finally settle down.

While the priest lectured about the evils of gambling in Atlantic City, the investigator pictured John Short. He imagined a man stealing a life and living without remorse. For a Catholic, that lack of guilt-fueled soul-searching bordered on the incomprehensible. If guilt did not give Short away, however, Brejack felt confident that something else would. Judging from what he already knew, the investigator figured John to be careless. "Somewhere along the line," he had told Nativo, "the bastard's bound to fuck up."

Brejack's job would be to pounce on that miscalculation and use it as a weapon of conviction. He knew that the perfect crime did exist; many people commit murders and leave no clues behind. But John Short was probably not one of them; sloppiness seemed to be a persistent trait in John's life, and some of that had to be present in the murder. Short's cunning, the investigator believed, would be overshadowed by his imprudence.

As congregants began lining up to accept the host, Brejack's mind still rattled around with images of a killer. After he took the thin, bland wafer in his mouth, Brejack blessed himself and asked God to give him the strength and conviction to see this case through. He prayed for the guidance and patience he would need to bring John Short to justice and avenge the death of Candy. No signals or signs greeted the request, though Brejack did feel a rush of self-confidence; he knew he had the faith and strength and talent to solve this case.

An hour later, after he and Lisa arrived at his mother's house for breakfast, Brejack piled his plate high with bacon and eggs. He sopped half a bagel with butter and soaked up a runny stream of bacon grease. Joining his brother Robert (a short, muscular, easygoing, forty-four-year-old man who worked as a machinist and was still saddled with the unfortunate childhood nickname of Rabbit) and his sister-in-law Patti, George seemed distant.

Rather than asking him what was wrong, Rabbit wondered about how it felt to be back in law enforcement. "It's beautiful," George told him. "I've got a couple of good cases going. But it's a murder from 1981 that I'm really interested in."

"Eighty-one? That's six years ago," said Rabbit. He whistled a long, single note of amazement, expressing the awe that he usually felt for his older brother. "How are you going to get him convicted now?"

"I'm going to do it," Brejack assured. "The evidence is there. It's just a matter of putting it together."

"We're so proud of you," Patti said. "It's nice to see that you're back to doing what you really enjoy. I always knew that you missed the police department."

"He's not with the police department," Rabbit corrected his wife. "It's the prosecutor's office."

"We're still proud of you," Patti said.

"Wait till I put this son of a bitch behind bars. Then you'll really be proud."

Hearing such language, especially after church, caused George's mother Christine to shoot her son a disdainful look as he topped his bagel with a forkful of egg. After he popped it in his mouth the conversation moved on, but his mother now smiled at him. Christine Brejack, a strong-willed matriarch and George's primary inspiration, had as much confidence in her son as he had in himself.

CHAPTER
11

Each morning, as George Brejack drove to work, he passed through the burned-out streets of Paterson. The daily journey reminded him of how low the city had fallen and how far from the housing projects he had come.

Nearly every day of his life had been spent in this place that had once heralded itself as Silk City. Through the 1950s it boasted the highest volume of silk production in the United States, and supported enough industry to keep the skies coated with a thick layer of soot. Back then the citizenry viewed it as progress rather than pollution.

By 1987, however, all but a few of the mills had ceased production. Many of them stood padlocked, living on as monuments to once-thriving times. The final blow to those productive days came with the race riots of the 1960s, which left square blocks of Paterson charred and abandoned. Neighborhoods that managed to escape total destruction might as well have been burned to the ground, as they became overrun with drug addicts, prostitutes, and a wide assortment of criminals.

While Brejack felt a certain amount of sentimentality toward his hometown, he harbored no illusions. The Paterson he remembered had nothing to do with the rich doctors' mansions that once lined the streets along Eastside Park—lush and welcoming decades ago, the park now served as a haven for crack dealers. As for the grand homes, they had long ago been abandoned and boarded over; their upkeep alone became unaffordable to anybody tough enough to brave the neighborhood.

While the city of his youth had been reasonably safe, Brejack's boyhood was dotted with violence and racism. He grew up in the Riverside Terrace housing project, an ugly spread of squatty garden apartments that resembled nothing so much as army barracks. Subsidized by tax dollars, it provided housing for families unable to afford the rent within the private sector. The projects created an underclass that was simultaneously supported and ostracized by the city's taxpayers. Riverside Terrace harbored a number of violent, hard-drinking tenants, few of whom would be considered role models for a child.

Nights in the Brejack home were rarely pleasant. George's father, John, was a thick-waisted, bulked-up, machine operator who drank heavily and regularly brutalized his wife Christine. On one night in 1945, though, the routine beatings took a turn for the worse. The four Brejack children—an older brother, a sister, and Rabbit, who was a year younger than George—huddled together in one of the bedrooms, holding each other as maternal screams penetrated the closed door.

Nobody remembered what their parents fought about, but it probably centered around John's ongoing affair with a young cocktail waitress. "You keep your fucking trap shut!" he shouted, smacking Christine squarely in the face. "I support you. This is my house. You don't tell me what to do."

She lay sprawled on the floor, her body beaten and abused, all too aware that calling for help would do no good. Domestic violence was a fact of life in Riverside Terrace, where an unwritten rule mandated that nobody interfere in another family's squabbles. Any man foolish enough to do that would most likely find himself decked by whomever he had tried to calm down.

Ironically, however, for all the physical clout that the

fathers wielded, the projects resembled a matriarchal society. Heroic women held many of the families together. They found the resolve to earn livings and keep their kids fed long after the bullying men they married had disappeared.

For the time being, the Brejack kids took comfort in actually having a father. That he abused alcohol and womanized and beat his wife didn't seem so bad. In Riverside Terrace, where many husbands worked like mules for minimal factory wages and carried untold amounts of frustration, the violence was all but expected.

At least John remained home and supported his family. That's the way Christine rationalized it. After this most recent beating, though, she had second thoughts. Lying on the floor with blood pouring from her nose, her face beginning to swell, her body aching from the physical onslaught, she clearly saw the threat against her life. How much longer would it be before one of these punch-ups proved fatal?

Blood stained her husband's mitt-like hands as he stormed around the apartment, bellowing. George, a skinny five-year-old boy with a brush cut of blondish hair, separated himself from his siblings and cautiously stepped out of the bedroom and into the hallway. His half-conscious mother lay stunned on the floor, unable to get up; his father stood out of sight, in the kitchen pouring himself a boilermaker. This allowed George the opportunity to surreptitiously open the apartment door and slip outside.

Not bothering to put on his shoes, and wearing only pajama bottoms, George emerged into the winter night. The Brejacks had no telephone, so he waded through the shallow snow to an emergency police box that had been set up in the projects' parking lot. After dialing the operator and asking for the cops, George announced that his mother had been beaten. He gave his location, then spent twenty minutes standing by the box and shivering in the snow. The other children remained huddled together, frightened and helpless. They listened to their mother's anguished moans and prayed that she would survive the physical punishment.

Two policemen finally pulled up—they always took a little longer in responding to a call from Riverside Terrace—and George led them to the apartment. They walked in to see John Brejack sitting on the couch with the radio on, a broadcast of big-band music blasting from the speaker. To the casual observer nothing seemed amiss, as Christine cried behind a closed bathroom door. Upon noticing the cops, John cursed his son and attempted to get away. But they grabbed him before he could reach the door, wrestled the big man to the floor, and cuffed his wrists.

The next morning Christine pressed charges, and the court handed down an order for John Brejack to stay away from his family. Policemen leading him out in handcuffs provided George with a final paternal image.

Disturbing memories from his youth often went through Brejack's mind as he read Wayne's reports on the Short murder. That his father's first name was John proved to be the most obvious and least compelling correlation between him and the man suspected of killing Candy. More importantly, Brejack's father and John Short shared a bullying brutality that they most often vented against women. Unfaithful to the vows of matrimony, neither of them particularly cared about the children that they inadvertently victimized. George categorized that disregard as the worst possible breach of faith between a husband and wife.

Christine Brejack scrubbed floors to support her family, and watched helplessly as George fell in with a rough crowd of friends who lived in the projects. Confronting schoolmates who looked down on them for their hopelessly lower-class lives, the Riverside kids retaliated with the violence that rumbled all around them. Project gang members stashed zip guns and regularly fought anybody who crossed them. On their home ground, white contin-

gents frequently rumbled with black ones. Frustration
ran so deep in Riverside Terrace that these kids used any
excuse for a fight, desperate to blow off steam and ex-
pend energy.

As teenagers, Brejack and his friends sipped quarts
of beer from cardboard containers. They intimidated a
neighbor into buying them limitless amounts of the brew
and sat in a small concrete park, unwittingly growing up
to be just like the irresponsible fathers that they de-
tested. In all fairness, however, the Brejack boys were
somewhat different. Christine struggled—often with limited success—to keep her sons out of trouble.

Each morning George delivered newspapers before
school, and spent Saturdays and Sundays setting pins
downtown at the Peerless Lanes bowling alley. Balls furiously whizzed along the polished wooden planks, and he
and Rabbit made sure to be out of the way. The job was
dangerous enough to leave a few coworkers maimed, but
it paid better than anything else that the Brejacks could
do for money, and Christine needed their financial help.
At midnight, when the shift ended, George and Rabbit
stuffed five dollars apiece into their socks and ran all the
way home, lest a rival gang stop the brothers and try to
steal their money.

After-school hours were taken up with city league bas-
ketball, baseball, and football. Nights were reserved for
getting into trouble. During his teenage years, in the
mid-1950s, Brejack and his friends hot-wired cars and
joy-rode them around the city. They indulged in petty
crimes and vandalized a closed-down gas station. They
were wreaking havoc near the pumps when a pair of
policemen caught them in the act. Later that evening, a
wearied Christine Brejack cried as she signed her son out
of a juvenile detention hall.

By his sixteenth birthday George had been expelled
from vocational school for having one too many fights.
Eager to work, he lied about his age and got a job in a
silk warehouse downtown. A year before Brejack was

licensed to drive a car he found himself behind the wheel of the company's truck, put there by a trusting boss who believed the oversized boy when he claimed to be experienced at making deliveries.

Even as he worked a full-time job, though, George seemed to be heading for nothing but trouble. He impregnated one of his girlfriends and was pressured into marrying her. The teenage couple moved into her parents' house and the union lasted less than two months. Beyond the fact that her father didn't care for Brejack's gruff, projects-style mannerisms—precisely the thing that had attracted his middle-class daughter in the first place—he absolutely hated hearing the bed springs creaking in the newlyweds' room. Never one to respect authority figures, Brejack left the house and arranged for a divorce.

He moved back in with his mother, and Christine saw a dismal future ahead of him. Still just a boy, her son already had one broken family to his credit. Dreading the possibility of George wasting his life on the streets of Paterson, she desperately wanted him out of the neighborhood and away from the bad influences. A friend of hers worked for the draft board, and she arranged things so that George would be plucked for the Army sooner than chance would have had it.

"Shit," he whispered when the draft notice arrived in the mail. "I don't know why they're so interested in me. There's not even a war going on. Nobody else is getting drafted till they're twenty-two, twenty-three."

"Maybe it's all for the best," Christine said, smiling, grateful that her friend came through as promised. "It'll do you some good to get away from here, to see something else besides Paterson."

"But who's going to take care of you, Mom?"

"Don't worry," she said with a wave of her hand. "I'll get by."

"I'll send you whatever I can," vowed Brejack, who

lived up to his word by donating half of each paycheck to the household.

In the spring of 1958 George gave notice at the warehouse and prepared to leave for basic training in Fort Hood, Texas. The place sounded as exotic as Timbuktu for somebody who rarely ventured beyond the confines of his neighborhood.

Before Brejack took off, his friends threw an outdoor party for him. They sat in the park and sipped their beer and said how sorry they were to see him go. Neighborhood girls, black and white, tongue-kissed their departing G.I. The sweet smell of marijuana, which had already infiltrated the projects, wafted into the sky.

"Here, soldier boy," one of the black kids said, passing a skinny reefer to Brejack.

"I'll stick with beer," he replied.

The kid shrugged and took another toke. He exhaled a plume of smoke and laughed hysterically for no apparent reason.

If Christine Brejack had any second thoughts about the bit of rigging she orchestrated with the draft board, one peek at her son's sendoff would have confirmed that she did the right thing. The projects were in the process of being transformed, and none of the coming changes would be for the best.

By the time Brejack returned from his two-year hitch in the service, the old neighborhood barely resembled what he had left behind. The streets had become increasingly dangerous and the projects themselves deteriorated, though most of his old friends still lived there. Killing time with menial jobs, they allowed their meager dreams to fade away.

Welcomed back like a war hero—even though he had come no closer to combat than daily workouts on the rifle range—Brejack regaled the local folk with tales from his time in the service. Stationed in post-war Germany, he had plenty to tell.

"The goddamned broads," he recalled over mugs of beer at a local gin mill frequented by factory workers like his father. "They're beautiful. And they love American guys."

"Did you get laid a lot, George?" they wanted to know.

"Like clockwork," Brejack responded. "Those big blond *frauleins* relied on us for booze. One dollar equaled four marks. We could have bought and sold their pussies if we felt like it."

Eventually, though, the stories got old, things returned to normal, and Brejack found a job driving limousines and hearses for a funeral home. Possessing a strong stomach for being around dead bodies, he spent weekends picking up extra cash by helping morticians with their prep work. The job paid reasonably well, but George wanted more. His days in Germany had given him a yearning for a position of authority.

Attracted by the uniform, the weapons, and the action, he toyed with the idea of becoming a Paterson cop. He watched the patrol teams driving by in their yellow-and-black cars, with the spinning cherries on top, and decided that Paterson's finest had a glorious existence. A rough-and-tumble guy with too much physical energy for his own good, Brejack decided to put his forcefulness to constructive use.

But in order to become a city policeman he had to pass a civil service test, and no tests were scheduled for several months. Then, just as he resigned himself to the long wait, a job became available with the housing police; it required nothing more than a willingness to work. Brejack jumped at the opportunity to join the uniformed corps who patrolled Paterson's projects. His Army experience, coupled with a lifelong knowledge of the area, made Brejack a shoe-in for the post. After a crash course in police science he got measured for a uniform, licensed for a gun, and assigned badge number 271 in September 1963.

Though the area he patrolled was far more dangerous than where he had grown up, Brejack found it easy to deal with the people there. He enjoyed helping out lower-class families with backgrounds very much like his own. Never forgetting the battles that had gone on in his childhood home, Brejack developed a soft touch for settling domestic altercations and an ability to handle mischievous kids.

However, when it came to dealing with the more violent situations—made inevitable by the encroaching drug culture and radical politics of the early sixties—Brejack never backed down. One evening, while patrolling his beat on foot, he heard the pained screams of an old man. Lying on the ground, a senior citizen clung to his wallet, struggling for both his life and his Social Security money. An assailant in his early twenties, skinny and sallow enough to be a junky, kicked and scrapped and grabbed at the calfskin rectangle.

"Hey, leave the guy alone!" Brejack yelled as he hustled over.

Annoyed by the intrusion, the mugger turned around and delivered a hard right to Brejack's stomach. Unaware that this heroin addict used to box professionally, the rookie cop walked into a sledgehammer of a body blow. He retreated a few steps, caught his breath, and came at the assailant with his nightstick swinging. He cracked the guy a good shot across the back of his head and made the arrest. Once it became known that Brejack had saved a World War II veteran with only one lung, the young patrolman received his first medal. Had he not intervened, the violent ordeal would doubtlessly have culminated in a killing.

While walking the beat he occasionally ran into Officer Chuck Nolan, the very man who had once arrested a younger, skinnier Brejack for vandalizing a gas station. Taking a special interest, Nolan encouraged him to stick with the job and to do well at the police academy. George did. He graduated with flying colors, got a job as a foot patrolman, and discovered his calling. In eighteen years on the Paterson police force Brejack worked his way up to the rank of detective, and also became one of the most decorated cops in the city's history. He developed a penchant for doing the right thing, and he proved to be a policeman with a heart.

Early in his career as a uniformed officer, Brejack found himself put to a test that proved exactly where his loyalties lay. One morning in the station, as he sipped coffee and ate a buttered roll, he saw a familiar face and name on the department's list of wanted criminals: Tommy White. This black man with deep-set eyes, skeletal face, and a slip of hair on his chin was a buddy of Brejack's from the projects. They had fought against each other, partied together, and, despite the racial difference, shared a certain amount of kinship simply because of where they had grown up. Now White was wanted for selling the heroin that generated funds for his own habit.

Not saying a word to anybody, George and his partner drove to the projects and easily found Tommy; he lived with his mother, and Brejack simply stepped up to the concrete stoop where they sat together. Before his emotions could get the better of him, he made the collar. At first Brejack feared that his earlier relationship with the man would get in the way, would soften him. But as he approached the apartment, Brejack knew that he'd make the arrest. He couldn't back down. He recognized that he was doing the right thing.

The police officer snapped his handcuffs shut around Tommy's bony wrists, momentarily recalling the times they had together and considering how odd it was that they would end up on opposite sides of the law.

"C'mon Brejack, gimme a break," White whined. "We been friends since we were little kids. You ain't gonna arrest me."

Eager to avoid a debate that he might feel compelled to forfeit, Brejack read the suspect his rights and led his boyhood friend to the patrol car, gently protecting the top of White's head as he guided him into the backseat.

"I'm sick," he pleaded, just before Brejack shut the car door. "Give me a break, please."

The eyes of project residents never left Brejack as he completed his job. Many of them looked at the one-time local boy disparagingly, as if by becoming a cop he had betrayed some secret tenet of the neighborhood. And in a way, perhaps, he had.

But law enforcement proved to be Brejack's salvation, and he worked cases with a brave, tireless devotion to maintaining order in the city where he had grown up. Over the years he developed an uncanny knack for putting together seemingly disparate pieces of evidence which resulted in arrests and convictions. This led reporters to dub him the "psychic cop," and for a long time Brejack insisted that he had a gift. "I don't know how I do it," he generally said with a shrug. "I just get a vibe and follow it. It's like somebody's sending me messages or something."

In one instance a group of officers had spent three weeks searching for the body of a raped and murdered eight-year-old Spanish boy. They practically turned an entire railroad yard upside-down in their quest. When a law enforcer complained that the corpse didn't seem to be there, Brejack eyed them and commanded, "Keep looking."

Finally, nearly a month after their search began, the officers gave up. Annoyed, Brejack scoured the vast, open area himself, then called to a veteran detective, "Did you look here?" the detective nodded. Ignoring him, Brejack investigated a remote corner of the lot. Beneath a plywood board there, the decomposing body was visible.

In other instances he showed up at murder scenes, inspected crowds full of onlookers, and each time picked out the one person who could lead him directly to the killer. After a fatal stabbing, Brejack made eye contact with a local resident and asked him what he knew about the murder. Unnerved by the big man's intimidating gaze, he said, "I saw a guy running down the street with a knife and a TV set."

"Do you know who that guy is?" Brejack asked.

"He lives in the neighborhood, right down there."

The man pointed to one of the beat-up old houses half a block away from where the crime had taken place.

Brejack carefully approached the building, noticed the door ajar, and nudged it with his foot. Inside he saw an empty bottle of Night Train on the floor. A TV game show played in the corner, and the handle of a bloody knife jutted out of the wall. The arrest went smoothly and contributed to the mythologizing of George Brejack.

Life as a member of the Paterson police department—particularly during his four years in narcotics—wasn't always so easy or so glorious. Despite being a crack marksman, Brejack prided himself on rarely drawing his gun. Instead his fists, his instincts, and his nightstick earned him the reputation of a feared and hated man on the city's streets. Brejack became so fascinated with the ways of the underworld that, long before he became a narcotics officer, he frequently initiated buy-and-bust operations.

This usually infuriated the department's narcotics commander, who hated the idea of an unseasoned cop horning in on his territory. Occasional reprimands aside, however, the extracurricular activities eventually paid off. In 1968 Brejack became a member of the narcotics squad. The post promised to deliver the department's highest degree of action, and Brejack did what he could to intensify the experience.

One Sunday afternoon, while driving with a civilian buddy of his on an errand in downtown Paterson, Brejack decided to slowly cruise through the drug-infested neighborhood known as the Fourth Ward. Familiar dealers lined the streets, pimps idled in garish Cadillacs, and dope-ravaged families struggled to get through another day.

As he turned a corner Brejack passed Chester Brown, one of the area's most notorious heroin dealers. Recognizing Brejack's face from the frequent rounds he made during the week, but neglecting to associate him with the uniform he usually wore, Brown gave the off-duty policeman a lazy wave of his hand. He assumed that any white man driving through the neighborhood would be there for only one purpose: to purchase narcotics.

Brejack returned the wave and continued driving. Then he told his friend, "I'm going back there to do a buy-and-bust with that guy. No matter what happens, just sit still and don't say a word."

His friend reluctantly agreed. Turning the car around, Brejack drove to the corner where the dealer stood. "Hey, man, how you doing?" he asked, rolling down the car window.

"What can I do for you?" Chester wanted to know. He dug his hands into the pocket of his suede ankle-length coat and leaned into the car.

"I need to buy a few things," Brejack responded.

"Who's he?" Ignoring his customer's request, the dealer pointed to the clean-cut man in the passenger seat.

"That's my partner," said Brejack

"Your partner? He looks like a cop."

"He's no cop. We did some time together, and he just got out of the can. Come on, get in the car."

Ignoring his better instincts, Chester took the backseat. As was the custom for drug transactions, Brejack began driving so that the sale could be completed in motion, making it more difficult to detect. Brejack took off in the direction of the police station, which was located about ten blocks away. Sliding the dealer a twenty-dollar bill for four nickel bags of heroin, the officer zoomed through an amber light. This further roused Chester's suspicions.

"Okay," he said. "You can let me off right here."

Intending to pull up in front of the station and make the bust there, Brejack continued driving. "I just want to go a few more blocks. You know—"

Chester cut Brejack off in mid-sentence by wrapping his hands around the officer's neck. Frozen with panic, the passenger unwittingly followed Brejack's earlier advice and remained motionless. Brejack slammed his foot on the brake and the car rocked to a short stop in the middle of Bridge Street, an avenue thick with stores and weekend shoppers.

He tried in vain to unclasp the fingers around his neck as his breath came in choppy gasps. Horns honked from the rear, and a patrolman happened to hear the racket before noticing a car stalled in the center of the street. He spotted two guys fighting and—never imagining that one of them would be an off-duty cop—decided to investigate.

Gun drawn, the officer emerged from his cruiser, pulled open the driver's side door of Brejack's car, and was shocked to see the narcotics officer in the front seat. At this point, of course, the masquerade ended. The man in the backseat suddenly let go of Brejack's neck and bitterly whispered, "Shit. I've been set up."

Cuffed and subdued, Chester was escorted to the police car, which Brejack followed to headquarters. As his friend regained his composure, Brejack led the drug dealer to the booking area and completed the arrest. During the following week the story generated a lot of laughs from other cops, but the narcotics' commander expressed displeasure.

That Monday he called Brejack down to his office. After extending congratulations on the arrest, the department chief explained that he had some problems with the approach that had been employed by his prolific subordinate. "What were you doing buying drugs on your day off?" he wanted to know. "Especially when you had a civilian in the car?"

Brejack shrugged. "The drugs are out there. I'm just doing my job."

"But you were off-duty," his exasperated superior replied.

Brejack shook his head and said, "I'm never off-duty."

After five years with the force Brejack became a detective. Colorful and controversial, his picture began appearing in the newspapers, and his childhood hopes came to fruition: People knew George Brejack, and most respected him. His unorthodox techniques drew scorn from the department's more conservative members, but Brejack didn't care as long as the promotions, commendations, and collars continued to roll in.

By the end of 1980 even his personal life had straightened itself out. With two divorces behind him, Brejack found himself entering his third year of marriage to a woman that he truly loved. Jill, a Waspy, thirty-two-year-old blonde with an efficient demeanor and a trim build, worked as an airline stewardess. She spent several days each week in transit, but compensated for the time away by joining George on romantic trips to Tahiti, Hawaii, and the Caribbean. For a guy who had done his only traveling via army transport, this life was nothing short of fabulous.

However, by the end of that third year problems became apparent. During her increasingly rare stints at home Jill suddenly turned remote; her thoughts always seemed to be somewhere else. She no longer found George's work-related anecdotes to be amusing. And whenever he suggested one of their little getaways, she always came up with a reason why it would be a bad idea.

Considerably more disturbing to Brejack was the difficulty he suddenly had in contacting Jill when she worked the New York-to-Los Angeles flights. Part of their routine when Jill went out of town was to end each day with a pre-slumber telephone conversation—the long-distance equivalent of a good-night kiss. On several occasions Brejack spent early morning hours calling her hotel room, receiving no answer, and crying himself to sleep. However, like many men being deceived by women they love, he initially chose to avoid confronting her, hoping that the problem (whatever it was) would mend itself.

Finally, after a few weeks of this, Brejack could no longer hold himself back. "You're never in your room anymore," he said over dinner. "I call there, the phone rings and rings, but there's no answer. What's going on?"

"Nothing's going *on*," Jill replied, annoyed to have her husband treating her like a suspect. "I've just been staying with my friend Ellen. I've told you about her; she's the one who lives in L.A. After a while you get tired of those hotel rooms."

"Maybe you should give me her telephone number. You never know when something might come up and I'll need to contact you."

Jill grudgingly wrote down her friend's number and taped it to the wall near the kitchen telephone. But even as George saw those digits, he could not trick himself into believing that she was being completely honest.

The next week, when his wife flew cross country, George put her word to the test. At two that morning he dialed her hotel room, received no answer, and then tried the number she had given him. Ellen picked up the telephone after a few rings, and George asked to speak to Jill. "Uh, she's not here now," Ellen said. "She ran out for a container of milk."

"Well," George replied, playing up his angst, "as soon as she gets in, tell her to call me. It's urgent. I must speak with her immediately."

Ellen agreed to do that and George hung up the phone. Five minutes later it rang. He grabbed the receiver and heard Jill's voice on the other end of the line. "You're back at Ellen's now?" George asked.

"Yeah," she said, her voice fraught with concern. "What's wrong? What's wrong?"

Without saying a word, Brejack hung up the telephone and dialed Ellen's number a second time. Once again the woman answered, and he asked to speak with his wife. "She's not back yet" came the response.

"You fucking lying bitch," Brejack whispered, slamming the receiver down and surmising that Jill was indeed having an affair.

A few minutes later, she called back and spoke through a veil of tears, refusing to reveal where she was staying. Once Jill returned, they had a huge argument; Brejack confronted her about the affair and she continued to deny it, but offered no explanation as to where she had been. Heartbroken, Brejack still hoped that things could be worked out. Aiming to accomplish that, he visited Jill's mother but failed to convince her to help patch things up. A session with a priest who had known Jill since she was a little girl also ended unsuccessfully. Both parties told Brejack that they would intervene only after Jill came to them and expressed a desire to save the marriage.

After a few uncomfortable weeks, in the spring of 1981, a month or so before Candy Short met her demise, Jill broke the news to George. "I'm bored with you," she said. "I want a divorce."

"Bored with me?" asked a resigned Brejack. "We've got a beautiful life together. Is it because I don't go out partying every night? Is that why I'm boring? We live in this nice house, we travel, we do things. How can you be bored?"

For a moment, Jill failed to reply. Then she blurted out, "I just am. I've spoken to a lawyer, and he suggested that we resolve things as quickly as possible."

Brejack was devastated. Jill represented his entire life. Everything he did revolved around her. He had envisioned the two of them growing old together, living off his pension. He looked forward to enjoying a pleasantly relaxed life that would compensate for his desperate earlier years. The lies and the affairs would pass, Brejack believed. She would get a kick out of such activities for a while, then come to her senses. He told her as much, but it was to no avail. Jill wanted out.

Efficient as ever, she packed and left him within the week. Shocked by her hasty departure, Brejack experienced his grimmest period during the coming three months. He couldn't concentrate on the job, and his number of arrests dwindled. When he did make a collar, Brejack expended his pent-up aggression on the defendant. His evenings became a string of Hungry Man dinners washed down with glasses of vodka on the rocks. Each night, after finishing his apple compote, he called Jill in her new apartment and begged her to take him back. She always said no.

Finally he could tolerate no more of it. Memories of his ex-wife haunted his house, his neighborhood, and his life. Brejack had to get away. That July he resigned from the police department, packed a trunk of clothing, and drove to Florida. His older brother John, Jr. managed a Trailways bus depot in the town of Ocala, and he agreed to let George stay at his house for a while. After a few weeks down there, however, Brejack received a call from Jill. "I want to see you," she said. "Please come back to New Jersey."

The reunited couple spent a passionate weekend together, each of them seeming to relish the other's company. Telling George that she made a big mistake, Jill discussed a reconciliation. She'd be willing to make the marriage work, but George would have to sell their house in New Jersey. She had recently convinced him to make her an official half-owner of the property, and Jill now wanted to cash out. Brejack protested, offering to sell the home and put the proceeds in an escrow account until their differences were fully resolved. But Jill refused to relent. She desired the money—that was nonnegotiable—and only then she would take George back. Ignoring his lawyer's advice, Brejack approved the necessary papers.

"Why don't you go to Florida? I'll straighten things out up here, then meet you down there in a few weeks," Jill suggested after consummating the deal.

"All right," said a now suspicious Brejack. "But how do I get a hold of you?"

"It would be awkward for you to call me where I'm staying now. But I know how to reach you. I'll be in touch within a few weeks."

Brejack disliked the arrangement, but he returned to Florida. A week later he was washing his new Harley Davidson in John's driveway when a sheriff's officer strolled up with a certified letter. It contained divorce papers. Not only would George lose his wife, but he had also been conned out of his house. In this case, the man who had once been touted as the "psychic cop" allowed his emotions to get in the way of common sense. Only now, looking at the papers in front of him, did he realize how stupid he had been. Unable to do much of anything else, he tried to rebuild a life for himself down south.

Ultimately, though, Florida proved to be anything but the paradise that George expected. During his first few weeks there, he discovered that John was in debt. "I need $25,000," he told George, "or else I'm going to be in trouble."

"I could loan you the money," Brejack cautiously allowed. "But it'll be coming out of my pension fund, and that's all I've got to retire on. So you'll have to pay me back."

"No problem," said his brother, sounding grateful. "I'll give you a grand a month."

To make matters worse, Brejack found it impossible to land a job with any of the Florida police departments. Ignoring a half-dozen glowing recommendations from Paterson, one police recruiter after the other told George that at forty-one he was simply too old to hire. But he had to find some kind of work. His savings began to dip perilously low, and sitting around the house, making small talk with his sister-in-law, would drive Brejack crazy.

Finally John offered his brother a job at the bus depot. It was a beat-up shed of a place, a converted wooden barn with dirt floors and a makeshift bay for the buses. Brejack hosed down the vehicles and tidied up their interiors. Not much of a challenge for a gifted law enforcer, but it provided pocket money and kept him occupied. At that point he would have done anything to avoid thinking about Jill.

The depot attracted unsavory groups of vagrants and misfits. Some of them crashed out for nights at a time on the benches. Others hung around outside and drank beer. Naturally, with his Harley propped in front, Brejack fell in with a group of would-be bikers. It did not surprise him to discover that most of them had shady pasts and criminal backgrounds.

As he had during his early days on the Paterson police force, Brejack found society's underbelly appealing. This time, however, he kept his PBA ring hidden and never discussed his previous career. That suited these new friends just fine; they revealed nearly nothing in the way of personal details, including their last names. Operating without a history served a secondary purpose for Brejack, as mention of the failed marriage practically reduced him to tears. Living from hand to mouth, maneuvering outside of the law that he had once upheld, and acquainting himself with a new environment all served to satisfy Brejack's desire to sunder any remaining links with Jill.

George found a woman—a runaway in her late teens who supported herself by having sex with local businessmen—and spent the last six months of 1981 raising hell in Ocala. He and his friends hung out in beer joints and listened to country music. They hunted rattlesnake and fished for red snapper. Occasionally there'd be brawls with outsiders or among themselves, but Brejack was up for that as well.

His most enjoyable evenings would begin after a couple of guys stole a pig from one of the local farms, put it on a spit, and roasted it. The group spent those nights in the woods, drinking beer, eating the freshly killed meat, and slipping out of sight in pairs. Sequestered behind trees, women grunted with delight as their greasy boyfriends went down on them.

George and Jody were a typical couple in this crowd. Neither one wanted a long-term commitment and they were both running away from things: Jody from abusive parents, George from the bad memories of a ruined marriage. In each other they found a strange, pathetic sort of solace. Like the others in that circle she snorted speed, and constantly offered George a taste. Strictly a beer and vodka man, he always turned her down.

Life was good in Ocala, a nonstop party fueled with schemes and scams and the odd bursts of violence. It was as different from his days with the stewardess as could be, and provided George with the ultimate escape. But he knew that it served only as a temporary existence. The job at the depot quickly became old, his salary there barely kept him above the poverty level, and he had no desire to pursue the illegal money-making opportunities that this new crowd favored. Brejack wasn't looking for *that* much of a change. To make matters worse, tensions were running high in his brother's house.

One night, after a two-day bender of heavy drinking, John, Jr., began arguing with Arlene for no apparent reason. When the shouting reached a head, George felt compelled to step in. "Come on, John," he said, putting a hand on his brother's shoulder. "You can't treat your wife like that."

"I'll treat her any fuckin' way I please," John said. He shoved George away and added, "I don't need some fucking freeloader telling me how to act in my own house."

"Hey," Brejack replied, stepping back, "this isn't

about you and me. It's about you and your wife. You've
got to calm down."

John grabbed a six-foot-high floor lamp that was used
to illuminate the living room and came at George swinging. George ducked out of the lamp post's range and
retaliated with a hard right to his brother's jaw. The blow
knocked John down and didn't leave him especially game
to continue fighting. From the floor he shouted up at
George, "You get the fuck out of my house! I don't want
you here!"

"Fine," George replied. "I'll leave. Just give me my
twenty-five grand, and you'll never hear from me again."

"I'm not giving you a goddamned dime. Just get out
of here."

Believing that he'd get his money back once the smoke
from this incident had cleared (in fact, the brothers
stopped speaking to one another after the altercation,
and John never repaid any of the loan), Brejack skulked
off to his bedroom and placed a late-night call to his
younger brother, who lived in New Jersey.

The telephone's ring jarred Rabbit from a deep sleep.
"George," he said, after recognizing a muffled greeting.
Head groggy and voice thick with sleep, Rabbit asked,
"How's it going down there in Florida?"

"Not so good," George reported. "I don't know what
the hell to do. I wasn't happy up north, so I came down
here to get away from things. Now I don't like it here
anymore either." Brejack finally broke down and began
crying. Through the tears he said, "That bitch took my
house. She broke my heart, Rabbit, and then she lied to
me."

"Why don't you come up here? Stay with us for a
while. Get your feet back on the ground."

Rabbit found it easy to believe that the domestic friction in Florida wasn't contributing to George's emotional
and financial recovery. He knew that a stable family environment was what George needed.

Two days after Rabbit made his offer, George decided

to take him up on it. Only Jody kept him in Florida, and he tried persuading her to make the trip north.

She thought about it, considered Rabbit's promised hospitality, then finally said no. "I can't deal with another family scene," she told George. "I'm here to get away from all of that."

As they spoke, a Grateful Dead song blasted from a boom box and a joint passed by them. Jody reached for it and took a long toke as she watched a fat woman with long, matted brown hair execute a modified Texas two-step. She gestured toward a cluster of bearded longhairs and explained, "Right now, this is my family."

George understood, but at that moment he realized that he too needed his family. Hiring a buddy who owned a pickup truck, George had his belongings hauled back to New Jersey while he rode his motorcycle north. He headed up to Rabbit's, for a new life and a fresh start. Returning to law enforcement seemed a likely option, but Brejack didn't want to rush things.

The Copacabana in midtown Manhattan was on its last legs. Disco music had been in its death throes since 1980, and now, during the first months of 1982, the club attracted a druggy bridge-and-tunnel crowd that still reveled in the previous decade's fad. Brejack couldn't have cared less about trends in music and fashion. From where he stood, anybody with the fifteen-dollar cover charge who wasn't armed could be admitted.

Working as a bouncer at the Copa—a job he secured through an old friend from Paterson—provided less intrigue than being a cop, but it was a lot more exciting than washing buses in Florida. It allowed him to retrench, rethink, and reestablish himself in the locale he called home. "Florida's a beautiful place," George liked to tell people, "but it's not where I live. I could never have stayed there."

That first year back in New Jersey was a strange time for Brejack. After running away from his problems, then

John and Candy Short prior to their marriage. *(Courtesy Joe Frank)*

Helen and Fred Austin, Candy Short, John Short, James and Adele Short. *(Courtesy Joe Frank)*

Fred and Helen Austin with their daughter. *(Courtesy Joe Frank)*

Joe and Betty Frank. *(Courtesy George J. Brejack)*

Judy Reiger and John Short. *(Courtesy Joe Frank)*

Left: John Short with his "mountain man" look. *(Courtesy Joe Frank)*
Right: John and Jesse Short in October 1981. *(Courtesy Joe Frank)*

George Brejack leading John Short into the Passaic County Jail on the night of February 2, 1988. *(Photograph by* Bergen Record*)*

Left: Captain John Nativo, Brejack's most vocal ally at the Passaic County Prosecutor's Office. *(Courtesy George J. Brejack) Right:* Steve Brizek, who prosecuted the case against John Short. *(Courtesy George J. Brejack)*

Aerial photograph of Willowbrook Mall's parking lot. It traces the circuitous route taken by John Short and Fred Austin. Notice that Short spotted the car from 333 feet away, yet he failed to see it from distances of 174 and 195 feet. *(Courtesy Passaic County Sheriff's Office)*

The front seat of Candy's car minutes after her body was removed. *(Courtesy Passaic County Sheriff's Office)*

Candy's gold-colored Cutlass with the rear bumper stickers visible. *(Courtesy Passaic County Sheriff's Office)*

The one-of-a-kind key fob found beneath Candy's body (right) alongside the type of key ring that belonged to her. The original was never found. *(Courtesy Passaic County Sheriff's Office)*

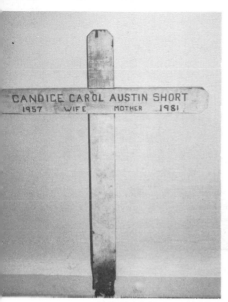

Using planks of wood, John constructed this crude cross for Candy's grave. *(Courtesy Passaic County Sheriff's Office)*

George Brejack and Steve Brizek doing research in Willowbrook Mall's parking lot. *(Courtesy Passaic County Sheriff's Office)*

John Short awaits his sentencing in Passaic County Jail. *(Courtesy Passaic County Sheriff's Office)*

turning his back on law enforcement, he finally felt secure enough to confront his emotional turmoil. At the time of his arrival at Rabbit's house, George suffered from the symptoms of a minor nervous breakdown and deep depression. Any conversation about his ex-wife still brought him to tears, but only after wallowing in misery could he begin the recovery process.

Sitting at the kitchen table one morning, before his brother and sister-in-law left for work, he held his face in his hands and voiced a number of regrets. "Things were going so well for a little while," George told Rabbit and Patti, a couple with seemingly endless patience. "It was like we had the world by the balls. Now I got nothing."

"One day at a time," Rabbit advised. "Take things slowly and they'll begin to turn around. You just want to get through each day."

Rabbit grabbed his brown lunch bag and left for the machine shop. The kids went to school, and Patti headed out to nearby Ramsey, where she worked as a housekeeper. Alone in his brother's big house, surrounded by trees in a secluded rural section of northern New Jersey, George retreated to the basement, where he spent the day sleeping in his makeshift room.

Little by little, as Rabbit had predicted, things did turn around. After three years the job at the disco led to a position as a private investigator for a lawyer. The gig paid well and provided Brejack with the kind of action he craved, yet it lacked the very element that had attracted him to law enforcement in the first place: the moralistic payoff that comes with police work. Instead of enforcing the law, Brejack found loopholes that would free the sorts of people he had once arrested. It lasted several months, until he found a job with New Jersey's utility company, Public Service Electric and Gas. There Brejack worked for the in-house security unit, tracking down embezzlers and petty thieves.

The work interested him, and provided the sense of

authority that was so central to his being. For the first time since the divorce, Brejack himself sensed that things were turning around. Within the year he left Rabbit's home and moved into an apartment in Paterson. On his own again, he dated quite a bit and regained his confidence. Then came Lisa. They went out for six or seven months before he convinced her that the two of them should live together. Eager for female companionship, Brejack rationalized, "You can look at it as a matter of convenience. We get along, we'll save a little money, and the two of us are together all the time anyway."

But less than a year after moving in with Lisa, Brejack felt professionally restless again. He reconnected himself with friends from the police department and constantly inquired after job openings. "I'd get you hired in a minute, but it would be tough on your finances," Paterson-based Senator Frank Graves told him. "You can't go back to your old rank, so you'd have to start off as a patrolman again. Maybe spend a few months at the Academy for some refresher classes. The salary would only be twenty-four thousand dollars."

"Twenty-four thousand dollars?" Brejack asked in disbelief. "I can't live on that."

He decided to wait until a more reasonable opportunity presented itself. Finally it did, in the form of an investigator's position with the Major Crimes Unit of the Passaic County Prosecutor's Office. As with any job in the public sector, getting hired there required some political string-pulling. Luckily for Brejack, Graves made the appropriate calls and put in a good word for the former delinquent. Brejack got the job.

Upon arriving at the Prosecutor's Office in the spring of 1987, George guessed that things would be difficult; he knew that the investigators there would not welcome competition from their cocky new colleague. And he was right. Too many people there knew about his reputation as a hotshot detective in Paterson, and they eagerly gunned for him, waiting for Brejack to make a mistake so that they could prove their point: You don't spend time away from law enforcement, and then come back, without losing something in the process.

Some guys wondered whether Brejack would be able to successfully operate within the confines of a regimented office rather than in New Jersey's equivalent of Fort Apache. Others simply believed that Brejack's string of solved cases represented nothing more than a lucky run of people, places, and events neatly stringing together. They didn't think that he'd still produce so many arrests.

Brejack intended to prove the nay-sayers wrong. The best way to do that, he knew, would be to solve a big case, preferably one that had stymied other cops. Ultimately, that was what made the Candy Short murder so appealing. So many years later, with witnesses scattered and one of the original cops dead, it looked like a dead end that no investigator in his right mind would venture near. The possibility of such complete failure could be overlooked only by somebody with a point to prove.

Even as he worked on other cases through the late summer and into the fall, Brejack remained obsessed with this one. He devoted every spare professional moment to it, and he knew that the investigation would eventually become an official priority as well as a personal one. In the meantime he tirelessly compiled evidence against John Short. Frustrated by other crimes that occupied his day, Brejack would not allow himself to slow down.

Little by little, he patched together enough information to convince his boss John Nativo that the investigation warranted more of a time investment. In the fall he received an unofficial go-ahead to focus in on the Candy Short murder.

"But don't work *exclusively* on that case," Nativo cautioned. "If word gets out that you're not handling current investigations, the shit'll start flying around this place."

Brejack thanked the deputy chief for his support and

went back to his office. By now the files had been organized, and Brejack compiled a list of important phone
numbers. He knew how to reach most of the people, and
had several sources to follow up with: Barbara Capalbo
and Diane Lovejoy topped his list of priorities. Capalbo's
name was written on a scrap of paper. Though she
claimed to have witnessed the prelude to the murder, no
report had been processed.

A Wayne police officer printed a transcript of Diane's
interview on sheets of legal paper, but Brejack did not
find the audio tape of that interview. Despite the fact
that she claimed to have had an affair with Short (not to
mention that he had apparently described the murder to
her before it happened), none of the original cops had
seemed eager to completely pursue her testimony. It was
the sort of police work that miffed Brejack. "They had
a beautiful case here, all the evidence was laid out in
front of them, but those guys in Wayne couldn't put it
together," he told Nativo.

"Don't be overly confident," the deputy chief cautioned George. "This isn't such an easy murder to solve,
and a jury will have to be convinced of Short's guilt.
Don't be too disappointed if he gets off."

"He ain't getting off."

He couldn't get off. If Brejack failed to get a conviction, he figured that he might as well go back to bouncing
at the Copa for all the respect he'd get in the prosecutor's
office.

CHAPTER
12

The house had originally been constructed for summer use. Canary yellow aluminum siding and a sturdy brick chimney were two recent additions that made it habitable year-round. Situated on a small block thickly packed with slightly shabby, Victorian-style homes, it was fronted by a small, scrubby lawn. The grass grew in sparse patches, like sprigs of hair on a bald man's head, and the nearby Atlantic Ocean left a briny residue in the air. During the warm months of June, July, and August, it was the scent of leisure, for summer afternoons in Ocean Grove were idyllic. Kids played in the cool surf, while their parents tooled around in speed boats and barbecued dinner when the sun began to set over the bay.

But as fall arrived, the town emptied out and the off-season atmosphere became subdued. Summer people shut down their beach homes, leaving behind a population of year-round residents. For all the refuge that Ocean Grove provided during the summer, winters there were dreary. Gray skies and freezing temperatures marked the months when bitter winds slashed across the beach and blew from one end of town to the other.

John Short never really minded it. He enjoyed the house, found the slower pace there appealing, and managed to establish the new life that he so badly wanted. At the moment, however, it was threatening to cave in. Oblivious to South Jersey's soft construction market, he spent money like crazy, snorting cocaine despite the expense of having a third child to support. Just maintaining a family of five was about as much as John could manage without the drug's additional financial burden.

Instead of kicking it or cutting back on his already cramped lifestyle, John underpaid his taxes. Then he dipped into a customer's escrow account and withdrew money that had been put aside to cover building expenses. In the process of snorting other people's money, John ignored the risks of embezzlement and reveled in a windfall of cocaine.

For the most part he kept his habit a secret, though one of the kids slipped and told Helen that Mommy and Daddy locked them out of the house while they put straws in their noses. John laughed, and explained that he and Judy were doing some spray-painting in the basement and didn't want their children to inhale the fumes.

But all that was far from John's mind this late afternoon. He sat down in the living room and turned on the television. After clearing a pile of newspapers from the coffee table, he laid out a turkey sandwich and a bottle of beer. A long time ago he never would have done that without using a coaster and place mat—Odessa, the nanny from his boyhood, scolded John for such things—but he no longer gave a damn about social niceties.

John watched the bottle sweat a ring of condensation onto the wooden surface. He tried to find something interesting on the tube and settled for the five o'clock news. A girl had been kidnapped from a shopping mall up north, and her unfolding story seemed to intrigue everybody.

About midway through the report, Short heard the doorbell ring. After a sip of beer, he walked to the front door and opened it a crack. He look out onto the porch.

"Yeah?" John said, his voice sounding croaky and tired. "What can I do for you?"

"I'm George Brejack, an investigator with the Passaic County Prosecutor's Office," said the big man with the stubby mustache. He held out a gold badge, which looked miniaturized inside his large hand, and practically pushed it through the door's opening. Brejack wore a snug-fitting, dark blue suit, under which a holstered pistol pressed against his breast pocket. "Are you John Short?"

"Yeah," Short said warily, not moving away from the frame of the door.

Brejack studied this man he had read so much about. He thought he had an accurate mental image of John Short. But this person cowering in the doorway barely resembled the over-confident cocksman that Brejack had pictured in his mind. He expected somebody more solidly built, not quite so wiry. The heavy, sloppy beard, which covered John's face like half a ski mask, also came as a surprise.

"We're going to be reinvestigating the murder of Candy Short, and I'd like to speak with you."

Brejack crowded the door, hoping to physically convey that Short wasn't dealing with some asshole who'd drive an hour and a half so that he could stand on a front porch. Finally, after a few seconds, the purpose of this visit registered in John's mind.

"Come on in," Short finally said, opening his home to Brejack and another investigator, a man by the name of Vincent Schraeger, who had tagged along in case Short got violent.

Brejack noticed the suspect's once hooded eyes suddenly opening wide. As he ushered the two men inside, his personality changed drastically. Suddenly he seemed friendly and eager to talk. No longer the scared, guarded man who had used his body to block entry to the house, John Short was attempting to be cordial. It's like the guy just woke up from a deep sleep, Brejack thought to himself, and suddenly realizes what he has to deal with.

Indeed, it's easy to imagine Short recalling his interrogation with the Wayne cops and flashing on their promise that someday, when he least expected it, the police might come calling—and the visit would not be pleasant. Was Brejack the Santa Claus with a badge and gun under his red coat that they had threatened him with?

Short offered the cops a couple of beers. They declined, and sat down on the couch. Their host shut off the TV as the little kidnap victim's face momentarily appeared on the screen.

"Damn shame what happened to that girl," Brejack offered.

"Yeah," John distractedly replied. "It's terrible." He settled his frame into an easy chair.

They discussed the purpose of this visit, and John claimed ignorance of Brejack's new investigation, adding that he had heard no additional news about Candy's death. Then he inquired after the diamond engagement ring that had been on his wife's finger at the time of the murder. The investigators agreed to find it.

Certain that John would intentionally tell them nothing of interest, Brejack wanted to milk the visit for as long as possible. He knew that the more he learned about the man—his tics, his speech pattern, the way he sipped from a bottle of beer—the more likely he would be to solve the crime. Brejack began by simply asking John how things were going.

"Fine," came the reply. "I've got my own construction company down here, with twelve men employed. Business is a little slow right now, but we're hanging in there while we wait to hear on a couple of projects. My girlfriend—about to become my wife, we're getting married soon—lives here with me, and we've got three kids. It's a nice life. A lot quieter than up north."

"Is Judy around?" Brejack queried, calling John's wife by name to demonstrate that background information had already been obtained.

"No," John said. He rolled his eyes upward and pointed his thumb toward the bedroom on the second floor. "She and the kids are up there, napping."

The three men conversed for a few more minutes, until

the investigators exhausted the few topics that would not alert John to the seriousness of their visit. As they walked toward the door, Brejack decided to leave Short with something to worry about. He turned to the suspect and asked, "Why did Candy go to Willowbrook on that night in 1981?"

"She went to the Sears there to buy me a pair of work boots."

"Oh," Brejack said, finding it odd that nearly everything he'd read about this case had Candy going to the mall for dance tights. "I guess that's why you suggested to Fred that the two of you go look for her at Willowbrook. You knew that Candy went to the mall that evening."

Short's inadvertent slipup opened a lot of doors in the mind of George Brejack; it was an unlikely mistake for somebody who originally told the truth. But he said nothing, choosing instead to enter it into the police report and put it to use another time.

The two investigators shook John's hand and departed on a friendly note, promising to get in touch with him when they learned something about the ring. John walked them to the curb, and as Brejack and Schraeger got into the unmarked car he made a request: "I know you're going to question a lot of people, but I'd appreciate it if you could avoid contacting my father. He's a very sick man."

"We won't talk to him unless we have to," Brejack lied just before they pulled away from Short's house.

As their car merged onto the highway, Brejack silently considered the last fifteen minutes. Though he would reveal nothing to Schraeger, Brejack had plenty of questions: Were Judy and the kids really sleeping upstairs, or had John simply wanted the lawmen to think other people were home? How come he originally told the Wayne cops that Candy went to Willowbrook to buy dance tights, when he now said that she'd gone there to purchase work boots for him? And why would a couple that lived together for six years suddenly decide to get married?

Brejack rolled these questions around in his mind as he halfheartedly kept up his end of a conversation about office scuttlebutt—something to do with the investigators who were racking up the most overtime. Schraeger wasn't what he would call a partner, as they worked together only occasionally, so Brejack dealt with him cautiously. As far as George was concerned this was his case and he would get the credit for solving it, not somebody who shared the driving down to Ocean Grove. But on the way back to Paterson, as they passed the housing developments and shopping strips that bordered the Parkway, Brejack and Schraeger's talk did turn to their encounter with the suspect.

"He acted friendlier than I thought he would," Schraeger offered.

"Too friendly," Brejack said. "I don't trust the prick."

Silence greeted the comment.

Like most of Brejack's new colleagues, Schraeger felt a certain amount of suspicion about the investigator. Not only had Brejack returned to law enforcement after a long enough absence to render him a virtual rookie, but the background that preceded this job was in itself questionable.

As far as the other investigators were concerned, the Paterson Police Department operated so differently from the Passaic County Prosecutor's Office that to them his experience there was all but worthless. Brejack had developed his style in a place where procedure was rarely enforced. In an understaffed, crime-infested environment, the only way of actually getting anything done was to be something of a renegade. But the prosecutor's office frowned upon such individuality.

College graduates with degrees in law enforcement made up much of the investigative staff. These people never wore uniforms, and they approached the job as more of a science than an art form. Idiosyncratic and instinctive, Brejack was gruff and poorly educated; he operated in a style that was diametrically opposed to that of his colleagues. He ignored their conventions and believed that only results mattered. But ultimately whatever they thought of him was irrelevant; Brejack accepted the job as a way of getting back to solving crimes, not as a route to a better social life.

"If somebody doesn't like me here," he often said, "fuck 'em."

In Brejack's mind, Jim Wilson fell into the same category as the prima donnas at the prosecutor's office. That feeling of distrust and dislike for one another was among the few things these two law enforcers had in common. Hardly on speaking terms before Brejack reactivated the investigation, the relationship between the two men grew downright chilly once word of his involvement reached the Wayne Police Department.

Wilson stood to lose face if Brejack managed to solve the Candy Short murder so many years after his crew had failed to do so. Considering that the patrol captain's day of retirement was approaching, it created a possibility that he would leave the force on a downbeat note. That was one reason why he could hardly have welcomed a call from Brejack.

"We met with Short," the investigator bluntly told Wilson, "and he says that you guys are holding on to Candy's engagement ring. He wants it back."

After checking on what they had in the evidence room, Wilson confirmed that two rings were there: the one that John Short wanted, and a signet with a curlicued C on it. He added that they had the gold Cutlass as well; it was being stored in a police impound area. Brejack wrote all of this information down, believing that some of it might come in handy later on.

"If he wants it back, all he has to do is come up here and claim it," Wilson explained. "It's his."

They discussed the case for a few minutes, and Brejack hung up with the distinct impression that Wilson wished to see it forgotten (a claim that Wilson would go on to vehemently deny). In spite of that, the Wayne police officer agreed to meet with Brejack during the next couple of weeks. But the promise sounded insincere, and Brejack correctly guessed that the meeting would never take place.

The next day he telephoned John Short and imparted Wilson's information. He maintained a congenial, friendly tone, as if the ring's discovery was the best news he'd heard in months. "Everything is here," he said. "Come on up, sign for it, and it's yours. Even the car."

"Yeah," Short said distantly. "I've got to put some time aside and pick that stuff up."

There was a moment of silence, then John Short unwittingly tipped his hand: In a too casual voice, he inquired about the progress of the case.

"Everything's going fine. We're just putting little bits of information together," Brejack responded. "We're working on the stuff that the Wayne police did six years ago. I hope to catch the guy who committed the murder."

"Yeah," Short said halfheartedly. "The bastard should rot in hell."

"You know, John, I think that you could help me out quite a bit." Brejack struggled to keep the warmth in his voice. "I'd like to arrange a meeting with you. Pick your brain a little bit and see what we can come up with. Maybe you remember some things that you didn't have the perspective to recall when the murder first happened. Putting a little distance between yourself and an event like this can go a long way toward sorting things out."

"I'll try to help you with whatever you need. I want to see this thing solved as badly as anybody, you know that." Another moment of silence, before John once again voiced what sounded like a personal concern. "Who do you think did it?"

"Hard to say. We have a few ideas, but there's nothing definite. You know, it could have been anybody."

The two men agreed to get together a few days later

at the Passaic County Prosecutor's Office. Aware that only the most naive (or innocent) suspect would agree to such a meeting, Brejack wanted to set the date for as soon as possible. Expediency would reduce the likelihood of Short reconsidering. If the suspect kept the appointment, Brejack believed that he would have him, that he'd get something out of the guy. But on the appointed day Short called to cancel.

"What's the matter?" an obviously disappointed Brejack wanted to know. "I thought you said today would be good for you."

"It *was* good for me, but something came up. I've got to see a client who owes me $107,000. What would you do if you needed the money?"

Brejack let out a sigh of acknowledgment, then agreed, "It's a lot of dough. But I'd also be concerned about the murder." He shifted gears and tried to sound as casual as possible. "So when can we reschedule for?"

"I can't reschedule. I spoke to my lawyer, a guy by the name of Pat Caserta, and he told me that I'd be crazy to see you alone."

"Do you want to bring Pat along?"

"I don't see the use. I cooperated fully with the Wayne police. I told them everything I knew. They questioned me for over five hours and treated me like shit." Not sure that what he said made much of an impression on Brejack, Short began to embellish: "One night they picked me up to give some blood samples, and they drove around like maniacs. The guy behind the wheel tried shaking me up by going ninety miles an hour."

Unmoved and disbelieving, Brejack asked, "Have you ever taken a polygraph?"

"They wanted me to, but I refused. I took one of those things a few years before and it was inaccurate. I'm too high-strung of a guy for it to work properly on me."

"You might want to consider the poly; it could do a lot to clear your name. And as far as being abused by the Wayne police, if it's true you could have filed a complaint against whoever did it. They're not allowed to scare information out of people."

"Look, I'm really busy," John said, as if he hadn't heard a word of Brejack's. "Judy and I are getting married, and we're having trouble with the band. They just canceled on us. I don't have time to deal with you guys right now."

"If you find the time," Brejack advised, "and you decide to come up here, just give me a call. We'll work something out at your convenience."

John Short said good-bye, and disconnected the call without placing the telephone receiver in its cradle. In the world of John Short, Brejack's arrival was completely unwelcome. Just when he was beginning to put the problems with Candy behind him, this had to happen. Some jerk-off county cop had to start busting his balls. He dialed Joe Frank's number, hoping to get a handle on exactly what this Brejack character wanted.

"I don't plan on going through all that shit again," he told Joe. "And I just hope they don't start bugging Candy's folks this time. Fred and Helen deserve better than that."

"I wouldn't worry about it, John," Joe said. He saw through Short's phony sensitivity, and tried to keep his emotions in check. Pleased by the possible enactment of long overdue justice, he wanted to keep from jeopardizing it. Joe had anticipated getting this kind of a call, and he was prepared to play it cool. "Those guys are on a fishing expedition. They don't have anything on you."

Short bought the lie. Before hanging up the telephone, he mentioned feeling slightly more relaxed about the situation.

Donna Olson Frangipane rarely thought about John Short anymore. On those days when she did, the memories came back with an ugly and violent tinge, like frames of movie film indelibly tinted red. She occasionally contemplated the dark side of their marriage, and the way it might have ended had she stuck around. She knew that even if she had survived the beatings, her spirit would have been snuffed out.

While she had managed to build a new life—which included a second husband and a home in a charmingly rural town on the western fringe of New Jersey—the three years she and Short had spent together lingered with the nag of an insistent but barely detectable odor. Still, Donna struggled to keep those memories closeted. She rarely discussed the previous marriage with her husband, her children, or anybody other than her best and oldest friend Alice Cooke. Donna viewed her years with John Short as an embarrassing secret.

On this particular morning, however, she would be spending an hour or so talking about that marriage. She had scheduled the conversation for a time when the kids were in school and her husband was away at work. Although she had agreed to the meeting, Donna did not look forward to it.

Irrational as it sounded, she still feared that John would come after her, seeking some kind of long bottled-up revenge. Maybe he'd find out that she spoke to the Wayne police when they investigated Candy's murder six years ago, or perhaps he'd get wind of today's discussion. Either way, she had no desire to find out how angry that would make him. John had never tried to contact her, and she had no reason to believe that he even knew where she lived, but Donna remained insecure. Never mind the assurances from the man who was coming to see her today, she wanted their meeting to be brief and painless.

A lake ran along the narrow, gently loping road that led to Donna and Peter Frangipane's small house. Brejack took in the placid scenery. It reminded him of his failed marriage and the rustic home he shared with Jill. Then he blocked those thoughts from his mind. Today was John's day, and he needed to devote his full brain capacity solely to the man he hoped to trap and capture.

As he pulled into the driveway in front of Donna's house, Brejack figured that whatever she might tell him would serve only as remote background information. More useful clues, he believed, might come in the form of other leads that she might provide. Donna surely knew some of John's old friends. Hopefully she would put Brejack in touch with them. He anticipated piecing together a psychological profile of Short—one that depicted a lifetime of abusiveness and showed him to be the likeliest killer of Candy—that left no room for doubt or question.

Brejack stepped out of his car and rang the bell. Donna greeted him at the door. The corners around her mouth were creased with worry, and she seemed resigned to performing a painful and difficult task. The woman displayed a seriousness of purpose that the other interview subjects had lacked. Brejack figured that Donna implicitly understood the importance of mounting a case against Short. She knew how bad he could be. Brejack appreciated that.

Considering that she recently had given birth to a second child—he slept soundly upstairs in his crib—thirty-four-year-old Donna had successfully maintained her figure and appeared reasonably satisfied with her life. As George entered the split-level house, with its contemporary furnishings and large-screen TV and stereo, he got the vibe that a happy family lived there. Unlike Short's house, it was neat and orderly.

Several days ago, a telephone conversation with Donna alerted Brejack to her embarrassment over what she had gone through with John. Respecting her reticence, the investigator now started off slowly, strolling through the background information that he had already cribbed from the Wayne Police Department's reports. "When we argued, John often used his hands," Donna said. "He used to beat me real bad. Sometimes I thought that he would break my bones or hospitalize me. But kill me? Never."

As they conversed, she kept her eyes on the ground or stared off into space. "When somebody at work told me about Candy's death," she allowed, "it was easy to believe that John could have had something to do with it."

She recounted a few of John's beatings—including one that had taken place in their car with Alice and her boyfriend along—and acknowledged that his physical abuse caused the demise of their marriage. More potentially helpful than any of her anecdotes was the address where she and John lived. Hearing this triggered Brejack to dig deeper into her ex-husband's past.

"Do you remember any of the guys he was friends with as a teenager?"

"The only one I can think of is Steve Gottlieb."

Though Donna did not know where Gottlieb currently resided, she gave the investigator enough information so that he could track the guy down through New Jersey's Division of Motor Vehicles. Brejack proceeded to do that, after he left Donna's place and returned to the prosecutor's office. He found out that Short's boyhood pal now rented an apartment in Clifton, only a town away from where Brejack himself lived.

As expected, Gottlieb initially expressed reluctance to comment on his friend. During a brief telephone conversation, he assured the investigator that he could add nothing to the case. Brejack refused to take no for an answer.

"There's only way I'll talk to you," Gottlieb finally conceded. "Everything I say has to stay off the record. You come see me, I'll be honest with you. I'll tell you whatever I know, but I don't want my name attached to it. I don't want John Short to think I'm creating any problems for him. This is all off the record, where it can't do him any harm. He seems to have enough problems without me adding my two cents' worth."

"Sure, Steve," came the unhesitating reply. "Whatever you say."

A couple of nights later, Brejack showed up at Gottlieb's garden apartment. Just after he arrived, at a few minutes past six o'clock, Gottlieb's girlfriend scooted out the door. A contractor whose thriving business was in the process of collapsing due to his alcoholism, Gottlieb had plenty of headaches already. The last thing he needed was a nosy cop. He snickered to himself as the investigator walked in with a beat-up fedora on his head and the telltale bulge of a gun below the breast pocket of his suit jacket.

This guy's a fucking cowboy, Gottlieb silently mused. Wearing clean blue jeans and a fresh T-shirt, sipping from a beer, he felt that he had no choice but to cooperate with Brejack. Cops made Gottlieb edgy, and he planned on handling this situation as cautiously as possible. After answering a few questions, his internal logic went, I'll get the guy out of my apartment and out of my hair.

Just under six feet tall, with a medium build and ruddy complexion, thirty-four-year-old Gottlieb had the robust look of an outdoorsman. This almost balanced out the wastedness that came from his compulsive drinking. As he entered the apartment Brejack stepped over a pair of muddy work boots on the floor. Pots of cooked food still occupied burners on the stove, and dirty dinner dishes floated in a shallow pool of soapy sink water.

Gottlieb pulled out a chair for himself, and then the investigator took his own seat at the room's small, round table with its spindly wire legs. "You sure you don't want a beer or something?" he asked.

Brejack shook his head no.

"And whatever I tell you right now is off the record? It goes no further than this room?"

Brejack agreed, then asked Gottlieb whether he'd ever seen John beat up Candy. "No. But I do know that he physically abused his first wife all the time. And from what I understand his current wife, Judy, is getting the crap beaten out of her on a regular basis as well."

"What makes you say that? Have you seen John lately?"

"The last time I saw him was at Louie Derringer's house, in upstate New York. The three of us were friends in high school, you know, and we occasionally get together with our wives and girlfriends and kids. I left early, but Louie called the next day to tell me that John whacked the shit out of Judy with a big heavy-duty, six-cell flashlight when she dropped the keys to their van. Louie wound up calling the police, who sent an ambulance so that Judy could be taken to the hospital and get stitched up." Gottlieb shook his head and took a long draw from the beer. "It's a shame that Louie's kids had to see something like that."

"How did you find out about Candy's murder?"

"I heard it on the radio," Gottlieb said. "And when I later discovered that John told people he was lost in West Orange I knew he was full of shit. I used to live in West Orange, and John came to visit me a few nights each week. Some goddamned truck that his parents bought him sat in my driveway for six months."

This revelation set off Brejack's internal sensors, and reminded him to begin looking for clues that might disprove Short's alibi. He continued pressing Gottlieb for additional information, and even as his source recounted John's indifferent behavior at the funeral, Brejack's mind wandered back to that one point. He suddenly realized that if he could disprove John's story about getting lost, the entire case for his innocence would come to seem increasingly indefensible.

After a half hour or so Brejack packed up to leave, surprised at how willingly Gottlieb had implicated his friend. Standing, the investigator casually tossed out a question that he had held himself back from asking any other source. "What do you think was John's involvement in the death of Candy Short?"

Steve Gottlieb pondered this for a moment, then he ran a hand through his slicked-back dark blond hair and said, "Like everything else I've told you tonight this is off the record, so don't put it in your report. But I think he killed her. I thought that from the second I heard about it."

"Why?"

"Because John Short is a violent animal," Gottlieb said, recalling what he had heard about John smashing Judy's head with a flashlight. "That's all I'm going to say. And if, in the future, anybody asks me about our meeting tonight, I'll deny that it ever took place. I'll deny that I ever met you. So don't write it up in your report."

Brejack buttoned his jacket and shook Gottlieb's hand at the door. After agreeing to keep their conversation confidential, he drove back to the office and proceeded to compose a detailed account of his meeting with Gottlieb. "Off the record," Brejack chuckled to himself as he two-finger typed. "The fucking guy doesn't know what it's like to deal with a real cop."

In stark contrast to Gottlieb's dualistic mixture of reluctance and candor were the words of Angelo and Mary Milano, the Italian-American couple from whom John and Donna had rented an upstairs apartment. As if reciting a tragic opera's libretto, they furnished Brejack with a dramatic chronicle of the beatings that had taken place above them. They offered detailed descriptions of Donna retreating to the streets and John storming around the living room without letup. None of this struck Brejack as particularly new or revelatory, as he had already heard similar tales directly from Donna.

Then Mary told him something that touched a raw nerve. "I'd be down here with my three children, and they made such a racket upstairs that the ceiling shook," said the fifty-eight-year-old woman. "It was just terrible. My kids huddled together in the corner, and I sat on the couch and cried. We heard her screaming as he punched and slapped her. Terrible . . ."

Mary Milano's voice trailed off and she grew a bit misty-eyed. George remembered those bad nights in the bedroom when his father brutalized Christine on the other side of the door. It nearly brought tears to the investigator's own eyes, strengthening his resolve to gather the evidence that would convict John Short.

On the way back to Paterson from the Milano house, he decided to stop at the Vincent Methodist Cemetery. He wanted to see Candy's grave, and he needed to get a look at the cross that John had constructed for her. Relatives had mentioned it in passing, but had never actually described the memorial. Even though nobody had gone into detail, Brejack expected to see something elaborate if not heartfelt. John, after all, was reputed to be an accomplished carpenter, with the ability to craft something beautiful, whether he truly wanted to or not.

When Brejack pulled up to her grave, the rickety white cross shocked him. It's like something you'd see on the burial site of a dead pet, he thought.

Brejack said a prayer for Candy, made the sign of the cross, and managed to kick over the flimsy grave marker so that it was no longer fully anchored in the ground. That night he called Helen Austin and suggested that the cross had been uprooted. "Probably blown over by the wind or something," he fibbed. "Would you mind if I took it for evidence?"

"Go ahead," she told him. "Do whatever you want with it. We've got a proper stone there anyway."

The next morning Brejack returned to the cemetery. He photographed the cross from a couple of different angles, then pulled it up, placed it on the backseat of his car, and drove to the Passaic County Prosecutor's Office. Wanting to keep the cross safe and out of sight—even though he found himself uncertain as to its practical use—Brejack stashed it behind his office door. He thought about the case actually going to trial, envisioned a jury listening to testimony, and couldn't imagine one that wouldn't convict John Short after seeing this shabby tribute he paid to his wife.

CHAPTER
13

Bony fingers worked Fred Austin's necktie into a fat knot. He saw his reflection in the bedroom mirror, centered the polyester triangle around his buttoned shirt collar, and squirmed in discomfort. Suits made Fred itchy, gave him the feeling of being penned in, but Helen had requested that he wear one.

"We want to look our best for Jesse," she said in a tone that approached scolding. "That's what you have to remember. We're going for Jesse's sake, not for John's."

"Just the same," he griped, "I could live without having to drive all the way down to Ocean Grove for this."

On a Sunday morning in the fall of 1987, Fred and Helen were preparing to attend John Short's third wedding, a celebration that neither one of them could ever have imagined being invited to. At least, not back when Candy was still alive. But as they'd come to learn, anything is possible. Even the most implausible scenarios could unfold and envelope them. Once ranking among the remotest of those was the possibility that John Short had murdered their daughter.

As the case progressed, however, the Austins' former son-in-law stood out as the likeliest suspect. While Helen still found the concept difficult to accept—though she grew increasingly willing to hear Brejack's theories—Fred wholeheartedly shared the lawman's suspicions.

Unlike the Wayne detectives, Brejack regularly chatted up the Austins and revealed different bits of information. It was simply his nature to blab, to fish for compliments and fresh leads by using what he already knew as bait. While the conversations rarely paid off with anything concrete, they allowed a legitimately friendly relationship to develop between the investigator and Candy's parents.

Dressed in their Sunday best, the Austins stepped out onto Passaic Avenue and got into the station wagon. Fred started the engine, cautiously backed down the gravel drive, and navigated his car toward the Garden State Parkway. He drove in silence, his mind flashing back a slew of images from the night at Willowbrook Mall. Helen primly sat alongside him, hands folded in her lap. Neither one of them particularly looked forward to this afternoon.

"Maybe it will all be for the best," Helen rationalized, as much to herself as to Fred. "What Jesse needs is a good, stable home. Maybe getting married again will have a calming effect on John."

"Yeah," Fred said. "Maybe."

Deep down, though, he believed that John was no good, and nothing had happened lately to turn that opinion around. If anything, Short's most recent behavior only served to confirm the negative view. Since the re-opening of the case John had become increasingly distant, and the episodes of domestic violence had escalated. The Austins saw less of him than ever, heard that he often inquired after his role in the investigation, and received sketchy details about the beatings that the future Mrs. Short regularly sustained.

One of the most disturbing of these reports came via a telephone call from Judy's mother; she contacted Helen out of concern for Jesse. No matter what John did, though, the situation remained the same: He had their granddaughter, and the Austins felt powerless to exercise any degree of control over him. All they desired was a good home for Jesse, and they would go along with any-thing that might encourage John to provide one.

As he made his way south on the Parkway, Fred squirmed in the driver's seat. He glanced nervously into the rearview mirror, as if expecting somebody to sneak up from behind. Finally his antsiness got the best of Helen.

"Is everything all right?" she wanted to know. "The way you keep jumping around and looking in the mirror is driving me crazy. I don't know who you expect to see."

"George Brejack's a persistent guy," Fred said, only one eye on the road. "I want to make sure the son of a bitch isn't following us to the wedding. There's no telling where he'll turn up."

He needn't have worried. While Brejack rejoiced over the union of John Short and Judy Reiger, his happiness had nothing to do with thoughts of the connubial bliss that awaited them. He viewed John's decision to marry Judy as a sign that the case was proceeding in the right direction. Why else would he have suddenly decided to tie the knot, unless it was to prevent Judy from being called to testify against him in court? It's what Brejack believed from the moment John revealed his wedding plans.

Encouraged, Brejack continued pounding away at the investigation, using the foundation of sources laid down by the Wayne police as a base on which to build. While retracing the steps of those cops, he also looked for fresh paths that might lead to unexpected places. Such was the situation with Steve Gottlieb and the Milanos. He saw those breaks as being at the crux of this investigation's eventual success, and explained as much to John Nativo one morning over coffee.

"All the people that John thought were his friends are turning against him now," Brejack said, standing in the chief's office. "It's beautiful to meet with these guys and hear them tearing their pal to shreds."

"It's not so different from when we were in Paterson," Nativo said, supressing a cough. "One thing leads to another."

"The funny thing about this investigation is that I know what happened. The information's still a little sketchy for me to actually verbalize it, but I've got a little version working itself out in my head."

"Keep talking to people, George. Ask them the right questions, and the answers will turn up. Maintain the footwork, keep pounding the pavement. It'll come to you."

Brejack lifted his cup of coffee and wandered back to his office, past investigators who lacked an appreciation for Nativo's folksy police wisdom. They did not share his faith in legwork and instinct.

Ironically, as Brejack's investigation into the Candy Short murder progressed, the atmosphere at the prosecutor's office became increasingly chilly. Most of this emanated from the department's chief of investigators, Max Swathmore. A grizzled man in his early seventies, Swathmore disliked Brejack from the start and fought tirelessly to keep him from being hired by the prosecutor's office. Only under pressure from Brejack's booster, Senator Frank Graves, did Swathmore acquiesce.

Now, with Brejack threatening to solve a case that his department had originally had a hand in botching, Swathmore had even more incentive to make life difficult for the investigator. Considering that he approved all expenses and overtime, it was an easy enough thing to do. Swathmore mandated that Brejack would not be able to collect overtime for this particular case, nor would he be reimbursed for mileage and dinner expenses.

Brejack said nothing. He simply persevered at his own cost and on his own time. Then, in case anybody in the department remained unaware of Swathmore's ill will, the commander erased all doubt. During a meeting Swathmore listened to the status of Brejack's case, stood up, and announced, "If George Brejack gets an indictment for John Short, I'll eat the fucking paper that it's written on."

Powerless to do anything about it, Brejack and Nativo listened without comment. Most debilitating of all was that Swathmore's bilious feelings trickled down to the lower levels. Brejack regularly overheard his colleagues complaining about him.

On the morning of his conversation with Nativo, the investigator strolled downstairs to the coffee machine. En route he passed the office of Thomas Perone, a young investigator with deep political connections. Everybody knew him as one of Swathmore's boys, and Brejack suspected that Perone had actually instigated a lot of the bad blood. What he heard as he made his way to the machine confirmed that suspicion.

"Brejack thinks he's the big wheel around here," Perone told a cop who sat alongside his desk. "The guy's trying to make a name for himself by solving that old murder. The case is deader than the woman who got stiffed."

"Yeah," the other guy concurred with a laugh. "He thinks he's gonna get his picture in the paper. Hell, he'll be lucky to have a job after this investigation goes belly-up. Six years ago the case went unsolved for a reason: There's nothing to hang it on."

"Psychic cop," Perone derisively said. "*Psycho* cop is more like it."

Unaware that Brejack was eavesdropping, they laughed wryly and changed the subject to sports. Annoyed, Brejack filled his coffee cup and proceeded back to the office. He considered confronting them, then realized the pointlessness of it; it would only lead to more problems.

Unlike most of John Short's friends, Will Lambert had managed to build an enviable life for himself. Looking back on those hard-drinking, freewheeling nights in the early eighties, he now saw his Coach Light antics as nothing more than a passing phase. Lambert likened it to the final throes of an arrested adolescence.

These days he was the ultimate family man. He rarely drank, stayed away from go-go bars, and devoted most of his nine-to-five energies to the job. The hard work paid off, and over the past six years Lambert came to own a small accounting firm. The company's profit allowed for a comfortably upper-middle-class existence, and he had recently purchased a vacation home on the Jersey shore. The house was small, but it came with a mooring where Lambert docked a motorboat. Life for him and his family had become both emotionally sweet and rich in material goods.

John Short had faded into a dim memory from his past. Then he received a call from George Brejack. "We're really swamped at work," Lambert amiably told the investigator, "so I'd never be able to meet with you during the week."

"How about the weekend?" Brejack persisted.

They scheduled a meeting for the Sunday before Thanksgiving. It brought George Brejack to a neighborhood full of recently built homes in Ridgewood, New Jersey. While many of the town's houses were oversized landmarks, Lambert lived in one of the area's newer dwellings. It was the model home that John Short had built and sold to him after the development slated to surround it never materialized. Despite his distaste for Short, Brejack found himself impressed by the detailing and fine craftsmanship that had gone into the structure.

A friendly man who likes to talk, Lambert ushered the investigator and a stenographer inside. They walked through the living room and entered a homey-looking den. Francis Lambert and the kids remained out of sight.

Brejack surprised himself by legitimately liking Lambert's open and engaging manner. Nevertheless, the investigator saw through the man's prudency. It covered the truth whenever Lambert referred to himself and his own dalliances during The Coach Light days. But that was all right. As Brejack thought to himself, *I don't care if the guy fucked mules in Tijuana. I'm only interested in what he has to tell me about John Short.*

On that end, Lambert delivered. Not only did he fill Brejack in on Diane Lovejoy, and alert the investigator to her importance in the case, but Lambert also revealed further inconsistencies in John Short's stories. "John told me that his wife was pregnant at the time of the murder," Lambert recalled, mentioning something that showed up in none of Candy's medical reports. "I asked him how he knew, and why he never said anything before. He told me that he found out as a result of the autopsy."

Brejack swerved the conversation back to Diane Lovejoy. From reading the Wayne police reports he knew that John had lied about his wife's murder before it actually happened, yet he hadn't realized how widespread the tall tale had become. For the record he wanted Lambert to confirm Short's liaison with, and feelings for, the go-go dancer.

Organized and prepared, Brejack produced the credit card receipts that Short had signed when renting his room at the Howard Johnson's. The suspect's former friend looked down at them and nodded. "Yeah, those receipts are from my Carte Blanche, but the signature's not mine. It must be from the night that John borrowed the card."

"Did John Short ever tell you about his feelings for Diane Lovejoy?"

"Yes. John told me that he liked her very much. He had a great time with her, and they spent a lot of afternoons and early evenings together. At first I just considered it infatuation, but maybe there was more to it. On several occasions she met John at my office."

"Were there any marital problems between John and his wife?"

"Just the usual things," said Lambert, either unaware or unwilling to reveal exactly what had gone on in the Short household. "He was going through what I would characterize as the seven-year itch. He had a hard time adjusting to a daughter and wife. I know that the cash flow from his business was not great. While I assume that there were money problems, John seemed to spend a lot at the bars. He partied quite a bit, and I saw him inebriated on many occasions."

"Can you describe John Short to me personality-wise?"

"I've seen John get extremely hot over minor problems. I remember seeing him throw hammers and kick down two-by-fours. On at least one occasion he was cursing so badly that I had to ask him to either calm down or leave the office. It was starting to bother people."

This topic of discussion caused Lambert to remember something else, a telling piece of information that he had practically forgotten. "A while ago I ran into Gail Hunter [Judy Reiger's sister, and the common link between her and John] and asked her how John and Judy were doing. She got all upset and told me that John had a terrible temper. Several times she personally intervened after he began slapping Judy around. Apparently this happens all the time, and Gail expressed concern for her sister's safety."

"Did John ever tell you how he was treated by the Wayne police?"

"John said that the cops from Wayne tried making him into a fall guy. They locked him in a room and psychologically abused him for twelve hours, not allowing him to make a telephone call or leave the room. John claims that they kept hounding him for a confession. He says that he later consulted a lawyer, who advised him not to discuss the matter with any policemen and to stay away from police stations without the lawyer's presence."

Brejack stuck around for a few more minutes, then headed home. Lisa was in the apartment preparing a lasagna dinner, but he wasn't hungry.

After a brief hello and a peck on the lips, Brejack retreated to the apartment's second bedroom, which he had fashioned into a study with two steel filing cabinets and an oak desk from the 1950s. On one wall hung a print of a bald eagle—for Brejack, the most majestic bird in the world—and a locked drawer held the investigator's firearms.

He sat behind his desk, looked up at that eagle, and tried to figure things out. A lot of his information fit together neatly, and painted a portrait of John Short as a disturbed and violent man. But none of it provided the irrefutable proof that a grand jury would require before issuing an indictment warrant. Brejack needed something that would successfully challenge Short's alibi about getting lost on the way to David Jones's house. The missing piece to this bloody jigsaw puzzle would be the one that placed Short at the scene of the murder when it happened.

He had several people who agreed to the improbability of John Short's losing his way on the winding mountainous roads of West Orange. But that alone meant very little—it came down to their words against Short's. And in a courtroom, where a reasonable doubt meant the difference between imprisonment and freedom, John would walk. At that rate, the best Brejack could hope for would be manslaughter, which, as far as John Short was concerned, would be as good as a not-guilty verdict.

Barbara Capalbo, the woman who thought she might have seen the argument that night at the mall, might be able to supply a touch of credibility to the case against John. And for Brejack, who had several forces working against him—a department filled with people eager to see him flop, a six-year lapse from the time of the murder, no eyewitnesses, and a victim's family that still harbored relatively little animosity toward the man who seemed likeliest to have killed Candy—tiny bits of credibility were all that he could hope for.

As the investigation progressed, his confidence remained intact even when the odds appeared to be stacked against him. People inside the prosecutor's office became aware of the time he was putting into the case, and

Brejack grew to be even more of a pariah among his colleagues. Most of his discussions with the other investigators concerned ongoing cases and stayed away from the more personal banter that cops regularly indulged in.

The murder of Candy Short consumed him, in much the same way his divorce had in 1981. Brejack fed on obsession, was fueled by intensity, and actually enjoyed the acidic, stomach-churning feeling that came with it.

Even at home, he spoke almost exclusively of the Short murder. It reached the point where Lisa seemed to occasionally experience pangs of jealousy for this poor, pathetic dead woman, and she regarded George with vague suspicion. What had happened to the solid fellow who poked around Public Service Electric & Gas looking for payroll cheats?

Upon getting involved with him, she could not have realized that Brejack became this way whenever he took on a big case. Still burning in his psyche were the excitement and inwardly driven motivation that had built his reputation as an officer while destroying his usefulness as a husband. However, whether the end results would be the same—for both his professional and personal lives—had yet to be seen.

Alone in his small room, Brejack could hear the television. On the other side of the wall, in the living room, Lisa was watching a videocassette of *Stop Making Sense* while dinner cooked. She reduced the volume of the Talking Heads concert film so that the band's Brazilian-inspired beat wouldn't disturb her boyfriend. But he still heard it and found the songs distracting. George struggled to phase out the music. It all seemed like a lot of noise to him anyway. That, he told his friends, is one of the problems with younger broads: Their music all sounds like shit.

He turned on WPAT and listened to an orchestration of "Nineteenth Nervous Breakdown." Music itself meant nothing to Brejack; he used it to block out the sound from the next room and to buffer the silence in his head.

It aided him in thinking clearly, and if there was anything he had to do right now, it was that. Using what he knew about the crime, Brejack constructed a scenario of events beginning with the night that Candy lost her life. Judging from the interviews and reports, the version he'd come up with was the only one that fit.

The way he saw it, John Short met a go-go dancer and decided he was in love with her. He hated his marriage and wanted to get out of it. But when he mentioned divorce, Candy routinely threatened to sue him for crippling amounts of alimony. After fabricating the story of his wife's death for Diane Lovejoy's benefit, Short realized that killing Candy would be more economical than divorcing her. He decided to do it exactly as he had told Diane. In fact, he wanted to commit the murder rather than meet with David Jones. But when Jones insisted that Short keep the appointment, he inadvertently provided an instant alibi. The fact that Short had been left in charge of his parents' Pinto—they were in Scotland at the time of the murder—made things even better; his truck could have been too easily identified at Willowbrook.

So he arranged to meet Candy at the shopping mall, told her to leave the baby behind because he wanted to be alone with her. Maybe they'd shop a little bit, then go out for dinner. He hooked up with his wife near Ohrbach's, where she usually parked the car, got out of the Pinto, and slid into the Cutlass's driver's seat as he always did. They conversed for a few minutes; maybe John hoped that she would somehow talk him out of killing her, rekindle some long dead emotion.

Obviously that failed to happen. After strangling his wife and stabbing her below the breast for good measure, he needed to dump the body. So he drove away from the stores, toward the woods that surrounded the mall. John dragged Candy out of the car and set her down in the dirt. Then he felt guilty; as much as he hated the marriage, he couldn't just leave her there. Confused, and suddenly realizing that he was in way over his head, John dragged Candy back onto the front seat, drove to the other side of the mall, and left the car in the spot where he and Fred eventually found it. Next, John dumped the contents of Candy's purse upon the automobile's seat and floor mats in order to create the impression of a bungled robbery, then walked back to the Pinto.

The whole thing took only about twenty minutes, which left John with enough time to drive back to his parents' house (thus avoiding detection on Joralemon Street), change his clothing, and wash up. Refreshed, he took the Pinto to Jones's home. Once there, John made a halfhearted inspection of what needed to be repaired (but neglected to give an estimate), and drove back to Passaic Avenue. He parked the Pinto near the apartment, retrieved Jesse from Betty and Joe, alerted Fred to the fact that Candy was missing, and orchestrated it so that her father would find the body. John later pleaded innocent to the killing of his wife, maintained that he was lost on the back roads of West Orange at the time of the murder, and moved in with Candy's parents in order to deflect guilt. Only after he came to believe that Diane had cooperated with the police did Short drop her.

Everything fit together so perfectly. Now it was just a matter of finding the people who could turn this scenario into an airtight case. He believed that Barbara Capalbo and Diane Lovejoy would both go a long way toward doing that.

Brejack sat in his study, lost in thought, contemplating the reactions he'd get from the women once he tracked them down. He considered phoning Barbara right then and there, but decided to wait until Monday. It might seem odd for a cop to be calling on a Sunday evening.

He scribbled a few notes to himself as Lisa softly knocked at the door. "Are you hungry for dinner?" she wanted to know. "It's ready."

Brejack grumbled a blasé acknowledgment, put the pad away, and followed her into the dining room. A platter of lasagna steamed on the table and Lisa opened a bottle of wine, the stuff that Brejack liked to call Dago Red. Not very hungry, George poked at his food and listened to Lisa's account of a visit with her mother in Queens. As she spoke, his mind tried to concoct the pieces that would complete the puzzle.

Memories of what she had seen in the Willowbrook Mall parking lot remained vivid in the mind of thirty-year-old Barbara Capalbo: A woman was cowering, a man banged on the dashboard, impending violence was clearly in the air. It irked Barbara that the Wayne police had taken her information so lightly; on December 1st she told Brejack that they hadn't even bothered writing notes during the interview.

Nodding, yet withholding comment on the original investigation, Brejack questioned her about that evening in June and notated what she said she had witnessed at the mall. That this version of her story matched the original telling left the investigator feeling immensely heartened.

As Barbara spoke, Brejack reached into a briefcase that he had taken to carrying around and produced a manila envelope loaded with snapshots. He carefully removed some of them. Crudely lit by a police photographer, they depicted Candy's gold Cutlass. "I want you to look at these, and tell me if the car in the picture is the one you saw at the Willowbrook Mall," Brejack said.

Barbara stared at the images for nearly half a minute. She hoped to identify them. Nobody wants to be dismissed as an unreliable witness for the second time. But she had to tell the truth. Taking a deep breath, she allowed, "I can't say for sure that this is the same car. It *resembles* the car that I saw."

Her response was not good enough to be entered as evidence.

Disappointment spread out across Brejack's face, but that did nothing to jog her memory. Acknowledging that she had witnessed a violent argument at the mall—during that time period, *in that car*—would have allowed Barbara to help make his case. It certainly would prove that whoever killed Candy had a deeply entrenched relationship with her; and the next logical step from there might be that the person in the car was her husband. Of course it also could have been her illicit lover, or an old high school boyfriend, or any number of other people. But as Barbara shook her head in the negative, none of that mattered. Brejack suddenly saw a central link in his length of chain splitting in two.

He had hoped it wouldn't come to this, but the investigator's options had dwindled. Brejack produced another snapshot, this one of Candy. Even as he handed it to Barbara, though, he realized the unlikelihood of her being able to identify the face. As anticipated, she shook her head for the second time. Barbara Capalbo looked at the investigator apologetically and admitted, "I can't say for sure that the woman in the photo is the one I saw in the car at the mall."

"Can you describe the couple that you witnessed arguing?" Brejack asked, his exasperation mounting.

"The woman was in her twenties. She had light brown hair, and was smaller than the man. He had brown hair, and seemed to be a few years older than her. From watching them for a minute or two it was obvious that they were a couple, you know, not like a father and daughter or something."

"Were you able to get a good look at the two people in the car?"

"No. They moved around so much, and their faces were so heavily shadowed, that it was impossible to really see them."

Brejack showed her several photos of men, one of whom was John Short. He could not have been terribly surprised when she failed to pick Short out of the lineup. But before dismissing Barbara Capalbo as unreliable, the investigator had to take one last shot. "Let me ask you something, Barbara. If we were to produce the car, would you be willing to come down and try identifying it?"

"Sure," she said without hesitation. "I just don't know that seeing it in person will make it any more recognizable."

Brejack hoped that it would, and a couple of weeks later he said as much to Andrew Webster. "We need to get the car out of storage," Brejack said, keeping the hopefulness out of his voice as much as possible. "I have a woman who witnessed the fight that preceded the Candy Short murder. She needs to identify the car."

"Who's the woman?"

"Barbara Capalbo."

"Capalbo? We've already questioned her. She couldn't even get the color straight. Come on, Brejack. You don't want us to pull this car out just so she can say that she saw a different-colored vehicle."

"I need the car."

"Give me a break. It's stored in a fucking flood site and is covered in mud."

"Get the car, Webster. This is a murder investigation, and we need it for a witness. We won't let you hold anything back. I'll get a goddamned subpoena if it comes down to that."

"Let me see what I can do," Webster said, hanging up the telephone and making Brejack feel like a ball-breaking son of a bitch.

On December 15th at eleven o'clock in the morning, George arrived at Barbara's house. They drove to the Wayne Police Department's parking lot, where a recently hosed-down Cutlass awaited them. As the investigator and his attractively petite, stylishly dressed witness walked through the detective room, they found themselves confronted by Andrew Webster. He appreciatively took in Barbara's form and introduced himself.

"I was one of the original detectives in this investigation," he told her.

She nodded and slowed down her pace.

"That's a nice skirt you're wearing," Webster said.

Fearing that the detective would gum things up, Brejack stepped between them and spoke softly to Webster, so that only he could hear. "Leave her the fuck alone. We didn't come down here to screw around with you."

All but dragged by Brejack, Barbara hurried through the parking lot to the spot where the car awaited them. Much to Brejack's surprise, Barbara required only a quick glance before identifying it as the scene of the argument. "That's the car," she confidently said. "It's a Cutlass, just like my aunt's."

"Don't you want to get a better look at it before making a positive identification?"

"I don't need to," she said, pointing at the bumper stickers that read CAPEZIO and I'D RATHER BE DANCING. "I remember the stickers. This is the car."

After a closer inspection, Barbara made an official identification. Her statement not only proved that the car had been the site of a violent argument, but it also contradicted one of Short's oft-voiced contentions. He had hypothesized that the murder happened at another location, and that Candy's dead body was, in effect, dumped off at the Willowbrook Mall.

The case had taken a very positive turn, although Brejack knew that a few major links still stood between him and a grand jury. He required something that would conclusively destroy Short's alibi and shed additional light on his motive for killing Candy. The likeliest person to aid him on that latter point, Brejack knew, was the very woman for whom Short supposedly had committed the murder.

Diane Lovejoy was a chameleon. She routinely changed her lifestyle and appearance in a manner that few women would be able to manage once, never mind several times in as many years. The daughter of a successful Manhattan psychiatrist, she grew up in a large prewar building on the city's Upper West Side and demonstrated an early aptitude for music. Her instrument of choice was the violin. Spotted on the street or at some social gathering, Diane easily would have been perceived as one of New York's privileged children.

Soon after receiving an associate's degree from Queens College, however, she married, divorced, and began go-go dancing in New Jersey. There, in one of the bars, she met an older man, a lawyer from Florida, and married him. After her second husband died of a heart attack, and turned out to be less well off than one might imagine, Diane found herself with no means of support and went back to dancing.

Her sexual allure was in full bloom when she met John Short and round-aboutly accepted his money in exchange for sex. She continued along that path for a few more years, dancing and flirting and doing whatever seemed right and natural at the moment. Then Diane discovered something that turned her on more than gyrating in her underwear: religion.

In 1987 she became a member of The Way International, a born-again Christian group in Pittsburgh. Diane spent her days waiting tables in a sandwich shop there, always carrying a supply of the little pamphlets that bore sketches of Jesus on the front. Nights were taken up with reading scripture and studying the Bible.

She and her three roommates congregated at the small church and disseminated the word of the Lord. Making penance for her wayward past, for all of the John Shorts that she had encountered, Diane devoted her life to Jesus and the church. She occasionally found herself thinking about Short, but never prayed for him.

Using a telephone number that one of the Wayne policemen had scribbled in the margin of a handwritten interview with her, Brejack contacted Diane's parents. Unaware of Diane's whereabouts, he hoped that they would lead him to her. Emily Graves answered the telephone and apprised Brejack of her daughter's current situation. The investigator listened patiently, then insisted that he would have to speak with Diane.

"Hold on a minute," Emily told him.

She placed her hand over the mouthpiece of the telephone and carried on a muffled conversation with her husband.

Dr. Patrick T. Graves cleared his throat and put the receiver to his ear. "What do you want with my daughter?" he asked in a deep, well-educated voice.

"There's an investigation going on. A woman was murdered, and Diane may have some information that can help us solve it."

There was a moment of hesitation, followed by a flicker of recognition. "Is this that John Short thing?"

"Yes, sir, it is."

Brejack practically sensed a scrim going up between them, as the doctor said, "Look, you people have caused my daughter enough aggravation. You asked to speak with her once, and ended up abusing her. Why in the world would she want to cooperate with you again?"

"I don't know what went on back in 1981, Dr. Graves. This is a whole new investigation. I'm very sorry if the Wayne police officers offended Diane, but you have to believe me. This is all legitimate and on the level, sir. She has information that can be extremely helpful to us. I need to speak with her. Please help me."

"Diane was already interviewed by these animals, who verbally abused and threatened her. Can't you use their interview? Records of their conversations with her must exist."

Brejack hesitated, then sheepishly responded, "You're not going to believe this, sir, but there is no statement. They took some handwritten notes and that was it. The original group of detectives failed to do the job that they should have done. Everything is different now."

"Finally Diane is happy. She has her life in order. I am not going to have it upset by you and your colleagues."

"Please," Brejack pleaded. "I need to contact her. It's

extremely important. I wish that you would give me an address or telephone number at which I could reach her."

"I can't do that," Graves concluded. "What I can do is give her your telephone number. If she feels that she wants to speak with you, she'll call. Otherwise, you're simply going to have to find yourself another witness."

Brejack decided to give it a week. He would wait seven days before recontacting the doctor and his wife by telephone or simply showing up at their Manhattan address. He believed that if he were to meet them in person they would find it impossible to turn him down. And if they did, well, then he would try another tack. Diane Lovejoy was that important. She provided John Short with a motive, and she had actually heard him referring to the crime before it happened. Her testimony would offer premeditative evidence that no grand jury could ignore.

Four days after Brejack's conversation with her parents, Diane finally called. Informed that she was on the line, Brejack grabbed the telephone and began to furiously take notes. "My mother told me to call you," she coldly informed the investigator. "So here I am. What can I do for you?"

"The Candy Short homicide case is being reinvestigated, and I'd like to speak with you about it."

"Forget it. I've had enough dealings with you guys. Last time you questioned me I was told that it would be very nice and friendly, and they tried to set me up. For six hours those cops from Wayne screamed at me. They accused me of having something to do with the murder, they wanted me to entrap John Short. It was a humiliating, upsetting experience. No way will I go through it again."

"Listen to me, Diane. What I'm involved in has nothing to do with those cops in Wayne. This is going through the Passaic County Prosecutor's Office. I report directly to the chief prosecutor."

"I don't care who you report to. Nobody's going to put me through that stuff again."

"In no way would you be disrespected, Diane. You have my word on that. I'd like to meet with you at your convenience. You can bring along anybody who would make you feel comfortable. It's all on your terms."

"Investigator Brejack," she began, "do you believe?"

"In God? Sure I do. I go to church every Sunday."

"Yes, but do you really believe in the Lord Jesus Christ?"

This was a conversation that Brejack wanted to avoid. He knew that no matter what he said, it would do very little to further his cause with her. "I believe in God, Diane. I pray every Sunday. Right now, though, this is very important. If you want to talk to me about God that would be fine, but I also want to discuss John Short with you."

"Let me think about it, and I'll get back to you. I want to consult one of the people in my church, a man who's a lawyer." The conversation seemed about ready to end when Diane cautiously added, "And please don't call my mother anymore. I've caused my parents a lot of grief over the years. Right now I'm trying to bring peace into their lives. Calls from cops are not consistent with that."

"It's the only way I have of contacting you," Brejack said, grateful for the opening.

Diane grudgingly gave him her telephone number and promised to be in touch.

A few hours later she called back and offered the investigator a narrow option. "I spoke to the man who's a lawyer, and he told me that it would not be a good idea to meet with you in person. Particularly in light of what happened with the other police officers."

"That's it?" asked Brejack, broken-hearted. "You're refusing to discuss this case with me?"

"If you prepare a list of questions and mail it to me, I'll answer them to the best of my ability and respond to you in writing."

Brejack held back his anger at this woman who once had danced in go-go bars and now had the audacity to advise him on how to handle an investigation. He begged and cajoled, trying to persuade Diane to reconsider, but she simply refused. Those were her terms. They were concrete, and he would have to live with them. Or not.

"Do you remember very much about John Short?" Brejack asked, hoping that a more casual approach would loosen her up a bit.

"I remember John Short as a widower. As far as I'm concerned, he was a very nice man."

Without further prodding, Diane gave Brejack her address (so he could send the questions in writing), then she added, "And just because you have my name, address, and telephone number, don't think that you can just drop in on me. If you do, I will not discuss this case with you."

He assured Diane that she had nothing to worry about and thanked her in advance for any aid she could offer. Pissed off and disappointed, Brejack was about to hang up the telephone when he heard her speak his name.

"Yes?"

"Jesus loves you," Diane said just before cradling the receiver. "God bless."

Brejack hung up and softly muttered, "God *damn*."

CHAPTER
14

Brejack witnessed the murder. He sat in the backseat of Candy's Cutlass, conscious of his surroundings—cars rumbling past, air thick with the oily scent from an adjacent highway, ugly rectangular buildings visible in the distance—but ignored by the couple up front. Like a voyeur at a sex show he was privy to intimacy, but he might just as well have been invisible. Fascinated and repulsed, Brejack saw John wrapping his fingers around Candy's neck, marking her with a chain of garish purple welts. As he squeezed, the woman gasped for breath and struggled to speak.

Despite his desperation to do something, anything, that would silence the choked-off grunts that Candy emitted, Brejack remained immobile, completely helpless. When John finally began smashing his unconscious wife's head against the dash, George reached over and hooked a finger inside the neck of the man's T-shirt. His fingers were sweaty and greasy at the same time, and Brejack could not maintain a grip. Then the screaming stopped. Everything turned fuzzy.

Brejack woke up.

Sweating and shaking, he scanned the dark bedroom and tried to regain his sense of place. Lisa, vaguely aware of a disturbance, knew all about the recurring dream. She cocked an eye and didn't bother asking what had just happened. Instead she curled alongside him so that

259

their bodies fit together like a pair of spoons. Brejack wanted to doze off again, but he couldn't. Day and night, the case dominated his thoughts.

During George Brejack's waking moments he likened himself to a masterful pool shark, his world to a giant expanse of green baize. Each element in the investigation was a different-colored ball, and he aimed to line them up alongside the pockets. As 1987 neared its end, Brejack's game took shape. His hard work began to pay off. Previously undisclosed names and dormant information came to the fore, creating momentum.

Even as Brejack saw the balls lining up, however, he knew better than to relax. Experience told him that he was still a long way from gaining an indictment against John Short, never mind collecting enough evidence to actually get the man convicted of murder. He spent long nights at his desk, reshuffling information and dealing out the facts like a chronic solitaire player, hell-bent on beating the deck. Maybe, the reasoning went, reconstructing the data in different ways would reveal which evidence could clinch a circumstantial case.

He took the work everywhere with him. Before George and Lisa closed their Catskill camp for the winter she hiked alone, now resigned to the fact that her boyfriend would not return to his old enjoyable self anytime soon. He spent endless afternoons trying to make sense of the information that had thus far been uncovered. Sometimes it seemed to be in a secret code that he could barely translate. And therein resided the challenge. Laying out the facts so that others would understand them— or, even better, *see them*—presented a hurdle that he had yet to surmount. But that obstacle stood in the visible distance, and once he approached it Brejack expected to soar magnificently and gracefully over it. He pictured himself as one of those paper-and-ink eagles that hung on the wall of his study.

The sense of victory that came with solving this case would be sweet for more than the most obvious reasons.

Once Short wound up behind bars, Brejack imagined, those guys at the prosecutor's office would finally shut up. They'd have no choice but to stop riding him. He'd no longer have to deal with the cold glances and petty derision. Whispers about the investigator wasting department time and money on a hopeless case would be squelched.

At least that's what Brejack believed on the good days. More often, he figured that he'd solve the case and nothing in the prosecutor's office would change. But that, too, would be fine; at least Brejack would have proven to himself that he still had his investigative gift. Whatever his colleagues might say, however jealous they might act, none of it would truly affect him.

In order to reach that state of grace, Brejack kept the faith and pursued potential leads long after they appeared to be dead ends; occasionally the diligence paid off. At least one afternoon each week, he dropped in on Fred and Helen Austin.

Brejack built a trusting relationship with Candy's parents, and ceased to worry whether their conversations were filtering down to John. During his months on the case he came to know the Austins' small dining room as well as his own. Breaking police procedure by sharing information with people directly involved in the murder, Brejack sat there with the couple and looked out on to Passaic Avenue as the afternoons melted into dusk earlier and earlier.

In turn, the Austins grew comfortable enough with George that they casually discussed the death of Candy with him. He revealed details about his own troubled boyhood, and gently dug for clues that would bolster existing allegations against John Short.

Those visits were routinely followed by a quick run across the gravel drive. There he'd have a beer with Joe and get another take on freshly culled evidence. As much as anyone, Joe and Betty Frank believed in Brejack and trusted his intuition. They agreed that John Short had to have committed the crime. Like the investigator, they wracked their brains to come up with the piece of information that would inextricably link him with Candy's killing.

Then, as if by magic, that evidential gem materialized in the form of an unexpected telephone call. On a post-New Year's afternoon. Brejack sat in his office, looking through a loupe at color slides of the apartment John and Candy Short had lived in. It was a tedious process, but Brejack saw it as better than doing nothing. Besides, he reasoned, if you reshuffle the deck often enough, you'll eventually deal yourself a perfect hand.

He closed his eyes and tried to place himself in the Shorts' living room. Drawing on his own experiences as a child in a dysfunctional family, Brejack could feel the tense, claustrophobic atmosphere of that basement apartment. He relived the constant threat of violence. Then the ring of the telephone roused him from his dark reverie.

"Prosecutor's office," he said, holding the receiver to his face with one hand and rubbing his temple with the other, hoping to massage away an oncoming headache.

It was Judy Halbert Chamberlain, Candy's girlhood friend, and she had a thought to share with the investigator. "I don't know if it's important or not, but there's something that bothered me after Candy's murder. I thought about it at the time, then it slipped my mind. Last night my sister and I were reminiscing about high school, and when I woke up this morning it came back to me."

"Okay, Judy," Brejack said, hoping that this would be more than another dead end. "What is it?"

"The keys. I can't figure out why nobody ever found Candy's keys."

"The Wayne cops found them. The keys were right under Candy's body." He reached for the report that had been filed from the crime scene and read the description to Judy. "See, the keys were discovered on the floor of the front seat."

"But those weren't her keys," Judy insisted. "And that's what bothered me. Candy's keys were never discovered."

"Would you be able to describe what Candy's key chain looked like?" Brejack asked, holding back his excitement, not wanting to build himself up for a letdown yet feeling that he was on the verge of an epiphany.

"Sure. It was a ring with her keys and a little rainbow colored flip-flop on it."

Brejack looked at the photograph of the key ring from the crime scene. It had a plastic, T-shirt-shaped fob attached to the ring. Immediately, he realized that correcting this tiny oversight could pin John to the scene of the crime. If those were John's keys.

"Are you going to be home for another hour or two?" he asked Judy.

"Yeah."

"All right, I'm on my way over right now. What you've just told me may prove to be very important."

Brejack swallowed three Tylenol, packed up the pertinent evidence, and ran downstairs to his silver Volvo. He drove through Paterson's rush-hour traffic to Judy's home and lost himself in the beautiful music of WPAT. Snaking through gridlock with a truly optimistic sense of purpose, Brejack experienced a rush of confidence that had been in diminishing supply since the earliest days of the investigation. The key chain could lead him to its conclusion. By the time he pulled up in front of Judy's two-family house, Brejack's mind was swirling with the possible ramifications of her revelation.

Judy greeted him at the door, and George Brejack tried to be professional and low-key. But he found it impossible to mask his exhilaration.

If she were to say what he thought she would say, the case could soon be solved. Sitting down on the couch, Brejack laid his belongings on top of the Chamberlains' nautically inspired coffee table and took out his note-book. This time, he kept the small talk to a minimum and focused in on one thing.

"Can you describe to me the kind of key chain that Candy kept her car keys on?"

"Yes. It was a little rubber and foam sandal. A flip-flop."

"Did Candy have any other key chain that she used?"

"Candy's only other key chain had a small picture frame on it, with a photo of Jesse from when she was a baby."

Brejack took a deep breath and fished around in his envelope. He pulled out a sandwich-size Ziploc bag. "Okay, Judy, I'm going to show you another key chain. This one has a white fob in the shape of a T-shirt on it. Have you ever seen this before?"

"Yes," she said, relaxing a little bit, pleased to have furnished the investigator with some useful information. "I saw the key ring and fob on John's desk in the Short apartment. I remembered commenting to Candy that it was cute and asking her if there were any more; I kind of wanted one for myself. She told me that it was the only one of its kind and that John used it. Somebody had sent it to him in the mail."

This was precisely what Brejack had hoped to hear. A one-of-a-kind key ring—a sample that the manufacturer had made up especially for Short—found under the murdered woman's body, meant that only one person could possibly have killed her. How else could it have wound up there? It placed John Short at the scene of the murder in as concrete a way as any piece of circumstantial evidence ever can.

Everything had gone so well that Brejack, always optimistic, decided to get Judy's take on another piece of evidence. He opened up a brown paper bag, one that seemed to be padded with something, and pulled out a faded yellow blanket. As Brejack unfurled it, Judy blanched visibly. She sensed it was the blanket that her best friend's corpse had been wrapped in.

"Do you remember this?" he asked.

"That looks like Candy's blanket. She kept it in the trunk of the car." Judy began crying, then she looked up at Brejack and said, "I remember it because we went on a picnic together in May. Candy, Jesse, and I met with Cindy [the oldest Austin daughter] and drove to a park near her house. That's the blanket that we used. Candy always kept it in her trunk."

Brejack did what he could to comfort Judy—even as he thrilled at the fact that the murderer had known the car well enough to look in the trunk for a blanket—then packed up his belongings and left the house. He wanted to run this information past a few other people before the day was out. Their confirmation would add credibility to Judy's statement, proving that she wasn't simply trying to avenge her friend's death.

When he arrived at the home of Joe and Betty Frank, they were clearing away the dinner dishes and invited George to join them for a beer. He did, then inquired after John's keys. Without hesitation, they confirmed Judy's story. A few minutes later, a similar scenario played itself out on the other side of the gravel drive when he asked Fred and Helen Austin about the keys and the blanket.

Helen brought George a cup of coffee and laid out a platter of cookies. One with green dots of sugar on top caught Brejack's eye. He grabbed it, took a bite, and washed down the sweet with a sip of coffee. The cookie was not nearly so soft and chewy as the investigator had expected it to be. "Helen," he said, "something's wrong with these cookies."

She blushed, then admitted, "They're a few weeks old. I made them for Christmas."

Brejack felt so good about the day's discoveries that he didn't even care. He reached for a second one, softened it up with some more coffee, and prepared himself for another long night at the office. He had to track down one of the guys that John had worked with and question him about the keys.

Back in Paterson, though, that wasn't so hard. A few well-placed calls put him in touch with Dan Solowe, the construction worker who used to assist Short in North Jersey.

"I heard that the case was being reopened," Solowe said, speaking in a sluggish, uneducated voice. "I probably can come see you tomorrow as long as I don't have a job. Let me give you a call in the morning, and we'll see whether or not it works out."

Brejack gave Solowe his office number and wearily made his way downstairs to the silver Volvo parked across the street. His body ached with fatigue, but he felt good—confident that the case would come together and result in a conviction. By the time he got home a sitcom was on TV and Lisa had already eaten dinner.

She accepted Brejack's kiss on her lips and distractedly told him, "There's some chicken in the oven. Let me heat it up for you."

Tension from the investigation had taken its toll on George's relationship with Lisa. She couldn't understand the many emotions that this case stoked, then fanned, then smothered; and Brejack lacked the patience to explain them. He ate in stony silence, before going to bed and dreaming about plastic fobs and key rings.

At eight-thirty the following morning Dan Solowe phoned as promised, agreeing to stop by forty-five minutes later. When Solowe entered the office, Brejack saw a slightly built man whose age hovered around thirty. He had greased-back hair, and a swagger that had once been equaled by John's. Though he affected the attitude of a tough guy, Brejack sized him up as a punk. The investigator put his personal feelings aside and treated Solowe like a respected member of the community, but the source clearly felt uncomfortable in the Passaic County Prosecutor's Office. Jumpy around cops and already tagged with a rap sheet for a minor infraction, Solowe gingerly approached Brejack's desk.

"I'm going to show you a key ring that has five keys and a fob on it," Brejack slowly said. "Have you ever seen this before?"

He handed it to Solowe. For a second or two Solowe rolled the keys around the palm of his hand, appearing to be contemplating allegiances as much as the object itself. Handing the evidence back, he stated, "No. I've never seen this."

Brejack didn't believe Solowe, but he swallowed the urge to tell him as much. Instead, he did what he could to keep the conversation alive.

"What kind of person was John?"

"He was weird. He had a Jekyll-and-Hyde personality. One minute he could be nice to you, lend you money, buy you lunch. But other times he could yell in your face, curse you out, damage job sites. When John got mad he was a different person. If he was driving and somebody cut him off, John would lose control and start chasing the guy. He'd tailgate him, curse, try to run him off the road."

Solowe hesitated for a moment, trying to recall a particular incident. "John was very strong for his size. He showed no emotion for anyone. It was like he only cared about himself." Then he softly muttered, "John did things that didn't make sense."

"Like what?"

"One time he showed me nude photos of his first wife. Can you figure out why a guy would do something like that?"

Brejack shook his head in agreement and chuckled along with Solowe. Once again the investigator held out the keys, dangling them by the T-shirt-shaped fob. He rephrased his question. This time Solowe reconsidered and responded differently. Careful to avoid the investigator's eyes, he admitted, "Yeah. They're John's keys. He used to carry them around all the time, kept them in the pocket of his jeans."

Further questioning revealed that on the two occasions Solowe had seen Short driving the Cutlass, that incriminating fob was hanging out of the ignition. Encouraged by the source's sudden willingness to cooperate, Brejack hoped to scavenge some additional information. "Do you remember a go-go dancer named Diane Lovejoy?"

"No, but John spent a lot of time in go-go bars. He threw his money around, and tipped all the girls really well. He was free with his money, especially if there were blond go-go girls involved."

"Do you remember any blondes in particular?"

As he asked the question, Brejack silently chanted *Lovejoy, Lovejoy* like a mantra. "About a week before Candy's death John had his eye on a blonde at The Coach Light," Solowe began, now relaxed and as comfortable with Brejack as he could be in the presence of any cop. "John saw her and he started telling everybody, 'I have to have her. She's sexy, she turns me on, it's love at first sight.' "

"Was this unusual behavior for John Short?"

"Even though John was married, if he had a chance to go out and get laid he would do it. Especially if, like I said before, the woman was a blond go-go dancer. Hot-looking blondes were his weakness."

This material was so good that Brejack had to get it on the record. He called in a typist and rehashed most of their conversation. At the conclusion, Solowe signed his name to the bottom of the transcript. It confirmed that everything he had just told Brejack was true.

Over the years countless men had lied to Diane Lovejoy. So many broken promises—of money, security, sexual prowess—had led her to develop a sixth sense for deception. It told Diane that her last conversation with George Brejack would not be the final one—regardless of what the investigator assured her. Brejack could not have agreed more. Unfortunately, he was having trouble coming up with a plan that would persuade her to cooperate.

Brejack knew that she would never listen directly to him. He had to get at Diane through somebody she trusted, somebody who could speak the words that would convey the importance of her testimony.

The problem hung in the back of his mind, and he routinely discarded variations on the most obvious tacks: physical force, family pressure, chicanery. Like a lot of men in the past, Brejack found himself obsessed with the seductive blonde. His desires, however, went beyond the flesh. He wanted her mind, her memories, her conscience.

On a Sunday morning before church, Brejack sat at the kitchen table and listened to the bells of St. Brendan's, which served to calm his troubled mind. Suffering from a string of restless nights, he stared off into the distance and sipped from a cooled-off cup of coffee. Lisa freshened it and radiated concern as she looked at her boyfriend's puffy, overtired face.

"Are you all right, George?" she asked. "You look terrible."

"You know I have a lot on my mind. I'm still trying to figure out how to handle the Lovejoy thing." He censored much of what he told Lisa, ever mindful of the policeman's superstition that sharing an investigation with your woman could jinx it. In a tone designed to sound apologetic, he added, "I just have to devise a way to reach out to Diane and get her excited about the case."

Lisa wrapped her arms around George's shoulders and hugged him from behind, providing the comfort that he secretly craved. Then neither of them said much of anything. They walked out to the car and proceeded to the nearby church where they prayed each Sunday.

As Brejack made the short drive through the suburban streets of Paterson, cruising past the cemetery that ran down Crooks Avenue, Diane was already inside The Way's chapel. There, among her fellow Christians, she lost herself in a search for salvation.

As promised, she said a prayer for George Brejack. She asked Christ to save his soul and give him the strength to see the way of the Lord. A similar plea was made for John Short. True to born-again form, Diane refused to see John in anything but the best light. When she remembered him it was as a widower at loose ends, not as the murderer that Brejack had described.

John Short did not go to church. He slept in on Sunday mornings, waking up in a haze of alcohol and cocaine, with a bitch of a hangover. He drank coffee and smoked Marlboro Lights, scanned the Sunday paper, and told Judy to shut those kids up. He had a headache that wouldn't quit. Suddenly John realized that he had to make a telephone call. He dialed the home of his boyhood friend Louie Derringer.

The telephone was answered by Sally Derringer, who reminded John that she and Lou were no longer together. John didn't bother asking for his friend's number and she didn't volunteer it. Instead he mentioned that he and Judy would be coming through upstate New York in the next few days and would like to stop by. Remembering her husband's festering dislike for John, Sally wasn't thrilled with the prospect, but she didn't find it all that threatening either. Louie, she felt, had a tendency to overreact; and considering how badly their marriage had ended, her ex was hardly in a position to judge others.

"Okay," she told John. "I'll see you two soon, and I'll let Louie know that you're coming up."

For some reason, though, she never got around to calling her former mate. If she had, he would have told Sally that John was far more dangerous than the benign hard-ass everybody perceived him as. Tipped off by an inquisitive call from Brejack, Louie knew that his boyhood friend was in mounting trouble, the kind of trouble that went beyond a little recreational dope-smoking or bar-room scuffling. Though the investigator remained relatively vague, he said enough to make it clear that John was a likely suspect in the Candy Short murder. Vowing to have limited dealings with John—an oath that the flashlight incident had cemented—Louie only hoped that John had nothing to do with the death of his second wife.

But he had no desire to find out firsthand.

Brejack believed that he knew the truth about that, and he spent the morning in church praying for the guidance to put Short behind bars.

Then, as the investigator bowed down on his knees, looking up to the priest on the pulpit, divine inspiration struck: *the church*. He would use Diane's church to convince her that cooperating in the investigation was the right thing to do. If she wouldn't listen to Brejack she would certainly listen to her priest or minister, or whatever it was they had out there at The Way International.

First thing Monday morning, Brejack placed a call to Pittsburgh and got in touch with Nolan Yogi, a soft-spoken man who empathized with the investigator's plight. "I'll talk to Diane," he promised after twenty minutes of Brejack's flattering persuasion. "I can't guarantee what her response will be, but I'll tell her what you've told me and see what she says."

The next morning Diane called and agreed to meet with Brejack. Over the telephone she sounded like a changed woman. Her voice suddenly brimmed with friendliness, and her attitude was cooperative. Whatever Yogi said to her certainly seemed to have worked.

Now Brejack had to convince the prosecutor's office to spring for a trip to Pittsburgh. Considering the headway he'd already made on the case, this should not have been a big deal. But Brejack's political standing within the department was hardly an asset. Put bluntly, most of the people there, particularly Max Swathmore, already had more of Brejack than they could stand. They found him to be overbearing and unduly cocky. The thought of feeding that cockiness was completely unappealing to them. Finally, though, after he'd gotten John Nativo to back him up, Brejack extracted a promise that the office would pay for a hotel and gasoline expenses, but he'd have to drive his own car.

Brejack's head buzzed with anticipation as he checked into the Pittsburgh Holiday Inn and called Diane at the sandwich shop. Never underestimating the importance of this witness, he now vowed to treat her with the utmost respect and coddling. Regardless of how outlandish her requests might be, he'd listen politely, nod accommodatingly, and promise to do what he could to make things work out. Considering her initial apprehension about this meeting, Brejack realized that the slightest show of discourtesy could turn her off.

As he listened to the beeps and clicks of his call being processed, the investigator also pondered the very real possibility that she might get cold feet and back out of their meeting. Maintaining his cool under those circumstances would require the utmost in self-control. Brejack readied himself for the possibility but tried to keep it out of his mind, so as not to fill his voice with perceptible angst.

"Hiii!" Diane sounded warmer than she had in any of their previous telephone conversations.

"It's George, Diane. I'm in Pittsburgh."

"Great! How's everything going?"

"Never better. I'm looking forward to seeing you tonight."

"Oh, yeah. Maybe we can have dinner together."

"Okay, Diane, why don't you meet me at six o'clock in the lobby of the Holiday Inn? There's a nice restaurant right here."

"That sounds perfect, George." Chipper as a sorority girl after pledge week, she added, "And I'm going to be bringing along my friend Ricky."

"No problem."

The conversation ended, and Brejack hung up. It was about three o'clock. After watching TV, napping, and showering, he put on his good suit, flattened down what was left of his hair, and adjusted his pistol so that it would be undetectable. Brejack looked at himself in the mirror for a long time, inspecting his face for the details that he never had time to notice at home. Tired flaps of skin ringed his eyes, his cheekbones stretched the flesh on his upper face into two little arcs, and loose jowls hung below tapered cheeks. He fiddled with his mustache a little bit, smiled at his own reflection, and mouthed, "You handsome prick."

As he said it, though, Brejack realized that his career was winding down. Approaching fifty, he couldn't spend the rest of his life chasing gunmen through the back alleys of Paterson. After a certain age a law enforcer becomes most effective in a supervisory capacity; Brejack knew that paper-pushing loomed in the near future. Realizing that this could very well be his last big case, his final shot at glory and the big headlines that come with it, Brejack vowed to make it a good one. He packed a few bulging manila envelopes into his briefcase, shut off the light in his room, and closed the door behind him.

Downstairs, in the hotel's lobby, Diane and Ricky Bruckner sat close to one another on an emerald-green couch and waited for the investigator. As was second nature to him, Brejack instinctively sized up his two dinner companions. While he expected Diane to be attractive, Brejack couldn't get over how untarnished she was by her former lifestyle. Her face lacked the hardened appearance that most go-go dancers find it impossible to shake, even after being out of the business for years. Belief in Christianity (and the lifestyle that came with it) had done wonders for Diane's physical and mental well-being. Indeed, wearing neatly pressed navy blue slacks and a white blouse, Diane looked like a prim, proper woman who recently found her rightful place in the church.

Her companion, on the other hand, was an easier read.

Short, bald, and spacy, Ricky Bruckner immediately struck Brejack as an ex-hippie.

After a brief introduction, the three of them proceeded to the dining room and stiffly took seats around a corner table for four. Rather than being his usually garrulous self, Brejack made polite small talk with Diane and Ricky, questioning them about Pittsburgh and the church. They discussed the weather, the Steelers, a bit about their own lives. The one issue they avoided was John Short. Brejack waited until after they'd ordered to raise that topic.

Beginning to relax, Diane candidly told the investigator what he needed to know. The relief of confession made her euphoric, and once she began talking she didn't want to stop. She had been keeping a lot inside since her liaison with Short, and Brejack was a sympathetic listener. Diane took him through her evening with John, explained how they'd met, identified a photo of the Cutlass (but remembered nothing about the key ring), and confirmed that he told her his wife had been murdered in the parking lot of a shopping mall. However, Diane now offered more detail than what she had given the Wayne police, elaborating on John's claim that Candy had been strangled and stabbed.

"What was John like on the evening that you met?"

"He seemed depressed and preoccupied," Diane said as she hungrily dug into a piece of swordfish. "He really didn't want to talk about what happened to his wife." She flashed the investigator a smile and added, "Or at least what he *told* me had happened to her."

"Did you intend to see him again?"

"Oh, yeah. He said that he and Jesse were going to take me to the Hamptons. His parents supposedly have a house there. We made plans to spend the weekend together."

"When did you learn about the true death of Candy?"

"The night that we were supposed to leave for the Hamptons. I waited for him at The Coach Light—that's where he was supposed to pick me up—but he never showed. So I drove out to a club in Belleville where I used to work. I asked my ex-boss there, a man named Tony, if he knew John Short. That's when I found out about Candy. He told me there was an article in the paper about John's wife being killed."

"Were you surprised?"

"Shocked is a better word. It was unreal to me. I couldn't actually believe it until I saw the article. And even then it didn't completely register. I didn't think it was the same John Short. But after a while it began to make sense. I mean, I hadn't heard from him all week, so I knew that something had to be up."

"What was the name of the club in Belleville?"

"The Red Shingle."

"Do you recall what kind of cigarettes John Short smoked, if any?"

"Marlboro Lights, same as me."

"Did you try to learn more information about the murder?"

"I went to the public library and looked up news articles." Her appetite gone, Diane poked at her food and met Brejack's gaze with a puzzled expression. "I couldn't figure out why he told me his wife was killed the week before they found her murdered."

Brejack had a hard time associating Diane with the woman who had rebuffed him on the telephone. She had started off the evening friendly enough, and then through the course of the meal she had softened even further. Brejack believed that he now had gained Diane's trust and could count on her to be in his corner during the investigation. As a result, he had no hesitation about asking her to come back to his room after dinner. He needed to take a formal statement and transcribe it on a portable typewriter.

Without asking permission of Ricky Bruckner (who had been virtually mute throughout the meal), Diane readily agreed to do it. As the three of them rode the elevator upstairs, she turned to George and said, "Since I've met you, I can see that you're a different type of person from the other officers. You're a nice human being. You understand people."

By the interview's completion, Diane had total faith in Brejack as a person and as an investigator. She answered his questions completely and truthfully, claiming to feel instantly close to him.

In an attempt to cement that new bond between them—if the case ever went to trial, Brejack knew, Diane would be an indispensable witness—he stopped at her sandwich shop the next morning before heading back to New Jersey. Brejack ate a heavy breakfast of bacon and eggs and watched Diane scurrying around behind the counter. After he finished the meal she gave him a hug, handed over one of her The Way pamphlets, and vowed that she'd help in any manner possible.

Less forthcoming was Tony, the go-go bar impresario. He wanted nothing to do with the police and pleaded ignorance to the investigator's questions. However, he did manage to sell Brejack two hats and a T-shirt emblazoned with The Red Shingle logo.

The weekend in upstate New York should have been a godsend for John Short. He needed to get away from the job, from the coke, from the cops. His life seemed claustrophobic, as if a small room's walls were slowly closing in on him.

This promised to be one of those increasingly rare chances to enjoy a few days without the kids yelling and screaming and driving him up the wall. He'd see some old friends, have plenty of drinks, and relax the way he did in the old days, before he'd ever heard of George Brejack. John and Judy planned on driving their leased Lincoln Continental through the wintry countryside, and the conclusion of their trip would be a visit with Louie and his ex-wife Sally. However, John had been vague as to exactly when they'd be arriving.

When they reached the town of Marcellus, John telephoned Sally, announced that he was five minutes away from her house, and reminded her of the invitation that had been extended to Judy and himself. Unprepared at the moment—and having expected far more advance notice as to the exact time of arrival—Sally realized that the last thing she wanted was a sudden visit from John Short. But she could think of nothing better to say than, "Okay, I'll be waiting."

Upon arriving at Sally's, John had assumed that Louie would be there, but he was nowhere in sight. "I'll try calling him in a few minutes," John said, hugging Sally and settling into the warm, comfortable house.

From the moment he walked inside, however, John gave the impression that something was bothering him. He acted skittish and preoccupied, his eyes darted around the living room, taking the place in as if he were scouting it for a movie location.

Suddenly he jumped up and decided that he would call Louie. Acting with an uncalled-for sense of urgency, John asked to use the telephone. Sally dialed for him and John reached Marcy, the woman to whom Louie was now married. He identified himself and asked whether his friend was at home.

Marcy was about to hand the phone to her husband when he motioned for her to cover for him, to say that he had gone out for the afternoon. She complied, and a disappointed John Short left a message before hanging up. Let down in a way that seemed disproportionate under the circumstances, John joined Sally and Judy in the living room.

They spent a few minutes talking about their kids, discussing work, and what their lives had become. Then, after forty-five minutes and a handful of Budweisers, John revealed something that helped to account for his behavior.

"Remember that crap they put me through when Candy was murdered? Well, it's starting up all over again." John sipped directly from a can and tried to hide his despondency over the case's current status. "Some hotshot cop from Paterson is trying to find the guy who killed Candy."

"Has he had any luck?"

"No. It's very difficult at this point to figure out who did it. There was no real evidence. It could have been anybody." John laughed with put-on bemusement, and shook his head. "I don't know what they expect to find. I'll help the cops any way I can, but if you ask me I think it's all a big waste of taxpayers' money."

Sally's kids played in a corner of the house, and Judy distractedly watched them. She had nothing to contribute to this conversation. John got up a couple of times and tried phoning Louie but he had no luck in reaching him.

"Where's your ex-husband hiding these days?" he asked Sally. "I hope he can squeeze in a few minutes to see me while I'm up here. After all, the guy was the best man at my first wedding."

"I don't know where Louie is," Sally said tersely, hoping that nothing in her voice revealed his general reluctance to see John. "He's been real busy with work and everything."

John nodded. He'd heard that line before. In fact, he'd used it himself on several occasions.

Despite her best intentions, Sally found it impossible to be totally unaffected by Louie's desire to avoid contact with John. After all, the two men had been friends for so many years, Louie knew him as well as anybody, and if he thought John was dangerous that should have been good enough for Sally. She had taken Louie's claims lightly until today, until she saw this intensely high-strung man sitting in her living room and insisting that he had nothing to do with the death of his previous wife. The more John drank and the darker it got outside, the more convinced Sally became that she should get him and Judy out of her house as soon as it was diplomatically possible.

Finally, when he asked whether she'd be able to put

them up for a night or two Sally had her chance. "I'm sorry," she told him, searching for an excuse (no matter how lame), "but there just isn't enough room. If I'd known you were coming it might be different. I'd be prepared."

Dejected, John insisted that he understood. And a few minutes later, he and Judy departed. They got into the Lincoln and drove to a motel where they spent the night.

If John was upset about Brejack's intensifying investigation, he could have consoled himself with the fact that the statute of limitations had already expired on every charge short of murder. Even if a jury found him guilty, the common wisdom went, they'd probably charge him with manslaughter, and he would go free. So, technically speaking, John couldn't lose.

That Monday morning, though, before embarking on the ride back to New Jersey, he called Sally Derringer at seven-thirty.

She answered the telephone, startled to hear John's voice on the line. In the wake of the previous afternoon, she wanted to forget about him. But here he was, back again.

"Sally," John said, standing in a phone booth alongside the loaded Lincoln. "I need to talk to you about something."

"I don't have time," she said, grateful for an out. "I'm running late for work."

"It'll only take a minute."

"Another time, John. I'm really late."

"Okay," he said and hung up.

The urgency in John's voice disturbed Sally for several days to come. She could not imagine what this important thing John had to tell her could be. Whatever it was, something in John's tone left her nervous. For the remainder of the week, Sally jumped a little bit whenever the telephone rang. Each time she answered with apprehension, and expressed relief when the caller proved to be somebody other than John Short.

At around that same time John placed another call. This one went to Detective Lieutenant Ernest Hutchinson, who headed up internal affairs at the Paterson Police Department. "I'm calling to register a complaint against George Brejack," said Short, who forgot that Brejack worked for the county. "He's harassing me and my friends, acting as if I'm already guilty of a crime that I didn't even commit."

"What sort of harassment is it?" Hutchinson wanted to know.

Speaking in an agitated, high-pitched voice, Short replied, "verbal and emotional. And you better tell him to knock it off, or else somebody's going to get hurt."

"I'll pass that on to him."

Later that morning, Hutchinson did as he promised. He sent a letter to John Nativo, who wasted no time in sharing a laugh with Brejack over the misdirected complaint.

Basking in his good fortune, Brejack observed that had Short called Max Swathmore instead of Hutchinson, the consequences would have been far more severe. "This case is *meant* to be solved by me," Brejack said. He sipped from his coffee, shook his head, and half joked, "He's going to hurt *me*? That prick's got a good sense of humor, but he does not realize the caliber of man he's up against."

Now it was Nativo's turn to chuckle. "Guess you're going to have to educate him, George."

CHAPTER
15

Elation swung to frustration, and back again. Each day George Brejack saw himself getting closer to building a case against John Short, yet the grand jury hearing remained elusive. Caught up in his optimism, he failed to see how anybody could find Short innocent. But regardless of what Brejack uncovered, Marty Kayne remained outwardly unmoved. Kayne, Passaic County's chief assistant prosecutor, refused to convene a grand jury until a case looked tight enough to win, and this one had a ways to go.

Like most successful men in his profession Kayne leaned toward conservatism, and he saw several gaping holes in Brejack's findings. Forty-eight-year-old Kayne's courtroom requirements contrasted sharply with his large framed, often rumpled appearance: He demanded that all cases be well organized, completely buttoned up, and tightly investigated. After scrutinizing Brejack's findings, Kayne was bothered by too many loose ends.

"We need more," he continually told the investigator. "What you've got is good, it says a lot about John Short, but unfortunately it doesn't prove that he killed his wife on the night of June 22, 1981."

"What else do you want?" Brejack wearily asked.

"Something that directly ties him in to the murder and disproves his alibi, George. It's too far from the date of the crime to rely solely on all of this sketchy circumstantial evidence."

Brejack could not bring himself to admit it out loud, but Kayne had a point. The investigation seemed to say more about John Short and his relationships with women than it did about the murder itself. While a motivation existed in the form of Diane Lovejoy, and while Short did appear physically and emotionally capable of committing the deed, nothing definitively pinned him to the crime and truly disproved his alibi. Lacking eyewitnesses who could absolutely confirm Short's presence at Willowbrook Mall, the investigator needed to slyly finesse his information into looking like more than it really was. He required something that would place Short at Willowbrook, and not on the back roads of West Orange.

He complained about this to Nativo, who offered his standard line of encouragement that concluded with, "Keep working the street, George. You never know what you'll find. Just remember that this isn't an open-and-shut case. I hope you won't be too disappointed if nothing comes of it."

"Don't even say that!" Brejack shot back, annoyed. "Short did it, and he's going down the pipe."

During his more paranoid moments, Brejack secretly questioned the long time it was taking to convene a grand jury. High-ranking people within the prosecutor's office had been part of the original investigative team, and they would look bad if Brejack were to solve the crime six years after it had been bungled. Politically speaking, it appeared to be in their best interest to keep this case from going anywhere.

Maybe that was Brejack's problem. Maybe he didn't know how to maneuver in the political cauldron of the Passaic County Prosecutor's Office. Most of the investigators there had started out at small-town police departments in the county and coasted in on heavy political connections. Brejack came from the inner city and lacked their kind of clout.

"This place is a fucking whorehouse," he told Nativo. "Everybody's looking for something."

"You have to work within the system," Nativo replied.

"Fuck the system," Brejack told him. "I'm here to solve cases. And that's what I'm going to do, whether these jerk-offs like it or not."

Brejack's refusal to operate by the office's unwritten rules of cooperation and mutual back-scratching served to further isolate him. Besides having his overtime and expenses cut off, Brejack now found himself threatened with a change of hours.

Swathmore wanted to keep the investigator working all day on new cases, allowing him to devote only evenings to the Candy Short murder. Of course that would reduce the likelihood of his solving the case, and Brejack told Nativo as much. Thanks to the older officer's diplomatic intervention, the change never went into effect. However, Swathmore's threat added urgency to Brejack's quest. Eager to keep moving, even when nothing new was turning up, Brejack recontacted sources, rephrased questions, and spent early evenings shooting the breeze with Fred and Helen. Continually reshuffling the deck, he hoped to deal himself a winning hand.

One afternoon at the Austins, the investigator heard what he perceived as good news. "John's in the hospital," Helen glumly told him. "Apparently he's had some kind of a nervous breakdown."

"All this pressure's finally getting to him," Brejack said, struggling to mask any hint of a victory smile.

"Will Jesse be all right?" Helen asked, her voice heavy with concern.

"Tell me where he is. I'll call down there and find out his status. Then I'll let you know what we can do about Jesse."

Upon returning to the office, Brejack telephoned the Jersey Shore Medical Center and told the patient-condition receptionist, "I'm a cousin of John Short's. I'm just calling to see how he's doing."

"Oh, Mr. Short is fine," she said, delighted to share

good news with a concerned family member. "He left here two days ago."

"That's just great," Brejack said, hiding his disappointment behind feigned ebullience.

"It's so nice when relatives call to see how our patients are doing."

"Yes," Brejack told her before he hung up. "It's nice to be nice."

Disappointed that he had lost the chance to somehow take advantage of his prey's vulnerability, George was still pleased to see the investigation generating enough intensity to affect Short so adversely. "Everywhere the prick looks, I'm there," he told Nativo. "You can't stand too much of that."

Apparently Short couldn't. Following his release from the hospital, he brutalized Judy to the point that she finally prepared to leave him. As usual, though, John convinced his wife to reconsider, even as his emotional condition steadily deteriorated. He spent most evenings at the go-go bars and turned increasingly sullen around the house.

While all of this remained consistent with John's prior behavior, and supported Brejack's contentions, it did nothing to provide the sort of information that Marty Kayne was demanding. Brejack had to find that on his own.

One evening during the early days of 1988, after everybody else in his department had left for the day, the investigator remained at his desk until after dark. Through the window, Paterson's nighttime streets seemed to have a creepy, desolate quality. Neon bar signs bathed the blacktop, and no pedestrians were visible. Brejack tuned his tabletop radio to WPAT and began inspecting several different snapshots of the Short domicile. Going through a routine that he now knew by heart, Brejack scrutinized the photos and tried to mentally recreate life on Joralemon Street. He saw the tweed couch, the clunky furniture, the bookcase in the corner of the apartment.

Brejack reached for the magnifying glass and trained it on the titles lined up in the living room. Nothing unusual there: a couple of Stephen King novels, a book on auto repair, building regulation guides, and a paperback about the Lamaze technique for delivering babies. Brejack stumbled over that last title like a drunk navigating a crack in the sidewalk. He had seen this photo hundreds of times and passed it by without a second thought. For some reason, though, it now gave him pause.

On its own, the book entitled *Thank You, Dr. Lamaze* meant nothing, but Brejack couldn't shake the feeling that the name Lamaze had some significance elsewhere in the investigation. He trusted his instincts and he knew that the most revealing details existed below the surface, deep down where meanings were difficult to discern. Brejack was tiptoeing through that sublime region when the telephone rang. Annoyed, he grabbed the receiver on the second ring.

"Prosecutor's office," he said tiredly, rubbing his eyes and partially grateful for a break from the intense head work.

"Hi, George. I just want to know when you'll be coming home. I'm making lamb chops."

Shit, it was Lisa, and he had forgotten to tell her that he'd be working late again. She had her boyfriend's favorite dish in the broiler, and obviously she looked forward to having dinner with him. Hearing her voice made Brejack want to go home. He belonged there; he yearned to be there. At this very moment, however, after thirteen hours at the office, Brejack was tottering on the brink of discovery. He could not quit just yet.

Keeping this case from becoming the number-one priority in his life proved impossible, and the relationship with Lisa had suffered. So wrapped up was George that he couldn't remember when they had last made love; Lisa would have been hard pressed to recall a recent conversation in which Candy's name had failed to come up. The way she saw it, George had sacrificed his life with a live woman for an obsession with a dead one.

"I'm sorry, Lisa," George said, his voice rich with heartfelt regret, "but I'm really tied up here. I just don't know when I'm going to be home tonight."

"Okay." She spoke in a flat, uninflected voice that told him it was anything but okay. "I'll just put your chops in the refrigerator. Dinner will be here when you get in."

"Thanks, Lisa." Brejack was ready to sign off and return to work, but he felt that something else had to be said. "Once this case is wrapped up, things will get back to normal. We'll spend more time together. It'll be like it used to be."

She told him she understood, then hung up the telephone. As George slipped back into the insulated cocoon of the Short case, it was clear that things would never be the same again. It was as if another woman had somehow come between them—sometimes she took the form of Candy, other times she was the job that he consistently brought home with him.

Eager to get back to the Shorts' living room, Brejack shrugged off the telephone conversation and reached for his magnifying glass. He inspected the photograph, and it continued to puzzle him. He had seen the name Lamaze before, and it tied directly into this case, but how? "Lamaze, Lamaze," he said out loud. "Where the fuck does that Lamaze come from?"

Brejack had only the vaguest idea of what the Lamaze technique actually was, but that didn't matter. He suddenly remembered that the name had to do with evidence discovered at the crime scene. Getting up from behind his desk and hustling through the tightly corridored halls of the prosecutor's office, Brejack made a beeline for the evidence room. He hoped to find something with the word Lamaze on it in one of the Ziploc bags stored there.

He had sorted through this material countless times

before, and come to know it well. This time, though, was different. This time Brejack was hoping to find something specific, something that had been previously overlooked or not recognized as significant. Tossing aside the five-cents-off coupons and the color snapshots of Jesse and Helen and Fred, he finally came across the right bag: It contained a business card for Susan Fishman's Lamaze classes. For a moment, Brejack's anticipatory high melted to disappointment. All this woman would be able to do, he figured, is offer additional confirmation about John's ineptitude as a husband. Maybe he wasn't really looking for this after all.

The investigator ran his fingers over the raised type and inspected the address on the bottom of the card: 351 Stone Drive, in West Orange. Then it hit him. "Holy shit!" Brejack whispered, his mind suddenly reeling with victory. "If Short went there for Lamaze training, then the cocksucker couldn't have gotten lost when he had to meet Jones on the same street!"

Before allowing himself to get too carried away, though, Brejack reined in his emotions. He acknowledged that the couple might not actually have taken classes on Stone Drive. Maybe Candy had only gone there to buy the book, or perhaps she had considered registering for Lamaze but never followed through. There were any number of possibilities. Brejack would explore them tomorrow morning. Then he would contact this woman, this Mrs. Susan Fishman, and find out how well she knew John and Candy.

By the time George got home to Lisa, his mind had come up with several plausible explanations for the card's presence. Though he recognized the futility of foraging into a future and past that he lacked the ability to control, he couldn't help himself. The investigator held to the superstition that by projecting positive emotions onto a situation he could somehow manipulate its outcome.

A movie of the week played on the television set, and Lisa sat erect on the couch. Munching from a bowl of popcorn, she stiffly greeted Brejack as he walked inside. "I put your lamb chops in the fridge," she told him, barely looking away from the set, trying to play down her unhappiness.

Brejack headed for the kitchen. He pulled a liter bottle of Pepsi out of the refrigerator, poured himself a glass full, then set the cold lamb chops on a plate with a glob of ketchup alongside them. Returning to the living room, he seated himself in a reclining easy chair and put his feet up, the plate resting in his lap. "What's the movie about?" George asked.

"Too complicated to explain now," Lisa said, eyes glued to the screen. "When a commercial comes on, I'll bring you up to date."

Brejack agreed to that, but he didn't really care. He believed that the scenes playing out in his mind were far more interesting than anything dreamed up in Hollywood.

Stone Drive was all but lined with money. Big, rustic houses with perfectly manicured lawns looked out onto the elevated, horseshoe-shaped street. Brejack passed the house of David Jones, the stone-and-masonry structure that John Short had visited on the night of Candy's murder. Then he proceeded to the top of the 'shoe and reached number 351, the Fishman residence.

He parked his car next to Susan's house and hesitated for a moment to collect his thoughts. Looking in the rearview mirror, he straightened his necktie before killing the ignition. Brejack made his way up the concrete path that led to the Fishmans' front door, admiring as he did so their lushly landscaped property. Inhaling the scent of freshly cut grass, Brejack told himself that it smelled like a golf course.

The telephone conversation with Susan Fishman remained fresh in Brejack's mind. Though she had acted pleasant and expressed a willingness to help with the investigation, Susan sounded dubious as to what she could contribute. "Didn't the Wayne police ever contact you?" Brejack asked, a little surprised.

She told the investigator that they hadn't and agreed to meet with him.

A vista of woodland surrounded the back of the house and a pair of tall bushes book-ended its front porch. Legal fees earned by David Fishman, one of Essex County's top trial attorneys, paid for the house and the upscale lifestyle that came with it. But his wife worked anyway, as she enjoyed teaching the Lamaze technique to young couples. Candy and John were among her first pupils, so she remembered them clearly. Candy, Susan had told George on the telephone, was a pleasant, upbeat, mother-to-be. The nurse recalled less about John.

Dwarfed by the shrubbery, Brejack pressed the bell and heard a melodic ding-dong. After a few seconds a Jamaican woman in a white uniform answered the door. For a second Brejack was taken aback; he had expected Susan Fishman to be Jewish. Then he realized that this woman was the maid.

"I'm Investigator George Brejack," he said, taking off his fedora while still outside. "Is Mrs. Fishman here, please?"

"She's expecting you," the maid said, leading Brejack inside. "Why don't you take a seat, and I'll let Mrs. Fishman know that you're here."

She brought him to a sitting room with a plushly cushioned couch and large windows that looked out onto the woods. Soothingly illuminated by the afternoon sunlight, it had a comfortably understated ambience. Brejack enjoyed this part of the job, gaining access to worlds he would never ordinarily be allowed into. Absorbing the sights and scents of wealth, George viewed the woods and silently wondered if deer grazed within eyeshot. It reminded him that he had missed the hunting season while working on this case.

Then he glanced up and saw Susan Fishman. An attractive auburn-haired woman in her mid-forties, she was dressed in wool slacks and a cotton sweater. Her comfort and poise immediately put Brejack at ease, even though the posh surroundings were as alien to him as the streets of downtown Paterson were to her.

"What can I do for you?" she asked, taking a seat alongside Brejack and offering him coffee or a cold drink.

Brejack told her that he wanted neither.

"What exactly is Lamaze?" he wondered, curious as to how the process worked and eager to savor this heady moment of anticipation.

"It's a course that couples take when they're expecting a baby. It helps them understand what's going to be happening during the pregnancy, labor, and delivery. Ultimately there's less stress, less pain, and the father actually coaches and supports the mother throughout the pregnancy."

"And John and Candy were learning this, ah, Lamaze."

Susan nodded.

"How often did they come here?"

"One night a week for seven weeks."

Brejack had brought along several photos. He was nervously fingering one of them when Susan's voice suddenly jumped an octave, as if she had just remembered something important. She handed the investigator an index card with dates and times written on it. "It shows exactly when their classes were held."

Brejack inspected the card and felt a flash of confidence. According to Susan's records Candy and John had taken the lessons during January and February of 1979. That meant that John Short had managed to find Stone Drive even on the darkest nights of the year. Considering that fact, how could he have gotten lost in the area during the dusky daylight of an early summer evening only two years later? Now Brejack hoped that Susan remembered John well enough to pick the suspect's face out of a lineup. From his stack of photographic evidence, George selected a piece of oak tag with head shots pasted on it. He passed this to Susan Fishman.

"I want you to tell me if one man on there is John Short."

She pointed him out immediately. "I remember him very distinctly now," she said. "That's him."

"You're sure?"

"Yes." Susan Fishman thought for a moment, trying to recall something specific about the couple. Then she told Brejack, "After Candy had her baby she called to tell me the exact time and date of the little girl's birth. Jesse, right?"

Brejack nodded.

"Why are you so interested in John Short in relation to his wife's murder?" Susan wanted to know.

"He's a suspect," Brejack said before thanking her and taking his leave.

Since he had known he'd be in the neighborhood, Brejack had made arrangements to visit with David Jones as well. Located down the block from the Fishmans, Jones's home was solid-looking. It sprawled wide and low, with a brick-and-granite facade. Jones, a distinguished, well-dressed, real estate man in his mid-forties, greeted Brejack at the door and ushered him into his study. From the chair on which he nestled his frame, George saw a patch of woods very much like those that bordered the Fishmans' home. This time, though, he noticed deer grazing in the yard.

Jones sensed the investigator's interest. "Every year I spend a small fortune having the back of my house landscaped. And without fail, those deer come over here to eat the plants." He chuckled, somehow enjoying the irony in that, then added, "Sometimes I feel like my backyard is the animal version of McDonalds."

Brejack appreciated that line, and found Jones to be a charming man. Unfortunately, however, he had not yet cooperated to the extent that Brejack desired. Up till now his typical response to every question had been a polite suggestion that they refer to the Wayne Police Department's notes. Jones insisted that he had told the first group of cops everything he knew. Over the last six years, he maintained, the facts remained unchanged.

True to form, Jones clammed up as soon as the subject shifted to Short. While he obviously felt sorry for the Austins, admired Brejack's tenacity, and might even have championed John's indictment, getting involved in a murder trial was the last thing that any man in David Jones's position wanted to do. He had a wide range of business concerns and his own life to consider. Becoming tangled up in a legal hornet's nest couldn't possibly lead to anything good.

Jones's wife Deborah, a trim, well-built, forty-something woman, joined them in the study. She brought a 7-Up for Brejack and a glass of water for herself. David drank nothing. A smart no-nonsense man, he obviously wanted to get this over with and have as few hassles as possible. As he had done during a previous interview with Brejack, Jones managed to be subtly evasive.

"How did you know John Short?" Brejack asked.

"It was strictly a business relationship," replied Jones. "I own a building in downtown Newark and John had done some light construction work there."

"What was he doing in your house on the night of June 22nd?"

"Satisfied with what he had done in my office building, I inquired about his working for me here. I wanted a deck for the back of my house, a few little things built for the inside, and some repairs needed to be done on the roof."

Brejack glanced back to where the deer had been grazing, and noticed that Jones had never bothered commissioning somebody else to build the deck.

"When did John originally plan to come by?"

"He agreed to meet me here between six and six-thirty. I wanted it to be light outside, so that I could show John exactly what needed to be done. I wanted him to look at the house and give me an estimate in terms of time and money."

"Was this the first instance in which John would have come to your home?"

"Yes."

"Did you have to give him directions?"

"Yes. We made the plans about a week before the 22nd, and I gave him traveling instructions at that time."

He confirmed at the last minute John had tried to postpone the meeting for another day, citing impending thunder storms. But Jones wanted to get together that night, and Short had grudgingly agreed to be there by eight-thirty or nine. In fact he pulled up to Jones's house in his parents' Pinto at about nine-fifteen. Recounting the story, Jones shook his head and said, "It was too dark for us to go outside and look at the house. And that's precisely why John was supposed to come here in the first place."

"Did John tell you that he got lost on his way to your home?" Brejack asked hopefully.

"I don't remember any talk like that."

"How was John dressed that evening?"

"I don't remember," Jones said, obviously growing tired of the questioning.

"I remember," his wife chimed in. "John wore a short-sleeved white shirt and chinos. He looked good."

Now Brejack asked the million-dollar question: "How did John behave?"

As innocuous as the question sounded, the investigator really wanted to know whether John Short had acted like a man who just strangled his wife to death in the parking lot of a shopping mall. But neither of the Joneses provided the answer he hoped for. Instead, they remembered nothing at all unusual about John. He seemed like a blue-collar worker checking out a job site. Nothing more, nothing less.

"The only odd thing," Jones acknowledged, "is that he never gave us an estimate. Not that night, and not ever." He gestured outside and admitted, "We never got around to having the back deck constructed, although another contractor fixed our drains and completed the interior work."

"Did John discuss anything about his family when he came here?"

"He told us that he had a two-year-old daughter," Deborah said. "But that was about it."

"Did Candy's name come up at all?"

They both thought about this for a moment, then Deborah remembered something. "He mentioned that his wife had gone shopping that night. On his way out John said something about having to pick up his daughter at the babysitter's house. I found it odd that his wife would be out shopping so late at night—it was around eleven o'clock when he left—but naturally, I didn't think very much of it."

"Did you have many dealings with John after the murder?"

"No," Jones stated. "None at all."

Satisfied that he had coaxed as much out of the Joneses as he could, Brejack thanked the real-estate man and his wife for their time. He and David stood at the front door of the house as Deborah went to get the investigator's coat. With the pressure off, David let his guard down and allowed a semi-amused smile to play across his face.

"I've got to hand it to you, George," he said. "You are an extraordinarily persistent man."

"If you ever get to know me, Mr. Jones, one thing you'll discover is that I never quit."

Jones nodded appreciatively and both men remained silent until Deborah showed up with the coat and hat. Brejack buttoned up his tan trench, turned to the couple and said good-bye, then headed to his Volvo parked at the curb of the fancy house.

On February 2nd, George Brejack got his grand jury. His panel of twenty-three men and women who occupied an empty courtroom spent five hours listening to a recitation of Brejack's findings. No judge presided, nor were spectators permitted to watch. Chief Assistant Prosecutor Marty Kayne made the presentation, and the panel of citizens (none of whom had experience in law enforcement) heard the evidence so that they could decide whether John Short should be indicted for the murder of his wife.

Brejack waited in the hallway outside of the courtroom. Trying to imagine Marty Kayne in action, he envisioned the attorney dismantling the chain of circumstantial evidence. In Brejack's mind, every link was tossed on a table for detailed examination, so that each member of the grand jury could see the craftsmanship that had gone into producing it. If, after hearing all of the information and seeing the reports and evidence, they reconstructed that length of steel, viewed its links as being unbreakable, then John Short would be indicted.

Nativo had already agreed that the arrest should happen as soon as possible, before Short got wind of it. Who knows what a man might do when he's desperate and terrified?

As is customary with a grand jury hearing, Brejack entered the courtroom only when his testimony was required. He spent the remainder of the day waiting outside the door. Andrew Webster and Jim Wilson sat across the hall from him. They too were among the police officers who had been called in for questioning this afternoon.

Not surprisingly, few words passed between the three men. For the most part, Brejack sat in his hard-back chair and sipped from a bottomless cup of black coffee. A couple of reporters he knew stopped by to snoop around and ask what was going on. Brejack revealed hardly anything at all, but he allowed that something big could be in the making.

They nodded and sporadically visited the upstairs room. Between chats with them, Brejack read the paper and realized the tiny degree of control he now had over the outcome. The investigator knew that he had gathered as much evidence against John Short as possible, had done his job; now the rest was up to Marty. Occasionally he glanced up from his paper and caught the eye of Webster or Wilson. Ten feet away, the pair discreetly conversed in a tight little knot. Brejack figured that their words centered on him, yet he felt powerless to curtail the talk.

Instead of speaking to them, George spoke to God; *Please, let them come back with an indictment for murder. I want to really give those pricks something to whisper about.*

Closing his eyes, Brejack thought of Max Swathmore. He fantasized about the old man following through on his promise to eat the paper that the indictment warrant would be written on. Brejack saw his father and John Short merging into a single figure of domestic evil. He thought about arresting the latter and paying distant retribution to the former. He'd be able to permanently bury bad memories of his old man, and the circle would be complete. On top of that was the respect he hoped to gain within the Passaic County Prosecutor's Office. Those who had once doubted Brejack's skills as an investigator would now have to accept his ability to break the big cases that nobody else could.

All of these things swirled in and out of Brejack's psyche as he waited for an answer. Finally, after five hours, at three o'clock in the afternoon, Marty Kayne emerged from behind closed doors. Brejack looked up expentantly, but the chief assistant prosecutor had very little to offer in the way of news.

"George," he said, "they've got all the information. Now they'll make a decision. Nothing to do at this point but keep our fingers crossed." He pointed across the hall to the men's room. "I'm going to take a leak. I'll be right back."

Five minutes after he returned from the bathroom,

Kayne was summoned back into court. "They must have a question," he told George, once again disappearing behind closed doors. Tension coursed through Brejack as he waited for the lawyer to finish up with the grand jury.

A minute later he did. "Something very unusual has just happened," Kayne said. "They've indicted him for murder. It's extraordinarily rare for a grand jury to come back with an indictment so quickly."

Pride and confidence overwhelmed Brejack, but he tried (unsuccessfully) to play it cool. "Of course it didn't take them long," he told Marty Kayne. "Look at the information we had to work with. I've constructed a beautiful case for you people."

Brejack went back into the courtroom to gather his papers, and a few grand jury members congratulated him on having put together such a convincing argument for the indictment of John Short. After thanking them, Brejack had no time to bask in the glory. He wanted to head right back to the prosecutor's office and start making plans for the arrest. As he'd told Nativo the day before, "I want this to go down nice. No surprises, no violence. We get the motherfucker out of his house, into the car, and we bring him here to a cell. No problem."

Just how much of a problem it might actually be, however, was on Brejack's mind as he made his way out of the courtroom. Not only did John seem unstable, but he had Jesse. During a recent visit with the Austins, Brejack had assured them that their granddaughter would emerge from this unscathed. If Judy seemed less than fit to care for the girl, Brejack had guaranteed Fred and Helen that Jesse would be delivered to the house on Passaic Avenue. Under no conditions, he assured them, would their granddaughter be placed in a foster care situation. Considering the support that the Austins had lent him, he owed the couple that much at least. Now Brejack hoped to make good on his promise.

He swung open the heavy wooden doors that separated

the courtroom from the lobby, nodded happily to the marshal seated at a desk there, and encountered a couple of reporters who wondered what was going on.

"Can't tell you," Brejack said with a shrug. "But it might be worth your while to get the information elsewhere. Like I said before, something interesting could be happening tonight."

Brejack revealed nothing else. Already he had told them more than he should have. But what the hell, he was in good spirits, and a little bit of positive publicity never hurt anyone. He hustled down the steps, planning on taking the short walk back to his office, when he encountered Wilson and Webster in the parking lot.

"I'm going to go with you tonight when you make the arrest," Wilson said, neglecting even to congratulate George on the good news.

"No you ain't," Brejack responded. "This isn't your case anymore. I don't want anybody going down there who doesn't have a clear reason for being there."

A combination of disgust and disappointment shadowed Wilson's face as he absorbed the news. Brejack did not feel like sharing the publicity or the credit with anybody else. While it might have been a courtesy worth extending had Wilson been more cooperative during the investigation, Brejack believed that under the current circumstances he owed the man nothing.

Back at his office, he arranged the trip to Ocean Grove. Five officers would pile into a pair of cars for the two-hour drive. Brejack wanted such a large group in case John Short got out of hand. It wasn't so much that the investigator feared getting hurt, but he wanted enough people there to keep John from turning violent in front of Jesse.

Late that afternoon, two unmarked cars pulled out of the police garage and proceeded toward the Garden State Parkway, the highway that led to their quarry.

As they passed the same scenery that John Short had taken in on his trip down there with Judy in early 1982,

Brejack tuned in WPAT on the car radio and simultaneously enjoyed the static-y babble of activity on the police band. Adrenalized with anticipation, Brejack experienced a heady rush of glee, realizing that his gift for investigating and solving major crimes had not been lost. Turning to John Nativo, Brejack said, "The magic is back. This bust is going to be sweet; it's going down like sugar."

Always on the cautious side, Nativo considered tempering George's enthusiasm, but decided to say nothing. This time, Brejack was on enough of a roll that he just might be right.

CHAPTER
16

As Brejack and his posse proceeded downstate, John Short's mind imploded upon itself. The process had begun long before the investigator became involved in the case. But the Neptune Township Police Department, which counted Ocean Grove as part of its jurisdiction, had only recently begun chronicling John Short's emotional unraveling. According to the department's filings, his growing violence first became public record at 3:01 P.M. on Christmas day in 1987.

During the preceding weeks tension had been escalating in the Short household. Money ran low, substance abuse increased, and holiday spirit eluded John. As Helen had done in the past, Judy's mother brought gifts for the kids; her son-in-law spent the eve of December 25th on a drinking binge. As Christmas day broke, John had yet to return home. While his children tore open their presents, he was still intoxicated from the night before and becoming drunker by the minute.

When he finally arrived home for what was supposed to be a late-afternoon dinner, Short was rip-roaring drunk. He announced his arrival by banging loudly on the door before letting himself in. "Merry Christmas," Judy said hopefully as John stumbled toward the kitchen.

Drunk and on the edge of a rampage, he loudly berated his wife.

"Where the fuck is my money?" Short wanted to know.

Judy stepped out from behind the stove, an apron tied around her waist. He grabbed the glass of Jack Daniels that she had been sipping from and downed it in a swallow.

"John," Judy told him. "I don't know what you're talking about."

"You know what I'm talking about. It's all going down the drain."

When Judy attempted to calm John down, he responded by pushing her against the wall. Slapping and kicking at his wife, John railed about their dwindling savings and his declining business. He cried and screamed, and Judy recalled the time last month when he suffered a nervous breakdown.

Had she not been on the receiving end of John's vitriol, Judy would probably have pitied him. The beating momentarily let up as John wheeled around and saw the platter on which the family's Christmas dinner rested. He grabbed its rim and threw the dish to the floor. Broken glass and turkey and brown gravy slid across the kitchen linoleum. John stepped in a puddle of gravy and let out a wail of frustration as he slipped and almost lost his balance. Footing regained, he smashed his open hand against the side of Judy's face.

The three kids scampered up to a bedroom as the fight grew heated enough that a neighbor heard it and called the police. By the time a patrol car arrived, the argument had moved outside. The violence had subsided, but John continued to yell in his bullying tone. Turning around and noticing two policemen approaching, he quickly simmered down and eyed them suspiciously. While he expected something bad, Short had been through so much lately that he didn't know how much worse it could get. John's only break was that neither cop happened to be George Brejack.

"Mr. Short," one of them said. "You've got to take it easy."

The other officer took Judy's arm, handling it like a

boat's rudder and steering her inside. By separating the couple, the cop created enough space for John and Judy to regain their composure.

Playing the role of the innocent, Judy said that John came into the house drunk and angry and that he began hitting her for no reason. In a separate conversation, John maintained that his wife wasted all of his money on drugs. Patrolman Mike Ferranti knew enough about Judy to suspect that there might be at least an element of truth in John's allegations, but he kept it to himself. From what he saw they both appeared intoxicated—though the altercation served to sober John up—and probably shared the blame.

As he typically did with victims of domestic violence, Ferranti sat down alongside Judy and explained her rights.

"You can press charges if you want," he told her.

She promised to stop by police headquarters the next day and do so. As Ferranti departed, Judy wearily stood up and proceeded to clean the mess that had been made in the course of the beating.

Heading outside, Ferranti saw John standing in front of the house. Leaning against his Lincoln and dragging on a cigarette, he seemed oblivious to the cold. "She denied what you told me," Ferranti said. "She claims that you came home drunk and were spoiling for a fight."

Short said nothing.

"Whatever happened, it seems to be over now," the patrolman continued. "If you have somewhere else to go for tonight, it probably would be best if you went there."

Tacitly agreeing, John got into his automobile and took off. He drove away from the house and in the direction of a strip of go-go bars. Perhaps he imagined that one of them would still be open as Christmas day turned into night.

During the month of January, the domestic squabbles increased in intensity and regularity. John's temper became quicker; Judy's ability to cope with the outbursts expired. Finally, after an argument that showed John's most violent side, Judy believed that she had no choice but to leave. She packed her bags and did the very thing that she had threatened to do so many times before.

But after a few days she came back. The marriage had been shaken at its foundation and its chances for survival seemed remote, yet Judy was not quite ready to give up. This on again/off again acceptance by his wife contributed to John's shaky emotional condition. Between his professional and personal lives, everything seemed to be falling apart. Debt-ridden and plagued by the mishandling of funds, the contracting business was on the edge of bankruptcy. John knew it would go the way of everything else, and he would be left with nothing.

He expressed this sentiment during the late morning of February 1st, when he went to the nearby Midlantic Bank to get a full reading on his finances. It all looked unbearably grim. He sat down in the cubicle belonging to Patricia Stone, the officer who handled many local business accounts. She explained to him that his credit rating was shot, and expressed concern about the speed with which he seemed to be exhausting the corporate account. Short, after all, had outstanding loans with the bank, so she had a vested interest in his solvency.

"I will not put up with things the way they are now," he told her matter-of-factly.

"What do you plan on doing about it?"

"Who knows, maybe you'll read about me in the paper tomorrow. That would make all the shits happy, wouldn't it?"

Short quickly got up to leave and didn't cause too much of a scene in the bank. Yet his implied threat of suicide or homicide or *something* horrible disturbed Patricia enough that she contacted the police. However, when two officers showed up at the contracting business, an agitated John Short demanded that they immediately leave the premises. They complied, then proceeded back to the bank with the intention of speaking to Patricia Stone.

She was not alone. William Milne, Short's foreman, also was waiting there. He too expressed concern for John Short's safety. "John's talked about this nine-millimeter pistol he owns," Milne explained, "and he kept telling me that he wants to get his affairs in order."

You didn't need to be a master sleuth to realize that these were the words and actions of somebody contemplating killing himself. Or at any rate, somebody who wanted everybody to *think* he was considering the act. After Milne went back to the office, where he could keep an eye on his boss, a policeman was dispatched to the Shorts' Ocean Grove home.

Judy could not have been completely surprised to see a cop at her front door. She let him in and he began questioning her about John's recent behavior. "John made out a will not too long ago," she explained. "Last week he told me that he wanted to be on the safe side. He's been drinking heavily and has been particularly upset about problems with the business. He's so tense that it's causing friction at home as well."

"Do you think he'd be capable of harming you or the kids?"

Judy shrugged, and the officer suggested that she spend the next couple of nights elsewhere, maybe with a friend or relative. Later in the day, Judy made plans to take her two biological children to her sister's house. As usual, Jesse stayed with her father.

That evening, as he did every Monday night, John Short bowled with some friends. Though he seemed distracted, he managed to roll three reasonably good games. Nothing seemed particularly unusual, until it came time to leave. Then John handed a teammate his ball and bag. "I won't be needing this anymore and I want you to have it," he said.

She accepted the equipment and waited until John was out of earshot before placing a call to the police. She asked that somebody check up on him, and once again a patrol car was dispatched to the home in Ocean Grove. Sergeant William Ritter arrived there to find the television on and John Short relaxing in his living room.

The man seemed as pleasant as could be, and he gave away none of the thoughts that were seething inside his brain.

After work on February 2nd, John and Jesse were home alone. Accepting the policeman's advice, Judy had taken her children to spend a few nights with her sister.

Ten-year-old Jesse had no qualms about being on her own with her father. She was a sensitive, caring child who possessed the maturity to see that John was in no condition to be by himself. Distracted and obviously upset, he sat in the living room and stared at the television set. Newspapers, soda glasses, clothing, and empty beer bottles were scattered around him, but he didn't care. John now lived with the emotional depth of a zombie. Simply getting through the day seemed to be as much of a struggle as he could handle. At work that afternoon, he acted moody and preoccupied. Upon arriving home the day before and discovering a note from Judy, which stated that she'd be away for most of the week, John had given vent to none of his characteristic rage.

On the night of the 2nd, father and daughter ate together and watched the five o'clock news on TV. Neither of them said very much. It was one of John's silent evenings, and when he acted that way people knew better than to get him worked up. There was never any telling what he might do. That may have been one reason Jesse retreated to the kitchen, where she sat at a table and drew pictures on a sheet of white paper. That's what she was doing at a few minutes before six o'clock when four officers approached the back door and knocked gently.

Jesse opened it, and they walked inside.

"Is your father here?" one of the county investigators asked.

"Yes," said Jesse.

As soon as the words escaped her mouth, the men stepped around her and went after John. Jesse cried a little bit but mostly sat very still, very stunned, eager to stay out of everybody's way.

The sudden siege came as a shock to both father and daughter. One minute the house was silent and still. The next minute cops were everywhere, swarming like army ants at a picnic. Law enforcers barged in through both entrances. In sync with the county guys, two local policemen scooted around the blotchy lawn, intending to block John's possible escape through the rear. After hearing about his recent suicide bids, and realizing that Short had both his daughter and the nine-millimeter pistol in the house, all concerned approached him cautiously. Everybody wanted to avoid a shootout with a man who might be desperate enough to use his daughter as a shield.

Wearing his lucky fedora, Brejack led the attack through the front. For a moment or two he figured that the door would need to be broken down, then he turned the knob and it opened easily. That's when troops charged in from all sides. As they burst through the kitchen and entered the living room, George already had his gun trained on John. Wasting no time, he began reading him his Miranda Rights.

"You are under arrest and charged with the murder of Candy Short on the evening of June 22, 1981," he shouted in clear, concise syllables as another cop snapped a pair of handcuffs shut over John's wrists. Spoken words had never sounded quite so good to the ears of George Brejack. "You have the right to remain silent. If you give up . . ."

Other cops checked the living room. They searched for weapons but found nothing within the immediate vicinity. The Neptune policemen might have been curious to toss the house for drugs, but the warrant applied only to the arrest of John Short. It permitted nothing more than a cursory look around the area near where he had been seated.

Cautiously, they sorted through items within reach and found nothing that could be considered dangerous or illegal. In fact, for all the planning and caution that had gone into making the arrest, John himself appeared to be remarkably docile. Dressed in a flannel shirt and blue jeans, with a bushy, overgrown beard masking his face, he looked tired and drawn. As Brejack read him his rights Short acted relieved, as if this were the inevitable conclusion to a long and tedious cat-and-mouse game.

Slowly getting up from his chair, he allowed himself to be led out to an investigator's sedan that idled at curbside. As her father left, Jesse, wearing jeans and a T-shirt, remained immobile in the kitchen. All the tumult and action left the little girl shocked and shaking as her world once again turned upside-down. First her mother died, and now her father was being taken away in handcuffs. Brejack couldn't help but recall his own final paternal memory. In both instances, nothing was what it was supposed to be.

Jim Wilson would have been pleased. The scenario that he had depicted for John six and a half years ago in the Wayne Police Department's interrogation room proved to be surprisingly accurate. As Wilson had predicted, the arrest came at a time when Short least expected it, and the incident exposed his daughter to a side of her father that no child should ever see. The sight of Jesse alone in the kitchen caused Brejack to remember the phone call he had placed to the Austins a few minutes before heading south.

True to his word, George made sure that Jesse wound up with Fred and Helen and not in a foster home. Standard procedures dictated that under the circumstances she should have been placed in the state's care. Had that happened, however, the Austins would have had a difficult time gaining custody. For their sake, George had asked one of the investigators from the prosecutor's office to scoop the girl up and drop her off with her grandparents. Jesse left in a car bound for Belleville while Brejack and John Nativo took Short to the Neptune police station for booking.

They hustled him in through a back door, grateful that wind of the arrest had not yet reached the media. It would be best to keep things as quiet as possible. At least that was the way most of the cops saw it. Brejack expected a crowd of reporters to greet them in Paterson. He had told the guys in the courthouse just enough to whet their appetites and make them eager to find out more. Yet he was also careful not to reveal so much that he could have jeopardized the arrest.

At Neptune police headquarters the appropriate officers signed the papers that officially made John Short a prisoner of Passaic County. "Do you want to call your lawyer?" one of his captors asked.

"No," Short replied, sounding dazed. "He's not in his office now."

A dense rain began to fall as the group of lawmen led their suspect out of the police station and into the backseat of the car. Everybody, including Short, acted inappropriately congenial. It was as if he had suddenly accepted that Brejack and the other cops were simply doing their jobs. A half hour beyond Neptune they stopped at a Parkway rest area. One of the cops ran into the Roy Rogers there and picked up four cups of coffee to go.

They proceeded back onto the highway and made small talk about the inclement weather. Nativo expressed relief that it wasn't snowing, and John responded, "It never snows down here."

For Brejack it was all too calm, too anticlimactic, not nearly confrontational enough after the months of work that had gone into solving this case and getting an indictment warrant for Short. "Now we're discussing the goddamned weather with this guy?" he softly muttered. "Shit."

But Brejack kept his feelings quiet. The last thing he wanted was to provoke an altercation with Short that would somehow queer the arrest and spoil the investigation.

Finally, after finishing his coffee—managing to sip it with his hands cuffed in front—and dropping the styrofoam cup to the floor of the backseat, John Short made it easy for Brejack. He provided the conversational gambit that the investigator himself wanted to initiate. Looking down at his lap, Short said, "I can't believe this is happening. What have you guys got on me?"

"John, a grand jury, a panel of twenty-three impartial people indicted you for the murder of your wife Candy," Nativo patiently explained, speaking in the patronizing tone that's usually reserved for a small child. "That happened today."

Stewing in the front seat, Brejack could no longer hold himself back. He turned his head and locked eyes with this man that he had gotten to know so well during the course of the investigation. In anticipation of what they knew would be coming, the other cops looked away and discreetly smirked. "John, your fucking *friends* signed statements against you," Brejack said in a terse, pissed-off voice. "We got eyewitnesses who saw you and Candy in the mall together. We've identified the key chain that was found underneath Candy's body. You remember that key chain, don't you John? It's a little white plastic thing shaped like a T-shirt?"

"I don't know nothing about a key chain," Short said, attempting to put across the same attitude that had worked so effectively with McCann and Webster and Wilson.

"How can you know nothing about it? You told the Wayne police that they were Candy's keys. Now you forgot about them or something?"

"I don't know anything about them. I don't know what you guys have on me that you can come into my house and try to destroy my life."

Brejack wanted to scramble over the front seat and

take care of John himself. Instead he settled for hollering in the suspect's face. "Know what we got? Know what we got, motherfucker? We have a statement from Diane Lovejoy. We found her in Pittsburgh, and she's a very nice lady. She talked a lot about you, John, about how you told her that your wife was stabbed, beaten, and strangled and left dead in a car. You told her that on June 15, 1981, a week before your wife actually died under those very circumstances. Do you remember that, scumbag? Does that ring any bells, motherfucker?"

For one of the few times in his life, John Short found himself at a loss for words. For a moment or two he momentarily stared straight back in the investigator's face. Then something strange happened. It was as if volts of electricity had suddenly been let loose through John Short's veins. His body convulsed. His arms and legs shook. His lips curled into a jerky expression. "Ungh, ungh," was the only sound that escaped from his mouth as a trail of spittle dribbled down his chin.

Brejack turned away and looked smug. Now he was satisfied. This was the sort of reaction he had expected to get from John Short. George thought about Fred discovering Candy on the floor of the car, and remembered the beatings that his mother had sustained at the hands of another John. The gibberish emanating from Short's mouth did nothing to compromise Brejack's feeling of victory. He only hoped that John would still be emotionally fragile by the time they reached the prosecutor's office. If so, maybe they'd be able to get a confession from him that night.

The rain continued beating down on the car as they progressed up the highway and into the county. Unable to keep from taking a final swipe, Brejack turned around and asked, "Hey, motherfucker, why don't you talk about the weather now?"

John Short said nothing.

The shaking subsided as his mind noticeably wandered. Trying to get as far away from this situation as possible, he attempted to ignore the world around him. John almost succeeded at it, too, until they pulled up in front of the prosecutor's office. There the reality of his plight became unavoidably intrusive. A cluster of newsmen, note pads and camera flashes at the ready, awaited them. Brejack bathed in the glow of strobe, pinning his eyes straight ahead, remembering that heroes never smile for the camera, as he led his prisoner up the steps.

Ten days after his arrest John Short walked out of the Passaic County Jail. His mother used the Ocean Grove house as collateral to raise the two-hundred-and-fifty-thousand-dollar bail, and Short retained Patrick Caserta to represent him in the trial scheduled to take place on September 9, 1988, at the Passaic County Courthouse. A former attorney with the prosecutor's office, thirty-eight-year-old Caserta handled a large percentage of drug cases, and murder hardly ranked as his specialty. But since John Short was already a client—Caserta had represented him in a minor civil skirmish—he agreed to accept the case.

The two men met in Caserta's office in downtown Paterson and discussed the tack that they would take in the trial. While he clearly hoped to win the case, the attorney's confidence was somewhat buoyed by the statute of limitations. He hoped that even if a jury found Short guilty, the charge would be manslaughter rather than murder. Were that to happen, the defendant would go free. He told his client this, and Short seemed a bit relieved.

Even as John Short began to feel reasonably secure with the situation, however, his problems were just beginning. For one thing he had slipped hopelessly into debt, and now found himself in the midst of a cash-flow crisis. Over four hundred thousand dollars in money owed to him by clients remained outstanding, and since his arrest many of those clients had simply refused to pay. John filed for bankruptcy, and realized that it would be a long time before he ever again owned a contracting business. Besides the financial burden, subtler problems plagued him as well. With Jesse gone and the law closed in all around him, John Short became not only monetarily broke but emotionally bankrupt as well.

Judy moved back to Ocean Grove with him, and his parents offered financial aid, but the future looked increasingly bleak. Had he known what Brejack was up to, John Short would have had even more reason to fret. Acknowledging the likelihood that John could escape conviction due to the statute of limitations, Brejack did what he could to plug up any remaining cracks in his case. While Short remained in jail, George traveled down to South Jersey and snooped around, hoping to find somebody who could tell him something incriminating.

Considering all of John's financial troubles, the Midlantic National Bank looked like a good place to start. At ten o'clock on the morning of February 9th, Brejack pulled into the parking lot that wrapped around the building, with its drive-through window and pair of A.T.M. machines, then ventured inside. Patricia Stone, the banking officer with whom John usually dealt, awaited him at her desk. She repeated the same story she had told the Neptune Township Police about John's despondent state. Brejack listened attentively, as if hearing the information for the first time.

"Do you know John's wife very well?" Brejack inquired.

"Not really," Stone told him initially. Then, after a moment of thought, the banker remembered a conversation that she and Judy had had just prior to the wedding. "It was odd, but she told me that John was a violent man and that he beat her on a regular basis. After hearing that, I paid more attention to him and noticed that he frequently had alcohol on his breath." She mulled over the implications of all this, then added, "Considering the way his finances had fallen apart, I can't say that I was completely surprised to hear him talking about suicide a couple of weeks ago."

"Did he ever mention anything to you about his second wife?"

"Never," Stone said, explaining that she and John had had limited dealings with one another. "But I do remember John having a conversation like that with a man named Kevin Johnson. Mr. Johnson is one of our loan officers, and he mentioned to me that John told him his wife had been murdered."

Johnson was obviously Brejack's man. The investigator found out that he worked at a different branch and obtained Kevin Johnson's direct line. A few minutes of conversation left Brejack eager to learn more. They set an appointment for February 17th, and Johnson suggested that Wayne Williams, another vice president at the bank, be present as well. He too had dealt with Short.

Brejack arrived early on the appointed day, eager to speak with these men who might provide further inconsistencies in John Short's telling of the events that had happened on the night of June 22nd at Willowbrook Mall. Dressed conservatively in a dark blue suit, Brejack introduced himself to the bankers and accepted the cup of coffee that Johnson's secretary offered.

"I'd like to discuss the conversation that you and John Short had about the death of his first wife," Brejack began.

"I don't remember anything about it," Williams immediately said, and for a moment Brejack feared that both men would clam up. Then Johnson came forward with the information that he had hinted at during their telephone conversation a week ago.

"Before John Short moved down here, I handled a business loan for him and asked why he was moving to the Jersey shore area," Johnson began. "He told me that he was trying to get back on his feet, that he wanted to make a clean start of things after his wife's murder."

"Did John tell you anything about the murder?"

"He mentioned that I probably read about it in the newspaper—which I hadn't. John told me that he and his wife had gone shopping together and split up once they got to the mall. They were supposed to meet one another later on. When his wife didn't return, John found out that she had been tragically murdered."

"Did he tell you when this was supposed to have taken place?"

"In broad daylight, during the Christmas season." Johnson looked away for a moment and appeared to be recounting the story in his mind before he added, "It sounded horrible. He cried as he told me about the incident. The whole thing seemed to upset him so much that it pained me to hear it."

"Was there anything else that John told you about Candy?"

"Only that they were high school sweethearts."

"Did John receive the business loan?"

"Yes."

"How big of a role did the situation with his wife play in his approval?"

"No role at all, Investigator Brejack. We don't give out loans based on people's personal tragedies."

Sensing that he may have offended the banker, Brejack told him that he understood. What Brejack didn't reveal was the importance of the information, which marked the first time that John had admitted being with Candy at Willowbrook Mall when she was murdered.

Steven Brizek read the case files with care. A small-framed, dark-haired, cautious and fastidious man, he saw this as his big chance to make a name within the prosecutor's office. Like Brejack, thirty-nine-year-old Brizek found the Short murder appealing partly because it promised a share of the glory that had as yet eluded him. Beyond the legal challenge of a high-profile circumstantial case, it would be his first murder—a fact that he had managed to keep from the investigator.

Upon meeting Brizek for the first time and finding out that he would be handling the case, Brejack responded with his usual enthusiasm. "Brizek, Brizek," he said, speaking like a man in deep thought. "That sounds like a Slovak name. Are you a Slovak?"

"Well, yeah," responded the lawyer, who had only recently returned to the prosecutor's office after a short stint in the private sector.

"Beautiful!" Brejack jubilantly told him. "So am I. With a couple of Slovaks working this case, we can't lose." Walking down the office corridor with Brizek at his side, Brejack cried out. "All *right*! Goddamned Slovaks are taking over this joint!"

Remaining true to character, Brizek said nothing. He simply smiled with a mix of sheepishness and embarrassment. In the courtroom he eschewed lawyerly histrionics for quiet, intensely focused dignity. Away from the bench he seemed downright shy.

Together, the two men made an odd and unlikely pair. The physical contrasts alone were startling: Brizek was slightly built, combed his dark hair over a bald patch, and leaned toward a loose-fitting, overly formal wardrobe. An aficionado of art and literature, Brizek quoted from Dickens and painted on weekends. His hero was Abraham Lincoln—a self-rendered oil of the sixteenth president hung above his desk—and he valued truth above all else.

As a youth, Brizek sang in the church choir and spent Sunday mornings serving at mass as a lector and Eucharistic minister. He grew up a loner, more concerned with schoolwork than with outside activities, and had few friendly dealings with rough-and-tumble Brejack types. In the Navy he made the rank of lieutenant, and cultivated an obsession for doing everything by the book. Brejack, conversely, spent as much time operating in the gray area as he did anywhere else. However, for all their differences (or more precisely, because of them) Brejack and Brizek complemented one another; each one compensated for what the other lacked.

After his visit with Johnson, Brejack came bounding

into Steve Brizek's office and blurted out the news. "I spoke to somebody who caught John Short in a lie! Short made his biggest fucking mistake when he spoke to this guy!"

"Oh, yeah?" Brizek said, fingering a silver-plated Parker pen. He looked skeptical as he asked, "What kind of a lie?"

"This guy Kevin Johnson, he made a business loan to John Short, and he recalled Short telling him that he went to the mall with his wife on the night of the murder. It's the first time he told that to anybody."

"Interesting," Brizek said, remaining outwardly unmoved. "We get a few more breaks like that and we'll be in great shape."

"We're in great shape already, Steve. This case was made for you to handle. You've got a beautiful situation here. It's open-and-shut. John Short is definitely going down the pipe. He's going to jail for killing his wife. You mark my words."

"I hope so," Brizek said, as a smile broke across his face.

He had never met anybody quite like George Brejack, and he found the investigator's optimism to be infectious. While curbing his own enthusiasm so as not to lose perspective of the truth, Brizek soon became as enmeshed in the life of John Short as George had been for the last six months.

They had endless conversations, arguing the fine details in their reconstruction of a murder scenario. Each man had his own theory on what happened that night at the mall, and it comes as no surprise that Brejack's take on those events was more fantastic, more deviously plotted than what Brizek imagined. Keeping their differences from getting in the way of the relationship, the lawyer and the lawman developed a professional respect for one another as they drove around the state and interviewed potential witnesses.

Brejack typically took the wheel and Brizek sat in the

front passenger seat; he sorted through papers, made last-minute preparations, and questioned George on additional information for the meeting. Brejack held up his end of the conversation as he maintained a steady speed of at least seventy-five miles per hour. This never failed to unnerve Brizek.

En route to a pre-trial interview with Kevin Johnson, Brejack momentarily took his eyes off the road and turned to the attorney. "The thing with Johnson," he said, "is that he's a nice guy, so he doesn't want to feel like he's ratting out Short. We play it cool with him and he'll cooperate. I think he's still got some useful stuff that he hasn't told us yet."

Brizek nodded and suggested that George keep his eyes on the road. "Maybe you should also slow down a little bit," he said in the manner of a nervous wife. "We're not running late. We'll get to the bank well before three o'clock."

"You think I'm going fast?" Brejack asked, gunning the accelerator.

"I haven't traveled at this speed since I flew home from England on my honeymoon," Brizek joked, getting to enjoy his role as Brejack's straight man.

"I'll show you fast, Steve. I'll give you a white-knuckle ride."

They both laughed at that, as Brejack shifted into fourth gear and goosed his silver Volvo into the passing lane.

CHAPTER
17

Witnesses changed their minds as the trial date neared. Their stories did not get reworked so much as their emotions did. Imagining themselves in court, answering a bunch of incriminating questions about a friend or acquaintance, became less appealing as the moment of truth drew close enough to be real.

Such was the case with Dan Solowe, a former employee of John Short's who had provided compelling details about his boss's carousing and violence. Most important, he had offered a vivid description of John's key ring with the plastic T-shirt-shaped fob on it. If he took the stand, Solowe had the power to virtually place Short at the murder scene. Brejack and Brizek could not afford to lose his testimony.

Brejack sat in his office, struggling to come up with somebody who could testify that the night of June 22, 1981, had indeed been so dark that John could not possibly have unwittingly spotted the Cutlass from three hundred and thirty-three feet away. He considered calling the Hayden Planetarium in New York City when a loud argument broke his concentration. Brizek, a mild-mannered man whose voice rarely rose to anything approaching a holler, sounded livid. Solowe was slated to be pre-interviewed for the trial this afternoon, and Brejack wondered whether the altercation tied into that.

Before he had a chance to find out for himself, the

assistant prosecutor knocked at the door and asked Brejack for help. "Dan Solowe's giving me a hard time," he said, suit jacket off and necktie askew.

"Maybe I'd better talk to him," Brejack suggested, not bothering to question the nature of the quarrel. Getting up from his desk, leaving behind the phone calls, Brejack followed Brizek into his office.

The door closed behind them, and the assistant prosecutor paced back and forth. Face flushed crimson, Brizek looked agitated, allowing himself a rare display of negative emotion—the very thing that can be suicidal in the courtroom. Sitting with his sneakered feet on the floor, ankles akimbo, and expression insolent, Solowe was aggressively unconcerned. In fact, he had the appearance of somebody who cared about nothing at all.

It was as if he had told Brizek something only so he could watch him react. Solowe's look of vague amusement annoyed Brejack, and predisposed him to smack some sense into the guy. But he knew better than to treat an innocent man that way, especially one who promised to be an asset in the courtroom. A better idea was to create the *impression* of impending violence.

"What's going on here?" Brejack wanted to know, adopting the tone of a high school principal who has walked into a boys' room filled with cigarette smoke.

"Dan says he doesn't want to testify," Brizek informed.

"What do you mean he doesn't want to testify?" Brejack asked.

He stood in front of Solowe and bore down on him from above.

His face reflected ugly and mean in the young man's eyes. Now looking scared, Solowe weighed his options with more care than he had exhibited when confronted only by Brizek. After several seconds he decided to reveal the true nature of his problem.

"The more I think about it, the less I want to take the stand against John. The guy's a friend of mine. I can't go up there and tell everybody all of these things about him." He hesitated dramatically, then added, "Besides, I'm not sure that what I told you is completely accurate."

"Number one, you told us those things under oath," Brejack quickly responded. "They'd *better* be accurate, or we'll nail you for perjury. Number two, you've got no choice but to testify. We'll subpoena your ass and get you up on the witness stand so quickly that you won't know what hit you."

"I was told by some people that I don't have to appear in court. They said I could leave the state if I want to get out of it."

Brejack decided to explain the situation to Solowe in a way that left no questions about where such a decision would lead him. "Look, jerk-off," he said, pointing a fat finger a few inches from Solowe's nose. "I worked too hard on this case for a guy like you to throw a monkey wrench into the gears. All I want you to do is show up in court and tell the truth. Just confirm what you told us in your statement. That's all I'm asking. Nobody wants you to lie. But if you refuse to testify, if you leave this area, you're going to have me on your ass. And that's about the last fucking thing that you want. I'll find you, Dan. Wherever you are, I'll find you, I'll track you down and throw you in jail. How's that for an option, Dan? You can spend a few nights in jail till everything gets straightened out, *then* you can be called to the stand to testify."

"All right, all right," he said, resignedly waving his hands in front of his face so that the palms were turned toward Brejack. "I know what kind of guy you are, and I don't want any trouble." He looked down at his sneakers and conceded: "I'll testify like you want me to. I'll tell them whatever it is that I know."

"Good," Brejack said with a smile. "Now you're being sensible. We don't want any problems, and neither do you." Then he added, "But if you get any more of these funny ideas, you better check with me before following through on them."

Dan Solowe nodded and Brejack turned to the assistant prosecutor. "See, Steve, there's no problem. Dan'll work with you. Just go back to asking your questions, and everything will be fine."

Brizek nodded and did as Brejack suggested, pleased by Solowe's newfound willingness to cooperate. "Okay," he said as the door to his office closed and the investigator disappeared. "Let's get back to that key ring. In the report you say that John had it with him nearly all the time. Is that correct?"

Solowe agreed that it was, and Brejack returned to his office feeling like a one-man cavalry.

Jeanne occasionally liked to shop at the Elmwood Park Flea Market. Located in an industrial compound across the river from Paterson, it attracted a lower-middle-class crowd and lacked the tony ambience to which Candy's older sister had become accustomed, but she didn't care. She enjoyed looking at the cheap knickknacks and T-shirts and bootleg cassette tapes that were sold there.

Browsing through a booth loaded with riotously colored silk flowers, she practically bumped into Mary Anne Seegers, a sister of Judy Short's. The two women exchanged a terse greeting and spoke uncomfortably for a few minutes, neither of them mentioning anything about the arrest. Then Mary Anne let something slip about John taking a vacation.

"Yeah, he'll be packing up and getting ready for his trip to Florida," she said. "He and Jesse are going to Disney World."

"He and Jesse?"

"Sure. That's what he's telling the family. They're going to spend a few days together."

"But he's not allowed to see Jesse," Jeanne insisted, dropping all pretenses. "It's a condition of his bail."

Mary Anne backed up a step and insisted that it was true. No longer concerned with shopping, Jeanne replaced the flowers she had picked out. She quickly left the flea market, intending to do something more constructive than stand there and argue. Upon arriving home, Jeanne barely had her coat off before she telephoned her mother. After hearing a recap of the conversation, Helen became concerned. Then she saw her granddaughter sitting contentedly in the next room, eyes glued to the TV, and gained a false sense of security.

"Jesse is here," she softly said into the telephone. "How could John get her, as long as she lives with us?"

"Who knows how he can do it?" Jeanne replied, thinking like the lawyers that she worked for and trying to find an angle. "Maybe he'll turn up at her school and notify the principal that she has to leave early, then they'll take off together."

"Oh my God," Helen said, her voice quavery. "I don't think he would do that. But it makes me so nervous even to think about it. Oh, I just don't know what to do."

"I know what to do. Give me John's mother's number. I'll call her and straighten this out immediately."

Helen obliged and Jeanne placed a call to Adele Short. Considering the recent turn of events, she was not at all pleased to hear from any members of the Austin family. As Jeanne recounted the conversation between herself and Mary Anne, Adele revealed the protective instinct that all mothers have for their children—even if the children happen to be pushing forty.

"You're making trouble," she told Jeanne. "I don't know what's the matter with you."

"I'm *not* making trouble," Jeanne responded. "I just want you to know what I heard."

"And I just want to tell you that it isn't true."

"Look, you go back to your son and tell him that I know exactly what he plans on doing. If, God forbid, something should happen to Jesse, we know where to find him."

"You're lying," Adele said, her rage rising to the surface.

"You're calling me a liar? If you were here right now,

I'd knock you down the goddamned stairs. I know exactly what I'm talking about, and so do you."

Jeanne slammed the telephone back into its cradle. Even though John wound up doing nothing remotely close to what his former sister-in-law feared, Jeanne never once regretted her conversation with Adele. Seeing it as precautionary, she believed that her action perhaps prevented John from kidnapping Jesse.

During John's trial, Jeanne and Adele eyed each other from distant ends of the courthouse lobby, but they never came close to exchanging even the most rudimentary nicety.

During the months leading up to the trial, Pat Caserta had little to do beyond devising ways to discredit the state's case against his client. There were few witnesses that he could rely on. The defense's success would rest upon his ability to cross-examine and hopefully trip up the forty-one people—including just about everybody whom Brejack had interviewed—that Brizek planned on calling to the stand.

The best way of doing that would be to know as much about Brizek's witnesses as possible. Hoping to achieve that, Caserta set up his own meetings with the major people who were scheduled to testify for the State. That's why he wound up spending the better part of a Sunday afternoon in December 1988 at the home of Fred and Helen Austin.

They desired nothing less than a meeting with John Short's attorney, but Brizek warned them that not cooperating with Caserta would make them look like hostile witnesses. So in effect, they had no choice. But did they have to do it in the house on Passaic Avenue? In the very home where Candy had grown up?

When he first scheduled the meeting, Caserta suggested dropping by.

"Can't we come down to your office separately, whenever it's convenient for each person?" Fred wondered.

"You can," the lawyer allowed. "But I don't know if you'd want to, particularly because you'd be bringing along your wife. I'm located in downtown Paterson."

After a few minutes of consideration, Fred agreed that maybe it would be best for Caserta to come to Belleville. Whatever the legitimacy of Caserta's concern about the neighborhood, one can imagine that he had other reasons for wanting to do it in the Austins' house. Besides the fact that they would probably be most comfortable there, it increased the likelihood that everyone would show up. Who knew if the family members would drag themselves out to Paterson? Caserta couldn't afford to take a chance, as these were among the State's strongest witnesses.

Eight people (Fred and Helen, Betty and Joe, and Candy's sisters and their husbands) sat in the dining room, drinking coffee and talking about anything but Candy, when Caserta arrived. He was accompanied by an investigator—a big, silent fellow, who was most memorable for his blow-dried blond hair, silk shirt, and pinkie ring.

"He will serve as a witness today," announced Caserta, a short, well-built, well-dressed, unpretentious and straightforward man who contrasted with his partner in nearly every way. "He'll write notes and listen to what you tell me. That way, if there are any discrepancies in court, he can take the stand as a witness."

They grumbled grudging assent to this arrangement, as Caserta and his investigator made their way into the living room. There, where the rest of the family members were unable to hear anything, each relative was interviewed individually. Fred caught a glimpse of the lawyer's colleague, then turned to Joe and whispered, "The guy looks like a Louisiana pimp."

They both had a big laugh over that while Jeanne took a seat alongside Caserta on the couch. Responding honestly, she told him everything she had told George.

As was his job, the defense attorney poked at the family's statements and nitpicked in search of weaknesses.

For the most part, though, they stuck to their stories. All of them had been through so much over the last seven years that it would have taken a man stronger than Caserta to sway them. That's precisely what Joe Frank maintained as he entered the living room.

In telling Brejack about the final argument he witnessed between John and Candy, Joe had described a situation that was clearly open to interpretation. Attempting to show him another way of seeing it, Caserta employed a little bit of common sense that bordered on condescension. "A lot of couples argue," he pointed out. "They say things that they don't really mean. How could you know that John really meant it when he told Candy that he would piss on her grave?"

"There were a lot of inflections," Joe replied, his patience nonexistent. "John meant what he said and so did Candy. They were going at it in a way that I had never seen before."

"You can't really say what's going through a couple's mind, can you?"

"Look," Joe snapped, "don't sit here and try to jerk me off. I know what I heard, I know what I saw. John threatened to kill Candy, and it was real."

Caserta did not expect to change anybody's opinion that night. He simply wanted to probe the vulnerabilities that were inherent in their testimony. And although they didn't intend it, Candy's relatives allowed their emotions to play precisely into his hand. The lawyer left the house knowing where the family's weaknesses and strengths were. Supposedly lured into discovering the body of his dead daughter, Fred would provide the most emotionally charged (and therefore the most damaging) testimony against John. If he wanted to win this case, Caserta would have to aim his biggest guns at the elderly, gray-haired man who described his years on a battleship during World War II as "a picnic" compared to what he had gone through after the death of his daughter.

*   *   *

While Caserta struggled to come up with ploys to reduce the prosecution's credibility—he believed that its case would be based primarily on events prior to the murder (rather than the murder itself) and the shock-value of the crime—Brejack and Brizek scrambled around to solidify their chain of events. They formally timed the route that John would have taken, and Brejack found several people who could attest to the defendant's knowledge of the area surrounding David Jones's residence. Whenever possible they questioned John's family, friends, and acquaintances who had been missed or intentionally avoided on the first go-round.

At one point the investigator turned up at the front door of James and Adele Short, where he was about as welcome as a bill collector. A crotchety, easily aggravated man with a thick, portly build and wisps of gray hair combed across his head, seventy-six-year-old James felt obliged to allow Brejack inside. But that did not mean he had to cooperate. George handed a business card to the suspect's father and took a seat in the living room.

"I'd like to ask you a few questions about John," the investigator said.

"My wife and I were in Scotland at the time of the murder, and that's all you need to know!" he angrily snapped, his voice thick with Scottish inflections. Before the next question, Short added, "Brejack, you are causing a lot of trouble for me and my son."

"I'm sorry you feel that way, but you should understand that I didn't cause any trouble. A murder took place, and I'm just doing my job."

"Your job . . . It's your job to come here and bother people?" Growing increasingly annoyed by the minute, he told Brejack, "I'm calling Pat Caserta. I don't think I have to speak with you."

Citing James Short's poor state of health, Caserta persuaded Brejack to leave John's father alone. He agreeably departed from the house, silently noting that James

Short had never once proclaimed his son's innocence. Eager to get more input from those who personally knew John, Brejack went on to contact a sister-in-law of Judy's. They spoke on the telephone for a few minutes, and she illustrated John's skill at camouflaging family problems.

"Did John Short ever tell you anything about his second wife's murder?"

"No. I found out about it last week when the article about the case was in the newspaper."

"How do John and Judy get along?"

"Fine."

"Do you have any knowledge of physical abuse in the Short home?"

"No," she concluded before hanging up.

The helicopter made a choppy ascent above Willowbrook Mall. Harnessed in, a New Jersey State Police photographer dangled out of the cavity where a door would ordinarily be. He focused his telephoto lens on the parking lot, and Brejack advised him on where to aim. The photographs were eventually blown up to 32″ x 40″ and marked to illustrate the course taken by John and Fred. Keeping his feet on the ground, Brizek took to reviewing all facets of the investigation and patching up any improprieties that might have occurred along the way.

For his part, Pat Caserta's options were limited. Since he could not absolutely prove Short's innocence, the defense lawyer primarily needed to make the jury wonder why all of Brejack's incriminating testimony had been altered since the time of the murder.

Even if he failed to do that, Caserta's client could still go free due to the statute of limitations on manslaughter. As long as the attorney convinced the jury to find Short guilty of anything but murder, John would leave the courtroom a free man. He'd be able to move back to Ocean Grove and rebuild his life down there.

*   *   *

At one point, as the trial date neared, Caserta seemed likely to get a break that would tip the scales of justice in his favor.

It began when Brizek called Diane Lovejoy to confirm everything for her day on the witness stand. The conversation moved smoothly until Diane inquired about the trial's media coverage. Responding frankly, and trying to prepare her for what she might encounter, he advised Diane that press attention was a possibility. "There are going to be reporters and possibly TV cameras," the assistant prosecutor said. 'You might wind up on television."

"Really?" she replied. "You mean the New York newspapers will be there as well?"

"That's possible," Brizek told her.

Diane concluded the conversation and spent the next few days contemplating all of that. She wondered whether she wanted to be portrayed on television as the woman who had slept with John Short in exchange for money. Not only would it destroy her hard-won self-esteem, but it would bring untold amounts of pain to her parents. She discussed this with Nolan Yogi, her lawyer friend from The Way International, and he suggested that she should do what she felt in her heart. Think about it long enough, he advised, and eventually you'll reach the right decision.

A few days later a letter postmarked January 5, 1989, arrived at the Passaic County Prosecutor's Office. Diane had written to announce that she could not bring herself to testify. She had a change of heart, and they would just have to live without her taking the stand. The text of the missive included quotes from Scripture and contained Diane's homespun rationalizing. It concluded with a plea for George and Steve to see the way of Jesus Christ.

Brejack read the letter and immediately telephoned the reluctant witness. Five seconds into the conversation, Diane explicitly stated her position. "I'm not going to be able to testify," she said bluntly.

"I thought we reached an agreement," replied Brejack.

"Well, I've changed my mind. Steve Brizek told me all about the TV cameras and the newspapermen. *The New York Times* might be there, for goodness sake! I can't have my photo in the *Times*. It would absolutely kill my parents."

"Steve exaggerated." Brejack hesitated for a heartbeat, hoping that Diane would reconsider. She didn't, so he added, "Look, I'm not going to lie to you. It's a big case. There'll be some newspaper coverage, but no TV and nothing national. If anything, it'll be a few of the local papers. That's it."

"Sorry, George." Diane slipped into her woman-scorned mode and refused to consider his request. "I've made up my mind. Besides, I'm leaving for Arizona in a few days and won't be in this area anyway, so I couldn't testify even if I wanted to."

"I just wish you'd think about it." He struggled to keep his voice level, to mask the anger and frustration he felt at having this happen now. Snipping their barely existent line of communication was the last thing that Brejack wanted to do. "I'll speak to you in a day or so. Maybe we can figure something out between now and then."

"Okay." Diane hung up without saying good-bye.

Brejack waited until the phone clicked dead, then slammed down the receiver. He kicked his wastepaper basket across the room, sending crumpled sheets of paper onto the floor. It hit the wall with a hollow thud, and Brejack looked for something else to vent his anger on. He left a few dents in the file cabinet, then felt calm enough to deal rationally with the recent turn of events.

"Diane backed out," he told Brizek, walking into the lawyer's office without bothering to knock. "She's leaving town in a few days, so you better get your ass in gear. File whatever papers we need to keep her in Pittsburgh or ensure that she'll be down here for the trial."

"She doesn't want to testify?" Brizek asked, unaware that his frankness had spooked her. "I'll get right on it."

He drafted and filed the necessary documents under the Interstate Witness Compact with the authorities in Pennsylvania. Because time was of the essence, they managed to complete all the paperwork within forty-eight hours. A day before Diane was scheduled to leave for Phoenix, two Allegheny County officers showed up at her home with a warrant for her arrest. They brought Diane before a county judge, who ordered her to appear as a witness in the case being filed against John Short. Were she not to comply, he promised, it would be viewed as a criminal act.

After agreeing to cooperate, and before leaving the courthouse, Diane placed a call to Brejack. In a voice that practically quivered with a little girl's fear, she apologized. "I'm sorry. I shouldn't have gone back on my word. You won't need to arrest me again. I'll cooperate just as I originally promised."

"That's all I'm asking from you, Diane. All Steve and I want is for you to go up on the witness stand and be honest. It's not hard, unless you make it hard."

"I'll cooperate, George," she repeated. "But Lord help you if things don't go as smoothly as you say they will."

"Don't worry," Brejack said as the conversation wound down. "We'll be there to protect and support you, Diane."

Lord help *her* if she doesn't show up, Brejack told himself. He contemplated passing that message on to Diane, then thought better of rocking the boat. Thrilled to have the final link of his chain solidly in place, Brejack wasn't about to say anything that might break it apart.

PART THREE

January 19, 1989

BURIED MISTAKES

"The State's position is that the defendant wanted his wife dead. He had a motive, and he had the inclination to kill her."
—Steven Brizek, assistant prosecutor for Passaic County

"Don't let [Brejack and Brizek] persuade you. They made a last-ditch effort to save face and salvage this case."
—Patrick Caserta, defense attorney for John Short

CHAPTER
18

Spend enough time in the company of criminals, and eventually you pick up their mannerisms. Regardless of one's economic level, something magnetic and charismatic about their world (if not their personae) rubs off like streaks of sticky, garishly colored paint. Nowhere is this phenomenon more prevalent than among criminal lawyers. Even with their Ivy League educations, and employment in one of the world's most lucrative professions, they invariably adopt the speech patterns and styles of dress that their socially inferior clients favor.

Every morning, in criminal courts across the country, attorneys drive from their sprawling suburban homes to some governmental neighborhood of a nearby city, park their Benzes and BMWs, and make the transition from Good Citizen to Good Fella. This rule of downscale envy permeates the Passaic County Courthouse, a modern glass-and-steel structure located across the street from the Major Crimes Unit. Sometimes, as the lawyers pass through the building's airport-style metal detectors, it's impossible to distinguish them from the accused that they represent. Only the snapped-shut, finely tooled leather briefcases, fat with transcripts and testimonies, give them away.

On the morning of January 19, 1989, the John Short trial reigned as the primary topic of discussion among the thuggish counselors. Pat Caserta had the court date postponed by four months so that he could further prepare for the case, and the general consensus among his colleagues was that he had an ace in the hole, that somewhere, somebody would prove John Short's innocence. Overshadowing Caserta's primary criminal trial experience (mostly drug possession cases), was his reputation as a scrappy, street-smart attorney whose abilities should not be underestimated. No white-shoe barrister, Caserta had put himself through law school by working as an IRS investigator. He served a four-year stretch with the prosecutor's office before jumping over to the other, more lucrative side in 1984.

Wearing pinstripes and affecting the oral tones of Mafiosi, criminal lawyers shared elevators to the upper floors where judges and clients and cases awaited them. On mornings like this one, with a big case slanted to commence, the attorneys invariably handicapped the outcome.

"It won't go further than today," one lawyer predicted, as the elevator door closed and the car began its ascent. "I don't care how inexperienced Caserta is with murders. Nearly eight years after the fact, this guy shouldn't even be tried."

"Don't be so sure," his companion replied, the man's voice resonating with a spectator's gleeful anticipation. "I don't think the county would have even presented the case if it didn't look like a sure win. Brizek's got to be coming in there with something."

"I don't care if he's got the 82nd Airborne. Eight years is a long fucking time. How can you support a witness's testimony so far after the fact?"

The elevator stopped at the third floor. Both lawyers stepped out and continued to converse (the topic now turning to the sorrowful New Jersey Nets) as the empty car rose two more stories. There, in room number 523, the honorable Judge Vincent E. Hull, Jr. planned on putting a stop to the speculation—in and out of the courthouse.

Since John Short's arrest nearly a year ago, the local media had been keeping the general public informed about the murder, the imminent trial, and the issues surrounding it. A few weeks ago, articles on the vagaries of circumstantial evidence ran in *The Bergen Record* and *The Herald News*, the area's two largest newspapers. The former offered an overview of these kinds of cases and included quotes from several defense attorneys. One of them pointed out, "Just the [eight-year] time span alone may be unacceptable to the jurors." However, it was the article in the *Herald* that seemed likeliest to influence the trial's outcome. Entitled "Time Is On His Side," it examined the possibility of John Short's going free even if a jury found him guilty of manslaughter.

A smattering of reporters and lawyers occupied the polished wood benches in the circular, oak-paneled room where Judge Hull planned on hearing testimony. But this morning, before the actual trial began, the prosecution and defense would have the opportunity to argue preliminary points. The most important issue revolved around the way in which jury members would be instructed regarding sentencing. Brizek believed that they should not receive the option of first- or second-degree manslaughter convictions, as it would trick them into believing that a prison sentence existed under those lesser charges. Caserta, on the other hand, argued that the jury's job was to hear the testimony, view the evidence, and, if need be, render a verdict of guilty. Nothing more, nothing less. Sentencing, he maintained, was the judge's concern.

Always a stickler for punctuality and known for running a tight, no-nonsense courtroom, Judge Hull stepped out from his chambers at precisely nine o'clock. A neat, small-featured, humorless man in his fifties, Hull ran a hand over the side of his finely parted, meticulously combed gray hair and viewed the courtroom. He was visibly annoyed that Pat Caserta had yet to arrive for the pre-trial hearing.

The judge killed a couple minutes by distractedly scribbling notes onto a pad and asking about Caserta's whereabouts before he retreated to his chambers. Ten minutes later, when the defense attorney showed up, Hull scolded him for his tardiness and curtly suggested that they get to the matters at hand. Trying to make up for his inauspicious entrance, Caserta quickly launched into his argument for the dismissal of charges.

"The Wayne Police Department did not file reports on interviews that led nowhere toward solving the case," Caserta began, making the point that a thorough investigation never seemed to have taken place. "Whenever I asked Officers Jim Wilson and Andrew Webster about those interviews, they insisted that Billy McCann [who's now dead] knew about them. There's nothing to back up what the witnesses are saying and to state why certain leads were not followed."

After complaining that the Wayne Police Department's slipshod investigation destroyed the opportunity to find Candy's true killer, Caserta went on to list a few particulars: a woman who worked at the Belle Maid Delicatessen failed to recall whether or not John Short bought cigarettes there at the time of the murder, yet she was never shown a photograph of Short that might have encouraged her to identify him; two people who claimed to have seen Candy's car earlier in the day at the Willowbrook Mall (which decreased the likelihood of her having gone there twice, and made the theory that she was murdered elsewhere and dumped off at the mall more plausible) were never interviewed by the Wayne police; and in a taped telephone conversation Billy McCann prematurely told Harry Austin (now mute and paralyzed) that John Short was his primary suspect.

"I'd like to attack the basis of that telephone conversation," Caserta stated. "I'd like to [ask McCann], 'You were after John Short from day one. Why?' I'd like to see what answer Detective McCann could give to that. There is no firm basis for his line of reasoning as far as the defense is concerned."

Hull listened, expressed confusion over why Caserta would have presented the last of his points, and concluded that, if anything, McCann's absence would actually put the defense at an *advantage*. "I don't foresee any problem with playing that tape or a portion of it," Hull said, "should what is on that tape be relevant for this case." He turned to Brizek and asked, "Mr. Brizek, is there any problem with having the tape played to demonstrate that at some point Detective McCann said the defendant is his key suspect?"

"Judge," Brizek declared, sure that such a move could only show that John was always the obvious murderer, "I would be so happy if that tape were played for the jury in its entirety that I recommend you play it in Dolby Stereo."

Even as this strategy took him nowhere, Caserta persevered. He steadily maintained that having certain people unavailable to testify (who would have been called to the witness stand had John been brought to trial in a timely fashion) hindered his ability to present a case. For those reasons, the defense attorney argued, John Short should not be tried. The case should be thrown out.

Following a few seconds of consideration Hull announced, "I'm going to render a ruling this afternoon, and it's going to be adverse to you, Mr. Caserta."

Forced to accept that his client would have to face a jury, Caserta next tried to alter the context of the jury instruction. Realizing that the expired statute of limitations evaporated any charge short of murder, he wanted the jury to have the option of returning a first- or second-degree manslaughter verdict without being told that it would be tantamount to an acquittal. Brizek, on the other hand, wanted the jury to consider only whether or not Short was guilty of murder; he argued against mentioning anything about the lesser offenses.

"The fact that my defendant can't now be charged with what he could have been charged in 1982 is a prejudice," Caserta said, maintaining that Short should not have to suffer just because the state had spent eight years mounting its case. "The jurors should not be placed in the position of having to make an all or nothing [guilty of murder or innocent] verdict. The defendant is constitutionally required to [having the option of being charged with the] lesser offenses. It would allow the jury to decide, perhaps as a compromise, that he's guilty of aggravated manslaughter."

"They're not being given all or nothing," Hull responded. "If the facts warrant it, they'll be told about aggravated manslaughter and/or manslaughter."

"But they're still going to see themselves as having only two choices: If he did it, he gets convicted of murder; if he didn't do it, he goes free. They're still faced with all or nothing, no matter how they come to that."

"The jury will have the benefit of all the factors if the evidence warrants it," the judge concluded. "The jury will understand that if they find the evidence to be sufficient only for an aggravated manslaughter situation, then they will find the defendant not guilty."

One might have thought that Caserta would be pleased with the ruling, as it made the State responsible for proving that John Short *purposely and knowingly* killed Candy. Those are the two words that define murder in New Jersey; premeditation does not enter into it, as that is not among the state's conditions for the charge. If Brizek failed to prove purpose and knowledge on the part of John Short, the ruling went, then the defendant would go free. But Caserta was not at all satisfied. He continued to argue that the options were really nonexistent, through no fault of Short's. Hull listened but refused to budge.

As the pre-trial hearing wound down, Brizek made one request: "I'd like to have Investigator George Brejack present in the courtroom, sitting at the prosecution's table and assisting me."

As expected, Caserta balked. "Investigator Brejack is intimately intertwined in the entire case," the defense attorney argued. "Not only has he taken statements from witnesses who have changed their testimony, but he's conducted aspects of the investigation on his own. He will be testifying as a witness to those aspects of his investigation, and the prosecutor's office has alternatives. They have a complete staff of people to sit with the assistant prosecutor and perform the function of an aide during the trial."

The judge considered the information, then he asked Caserta, "Is the credibility [of the prosecution's witnesses] going to be attacked?"

"In some instances, yes."

"And we have situations where there may be prior inconsistent statements?"

"Yes."

"Investigator Brejack will not be allowed in the courtroom," the judge ruled. "He'll be subject to the sequestration ruling."

The three men wrapped up a few more loose ends, and Judge Hull warned Brizek and Caserta to refrain from talking to reporters. "The comments you make about this case are going to be done in this courtroom and not to the press," he stated, adding that he had seen a recent newspaper article in which Brizek was quoted. "We're not going to have interviews conducted before the trial or once we get involved in the trial. Anything you're going to say is for the record, here in the courtroom."

Despite this final mild wrist-slap, Brizek was heartened by the pre-trial hearing's outcome. That Brejack would not be able to sit in on the proceedings disappointed him, but he realized that the request had been a long shot anyway and decided instead to have Fred Smith and Peter Lackland there. They were adept investigators and would do a fine job of running information in and out of the courtroom. Brizek won the more important motion: The jury most likely would be advised that a guilty verdict on either of the lesser charges would result in no prison time.

Soon after leaving the courtroom, as he sat in his office and enjoyed one of his wife's homemade bran muffins for lunch, Brizek felt as sure as he ever allowed himself to feel. Brejack, who was seated alongside him, wanted to hear all about the pre-trial hearing. While Brizek kept his positive projections buttoned up, and maintained an air of uncertainty, the investigator would tolerate no negative words.

"You've got to think positive," Brejack said, chewing his way through a cheeseburger. "Everything we have points to John Short as the killer. What the hell can Pat Caserta have on us?"

"We'll see tomorrow," Brizek replied cautiously. He kept the crumbs from touching his desk and replayed the morning's session in his mind, analyzing the nuances in Judge Hull's responses and searching for possible weaknesses in Caserta's presentation.

The tacky summer-weight suit had to go. Pat Caserta believed this as soon as he saw what John planned on wearing to court. "I suggest that you dress in a tweed jacket and maybe a pair of beige chinos with a blue Oxford cloth shirt," Caserta advised, warning John that his attire could strongly influence the jurors. "Something professorial would make you more sympathetic."

"I have a suit that I want to wear," replied John, who had already gotten a decent haircut and shaved his beard in preparation for appearing before Judge Hull. "I'm going to wear it."

And he did. On the first day of the trial, in the dead of winter, Short arrived in court dressed in a powder-blue seersucker suit, something that was totally inappropriate for the season—or any time of year in a courtroom. Beyond his attire, though, the defendant came across as a man with plenty of problems. Timid, and humbled by the magnitude of the fix he was currently in,

John Short hardly came off as the braggart of a decade ago.

Physically shrunken, Short appeared to have exchanged his swagger for a mien of jittery insecurity. The last twelve months had apparently wreaked havoc on John's physical and emotional well-being. This debilitation surprised Brizek, who, after hearing so much about the man's brutal and violent personality, had expected to see a more confrontational, more formidable defendant. Instead, he encountered somebody who meekly made small talk whenever they inadvertently met in the men's room. The fact that Short's wife and mother escorted him into court each day (John's father remained conspicuously absent during the entire trial) further added to the defendant's overall look of fragility.

Two very different women drawn together for a common cause, Judy and Adele nervously watched the proceedings designed to systematically tear down a man they both loved. From the start Adele watched her son protectively, while Judy continually attempted to make eye contact with various jurors. As the trial progressed one can assume that their love for John remained intact, though the emotion had to have been fraught with disrespect.

Like most trials, this one started slowly. The first few days were taken up primarily with testimony from police officers who were at the original crime scene, and with expert witnesses grappling over the fine points of Candy's death. Clinton Hatchet, an astronomer from New York City's Hayden Planetarium, swore that the night of June 22, 1981, was an especially dark one, with few stars to be seen in the sky, which further hampered the already limited visibility in the mall's parking lot. Dr. William Van Vooren, the medical examiner who had first looked at Candy's body, stated that the victim had not been raped, and estimated the time of her death to be between seven and eight o'clock. A General Motors employee confirmed that the keys found beneath Candy's body were duplicates, which made it clear that the originals—i.e. Candy's keys—had never turned up.

Not until day three, January 25th, when Brizek was scheduled to call John and Candy's friends and relatives to the stand, did anybody expect things to get interesting.

Reporters, lawyers, and a handful of crime buffs regularly checked in to see who was testifying and to decide whether it would be worthwhile to sit through the proceedings. As a result, an unusually large turnout of spectators crowded the hundred or so seats on the morning of the 25th. Scheduled to be called to the stand were Judy Chamberlain, Candy's two sisters, her aunt Geri Austin, and a pair of Short's friends. Revealing as their testimonies had the potential to be, however, the day was slated to close with the trial's star attraction: Diane Lovejoy.

Behind the closed doors that kept upcoming witnesses ignorant of courtroom activity, the day's drama began unfolding when Dan Solowe stepped up to the stand. Below him, at the front of the courtroom, John Short sat at the defense's table—face drawn, and expression dour. He made no direct eye contact with any witnesses, and emotionally distanced himself from the proceedings.

Uncomfortable with the prospect of contributing to a former friend's demise, Solowe tried in vain to avoid answering Brizek's most incriminating questions. But the lawyer proceeded with an unflappable sense of mission. Grudgingly, Solowe identified the piece of T-shirt-shaped plastic on Short's key ring, but when it came time to acknowledge his former employer's involvement with Diane he claimed to have no recollection.

"Would you like to refresh your memory by looking at the statement?" Brizek asked, handing the witness a transcript of his interview with Brejack. "The bottom of page two in particular?"

Solowe did as he was told, then glanced up and sheepishly muttered, "Lovejoy."

At Brizek's urging, Solowe recounted everything he

had originally told Brejack about John's feelings upon first meeting Diane. Coaxing the words out, the attorney worked Solowe (and the prosecution witnesses who followed) with a soft, relaxed touch; he knew exactly what they would say and possessed the backup to correct any of their mistakes. Pat Caserta—who would later maintain that Brizek and Brejack "constructed the trial through heavily scripted testimony"—lacked that sense of certainty, yet he persevered with his own strategies.

As he did with nearly everybody who took the stand, Caserta attempted to discredit Solowe's testimony by asking questions that insinuated manipulation on the part of the prosecutor's office. After getting Solowe to agree that the statements he made in court had been rehearsed and literally highlighted in red so that he could remember them, Caserta went in for what he hoped would be the kill.

"When Detective Brejack first called you and brought you into his office, you had virtually no recollection of these events, is that true?" Caserta's voice boomed with accusation as he shifted into his pit-bull mode.

"To some extent. I mean . . ." Solowe stammered, no doubt recalling Brejack's warning about perjury.

"Detective Brejack told you about this investigation, what he was doing, what he had done, what his thoughts were on the case. Right?"

"Yeah."

"Then he began to ask you questions?"

"Yeah."

"And then you began to remember things?"

"Exactly!"

Caserta successfully made his point; the witness had been influenced by Brejack. He laid the foundation for his defense and continued by exposing the fact that Solowe could not remember what he had worn, where he had gone, what he had done on the day in question. So, why would he remember his boss's keys? Perhaps because it had been planted in his mind by Brejack and

Brizek? This point was driven home when Caserta questioned Solowe about returning to the prosecutor's office and attempting to back out of appearing in court. The picture he painted for the jury was that of a man who had been strong-armed into testifying against a friend.

On the redirect, Brizek struggled to patch up the damage. He steered Solowe toward acknowledging his understanding of the consequences of inconsistency, and asked him if his original statement was the absolute truth. Yes, Solowe assured the court, it was.

Despite Brizek's efforts at damage control, it was hard to believe that Caserta's cross-examination hadn't succeeded at planting doubt in the jurors' minds.

In the well of the courtroom, a low area in front of the judge's perch, Brizek had propped an easel with a four-foot-square map that depicted parts of Passaic and neighboring Essex Counties. Centering on West Orange, the map highlighted Willowbrook Mall; the Austin, Frank, and Short homes (John's and his parents'); and all streets leading up to Stone Drive, where the Joneses and Fishmans both lived. At first the jurors were curious as to its purpose; it seemed odd, and meant nothing to them. Brizek enjoyed presenting this little bit of mystery. Eschewing verbal hot dogging, he found the visual tease to be a comfortable and effective form of showmanship.

When a reluctant Steve Gottlieb was called to the stand, the twelve folks in the jury box received their first inkling of what the prosecutor planned on doing with the images. But first Brizek had a few questions. He established Gottlieb's close friendship with Short, and used him to dramatize the defendant's lack of emotion at Candy's funeral. Then Brizek called the construction worker down to the well, where the easel with the photographs stood.

"I am pointing to a green circle with the letter 'G' inside of it," he began. "Please look closely at that location and the roadways which are labeled immediately around it." He paused long enough for everybody to look, then added, "Now tell the jury, if you can, what that dot corresponds to."

"That's where I used to live," Gottlieb said, referring to an address in West Orange, not far from Jones's domicile, and acknowledging that Short frequently had visited him there.

"For the record, it signifies the location of your home, at 35 Robertson Road, between 1972 and 1975."

"That's correct."

"Thank you. You may resume your seat."

Nobody quite knew what Brizek was getting at, and he preferred it that way, at least for the time being. Allowing the jurors to experience the same process of discovery as a criminal investigator was part of his strategy. As the trial progressed, the map became crowded with stick-on dots. Augmented by testimony from Susan Fishman, David Jones, and a handful of others who had worked with Short in and around West Orange, there would soon be ample proof that John Short was well acquainted with the roads that led to Jones's house. It would, Brizek believed, show that Short could not have gotten hopelessly lost for over an hour on the night of the 22nd. The marked map provided the sort of compelling circumstantial evidence that was designed to withstand Caserta's attempts at discrediting testimony.

When Caserta cross-examined Gottlieb, he keyed in on John's background and his past. He intended to prove that the defendant's blasé behavior at the funeral was not at all out of character for John. He began by asking about the emotional environment inside James and Adele Short's household. Gottlieb replied by recalling James's sternness. The logic went that it would account for an overall lack of emotion on the part of the man's son.

Indeed, for anybody who saw Short in court, the testimony was superfluous. He sat at the table alongside Caserta and stared at invisible points in the courtroom, an expression of indifference on his face. Alternating each day between two equally inappropriate blue suits, he seemed removed enough to be attending the trial of somebody he barely knew.

Nevertheless, Brizek objected to Caserta's line of questioning. Approaching the bench and speaking softly enough so that the jurors would not hear him, Brizek said that he had information which "indicates that John Short has a history of exhibiting a great deal of emotion."

Hull turned to the jurors and asked them to leave the courtroom while he ironed this wrinkle out with the two lawyers. "If the defense is taking the position that John Short is a man of peaceful, stoic character, I can bring up how he abused his first wife, how he throws hammers off of roofs when he's upset," Brizek said, agitated. He added that he would raise all of these points if the defense continued on the course it seemed to be taking.

Caserta maintained that the witness was expected to simply say, "John often tried to be a macho kind of guy, emulating his father, but at times he was also emotional." In the end, that's all he did say, and Brizek never had the opportunity to retaliate as he had threatened.

The next witness to be called was Geri Austin. She explained how she saw Candy nearly every day for a two-year period, and recalled spotting bruises on several occasions. Geri also supported Steve Gottlieb's allegations about John's behavior during the funeral, and the fact that Candy's key ring and fob were different than the one found at the scene of the crime. Because the victim's flip-flop sandal key chain never surfaced, Brizek borrowed his wife's key ring, which happened to be of an identical design, and showed it to the jurors. It was a small, rainbow-colored beach-thong with a silver ring attached to it, the sort of item that could be found in most any five-and-ten.

Caserta began his cross-examination by attacking Geri Austin. He wondered who made her the arbiter of how people should behave at funerals. He pecked away at her testimony, pointing out that individuals grieve differently. Undaunted, Geri stuck with her original statement. "Being able to turn the tears on and off like a faucet is not what I'd call normal behavior at a funeral," she said.

Playing a dangerous game of pushing the state's witnesses to the brink of lashing out, Caserta continually risked looking like a bully. Regardless of how anyone else viewed this case, it was difficult for the jurors to not feel sympathetic toward the Austins, an obviously upstanding family that now had to deal with the senseless murder of a loved one. If Caserta shoved too hard, these witnesses would inadvertently elicit pity that had very little to do with the actual case but could have a major impact on the verdict.

Stepping back from his questioning about the funeral, Caserta next accused Geri of having a selective memory. He pointed out several other details from eight years ago and found it curious that she had failed to remember those. "Do you know what *Jeanne's* key ring looked like?" he asked, his voice flushed with innocent curiosity as he referred to Candy's sister.

"No, sir," Geri said without a trace of timidity in her voice. "But I remember Candy's just because we used to tease her that it would fit her foot [because her shoe size was so small]."

As if he couldn't quite grasp this, Caserta reiterated his question about precisely why she remembered the key ring before dismissing Geri from the witness stand.

She was followed by Candy's oldest sister, Cindy Austin McCumber, who backed up Geri's testimony about the bruises. Though she and her sister had not been especially close, Cindy saw Candy at least once a month and on those occasions managed to notice marks. She recalled going to Willowbrook Mall with Candy, and pointed out that they always parked in a specific area other than where the Cutlass was found on the night of June 22, 1981. Brizek smiled and marked another spot, this one on his aerial photograph of the Willowbrook Mall parking lot, which rested on a second easel.

Following Cindy's testimony, Judy Chamberlain was called to the witness stand. She walked through the door at the rear of the courtroom and proceeded past a mix of spectators and reporters, none of whom had turned out to see her. They were there for The Diane Lovejoy Show; the former go-go dancer promised to be the juiciest witness to date.

But the spectators first had to sit through Judy's testimony, which initially centered on her best friend's parking habits and the key rings that Candy and John each had used. A more enlightening verbal turn came with Brizek asking Judy about Candy's shopping proclivities.

"Do you know where Candy customarily shopped for dance clothes?" Brizek asked.

"Yes," replied Judy. "It was at the Capezio [factory] outlet in Totowa, New Jersey."

"Why did she shop there?"

"The items were sold at a discount price."

"Do you know the hours of business at the Capezio outlet?"

"Noon to four on Saturdays only."

"On all the times that you went shopping with Candice Short after the birth of her daughter, did she ever go shopping without Jessica?"

"No."

"Is there any exception that you recall?"

"Just once, when we went looking for bridesmaid dresses for my wedding."

"Did Candy ever park in the vicinity of Sears [where the car was ultimately found] when she went shopping at Willowbrook with you?"

"No."

"Did you ever go shopping with her at Willowbrook during the week?"

"No. We always went on weekends."

"Did you go daytime or nighttime?"

"Daytime. Never at night."

Brizek used the questions to serve a dual purpose: They showed that Candy had not made a routine trip to the mall which went terribly awry, and they also detracted from the likelihood of Candy *ever* going there to buy tights. If Brizek could prove that enough of John's contentions seemed inaccurate, it would logically bring into doubt his version of the circumstances surrounding the June 22nd murder. Judy went on to establish that the yellow blanket had been stashed in the Cutlass's trunk for years, and that the key ring with the T-shirt-shaped fob indisputably belonged to John, not to Candy.

On his cross-examination, Caserta took issue with Judy, citing inconsistencies between the statements she made today about shopping with Candy and what she had told the Wayne police in 1981. According to their reports, the friends had gone to the mall together only a few times, and Candy's parking patterns were more erratic than Judy now maintained. Additionally, when Brejack first met with Judy and showed her the blanket, she did not remember it being in the car. "You had interviews with Detective Brejack beginning in October of 1987 and they continued through January of '88," Caserta continued, using the investigator's old title in a pejorative way. "You gave statements, and you were interviewed again. Then he'd come back later, take another statement, and the more you saw of him the more you remembered?"

"That's right," Judy told him, meaning nothing more than that the questions jogged her memory.

To further build a case for Brejack coercing and leading witnesses, Caserta played a cassette tape from the interview with Judy. It contained the sound of paper rustling. The lawyer alleged that Brejack had written out statements for her to recite. In response, Judy claimed that Brejack had taken notes for himself but had done nothing to influence what she said.

Despite a series of answers that failed to support Caserta's claims of underhandedness on the part of Brejack, his questioning did expose a less savory side of the lawman's investigative technique. As Brejack waited outside the courtroom, spending a few minutes in the lobby with the Austins, crucial links in his chain of circumstantial evidence were slowly eroding.

CHAPTER
19

A royal pain in the ass. That was George Brejack's opinion of Diane Lovejoy. Every step of the way, she had presented problems. When the time finally came for her to make the trip to Paterson from her new home in Arizona, she turned down the county's offer of an airline ticket and decided to drive. Special considerations were made to cover the mileage. Then, a week before the court date, she called George and raised another issue.

"I'm going to get tired along the way," she said. "I don't want to fall asleep behind the wheel."

"So drink coffee," Brejack suggested.

"I need a Thermos to keep it in. Will you guys be able to reimburse me for a Thermos?"

"Sure, Diane." Brejack knew that the accountants would never view Diane's Thermos as a reimbursable expense, so he resigned himself to the fact that the money would come out of his pocket. "Get whatever kind of thermos you want and I'll pay you back."

Once she arrived in town, Diane turned down the offer of a hotel room and opted instead to spend two nights with a friend from the church. Since there was no need to cover her lodging, though, Diane expected something else. She wanted the prosecutor's office to furnish her with a more generous per diem. Brejack, Brizek, and Nativo each kicked in thirty-five dollars so that their star witness could afford to eat while she waited to take the

351

witness stand. They all knew that any inconveniences would be more than compensated for as long as Diane came through in front of the jury.

Pat Caserta must have realized this as well as anybody. Before Diane was called in to testify, he made a big deal about the county funding her trip and the spending money that she had required. In typical form, Brizek explained everything to the penny, satisfying the judge and mollifying Caserta. With nothing left to complain about, the defense attorney muttered, "I just wanted to make sure that they didn't do her hair and take her shopping." Under his breath he added, "I assume that they didn't."

Diane drew a big crowd on the afternoon of January 25th. In much the way that Brizek anticipated, a lot of people were curious to see the woman who had stolen John Short's heart and supposedly driven him to kill his wife. She walked down the aisle of the courtroom dressed in a navy blue skirt, with a matching jacket and white blouse. She peered through oval-shaped eyeglasses, and shoulder-length blond hair framed her sharp-featured face. Diane took the stand, Judge Hull swore her in, and the questioning began.

Brizek led Diane through her entire relationship with John Short, and she proved to be a surprisingly adroit witness, answering his questions in a serious, straightforward manner. She recalled John's telling her that Candy had been murdered, and her initial surprise that the killing had (supposedly) taken place so soon before they had met.

"Did you make any effort to contact John Short after you learned that his wife had actually died on Monday June 22nd?" the prosecutor wanted to know.

"I had a number for him in my phone book, and I tried calling several times," Diane remembered. "But I received no answer. My main way of trying to reach him was through Will Lambert, who I saw a couple of times that week at the bar. I gave him several messages, requesting that John contact me. At that point I did not believe that he killed his wife. Later on I composed a letter to him and returned the hundred dollars [that Short had paid Diane in exchange for sex]."

"Did John ever contact you?"

"No."

Brizek finished his questioning and stepped away from the front of the courtroom. It had been a strong session for the State. Diane came across as articulate and credible. No one in the jury box questioned her sincerity or reliability.

On this particular day she seemed more like a born-again Christian than a go-go dancer, and none of that was lost on those in the courtroom. If they had initially viewed her with skepticism, or even contempt, by the conclusion of Brizek's questioning Diane had earned their respect. In trying to tear apart the image Diane had just built for herself, Caserta faced a tougher battle than anyone could have anticipated prior to her appearance.

But he had one night in which to think about it, as Judge Hall closed out the day's session following Brizek's examination of Diane. After the jurors had exited the courtroom, both lawyers stuck around to discuss the accuracy of Dr. William J. Van Vooren's testimony. One of Brizek's first witnesses, the doctor who had examined Candy's post-mortem body on the night of the murder testified as an expert on digestive matters, and maintained that the partially digested dinner found in Candy's stomach served as proof that she was murdered one to two hours after eating. Considering that she had dropped Jesse off after dinner, that would make the time of the murder approximately seven o'clock P.M.

This information had been accepted both by Caserta and the court. Following that day's testimony, however, Brizek confirmed through Dr. Corrie May (the medical examiner from nearby Sussex County) that Van Vooren's theory was not widely recognized; he then revealed this finding to the judge and defense attorney. Besides being the ethical thing to do, it also eclipsed the possibility of Caserta discovering the discrepancy and using it to his advantage. Brizek suggested that Van Vooren's testimony should be disregarded by the jury.

Caserta, naturally, agreed to this, as did the judge.

The next morning Brizek asked the court to strike Van Vooren's testimony and requested that the jurors ignore it. Pleased with the assistant prosecutor's gentlemanly style, Judge Hull turned to Caserta and said, "You may start with your cross-examination of Miss Lovejoy."

Reacting as if Hull's words had been the bell in a boxing ring, Caserta came out swinging, determined to discredit the witness's testimony in any way possible. He began by picking at the double entendre inherent in there being a go-go dancer named Lovejoy. "Is that your real name?" he wanted to know, asking a question that had to have crossed the mind of everybody in the courtroom. "Or is it a stage name?"

"No. It was my married name," Diane primly replied, showing nary a hint of embarrassment.

Caserta questioned her inability to distinctly remember many of the details just after Candy's murder, and furnished her with a transcript of the Wayne Police Department's interview. Like many of the witnesses, Diane's recollections had been rekindled soon after she spoke to Brejack. The revised testimony would have made her seem slightly irresponsible had she not already been so credible on the stand.

Making sure that the jurors understood the transformation Diane had undergone over the last several years, Caserta asked her to describe The Way International's purpose. It alerted the court to the fact that she wasn't merely a woman who went to church each Sunday, but was a born-again Christian, a fundamentalist.

Caserta then went after Diane's testimony to the Wayne police. "You discussed the subject of John Short three times with them before you mentioned anything about Candy being mugged," he said, referring to a taped conversation she had had with Webster and McCann.

"I'd have to check the transcript notes in order to be positive as to when I said that."

"Well, I've already done it, Miss Lovejoy," Caserta replied, relishing the sound of her name. "You don't say anything about mugging until the second tape."

"Was that a question?" Hull asked, a little testy.

Brizek jumped up, annoyed at Caserta's assumption. "Well, I don't think—"

"I don't recall, sir," Diane said, cutting him off.

"I don't think it's fair to ask the witness that unless we take a half hour, an hour, and let her read the transcript," Brizek said, spitting the words out like bile, as if the task would be offensive to him.

Ignoring his adversary, Caserta continued, "Well, yesterday, Miss Lovejoy, you remembered everything the prosecutor asked you, right? You had that outlined, and you were prepared to go with it. You specifically told us that you were so certain of those things because you had reviewed them in such detail. Isn't that true? Didn't you say that?"

"I did not claim yesterday that I remembered everything from the tape or the transcript. I did claim that I had reviewed them. And there were a number of occasions where I said, 'I really don't know,' or 'I don't recall.' "

Aiming to expose the heavy prepping that had preceded yesterday's court appearance, Caserta went on to explain how Diane had had to be coerced not only to give a statement but also to testify. He revealed that when the Wayne police had first questioned her she had stated nothing about John's mentioning that his wife had been strangled and stabbed; that didn't come out until she met with Brejack. Caserta went into detail about her having been subpoenaed in Allegheny County, and maintained that Brejack had tricked her into agreeing to meet with him. He discussed the expense money she received from the state, and alleged that John was not the first man with whom she had engaged in sex for payment.

All of this was designed to diminish her standing in the minds of the jurors. But it failed. Regardless of what Caserta said, the jury members could not make the leap of faith that would allow them to see this pious woman dancing in her underwear above a crowd of lecherous men. Instead Diane resembled a confused, emotionally ravaged girl who had escaped to the church only when she had nowhere else to go.

It was a pathetic image, and it became even more so when Caserta questioned her about her actions immediately following the murder. "You visited the library [after discovering that Candy had been murdered] and went through the newspapers there?" he asked. "You read all about the case?"

"Yeah."

"Now, having read about the case, and knowing what you knew from your conversations with John Short, you continued trying to contact him, right?"

"Yes, sir."

"You left messages with Will Lambert?"

"Yes, sir."

"You left messages at The Coach Light?"

"Yes."

"As a matter of fact, when you met with the Wayne police you were still trying to contact John Short, right?"

"I would have to say probably. Knowing how I felt about it, if there had been an opportunity to see him, to talk and find out what happened and how he was and all that, I would have probably taken it up. However, under the circumstances that the Wayne police recommended, I did not want to see him. They offered for me to do something—"

"Against John?" Caserta asked, referring to Wilson's suggestion that she trap him into a confession.

"Yeah."

"And you weren't going to do that?"

"No."

"Thank you for coming, Miss Lovejoy."

When Brizek's turn came to reexamine Diane, he approached her with the intention of further improving the former go-go dancer's image. Although she had stood up well under Caserta's pressure, the defense lawyer had questioned Diane in such a way that her testimony looked forced. The most important issue for Brizek was that when the Wayne police first questioned her, she failed to mention John telling her the exact way in which Candy supposedly had been killed. Brizek asked Diane to elaborate on this point in a way that Caserta would have discouraged.

"To the best of my knowledge," she began, "this original transcript of the tape, the tapes that were done when the Wayne police originally questioned me, are accurate and true. They were the closest to the incident of, you know, in this, of this being what one of the officers were writing while this was being taped. They're accurate to the best of my knowledge at that point, which is a week or so later. Now, eight years—"

"Before you get to that, and we will get to that, I need to ask one other question. When you said that John Short did not specify the manner of death, do you mean that he didn't go beyond the word 'mugging,' or do you mean something else?"

"All right, he did not go beyond the word mugging."

In his effort to stem the headway that Caserta seemed to be making with the witness, Brizek sculped questions which established the fact that Diane's more detailed testimony had not been prompted by Brejack. "The details beyond the word 'mugging' that you gave the investigator," Brizek wanted to know, "may have been the result of what you learned in the intervening six and a half or seven years, from reading this or hearing about various aspects of the investigation?"

"Yes, sir," Diane said, once again resembling a model citizen.

Brizek established that during recent months she had reviewed the material that had been obtained from the Wayne police, and devoted a good deal of her time to thinking the events through. "And," the assistant prosecutor continued, his voice booming into the jury box, his eyes making contact with the twelve people who would decide John's fate, "based upon your reflection of this incident, the consultation of the seven-year-old interview with the Wayne police, what did he tell you about the murder of his wife?"

"That she did not come home from dancing lessons one night, and that she was found mugged [and murdered]. They never arrested the person who did it."

Brizek's concern was that at a later date Diane had told Brejack that Candy was found "attacked, beaten. I don't remember whether he said 'strangled' or 'stabbed' or both." In the course of that conversation with Brejack she had added that John had told her about Candy's being found "in a parking lot in a shopping mall." The prosecution wanted Diane to completely refute that information—so as not to confuse the jurors and to dispute the claim that Brejack had coerced her—to stick with the original telling that had been tape-recorded by the Wayne police, in which she had no exact memory of how John prematurely claimed his wife had been killed.

"From the outset, you always included the caveat that the details beyond John Short saying to you that Candy was mugged [and murdered] could have come from some other source?"

"Yes, sir."

"And after consulting your tape-recorded statement, you now know that you developed those details from other sources but that John Short did tell you his wife was mugged [and murdered]?"

"Yes, sir."

That's how it was left when Brizek finished with her.

The varying testimonies had been explained in a way that the jurors could believe and accept.

During Caserta's final examination of Diane, he once again raised the point of the inconsistencies in her testimony. Diane expressed confusion over exactly where the story of the supposed cause of Candy's death had originated, acknowledging that somewhere along the line she had heard about John's wife being strangled, murdered, and beaten in a shopping mall parking lot. Whether that information had come to her at the bar of The Coach Light—before the murder even took place—or in the interrogation room of the Wayne police station, or from Brejack (as Caserta contested), was a matter that would remain open to speculation.

But if the defense lawyer had his way, it would not be a dead issue. It clouded all of Diane's testimony, and caused the jury members to wonder what they could believe from her. Caserta continually tried and failed to extract an answer from Diane Lovejoy, before he finally allowed her to step down from the stand. As she exited, spectators in the crowded courtroom craned their necks to watch her leave.

Besides John, the people who were most interested in the outcome of this trial were not privy to it. Because the Austins would be called in to testify, they had to follow the rules which prohibited witnesses from viewing the courtroom proceedings, lest their testimony be compromised by the words of other witnesses. Each day the Austin family arrived at the courthouse and waited on the black marble benches in the lobby outside of the courtroom. They were desperately eager to find out how the hearing was progressing, but they had been explicitly instructed against peeking inside or even discussing the case among themselves.

"If anybody hears you doing that," Brizek warned, "it could lead to a mistrial."

The Austins—who were often joined by Betty and Joe,

as well as Helen's sister and brother-in-law from Pennsylvania—heeded his advice. They conversed about the same mundane, everyday things they would have discussed had they been sitting in the backyard on Passaic Avenue instead of in the Passaic County Courthouse. Nevertheless, it was difficult for them to reserve comment as Diane sauntered by, probably unaware that they were Candy's parents. But they managed to do as Brizek had requested.

Also honoring the prosecutor's wish was Brejack, who spent limited amounts of time with the Austins and generally maintained a healthy distance from the courtroom. Most of Brejack's energies were expended behind the scenes. Working from master lists that Steve Brizek had drawn up, Brejack called all witnesses who were due to appear the next day and made sure that they'd be there. Even though the task kept him occupied, he had a hard time thinking of anything beyond the eventual outcome of his case. But he knew he had to wait. Like the Austins, the investigator was scheduled to testify. And despite Brizek's best efforts to gain him admission to the courtroom, Brejack found himself forced to follow the same rules as everybody else. He avoided discussing the case, and barely associated with the others who would be called to the stand.

Unlike Brejack, who actually had a job to do, the Austins all but viewed this *as* their job. They certainly saw it as their responsibility to be in court everyday. Besides, they felt more comfortable outside the courtroom, maintaining a daily vigil, than they would have at home. In the courthouse, they had at least the illusion of participation as witnesses paraded past them all day long. The Austins recognized some and greeted them discreetly—always cognizant of Brizek's warning—while others appeared to be complete strangers.

Will Lambert fit squarely into the latter category. Although they had heard his name, the Austins' single brush with the man took place on the day of Candy's funeral, and that entire period remained a mental blur.

They looked on silently, helplessly, as Lambert's courtroom entrance followed Diane Lovejoy's departure. The two former friends greeted one another with a brief hug but exchanged few words. Unable to get over how fit Lambert now looked compared to the bloated, beerbellied man she remembered from their Coach Light days, Diane attempted to chat him up about Jesus before realizing that Lamb had no time to languish.

He gratefully begged off when the bailiff called his name.

Strolling into the courtroom dressed in a conservative suit and a fashionably flashy, fifties-style necktie, Will Lambert presented a startling contrast with his old friend. It made you wonder whether the two men had ever really known each other, never mind shared significant moments of their lives. John Short sat at the defense table, miserably trapped in a nightmare. Struggling for his freedom, he watched friends and acquaintances stepping up to the stand and offering testimony that seemed custom-tailored to do him in. He sat alongside Caserta, looking too exhausted to rally any kind of response.

Reserved, and uncomfortable in his current role of turncoat, Lambert still served as a valuable witness for the prosecution. He recalled Short's initial encounter with Diane, the borrowed Carte Blanche card, and the story of Candy's premature death. It began circulating, he said, the morning after Diane and John slept together. More damaging, though, was the conversation that Lambert next recounted, in that it revealed Short's tendency to embellish and alter the story of his wife's murder.

Was it because John couldn't keep his fabricated alibi straight?

"Did John Short give you any details about how his wife had been killed, what condition she was in when she was found?" Brizek asked.

"We were out at lunch when he told me she had been

raped, and stabbed with a sharp object," Lambert said. "She was also strangled. And whoever committed the crime had been so violent that they knocked an eye out of its socket."

"Did John Short explain to you where he was the night his wife was killed?"

"Yes. He said he was going from his home to a meeting at Mr. Jones's house in West Orange. He was driving over there and had gotten lost."

"Did he say for how long a period of time he was lost?"

"Yes. It was approximately two hours. John said he was riding around, looking for the house for two hours."

Lambert went on to recall John's on-again/off-again emotions at the funeral—"shifting gears," he called it—his lie about Candy being pregnant at the time of the murder, and the theory that the actual killing had happened someplace other than Willowbrook Mall. Brizek also had Lambert confirm John's plan to take Diane away for a weekend—something that he would have been hard pressed to pull off as long as Candy remained on the scene.

When Caserta's opportunity came for cross-examination, he had his work cut out for him. But the defense attorney was well prepared with this witness, and he planned on using Lambert—who was always willing to reveal more information than anybody had requested—to weaken the State's circumstantial evidence. Apparently Lambert had told Caserta about a situation in which a family friend inadvertently predicted her spouse's death just prior to the described event actually transpiring.

When he was asked if he remembered this incident, Lambert acknowledged that he did.

"You thought to mention it because it's similar?" Caserta asked.

"Involving John Short?" Brizek interrupted, challenging the relevance of the defense's question.

"I'm not certain yet, Mr. Brizek," opined Judge Hull.

Further discussion revealed that Lambert's story did not involve John Short directly, and Brizek objected to it on that ground. The lawyers stepped to the bench and discussed the matter with Hull, who listened to both sides before requesting that the jury members leave the courtroom. He then asked Caserta to pursue his line of questioning without the jurors present, so that he would be able to make a decision as to whether or not the statement should be admissible.

"Mr. Lambert," Caserta began again. "Tell us about those similar circumstances."

"Okay. My mother's lady friend, who lives across the street from us, was having an argument with her husband one day and told him to 'go drop dead.' That afternoon, the man literally dropped dead. He fell down a flight of stairs as a result of a heart attack. Because of that [after hearing that John had lied to Diane about his wife being murdered], I told him, 'You're crazy saying something like that, because things happen.' "

Caserta's point was that other coincidences of this sort have taken place, that there is a precedent. The untimely death of Candy, he maintained, had more to do with fate than with his client.

After a bit of arguing back and forth, the judge decided against allowing the jury to hear this, as Lambert had not directly told John about his neighbor across the street. It spoiled what could have been a plus for Caserta; the coincidence angle would have made the circumstantial case—which by its very nature had limited stability—appear flimsier.

Other witnesses called that day—Donna Olson Frangipane, Dennis King, and Jeanne Austin Suarez—further verified John's familiarity with West Orange, his infatuation with Diane Lovejoy, the fact that Candy never bought dance tights at Willowbrook, and that at the time of the murder she didn't even need a new pair for her upcoming recital (the Wayne police had discovered a recently opened package in her bedroom back in 1981).

By the time Brizek called Jeanne to the stand, the jury members had a better idea of why he had placed the easel and photographs in the well of the courtroom. The dots that traced roadways in and around West Orange now made sense. Through various pieces of testimony they came to understand John's familiarity with the area, and learned why the State had difficulty believing the story that he had gotten lost there.

All of that information, however, was concrete and objective. Jeanne's testimony would turn out to be emotionally charged. But it didn't start out that way. Initially she answered Brizek's questions about the day of the murder in a clear and straightforward manner. Besides the fact that it obviously had been rehearsed, Jeanne had long ago committed to memory the events that preceded her sister's death.

Then Brizek did something that changed everything: the way the jurors viewed Jeanne, the way they judged John, and the manner in which they viewed the marriage. He introduced into evidence a white wooden cross. In the austere setting of the courtroom, it seemed as insubstantial as a toy. Brizek held it with both hands, as if anything less than this delicate treatment would cause the cross to snap in half.

The room turned eerily silent as he raised it and asked, "Mrs. Suarez, do you recognize what this is?"

"Yes, I do," Jeannie said in a small voice, struggling to hold back a wellspring of tears.

"Please speak up," said Brizek, now all business. "What is this object?"

"This is the cross that John made after Candy died. He put it on her grave."

"How long did it remain there?" Brizek asked, not needing to elaborate on its inadequacy for a human burial plot.

"Years."

"Did you ever discuss with John Short the subject of getting a more suitable grave marker for his wife?"

"Yes, I did."

"Did he ever get one?"

"No. I had to get it myself."

"Did you have any discussions in which John Short expressed to you whether he intended to get a grave marker or not?"

"Yes. He did intend to get a grave marker. He told the family that we would have to wait at least a year, for the ground to settle, before one could be put in. When a year went by and still nothing was done, I approached him and he said he would get it. But he never did. That's why I took it upon myself to have the grave marker ordered."

Against testimony like that, Caserta faced a no-win situation. Attacking the witness in too heavy-handed a manner would make him look like a fiend, and laying back would do nothing for John's case. He resorted to the best possible ploy in this sticky situation and tried to subtly discredit Jeanne's testimony, proving that her memories from 1981 were selective, and bringing up Tony Mancuso. Caserta informed the court that Jeanne had called Tony at midnight (when Candy failed to return from the mall on June 22, 1981), mentioned that Mancuso had recently moved into his own apartment, and alerted the jurors to the fact that rumors of a liaison between the former high school sweethearts swirled through the area following Candy's death.

Despite Caserta's valiant effort—which was successfully impeded by an objection from Brizek—the defense took a whipping that afternoon. And as the judge ended the session, John Short left the courtroom a battered and beaten man. Trailed by his mother and wife, he headed out to his car and embarked on the long ride back to Ocean Grove for the weekend.

In coming days the other Austins provided equally stirring testimony under Brizek's well-plotted examination. When his turn came to cross-examine them, Caserta followed through on his plan to show the inconsistencies in their statements from 1981 as compared to 1987. And he scored solid points. In most every instance, there were items and emotions that had drastically changed. One of the most damaging of these revisions had been made by Joe Frank, who originally maintained that "John and Candy argued over mundane things. . . .[They didn't] throw pots and pans around like *The Honeymooners* on TV."

Caserta read that passage from Joe Frank's original statement to the Wayne police. In light of Joe's recent retelling of the couple's most incriminating public argument—the one that ended with John vowing to "piss on [Candy's] grave"—the inconsistency was glaring. He admitted to Caserta that he had failed to reveal that incident to Webster and McCann.

Strutting with the adrenaline of victory, the lawyer proceeded on sheer momentum, continuing to verbally pummel Joe long after his point clearly had been made. "Why didn't you say to the Wayne police, 'Gee, they just had a big fight. She said she's leaving him, and he said he's going to piss on her grave'?" Caserta wanted to know.

Joe had no answer. He could have gone into a longwinded explanation about how your perspective changes over the years, how he was so close to the couple that it wouldn't have seemed right to reveal their personal problems to the police, but he just didn't have it in him. Instead, the witness responded sheepishly: "Uh-hum. I don't have an answer for you."

For all the changes of perspective, though, each family member came to the witness stand with a heavy emotional stake in the proceedings. They answered questions as if their own lives hung in the balance. However, nobody's testimony would be more crucial than Fred's. Simply because he had discovered the body along with John, and could testify to the State's parking lot's logistics, he carried the potential to be the most deadly witness.

In physical terms alone, Fred Austin won the jury's

compassion. He was a stooped-over, skinny, gray-haired man who had physically aged well beyond his sixty-four years. Maybe the ceaseless Lucky Strikes had as much to do with his condition as the death of his daughter did, but nobody could have guessed that just by looking at him.

Hobbling to the stand with a cane for support, Fred looked like a man whose life had been ravaged by this murder. Though the age difference between him and Helen was marginal, she appeared considerably younger and virtually unscathed by what had happened. Fred carried the emotional weight of Candy's killing in a way that had virtually turned grief into a physical, fleshy thing.

The dealings between Brizek and Fred went smoothly. Fred answered the questions with a sureness in his voice, maintaining that he had caught a final glimpse of Candy alive when she dropped Jesse off with Betty and Joe. It was between six o'clock and six-thirty on the evening of June 22, 1981. Fred knew this because he glanced up from *Chico and the Man* and saw her through the window. Employing a marker to retrace their route on one of Brizek's aerial photographs, Fred stuck to his story about what had happened later that night when he and John discovered Candy's body at the mall.

He explained how John had spotted the car from the other side of the lot, and described the visibility as being "darker than coal." When they pulled up alongside the Cutlass, Fred said, John immediately smashed the glass on the passenger side. Yet the older man still could not recognize even an outline of his daughter's body.

"Where were you when John Short opened the passenger door after the window was broken?" Brizek asked.

"I was coming back around to my daughter Candy's car."

"And what occurred next? Tell the jury what happened."

"Well, John opened the door and said something to

the effect of 'Is she alive?' He grabbed her in his arms and held her."

"What did you do?"

"I went around to the other side, tried to find a pulse, but I couldn't."

Steve Brizek wound down his direct examination by having Fred state that he would never have discovered the body without John's coaching, and that he had never had any problems with his eyes or with night vision. Before finishing up, there was one more point that Brizek needed to make. It had gotten lost in Fred's recounting the story of the body's discovery. For that, he required the witness to read the statement that he had made to the Wayne police during the predawn hours of June 23, 1981.

"Having read that section of your previous answer, does it refresh your recollection as to what, if anything, John may have said he was able to see in the car [immediately] before he smashed the window?"

"I see it written . . . the car but . . .," Fred said, sounding flustered.

"Take your time," Brizek gently suggested.

" 'She's in the car,' he said to me," Fred finally got out.

"Before or after he smashed the window?"

"This is before, because he asked me for the hammer."

"Did you see her in the car?"

"No, no."

"I have no further questions," said a stoic but obviously victorious Brizek.

As expected, Fred Austin provided the State's most heart-wrenching testimony. Unlike some of the other people who had taken the stand, he was a completely sympathetic and believable witness. His description of the night at the Willowbrook Mall damaged Caserta's strategy in that it made the basis for his defense seem trivial. The shading of testimony over a six-year period came to look like little more than a technicality now that this man had spouted such a convincing recollection of John Short leading him to the body of his dead daughter.

If Caserta planned on following his tack of discrediting the State's witnesses as he cross-examined Fred, he would be treading in dangerous waters. Fred Austin had won the jurors over, and pushing the frail man too hard could be detrimental to the defense. Pushing him hard enough to create just a tiny bit of doubt as to the precision of his memory, though, was what the attorney needed to do. And he intended to pull this off in a way that would not offend the jury.

Rather than keying in on Fred, Caserta began by making Brejack appear manipulative, wondering who had done most of the talking during their meetings together and being somewhat chagrined by Fred's response of "Fifty-fifty."

Referring to the breakfast interview at the Tick Tock Diner, Caserta asked, "Did Investigator Brejack explain to you what happened at Willowbrook?"

"I don't understand you," Fred replied.

"Did Investigator Brejack ask you to describe the route, or did he suggest what the route was and ask you to agree with it?"

"No, no. I described the route to him."

After confirming that the path Fred had depicted for Brizek was the correct one, Caserta began pecking away at the details of the witness's testimony. It almost sounded cruel, the way Caserta scrutinized bits and pieces of what Fred Austin had told Brejack and Webster, then tried to trip him up by raising discrepancies.

"Do you remember telling the Wayne police, Mr. Austin, that you swung right into the parking lot?"

"I remember saying things to that effect, but everything—swinging into the parking lot, how we got into the parking lot—it's all a blur. After we discovered the car, you know, my mind was moving pretty fast."

"Okay, but I'm talking about before you discovered the car."

"I don't understand what you're talking about."

Caserta raised questions about details of the parking lot, the placement of construction barriers—which, he condescendingly recalled, Fred had referred to as "gizmos"—and whether or not a curb had existed in 1981, as a way of showing how Fred remembered only things that incriminated John. The lawyer aimed to prove that Fred remembered details about the defendant's behavior but failed to recall the exact structure of the parking lot. This was designed to call into question the integrity of the State's case against John Short. He even went so far as to ask how Fred had managed to find his way back to Candy's car after he'd driven to the telephone booth and called the Wayne police.

Details from the night on which Candy's body had been discovered got pulled out of the report like body organs in an autopsy. As Caserta held each one up and scrutinized it—"Do you recall the tractor trailers parked in the lot?"; "Before John opened the door, you did not see the 'blanket [in which Candy was wrapped]?"; "Your position in terms of Candy's car was not a forty-five-degree angle?"—Fred became increasingly confused and emotional. His voice turned shaky in the perfectly quiet courtroom.

Caserta proceeded shrewdly, knowing that his incessant questioning combined with Fred's apparent old age was calling the witness's credibility into question—even if it was at the expense of his own popularity with the jurors. He raised questions about Fred's eyesight—yes, it turned out that he had a cataract; yes, he ordinarily wore contact lenses; no, he did not have them in on the night of the 22nd—and produced one of several drawings that Candy's father had sketched. It looked like the penciled equivalent of a rambling and unstable mind.

"I was only scribbling to make a point," Fred insisted, acknowledging that it was the drawing he had made for Brejack on the back of the Tick Tock place mat and maintaining that he never expected it to turn up in court. "There's no detailed maps [on this paper]."

Caserta produced another drawing, one that Fred penciled for the Wayne policemen on the night of the murder. The lawyer referred to it and questioned the position of the cars. "Like I say, it's all scribbling that I've made [while] talking to George or to Wayne or whoever." He scrutinized the lines and concluded, "This is probably representing Candy's car, and this is the way we approached it when we first got there."

The cross-examination was taking its toll on Fred and on the State's case. It colored what had previously looked like a black-and-white situation, posing many more questions than it answered. Caserta knew which buttons to push in order to make Fred look mentally incompetent. The questioning proceeded in this manner after a lunch break, when further inconsistencies of detail emerged. Ultimately, Caserta wanted to prove that John had not told Fred to make the turn that led to Candy's car, that Fred had not come to this conclusion until he was interviewed by Brejack.

"In the interview with the Wayne police, when you were asked what John said when he spotted the car, the answer was 'There's the car,' " Caserta said. "Is that correct?"

"Yes."

"It was not until your second or third meeting with Mr. Brejack that you began to give the answer of, 'The car is back there.' Is that true, Mr. Austin?"

"Things came back to me then."

"Don't you understand, Mr. Austin, that what they've done—"

Brizek cut him short by objecting, and Caserta rephrased the question. Brizek objected again, this time with more heat in his voice. "This is no time for a debate with the witness!" he protested.

"Let him finish so I can rule on it," the judge told Brizek. Then he turned to Fred Austin and instructed,

"Don't answer the question, however, until I decide whether you *should* answer it."

Caserta couched this all-important inquiry in the most benign language possible: "Don't you recall, Mr. Austin, that your memory changed after you met Detective Brejack?"

Judge Hull gave Fred the nod to answer, and the witness replied with a simple and certain, "No."

"Detective Brejack offered you a solution to these—"

"No."

"He convinced you that John Short was responsible?"

"No."

"He put words in your mind?"

"No."

"I know you mean these things, Mr. Austin," Caserta tried to reason. He obviously was losing ground here, as Fred remained immovable on how he had come to alter his recollection. Running out of workable strategies, the defense lawyer resorted to exaggeration: "But don't you realize that they are one hundred and eighty degrees different from what you said back then?"

"Can I answer you in a lengthy thing?" Fred Austin nervously asked.

"In a lengthy thing?" echoed Caserta. "Will it be different from what you [originally told the Wayne policemen], Mr. Austin?"

"What I said back then . . . I was in a state of mind . . . I had just lost my daughter," Fred began. He held one hand over the other to keep its shaking hidden from those in the courtroom, and mustered all his courage to speak out in this intimidating environment.

"I know that, sir," Caserta condescendingly interrupted.

"Let him speak," responded Brizek, anticipating that Fred's words would represent a considerable break for the State.

"What I said then, I rambled on for an hour and a half. Half the things I said were not clear in my mind.

Nobody went over those Wayne statements with me to clarify that what I said was off the top of my head."

"All right," Caserta patiently responded. "And over the course of the seven years, before you met Detective Brejack, you went over it many times again?"

"I went over it thousands of times in my mind."

"In a better state of mind than immediately after Candy's death?"

"That's right."

"Yet until you met Detective Brejack and had hours of conversation with him you never took the position that you're taking here in court today?"

"No one ever asked me."

"No one ever put it in your mind. Is that what you mean to say, Mr. Austin?"

"No, I'm not."

"Thank you, Mr. Austin," Caserta said by way of concluding then retreated from the well of the courtroom and returned to his seat alongside John Short.

Speaking to the lawyer's back and realizing that his audience had suddenly become inattentive, Fred had one last statement to make. And he refused to let the legal system's conventions quash it. Unbidden, he repeated: "No one ever asked me about it."

The reexamination was brief—Brizek asked questions which confirmed that Fred reached his conclusion about being "led to Candy" independent of Brejack—and Caserta chose not to recross, perhaps fearing another reprimand from Fred. He had pushed the witness too far—lost control of him during the last few minutes of the cross-examination—and it resulted in irreparable damage being done to his defense of John Short. As Fred Austin stepped down from the stand and hobbled out of the courtroom, most of the jurors viewed him as someone to be pitied.

CHAPTER
20

The Jury Box was a small luncheonette located across the street from the Passaic County Courthouse. Cramped but homey, and manned by an overly friendly Greek cook, the restaurant drew a heavy lunchtime crowd. On most days of the trial, John Short retreated there during his noontime breaks. Taped to the walls above him were yellowed newspaper clippings of county investigators making collars, and he completely missed the irony that one of them contained a shot of Brejack. Short typically occupied a window table and absently stared out into the street.

Usually he ate alone. Occasionally his mother or wife joined him. Both women attended every day of the trial and publicly supported John in whatever way possible. The one person conspicuously missing—from both the courtroom and the Jury Box—was John's father. Speculation around the Prosecutor's Office was that he cut off all contact with his son as soon as the arrest had taken place. Brejack liked that theory, although only John and James Short knew the truth.

Despite the good bit of notoriety he gained as a result of the trial, John generally managed to enjoy his lunch without anybody bothering him. It should have been the one time all day that he could truly relax. But even then, after spending the morning hearing people he'd once trusted trashing him from the witness stand, John could not unwind. He drank countless cups of coffee and chain-smoked from one end of the meal to the other. Looking out through the plate-glass window, John watched the pedestrians passing by, dragged on cigarettes, nibbled a sandwich, said very little.

Intentionally or not, before his fate had been decided, John already had the markings of a guilty man. It was in the haunted glaze of his eyes, in the hunched way he walked, in the jumpiness that had become part of his persona. Even if John emerged from the trial without a prison sentence, he would still be a virtual shadow of his former self. This experience of having your past—whether it's real, fabricated, or exaggerated—thrown up in your face for three weeks would be enough to diminish anyone's ego, id, and soul.

The jury members, for their part, had mixed feelings. While Pat Caserta hardly exhibited a likable courtroom presence and Steve Brizek convincingly portrayed the defendant as a brutal man, the evidence presented by the State had consistently proven to be somewhat off. Stories had changed over the years; formerly reluctant witnesses had suddenly become willing to talk. It reached the point where the jury members had a hard time figuring out whose testimony to believe and whose to dismiss. In their eyes, nobody looked all that great.

As the trial went into its second week, most of the twelve jurors began to approach their task with a new sense of seriousness. They wanted to do the right thing, even though all of them knew that finding Short not guilty would be the easiest, least emotionally taxing decision (as it would eliminate the risk of imprisoning an innocent man). Days piled on top of one another, and the information began to come together. But even as a picture formed, these jurors discovered that the pace of justice can be stupefyingly slow. They were regularly marched in and out of the courtroom, often left to spend hours sitting in a drab, cinder-blocked space, waiting for the trial to resume.

Some of the jurors used the down time to read, others spent it on the telephone. One woman knitted, a man wrote in his notebook about the case. On his pad he printed something that the other jurors would soon come to realize as well: "In spite of the inconsistencies, Brizek is beginning to make the more impressive showing."

Even if the early part of the trial—which had been taken up with countless reviews of the possible routes Short could have driven from the mall, to his parents' house, to Jones's house—seemed like a boring case of overkill, assistant prosecutor Brizek did appear to have his facts down pat. He knew the points he wanted to make, treated witnesses with respect, and lacked the nastiness that they perceived in much of Caserta's courtroom behavior. Brizek's formality made him seem trustworthy to the jurors. Even the way his shoes squeaked as he walked from the State's table to the jury box—the assistant prosecutor conducted much of his questioning on his feet and in motion—was found to be strangely endearing.

What most surprised the jurors was that they actually enjoyed their roles as arbiters of justice. If nothing else, each person knew that it would make an interesting story for a long time to come. Even with all the waiting around and spates of boredom, they found something exciting in the process and felt honored to be a part of it. The attention from the court, the media write-ups (which they had been asked to avoid reading), having two powerful speakers communicating directly to them—it all added up to a sense of importance. And although their positions had come to them primarily by luck, the jurors felt chosen. At the moment, as the trial progressed and they remained in the spotlight, the dozen men and women seemed legitimately glad to be there.

George Brejack remembered a time when sitting on the witness stand, facing down a panel of jurors, had been second nature. During his days as a detective in Paterson he had appeared in court frequently enough to feel completely at home under the interrogative gaze of a defense attorney. But that was nearly a decade ago. When his turn came to testify in the case that he had spent more than a year putting together, Brejack experienced unexpected pangs of anxiety.

Dressed in his dark blue suit, with a white shirt and a subtly patterned necktie, he stood outside of the courtroom and made small talk with the Austins—all of whom had already been called to the stand—simultaneously hiding his nervousness and keeping the conversation away from the trial. When the bailiff called his name, Brejack apprehensively proceeded toward the witness stand. Though it was late in the day, a good number of reporters remained in court longer than they ordinarily would have. They remembered that George Brejack made good copy.

Brejack's testimony had the potential to be as damning as Fred Austin's. Not only would he deliver an emotional report on everything that had been uncovered about John, but the appearance of the investigator gave a face and personality to all of the prosecution's information. If the jurors viewed him as likable and believable, then the evidence he gathered would be perceived in kind. Conversely, if Caserta succeeded at making Brejack look like a heavy-handed operator (the lawyer believed that the charming and coercion of witnesses had run rampant through Brejack's investigation), then it would augur well for John Short.

But before Caserta had a chance to attempt that, Brizek embarked on the State's direct examination. In the course of working closely with one another, the two men had developed a synergy that was evident from the jury box and gave the Q & A a natural flow. On top of that, Brejack knew the background of this case better than anybody in the room, and his sense of authority overshadowed any stage fright he may have felt.

Brizek started off by asking the investigator to identify aerial photographs of Stone Drive and the Willowbrook

Mall parking lot. In doing so, Brejack described the circumstances under which the images had been shot and used a Magic Marker to signify the locations in relation to one another.

Once the jury had digested that information, Brejack recounted his re-tracing of the route that John Short might have taken on the night of the murder. By his estimation, it took eighteen minutes to drive from the house on Joralemon Street to Willowbrook Mall, and the traveling time between James and Adele Short's house and Jones's was sixteen minutes. Brizek also had Brejack trace the path that John supposedly had taken from the mall to his parents' house (fourteen minutes) after the murder had been completed.

The jury now understood clearly that John would have had plenty of time in which to commit the murder, clean himself up in Bloomfield, and make it to the meeting with Jones by nine o'clock. Important as that may ultimately have been, however, it was all relatively dry, technical information. It was not what drew the crowds to the courtroom. As Brizek finished questioning Brejack on the topic of timing, it became obvious that the more interesting information was yet to come.

Whispering and paper-turning rustled through the courtroom as he got to a juicier topic: Brejack's dealings with John Short. Brizek asked the investigator what Short had said to him just before he and Vincent Schraeger left the Ocean Grove house at the conclusion of their first visit.

"He was asked how he knew to drive to the Willowbrook Mall with his father-in-law on the night of the murder," came the response. "John Short answered, 'Oh, Candy went to Sears to buy me a pair of work boots.'"

This was precisely the discrepancy that Brejack had noted on the auspicious day more than a year ago when he had paid a surprise visit to his prime suspect. He had felt then that the information eventually would come in handy, and Brizek demonstrated exactly how handy before turning the questioning to the night of the arrest. "Can you tell the jury what occurred on the ride up the Parkway? What was said by Mr. Short? What was said to you?"

Before Brejack could formulate an answer, Caserta brusquely objected to the question. He requested a sidebar with Brizek and the judge, and the three of them began a conversation that the court and jury were not privy to. Hull excused the jurors, and Caserta complained about having had no prior knowledge that the State would raise this point about the car ride north. Additionally, he had never been furnished with the police report from that night.

Anticipating that this would be time-consuming, and seeing the afternoon winding down, Hull adjourned court and sent the jury members home. Brejack felt that he had done an admirable job, as he proudly stepped off the witness stand and left Brizek behind to hassle with Caserta and the judge.

Later that night, over dinner with Lisa, George said very little about the trial's progress, and she chose not to press for details. Even as the Candy Short murder wound down toward its conclusion, the dynamic of George's relationship with his girlfriend seemed to have been irrevocably altered by the investigation. The distance between him and Lisa had widened, and she questioned whether she really liked being involved with such an obsessive man. Brejack harbored the belief that Lisa was simply jealous, that she didn't like competing with the attention he received outside of their home.

Whatever the case, they increased the physical and emotional distance between them. Lisa spent the evening reading a paperback, and George turned in soon after dinner. The tension that built up during his day in court had yet to dissipate, and it kept him awake as he struggled to win a good night's sleep. The cross-examination from Caserta promised to be rough, and Brejack wanted to be well rested.

That next morning, Judge Hull instructed Brizek to stay away from questions involving the police report that Caserta had not seen. Then he asked the bailiff to fetch the investigator. Possessing more self-confidence than he had displayed at the start of his first day on the stand, Brejack made his way to the front of the courtroom with his back arched and his head held high. Something about his newfound bluster annoyed the jurors. He seemed too arrogant, too sure of himself (despite the fact that he really wasn't) under these tense circumstances. And they reached that conclusion without having had the opportunity to see him flashing a thumbs-up sign to the Austins as he passed them in the hallway.

Wearing a pinstriped suit that day, Brejack now had a red power tie around his neck. The investigator couldn't have known that it made him look terribly arrogant to at least one juror. And even if he had been made aware of it, Brejack wouldn't have cared. The trial was coming to an end, and he remained as certain as ever that Short would be convicted of murder. Now he only had to stand up to this last round of questions on the witness stand.

As a result of Hull's ruling, Brizek had lost out on the opportunity to examine the issue of Short's unstable behavior (when he began to seize up in the car, for instance) and settled for asking Brejack only a few more questions. Like those that had preceded them, these centered on possible routes that could have been taken by Short and locations of sites near the Jones residence. Within the few minutes it took for those questions to be answered, the improbability of John getting lost on the night of the murder had been further solidified.

Far more challenging for Brejack would be the questions proffered by Pat Caserta. From the cross-examination's start, Caserta approached the investigator with an aura of skepticism that he hoped would rub off on the jurors.

The defense attorney tried to sway them to join him in the suspicion that Brejack had never fully investigated the case, John Short had been his only suspect from Day One, and the investigator had taken the case on because it would make for an easy, headline-grabbing arrest. From the way the trial had been going, Caserta was not far off track in his allegation that much of the State's testimony was based on emotions as well as legal findings. Using Brejack as an unlikely ally, he struggled to make the jury believe the same thing.

Caserta spoke with an aloof civility, as if this conversation were a terrible chore but he had tacitly agreed to be polite. Camouflaged disdain was volleyed back and forth, with Brejack acknowledging that he paid next to no attention to the Wayne Police Department's reports, and that he hadn't even bothered to read the transcriptions of the audio-taped interviews once they became available.

In questioning the investigator, Caserta manipulated him into acknowledging that he opted not to pursue the people who owned the Belle Maid deli—even after it became clear that the couple never truly acknowledged whether they sold cigarettes to John at a time that would have made it impossible for him to have committed the murder.

He let the jury mull over the fact that Brejack had neglected to follow up on something that might have worked in John's favor, and reminded them of how far out of his way Brejack had gone to track down Barbara Capalbo—a source with the potential to have exactly the opposite effect on the defendant's case. The information made it clear that Brejack had never wanted to exonerate Short, and Caserta's next point neatly capped the previous one.

"Did you find notes concerning people who had called in [to the Wayne Police Department] and reported incidents in the Willowbrook parking lot that night?" he wanted to know.

"There's a possibility that those things exist," Brejack acknowledged, "but I can't remember. There were so many scraps of paper and pieces of notes in that file that I can't remember everything, Mr. Caserta. I'm sorry."

"No, that's all right," Caserta said, glad to see his point being made and eager to move on to his agenda's next item. "Did you happen to see a note that identified an individual by the name of Steve Steinhoff, who told the Wayne police that he spotted the victim's car on Route 46 eastbound at four-fifteen P.M.?"

"I don't remember that."

Caserta mentioned a few other potential sources that Brejack had ignored, then he questioned the investigator's motivation for visiting Candy's grave site and "taking the cross, which you claim was on the ground, and confiscating it as evidence."

"Somebody told me that John had made a cross, a homemade cross," Brejack explained, eager to get in more than simply what Caserta wanted to know. "I was just curious to see it." Recognizing the opening, Brejack quickly made his move, nimbly sliding the additional information through Caserta's hard defensive line. "I looked at it and couldn't believe somebody would do something like that to a grave. But when I thought about the things I had already learned about this man in the course of my investigation, it was, like, consistent. So I came back. I spoke to [chief assistant prosecutor] Mr. Kayne about it, called Mrs. Austin. She said, 'If you want to take it, take it.' So I took it."

Surprisingly, Caserta did not interrupt Brejack as he swerved away from the exact question that had been asked, but that's not to say that the tangential response failed to disturb him. Pivoting toward Hull, the defense attorney immediately requested a conference with Brizek and the judge. They spoke in private for a few moments before the jurors were asked to leave the courtroom.

After the question and answer were read back to the court, Caserta looked at Hull and said, "Judge, I don't think anybody on this side of the courtroom is unaware that Detective Brejack has a reputation for volunteering information from the witness stand that is not responsive to the question."

Sitting alongside Hull, Brejack viewed this as a supreme compliment and barely suppressed a smile. "That answer can be strictly construed as responsive, but it's clearly an attempt by the detective to sneak in information," Caserta continued. "I want Detective Brejak instructed by the court to be responsive to the questions and not play games with me."

Judge Hull agreed with this and advised Brejack appropriately. "It would be most unfortunate," he stated, eyeing the apparently chastened witness, "if I had to terminate this trial and try it again because of an answer that goes beyond the question asked."

"Yes, your honor," Brejack softly said, realizing that Hull's threat coming to fruition would be among the worst possible outcomes. By the time the jury had returned to the courtroom, he decided to answer Caserta's queries in a manner more consistent with the court's wishes.

The jurors resumed their seats in the box, and Caserta went back to questioning Brejack's willful refusal to pursue all the bits and pieces of evidence relating to the murder. He mentioned that the Wayne report referred to Sears' employees who might have noticed the car with Candy's body in the store's employee parking lot. Brejack replied that he hadn't interviewed any of them.

Incredulous, Caserta wanted to know, "You read Wayne's reports, didn't you?"

"Mr. Caserta, I read the reports, but I didn't go into them because I wasn't impressed by them. I took names and locations, but there wasn't that much to read. It was just light things."

"So, more or less you started anew?"

"I started my own investigation, and I [also] talked to

people that they spoke to. I went deeper into things and explored other areas."

"Now, one of the things that existed were the names, addresses, and telephone numbers of two men who were parked in their tractor trailers right near the scene where Candy's car was found. Is that so?"

"I don't remember that," Brejack said, responding in a way that did nothing to help his own credibility but certainly served to deflect a potentially damaging attack from Caserta.

And that's the way the questioning proceeded. Caserta brought up various witnesses, mentioned the ways in which their stories had changed over the years, and wondered about a seemingly subjective method of report-filing.

Listening, nodding, Brejack answered the questions he could and pleaded ignorance on the others. Caserta hinted at the strong-arming that Brejack supposedly had employed against Dan Solowe, and raised the issue of the Interstate Witness Compact Act having to be invoked in order to ensure Diane Lovejoy's presence on the witness stand. This was designed to cast doubt on the veracity of her testimony. In fact, the former go-go dancer presented a major stumbling block for the defense, with the jurors viewing her testimony as surprisingly credible. Diane's words all but pegged John as the murderer, even though the reports still had enough gray areas—changes in her exact story, and an overall whiff of uncertainty as to what John had said when—that Caserta thought he could use them to sway the jurors. He attempted this by exposing the various phrasings that Brejack used in his reports.

"Is it fair to say that in writing your reports you would sometimes characterize the recollection of the witness?" Caserta asked, having just cited that very aspect of the Susan Fishman report, which stated that some of her memories were "vague."

"In that report I did it," Brejack said. "Yes."

"When you took statements from Diane Lovejoy, did you recall her ability to recollect? Was she firm in her recollection? "

"Whatever is on the statement is what she remembered."

"Do you recall how vague or firm she was in her recollection of the events concerning her meeting with John Short on June 15, 1981?"

"If you show me the statement I can tell you what she told me she remembered about him."

After a bit of fumbling, Caserta produced the appropriate set of pages and handed it up to Brejack. The investigator looked it over and waited for the question. "What I'm after here, Detective, is anything in your report which indicates that Miss Lovejoy was uncertain or vague in her recollection of these events."

"When you say 'events,' you're talking about June 15th, June 18th?"

"The entire time she knew John Short that week," Caserta said, his patience beginning to run out. "June 15th to the end of the week."

"Would you like me to read the report? I don't understand exactly what you're getting at. Her facts are in the statement. This is just a report from the interview."

Finally, when it became apparent that this verbal jousting would lead nowhere, Judge Hull felt compelled to jump in. "Read the report to yourself, and tell us whether there is any uncertainty on her part or whether you had to refresh her memory with anything in order to get the information that appears in the statement."

"We did bring the Wayne Police Department's notes to Pittsburgh," Brejack allowed. "She went over them in order to refresh her memory. We did that. Is that what you're talking about?"

"I'm asking you if you recall the *quality* of her memory," Caserta said, executing a slow burn. "Now you're saying it was refreshed after she read the notes." His voice angrily rose as he asked Brejack, "Is that correct? Is that correct, *sir*?"

"Well, I'm reading the report."

Brejack studied the words that he had typed himself, then signaled that he had finished, and looked up to face another question. "It's true, is it not, Detective Brejack, that in your report you make no characterization as to her recollection of the events after she gave them to you?"

"I don't understand you, Mr. Caserta."

"Sure you don't?" Caserta skeptically asked, attempting to show the jury that Brejack was intentionally avoiding cooperating.

"She remembered what happened and she told me," Brejack simply said.

"And she remembered it well, and *firmly*, right?"

"Well, I don't know what you mean by 'firmly.' "

After hearing the question rephrased several more times, Brejack acknowledged that, yes, Diane did remember the events firmly. All she told him she recalled exactly.

The fact that it had taken so long and so many questions for Caserta to get Brejack to give him a straight answer on this matter should have given the jury members something to think about. It was Brizek's job, on the redirect, to smooth out these bumps that Caserta managed to successfully introduce into the trial.

He started off by making it clear that in Diane's original statement to Brejack she had discussed John telling her that his wife had been "strangled or stabbed or both." By going through a good deal of Diane's testimony, and later bringing up Brejack's dealings with Barbara Capalbo, Brizek was able to make the point that the investigator's information had been legitimately obtained.

By the time Brejack stepped down from the witness stand and exited the court room, his testimony had brought a good deal of legitimacy back to the prosecution's case. While the jurors were hardly impressed by

Brejack the man, his skills as an investigator were undeniable. His testimony struck with a commanding resonance. The way he told it, the witnesses were neither coerced nor compromised. When he left the courtroom and mouthed the word "beautiful" to the Austins, it was more than simple boasting. Brejack knew that he had completed his role in seeing the investigation through: He had done all he could to ensure the conviction of John Short.

Later that morning, after the court proceedings broke for lunch, Caserta, Brizek, and Hull remained in conference. They needed to go through fifty pieces of the State's evidence that would be made available to the jurors once they began deliberating. Caserta objected to several of the items being entered—Candy's bra, the purse that had been dumped out at the murder scene, and a replication of the flip-flop key ring—and in each instance he was overruled.

When Brizek held up the cross and requested that it be entered as well, Caserta objected in the strongest possible way. "Judge," he said, realizing the damage it stood to inflict on his client, "the cross should not be entered. Its emotional impact far outweighs any probative value it could have. Apparently [the prosecution maintains] Mr. Short's woodwork skills were such that the cross is a poor example of his otherwise tremendous skills, and I don't think there's testimony to support that. Mr. Lambert's testimony was that he built him a good house and that he had skills in that regard. But to bring in the cross from the grave, I just think is inappropriate and irrelevant."

The judge listened to what Caserta had to say, then turned to Brizek and asked for his response.

"The State's position in these proceedings is that the defendant wanted his wife dead," Brizek began. "The state is going to argue he was disenchanted with his wife. He was enchanted with someone else. He had a motive and he had the inclination to kill her. The cross, together with other evidence—evidence of bruises, evidence of statements to his wife—are all consistent with that point of view. The cross is tantamount to a statement by the defendant: 'I hate my wife. I'd just as soon see her dead. I have utter contempt and disdain for her.' If he had said that in writing it certainly would be admissible. He said it in other ways. This cross speaks volumes, and it should be admitted."

"It will be marked in evidence," Hull decided, in much the same way that he agreed to let just about everything else be admitted as well. This included a photograph of John, Candy, and Jesse together. It was ostensibly a way of showing John and Candy's height difference and hair colors, in support of Barbara Capalbo's testimony, After Caserta complained that the image of their daughter would inappropriately sway the jury, Brizek agreed to block Jesse out from the photograph with a strip of black tape.

After lunch but before the jurors returned, Caserta made another attempt to get the case dismissed from court. "Let me first renew my application for dismissal based upon the inordinate delay of the presentation of this material," the defense attorney began. "The State has no justifiable basis for the delay. This is a case wherein the matter is 1981, and the positions of the witnesses are 1981 versus their positions today in 1988."

Caserta argued that there was nothing that indisputably pointed to John Short as the murderer of Candy; he added that what had been presented was all old enough to be deemed unreliable. With the jurors absent, he enumerated each piece of testimony that had changed substantially since the people were first questioned in 1981.

He maintained that one particularly critical change was involved in Barbara Capalbo's testimony. If the jury were to believe her—despite the fact that she initially mistook the color of the car—it would come very close to having an eyewitness. But, according to Caserta, hers was only the most blatant case of memories having been altered. "If you take every witness who was interviewed in '81 and interviewed today, their positions are different," Caserta argued. "Some are different on special points, some are substantially different. We're without Detective McCann to go into any of the statements taken in 1981 in terms of exactly what the witnesses said."

"I still don't see how you're prejudiced in that regard, and that was my finding before we started this trial," Judge Hull replied. "With respect to Miss Capalbo, you have the benefit of the information which was in the police notes, in which she described the vehicle as being a different color."

Though he didn't say it, Caserta felt certain that Barbara Capalbo had lied on the witness stand. He repeatedly maintained that if McCann were still alive—as he would have been, if the case had gone to trial at the time of the murder—then a lot of these vagaries could have been resolved. McCann would understand the squiggles of lead on Fred Austin's map of the parking lot; he would be able to discount Barbara as a witness; he would explain exactly what Diane Lovejoy had remembered John telling her that night at The Coach Light.

Brizek disagreed. He insisted that the defense had ample opportunities to address inconsistencies. Caserta's request to have the case dismissed, Brizek maintained, was absurd.

After brief consideration, the judge agreed. The trial, he announced, would resume as planned. With Brizek's list of forty-one witnesses completed, Pat Caserta now had the opportunity to call his first batch of people to the stand. Then the trial would continue on Monday, with everybody getting Friday off, as the day is traditionally put aside for sentencing in the Passaic County Courthouse.

Pat Caserta called his first witness. Her name was Andrea Stanton, and, like Barbara Capalbo, she and her sister had been at Willowbrook Mall on June 22, 1981.

Like the Capalbos, they too had seen something that disturbed them. "My sister Julia and I parked our car in the lot near Bamberger's," Andrea began. "And a man pulled in at around the same time, in the aisle across from us. Julia and I were getting my four-year-old son ready to leave the car when we realized that the man wasn't getting out. He rolled the windows up, he locked the doors, he made all the motions of leaving his car but never actually did it. We didn't leave our car until it seemed safe."

"What made you feel it was then safe to get out of the car?" Caserta wanted to know.

"We waited until after the man circled us and headed in the direction of Stern's. When he hit that corner, when we felt he was a distance away, we made it inside the mall safely."

So disturbed was she by the man's presence that Andrea copied down his license plate number and reported it to the police. On the statement she made to them, it was noted that he was there between six-thirty and seven-thirty, precisely the time in which Candy was said to have been murdered. Caserta had her confirm all of this and concluded his questioning, leaving the jury to wonder why the Wayne detectives (and Brejack, for that matter) failed to follow up on a suspicious character who might have been the killer of Candy.

In his cross-examination, Brizek attacked the witness for her willingness to see the man as being so suspicious. He didn't even bother raising the issue as to whether or not the man may have been the murderer and whether or not her lead *should have* been followed up. He refused to acknowledge that her suspect might have been truly dangerous. Brizek accomplished this by making the woman look foolish.

"Now, when you pulled in, his windows were down and when you observed him he rolled up his windows," Brizek asked in a controlled, condescending tone that he rarely used in the courtroom.

"Right," Andrea said, intimidated from the start. "We thought he was sitting in the car."

"He rolled up his window *once*?"

"Right."

"He wasn't rolling them up, rolling them down or anything?"

"No, no."

The conversation proceeded to the point where she acknowledged that he didn't actually *do* anything that would make him suspicious. But he did sit there. And he *was* watching them.

"Figuring out, maybe, why *you're* sitting in *your* car?" Brizek asked, rousing a chuckle from the jury box.

"While we were—," she stammered, openly embarrassed by the lighthearted way in which Brizek treated her testimony. "Before we realized he wasn't getting out, we were busy getting my son out of his car seat and things like that. We had a reason to be, you know, sitting in the car."

"What reason?"

"We were getting my son, you know, getting things organized to get out."

"And then he pulled away?"

"After sitting there for quite a bit of time and watching us, he pulled away. He circled the aisles a few times, then he left the area."

"That's it?"

"That's it."

On redirect Caserta had Stanton confirm that nobody had ever contacted her in an effort to follow up on this man as a possible suspect. After she stepped down, Caserta called Andrea's sister to the stand. Julia Mahoney told the story in a dramatic tone, relating how the man had looked at them through his rear view mirror before pulling away, how they had reported the incident to a security guard inside the mall, and called the Wayne police a day or two later, after reading about the Short murder in the newspaper.

Because she remembered the car as a light colored Oldsmobile—the same make of car that Candy's body had been discovered in—Brizek wanted to confirm that this was not the crime scene. He did it on the cross-examination by asking her whether or not there were any stickers on the rear bumper. She said no. He further discredited the witness by having her explain that her husband had recently been mugged and that she was especially uncomfortable about walking through parking lots.

As soon as court adjourned for the long weekend, Brizek dispatched Smith and Lackland to round up the witness who could refute the Stanton/Mahoney testimony. He promised to join them in the hunt after returning from a farewell dinner he had to attend for a departing assistant prosecutor.

Later that evening, at a nearby steak house, Brizek found himself confronted by Ronald Fava, Passaic County's head prosecutor. "I want to talk to you for a minute," Fava told him. "I understand that you were pretty rough on Andrea Stanton and Julia Mahoney today."

"Not *excessively* rough," Brizek said, about to formulate a response, eager to stay out of trouble with his new boss.

"Both of them complained about you this afternoon." Fava hesitated for effect, then pumped Brizek on the back. "Keep up the good work."

CHAPTER
21

The weekend had been anything but restful for Steve Brizek, Peter Lackland, and Fred Smith. They took advantage of the trial's three-day respite and devoted their time to sorting through police records and operating computer link-ups with the New Jersey Division of Motor Vehicles. It was the only way to disprove the sisters' claim that the man in the car was up to no good at the mall.

But it went deeper than that. Experience told Brizek that if Caserta had used the Wayne police reports to find Thursday's pair of witnesses, then he would most likely be calling Dale Servino to the stand as well. Servino had also reported seeing a suspicious character at Willowbrook Mall on the night of Candy's murder. Because the complainants had been quick-witted enough to record the offender's license plate numbers, Brizek and the investigators had a fighting chance to find those people and undermine the claims of Caserta's witnesses. Working against them, however, was the fact that the incidents had occurred nearly eight years ago. The vehicles could have changed hands any number of times, and the original owners might have died or relocated long after selling their cars.

Brizek believed that Caserta's ploy was a red herring. Were it to go unanswered, though, the testimony of Andrea Stanton and Julia Mahony, combined with what he anticipated from Servino, could be just enough to prevent one juror from finding John Short guilty, leaving the prosecution's case lost in a hung jury. But as long as Caserta's sources were alive and reachable, Brizek believed that Lackland and Smith would track them down.

From what Andrea had said on the witness stand, Brizek felt reasonably secure that the man she saw at the mall had meant her no harm. As long as they had him in court on Monday morning, the jury would know that as well.

The big surprise on February 6th, the Monday when the trial resumed, was the absence of John Short. Up till then he had appeared in court every day, precisely on time, with his wife and mother beside him. Today, though, Adele and Judy arrived punctually and the defendant was nowhere to be found. Word of this filtered out to Brejack, who feared that Short had committed suicide. "I could care less if the prick brodied himself," he told John Nativo. "I would just hate to see this beautiful case go down the drain."

The chief agreed that it would be a shame and suggested that Brejack place a call with the State Police to see if there had been any accidents on the Parkway. None that might have involved John had been reported. Just as Brejack began considering the possibility that Short had simply taken off, Judge Hull testily announced that they would begin the trial without the defendant.

It wasn't the way he liked to run a courtroom, but Caserta's first witness had limited time and the defense lawyer maintained that John was on his way. "Ice," he guessed, "is what's slowing him down. There's a lot of ice on the Parkway, and John has a long drive from Ocean Grove."

The jurors entered the courtroom and remained oblivious to John's absence as Caserta's first witness of the day took the stand. True to Brizek's instinct, it was Dale Servino, the automobile salesman who had filed a complaint with the Wayne police just after the murder.

Asked by Caserta to describe what happened, he said, "My wife and I walked into the mall, and it seemed like somebody was following us. We entered a store and he was ten feet away. When we left the store he was still behind us. So I walked toward him, like in a rush, and he took off around the corner and disappeared. I thought it was kind of strange and decided to keep my eyes open. Then, as we drove home on Route 23, I looked in my rearview mirror and saw the same guy behind me. I jammed on the brakes and swung the car around, so that he could pass me, which he did. I wanted to follow the guy and pull him over, but my wife thought that was crazy. He could have been some kind of a nut."

"Now," Caserta wanted to know, "did you later see an article in a newspaper?"

"The very next day. The very next day I read something, which said, 'If anything out of the ordinary happened to you while you were in the shopping center, call the police.' Being the citizen that I am, I did that and gave them the same information that I just gave you."

Servino acknowledged that he had reported the man's license plate number to the Wayne Police Department, but, to the best of his knowledge, no follow-up investigation had taken place. Like much of the testimony that Caserta elicited, this was designed to make the jury question the thoroughness of the search for Candy's killer, to prove that the law enforcers had gone after only the most obvious suspect and neglected to fully investigate the case.

When Brizek's turn came to cross-examine the witness, he proceeded with the same strategy that he employed against Andrea Stanton and Julia Mahony. Approaching Servino with doubt in his voice, Brizek aimed to discredit the man by showing that it could have been paranoia rather than true fear which led him to telephone the Wayne police.

"Were you able to recognize the face of the individual?" Brizek asked, referring to the tailgating incident.

"No," Servino replied.

"So you can't tell the jury that it was the same person [as in the mall], correct?"

"I would say it was the same person from what I saw in terms of the color scheme that he had on. I remember that he wore a red bandanna around his head."

"Was he doing anything unusual such as tailgating you or—"

"Yes."

"—beeping his horn at you."

"No, no. He was just coming up too close in back of me. He was directly behind my car."

"So he was driving behind you."

"Correct."

"And you jammed on your brakes."

"That's correct."

"Why did you do that?"

"For the simple reason I got a little excited. And when I get a little excited, I get a little angry. I was going to ram him."

"So after you jammed on your brakes and pulled over, he passed you, and you began tailgating *him*?"

"That's correct. I was going after him."

During his redirect, Caserta tried to reestablish the witness's credibility—to make him look like something other than an obsessive crank—by having him point out that he now remembered very little of the incident, and it was only a rereading of the complaint he had filed that recharged his memory. This only minimally made the person "tailgating" Servino seem to be a likely suspect, and the case would have proceeded with Caserta's next witness had John Short shown up.

At ten-fifteen, aware of the defendant's continuing absence, Judge Hull suggested that the jurors take a half-hour break in the hope that he would arrive by ten-forty-five. Once the jurors were out of the courtroom, he looked down at Caserta and asked, "Have you heard any word from Mr. Short?"

"No, I haven't," Caserta admitted. "Some of the people out in the hallway gave me different reports as to the road conditions on the Parkway. One fellow said it was bad. Another person told me he had no problem."

An investigator was dispatched to call downstate to some of the local police departments and check on the Parkway's condition. He came into the courtroom a few minutes later and announced that it was all clear. This gave everybody—including John's mother—cause for concern. Hull considered the circumstances for a moment, then asked Caserta when he had last heard from his client.

"There was a message," the defense lawyer said. "I got to my office before eight this morning, and when I called home to look for a message from my investigator, I discovered that John Short had called me. His mother said she heard from him at a quarter to eight. He was supposed to be leaving then. I just don't understand it."

"Have you tried calling him by telephone at his home?" Hull asked.

"Yes I have. I contacted my investigator and asked him to find out if there was a problem with John. Because he wasn't up here, I assumed that he would be at home. The investigator called and got an answering machine. But I can't imagine that he would still be at home."

"Well, being that it's now twenty-five minutes after ten, if he were home and there was a problem, I imagine that we would have heard from him."

"I think the same thing," Caserta said with a mixture of embarrassment and resignation. "I can't imagine that there could be such a problem."

During his years as Candy's husband, John's disregard for punctuality had reached legendary status. He had made people wait all the time. The Austins knew more about this side of John than they cared to. Today, as he forced the court to wait, those acquainted with John Short found it very much in character.

*   *   *

Because closing arguments were scheduled to begin that afternoon, Brejack elected to spend most of Monday in the courthouse. It was the one part of the trial that he anticipated being allowed to see, and he didn't want to miss it. But now, Short's disappearance created a potential glitch. The possibility that he had made a run for it or killed himself loomed increasingly large in the mind of George Brejack.

He said as much to Joe Frank when he spotted Candy's family members sitting outside the courtroom, waiting to go in and witness the trial's conclusion. Joe, however, insisted that George's fears were unfounded.

"John's not the suicidal type," he said. "The guy's got too big of an ego for that."

George said nothing. He looked around for a moment, checking whether or not Short had shown up, then turned back to Joe. "I have to take a piss," he said, and headed down the corridor to the bathroom.

Brejack walked in on an unexpected scene. Standing near one of the sinks, sweating and shaking, and visibly in no condition for a court appearance, John appeared to be on the verge of another nervous breakdown. "I-I-I-I'm sc-sc-scared," he told Pat Caserta, trembling and holding back a flood of tears.

Trying to calm his client, Caserta did not welcome the investigator's presence. Brejack didn't care. "What's going on here?" he asked, in a loudly aggressive tone that served to further upset John. He approached the two men and continued, "They're waiting for you in the courtroom. Why don't you get in there? Judge Hull wants to complete the trial."

"Come on, George, give us a little bit of privacy," Caserta said, concerned about the ill effect that Brejack's intrusive presence could have on his client. "We'll be in the courtroom in a couple of minutes."

Reluctantly, Brejack left and notified the Austins that John had indeed shown up. Within fifteen minutes Judge Hull also knew this, and the trial resumed. John explained that he had been held up because his car had broken down on the highway, although there appeared to be more dire circumstances than that which caused the delay. To all appearances, the defendant seemed to be recovering from an all-weekend bender. This was lost on the members of the jury, who barely took note of Short's presence and had not been informed of his lateness.

The trial proceeded with Caserta calling Will Lambert to explain his vagueness about whether Short had personally done the carpentry in his home; this testimony was designed to show that the defendant was *not* an expert carpenter who could have easily fashioned a beautiful marker for Candy's grave.

On cross-examination, Brizek asked the questions in such a way that Lambert contradicted himself by admitting that John did possess carpentry skills. Whatever the case, it all seemed to be something of a moot point now that the jurors had seen the cross and heard emotionally charged testimony from the Austins. They shared the feeling that if you don't like somebody you do nothing about their grave. If you hate that person, you desecrate it. And for all intents and purposes, that's what John appeared to have done with the cross.

The calling of Caserta's next witness, however, promised to shed more positive light on John's innocence— or at least it would contribute to the argument against convicting him of murder. Phyllis Rosco was married to the owner of the Belle Maid Delicatessen, the store where John claimed to have purchased a pack of cigarettes during the time of his wife's murder. She maintained that the Wayne police had questioned her, asking whether or not somebody had come in and purchased Marlboro Light cigarettes on the night of the killing.

She told them that a lot of people buy that brand on any given evening. However, Phyllis did remember one particular customer, a man who could have been John Short. A few days later that man returned, and Phyllis's husband jotted down the license plate number of the car he'd gotten out of. She reported this to the police, but the lead was never followed up. This added weight to Caserta's allegation that investigators had never seriously inquired as to whether or not John might have been in the Belle Maid that night. Once again, Caserta called a witness to the stand who pointed out that from the investigation's start, John Short had been the only serious suspect.

Brizek tried to reverse this by asking Phyllis Rosco whether John Short had personally tried to disprove his guilt. "Did he ever come up to you and ask if you remember him buying cigarettes on the night of the murder?"

"No," she told the assistant prosecutor.

Later, Sam Rosco, Phyllis's husband, came to the stand and supported her testimony. Caserta's position was further reinforced when the lawyer inquired, "Did you ask the police to provide you with further information so you or Phyllis could determine whether or not he was in?"

"I said," Sam replied, "we would be able to tell better if we either saw him personally or saw a picture of him."

"And what did the police do in response to that?"

"Nothing."

"During the telephone conversation with the officer, you indicated to him that you had a license plate number. Did he take it?"

"No."

In his cross-examination, Brizek asked Rosco to once again confirm that John, who had regularly shopped in the store, never asked them whether they remembered seeing him there on the night of the murder.

The final witness called before the lunch break was Elizabeth Austin, Betty Frank's mother and the great-aunt of Candy. She lived with her daughter, and was the person with whom Candy had left Jesse before heading to Willowbrook. Maintaining that Candy had told her John was busy that night and would not be meeting her at the mall, she had the ability to place further doubt in the minds of the jurors.

Brizek successfully argued that her statement was hearsay, and Judge Hall agreed that it should not be entered into the record. Before Elizabeth had a chance to say much of anything, she was dismissed from the stand and the court broke for lunch. An hour later Caserta opened the afternoon session by calling a pair of witnesses who had telephoned the Wayne police on June 24th. They had reported seeing Candy's car in the vicinity of the Willowbrook Mall at four-thirty on the day of the murder. The inference was supposed to be that Candy would not have gone to the mall twice in one day, so she was obviously murdered elsewhere and left in her car at the mall. It didn't make much sense, but the testimony had the potential to further cloud issues in the minds of the jurors.

After Andrew Webster was uneventfully called to the stand—he failed to recognize the photograph of the interior of Candy's car—the defense rested and it became official that John would not take the stand.

The bulk of the evidence that Caserta submitted for the jury went uncontested by Brizek; the most important piece he objected to was a tape recording of Brejack interviewing Judy Chamberlain in which the rustling of papers can be heard. Earlier in the trial, Caserta had wondered whether the papers were indicative of Judy Chamberlain reading from prepared statements (which she denied). Judge Hull overruled the objection and the tape was found admissible.

With all of that settled, Hull announced that summations would be held the next day, and he asked Brizek to call the first of his four rebuttal witnesses to the stand. This was a sweet moment for the prosecution and a tense one for Caserta. Brizek's people were poised to clear the defense's red herring out of the water.

First up was Phillip Manetti, Jr. Rather than saying exactly who he was, Brizek asked him for his license plate number (402 KRX), what he often wore when he drove (a red bandanna), and the road he routinely took home from Willowbrook Mall (Route 23). Manetti had no recollection of a driver in front of him slamming on his brakes on June 22, 1981, nor did he remember having an altercation with anybody at the mall. It crippled one of Caserta's suggestions of who else might have murdered Candy that night.

Brizek next called Andrea Stanton to confirm the license plate number of the suspicious car that she spotted in the Willowbrook Mall. Satisfied with her response, the assistant prosecutor had the owner of that automobile take the stand.

Alex Stevens of Pompton Lake, New Jersey, was a mild-looking house painter who lacked the mien of a murderer. Stevens explained that in the early eighties he had routinely picked up his wife from work at the Willowbrook Mall. Because he was self-employed and put in irregular hours, Stevens often had to kill time in the parking lot as he waited for his wife's workday to end. Yes, he did at times sit in the car, playing around with the windows and people-watching, simply out of sheer boredom.

After Stevens told Caserta that he had never been contacted by the Wayne police, Brizek called Theresa Stevens to the stand, and she backed up her husband's testimony. In the end it became abundantly clear that both of the menacing people brought to life by Caserta's witnesses were harmless. While all of this still cast shadows of doubt on the original investigators (who failed to pursue these leads), ultimately it detracted from the defense's case.

With the evidential portion of the trial completed, Judge Hull dismissed the jurors and asked them to return at nine o'clock the next morning in order to hear the lawyers' summations. Once the jury box cleared, Caserta had a final opportunity to argue that "the jury be given the options that they would have been given had Mr. Short been prosecuted [in a timely manner]. My position is that the jury should be charged as though this case was being tried within the statute of limitations."

In other words, Caserta maintained that the jurors should have the opportunity of rendering a verdict on a charge of first- or second-degree manslaughter even though the statute had already expired on those offenses. After the judge assured Caserta that that would not happen, the defense attorney argued on. "I'm asking the Court to point out that the State's proof indicates that the defendant may have been with the victim just prior to her death and they were engaged in a violent argument," he pressed, contradicting a stand he had taken throughout the trial. "And if the jury finds the violent argument such that [Candy] was killed in the heat of blood, in the passion of the moment, then that would reduce a murder charge to manslaughter."

Brizek offered a long rebuttal against this, reasoning that from the nature of the injury—the victim being strangled and stabbed through the chest with a screwdriver—the murder "is a knowing and willful act by definition. You don't accidentally or recklessly stab somebody through the middle of the chest. So there would be no basis for instructing on reckless manslaughter or reckless aggravated manslaughter."

The judge listened to what both lawyers had to say, then announced his decision. It was a decision that he had reached before hearing these arguments. He planned on allowing the jury members to return a verdict of guilty or not guilty of murder only. They would be apprised of the situation in regard to the statute of limitations and informed that unless they believed, beyond a reasonable doubt, that John Short had purposely and knowingly committed the murder he should be found not guilty.

In adjourning court, Judge Hull announced that the sequestration ruling, which had kept Brejack and the Austins out of the courtroom so far, would be lifted for the lawyers' final statements. Neither man had a problem with that, and they both promised to be in court at nine the next morning.

CHAPTER
22

Steve Brizek wore his lucky necktie. He always selected the dark blue tie on summation days. For this, the trial's final day, the courtroom was packed with spectators who included Brizek's wife, parents, and mother-in-law. Not far away from them, like an esteemed family in a small-town church, the Austins occupied an entire pew-like row. Too keyed up to accomplish anything at the office, Brejack came to the courtroom at seven-thirty that morning and staked out a ringside seat for himself. Never big on discretion, he selected a second-row vantage point, eager to be up close and personal when his hard work finally paid off.

As certain as the investigator was of anything, he remained convinced that John Short was guilty. He also maintained an unfounded belief (especially since he had seen none of the trial) that the jurors would agree. As the trial's third week neared completion, excitement in the courtroom was running high. Nearly palpable tension between the Austins and Shorts could be sensed as members of both families warily checked one another out from opposite sides of the courtroom. Meeting under these macabre circumstances was something that neither family could have anticipated—not after the marriage or the murder.

When Caserta began his summation at a few minutes past nine o'clock on the morning of February 7th, the pressure level in the courtroom dropped considerably. The audience members could now focus their attention on the defense attorney instead of each other. He first reiterated that John had been mistreated by the police from the very moment they arrived on the scene at the Willowbrook Mall. "The Wayne police told him, 'You're the subject of the investigation. You're the suspect,' " Caserta told the jury, looking directly into their eyes, hoping to reach the conscience of at least one juror and make it impossible for him or her to find the defendant guilty. "Yet no investigation had been conducted on their part."

He went on to discuss the ineptitude of the Wayne detectives—"They ignored evidence, destroyed evidence, overlooked evidence," he passionately lectured. "And in nearly every instance it worked to John's detriment"— before time-tripping from the past to the present, to Brejack's rejuvenation of the investigation. After all, the doings of McCann and Wilson and Webster now amounted to ancient history. If Caserta was to win the jurors' sympathies, it would have to be at the expense of the most recent effort. In order to discredit it, he had to attack the prosecution at its core. He had to go after Brejack.

Portraying Brejack as a maverick desperate to reenter law enforcement with a splash—a fairly accurate depiction—Caserta stated that the investigator had taken the case on primarily because he'd be able to easily shape old hearsay and new misinformation against John. After discussing Brejack's ability to sway witnesses, Caserta launched into an impassioned diatribe against the vagaries of circumstantial evidence, citing the belief that the earth was flat as the ultimate circumstantial mistake: "If you take a narrow and restricted view of circumstances, your limited view forces you to believe something that's not true."

In much the same way as Brejack likened a circumstantial case to a length of chain, Caserta compared it to a paint-by-number painting. In this particular instance, he maintained, the little areas of color did not add up to a credible picture of guilt. He argued that, at the time of the murder, nobody had come forward and accused John of killing his wife, or even mentioned the fact that the defendant and victim had a bad marriage. In fact, Betty and Joe's recollection of the argument that had concluded with John promising to piss on Candy's grave didn't come to light until Brejack got started.

"I don't deny that the fight took place," Caserta earnestly pointed out, going on to explain that the family eventually became susceptible to suggestion. "That's not the defense position in this case. The point of the matter is that as time went on the fight's significance grew. [But] I don't blame Ms. Frank and Mr. Frank for that, not at all. Mr. Brejack gave them and the Austin family hope that Candy's death would somehow be explained."

He dismissed the State's theory that John had killed his wife because it would be cheaper than divorcing her— "What did John have at the time?" Caserta wanted to know. "A basement apartment and two pickup trucks?"— and he did not see Diane Lovejoy as a suitable motivation for a man to commit murder. Caserta characterized her as a "hooker," and held fast to the theory that Candy's death having come so close to John's lie about it was simply a horrible coincidence. "It was a rather bizarre situation," he contended. "Have you never in your life heard somebody say something and then it came true? Have you never heard of a circumstance where somebody predicted ill for a loved one, and, heaven help us, that person dropped dead? It happens. It's bizarre, but it happens. Right?"

The question was rhetorical. *These things do happen. Strange events can transpire.* Less mysterious, Caserta maintained, was the prosecution itself and the techniques it had employed to build a case against John. "Diane Lovejoy shows you the corruption of the prosecution of this case," he said. "People were put on the witness stand not to speak with you, not to tell you the truth, but to recite a rehearsed script. I hope you saw that, because it's as clear as the day is long."

He pointed out how Diane's telling of her nights with John Short had evolved, maintaining that Brejack originally had promised her that she would never have to appear in court and personally charmed her into making her statement. The way Caserta told it, the case had been built through emotional seduction and physical coercion. He continued to claim that Judy Chamberlain had read her statement from a script (ignoring her acknowledgment that the rustling of paper on the audio tape came from Brejack taking notes) and that Brejack ignored the original police work because it would have forced him to look beyond John Short for a suspect. Caserta expressed dismay at the fact that Brejack had managed to miss the names of people who could have supported John's innocence.

"But somehow, with his supercop talent, he decides to go and find, of all people, Barbara Capalbo," said Caserta, sounding sad and disgusted with this woman who he believed had lied on the stand. "And somehow he knew what a willing, cooperative witness Barbara Capalbo was going to be. Somehow he got Barbara Capalbo to take a light blue car in June of 1981 and call it a gold/brown car before this jury in 1989."

Point by point, Caserta dismantled the case that the State had constructed against John Short. He maintained that John had had no idea that David Jones lived on the same block as Susan Fishman until after he got there. He discussed the impossibility of committing a daylight murder in the parking lot of a well-trafficked shopping mall. Caserta pointed out that John Short's nervousness as he and Fred had approached Willowbrook Mall stemmed from the knowledge that the closer they got to their destination, the further they went from simply finding Candy's car broken down on the highway. And as for Fred's testimony about John knowing where the car was parked, the defense lawyer reiterated that none of this information had come out before Brejack began questioning people.

Perhaps hoping to compensate for having roughed up Fred Austin on the witness stand, Caserta swerved away from the subject at hand and offered an aside. "I hope you don't think that I ever meant to imply that Mr. Austin came here to lie to you," Caserta said, his voice dripping sincerity. "I told you at the beginning of this case that he's a good man, and I hope he's shown you just what a good man he is. I just have to go back to the fact that he's a father whose daughter was murdered brutally, and he has sat for years with no answer to that crime. And when he was asked questions by somebody who suggested answers to him, telling him that they could resolve his heartache, he adopted the position of George Brejack without even realizing it. That's what happened to Mr. Austin.

"And it's a shame that in order to obtain a conviction in a case, in order to make a comeback as a cop, that George Brejack would mislead somebody this far. I don't know. . . ." Caserta's voice markedly trailed off, as if he were in search of a rationale. "George is not—you saw him on the witness stand—he's not a bad person. I don't think he set out to hurt the Austins. But the fact of the matter is I think his overzealousness and selfishness perhaps brought him to the point where he saw a case coming together and he pushed it a little too far and a little bit too much."

After this relatively sympathetic description of two people whom Caserta had already painted as being pivotal in what might turn out to be a gross miscarriage of justice, he turned back to tearing down the State's case against his client. He pointed out that investigators found no direct evidence—hair, blood, skin—linking John to the murder, then attempted to refute one of the most damaging bits of evidence: the keys beneath Candy's dead body.

Caserta laughed at the notion that killers always leave

something behind, likening it to "a dime-store novel" plot and insisting that there was no way to truly prove who owned those keys. Despite witnesses who maintained that they belonged to John, the lawyer insisted that the keys could very well have been picked up and used by Candy. "Maybe Jesse was playing with Candy's key chain, the flip-flop sandal somehow fell off, and Candy took the [T-shirt-shaped] key fob and used it," Caserta hypothesized with a shrug. "And that's all there is to it."

He emphasized the importance of Brizek proving all of his points beyond a reasonable doubt, warned the jury members that they would not be able to consider manslaughter as a charge, and punched holes through the circumstantial evidence that the State built its case on. "They've thrown in some ringers, some icing on their cake, some things that really shouldn't be there," Caserta said, ticking off the cross, reports of John's uncaring attitude at the funeral, the bruises on Candy's arm. "Candy married John Short on a certain date; after that date we saw bruises on her that were—in the exact words as Mr. Brizek asked the question—'not similar to bruises they had seen on Candy before the marriage.' So what? What does that have to do with anything, except to suggest to you, 'My God, John was beating his wife, he probably did kill her, we can't let him get away with that murder.' *There's no evidence in the case that that ever happened.*"

He railed against Brizek "daring to question the way another man grieves" and deemed the inclusion of the cross as evidence to be "despicable." "To say that because he fashioned a cross with his own hands means that he didn't care is horrible," Caserta continued, going on to question the assumption that John Short is a master craftsman based on the fact that his company constructed Lambert's house. "When Mr. Brizek was done, you would think John Short could have carved and *should have* carved an ornate cross out of heavy lumber, when all he did was put something on the grave to mark it so it wouldn't be bare. And sure, in 1989 people can come to this courtroom and say, 'How dare you do such a thing?' But who are they to point a finger at anybody?"

Reaching a conclusion, Caserta used his witnesses—admitting that they may have seemed a little bit silly—to show how little effort had been put into finding any other suspect. "The failure of the Wayne Police Department gives the prosecutor an out," Caserta said. "It makes Detective Brejack look good 'cause he can say that he showed up the Wayne Police Department. And for everything that's lacking in the case, the prosecutor can say, 'Look, don't blame us, don't blame my staff. Wayne didn't do it, it's their fault.' But he still has to prove his case to you, *no matter whose fault it is that he doesn't have a case.*"

The defense attorney maintained that witness testimony was scripted by Brejack and Brizek, then went on to explain the importance of viewing each piece of circumstantial evidence independently, inspecting the information from every possible angle and taking none of it for granted. He emphasized the seriousness of their decisions, and the impact that it would have on John Short. "Don't let [Brejack and Brizek] persuade you, ladies and gentlemen," Caserta pleaded. "Don't let them use you as a vehicle to cover their own inadequacies. You see what happened here: They negligently allowed the statute of limitations to expire on all of the charges but murder. They made a last-ditch effort to save face and salvage this case."

He got close to the jurors and spoke to them in a confidential, intimate manner, as if they were all on the same side. "But, ladies and gentlemen, before you tell John Short that he murdered Candy, do what you were brought here to do, what you swore on this Bible to do. Consider the evidence. Look for the facts. Tell Detective Brejack and Mr. Brizek, 'We're sorry, fellows, but you're not going to use us to cover up your failings; that isn't going to happen with this jury in this case. We're not going to convict John Short on this kind of evidence.'

"When you think about that, ladies and gentlemen, remember this: John Short was indicted in this case and charged with killing Candy, murdering Candy. He replied to that by saying he was not guilty. He is not guilty. He did not kill Candy. He did not kill Candy, and they can't prove that he did."

Save for a quick "thank you," that was how Caserta concluded his summation. The courtroom remained quiet. No doubt the spectators were considering what he had said and wondering how they would be reacting to it if they were sitting in the jury box. As for the man whose freedom hinged on the jury's decision, he remained expressionless, appearing dazed and distant from the critical argument that had just been presented.

At the prosecution table, Brizek shuffled through some papers and prepared to make his statement. Before he had a chance to rise, however, the judge called for a mid-morning recess, and told the jurors to file out ahead of the room full of spectators. Both groups were grateful for the opportunity to stretch their legs and have a smoke before Brizek launched into his summation.

Steve Brizek is a small and unprepossessing man. His exceptionally pale complexion frequently prompts colleagues to ask whether or not he's feeling all right. This irks Brizek, as he had grown up hearing the same question from his mother on a regular basis. Once he enters a courtroom, however, the assistant prosecutor is a powerhouse. His demeanor could be described as refined and polite and gentlemanly, but he also possesses an imposing side that reveals itself when least expected. Intelligent and quick-witted, he makes a good case for not judging people by initial physical impression.

In summations, Brizek tends to be particularly strong. A loner by nature, he shines when given the opportunity to speak solo in front of the court. His tone on this particular day was eloquent and his physical presence suddenly seemed imposing. It was the impression he intended to leave the jurors with this afternoon, as he fingered the lucky necktie and launched into his final monologue. It would be his last opportunity to bring John Short to justice.

Brizek began by pointing out the validity of circumstantial evidence, speaking of how it can prove more than direct evidence, because of the many pieces that fit together and present a stronger image than any single eyewitness's report could provide. He also reminded the jurors that the State's job was not to prove *how* John had killed his wife, but only *that* he killed her. After establishing that, Brizek went on to suggest a possible scenario for what had occurred in Willowbrook's parking lot. He described John murdering Candy, Barbara Capalbo witnessing the preliminary beating from a distance, John leaving the body on the floor of the car and arranging for its eventual discovery.

Standing at the front of the courtroom and facing the jury, Brizek asked them to consider the facts as a whole, not to view each one independently as Caserta had suggested. He wanted them to see the trial's outcome as a completed jigsaw puzzle. "There are thousands of pieces, and the pictures that these puzzles portray can be rather complex," he said. "There'll be a picture of a forest with hundreds of thousands of leaves. If you take one of those pieces and determine whether it will be useful in assembling the puzzle, your answer is going to be no. It's the same thing with this case. First put all of the pieces together. Stand back and see if the picture that I suggest those pieces portray is actually there." He hesitated dramatically, then added, "The picture that I suggest is that the defendant murdered his wife on June 22, 1981."

Like a father doing a jigsaw with his young son, Brizek intended to help the jury through and show them where all the pieces fit. If it went the way he hoped, the jurors' job would be simple. The completed puzzle's picture would irrefutably condemn Short. Brizek eloquently described the relationship between John and Diane, explaining John's desire to spend the weekend with her. "He's *enchanted* by Diane," the prosecutor said, savoring the word like a sweet. "He lamented, 'God, where were you *five years ago*?' Now, did he just pull that figure out of a hat, or is there significance to that figure, *five* years ago?" He paused as if waiting for a response, then answered the question himself. "It's the latter.

"Donna Olson Frangipane, John Short's first wife, testified here, and she told you that she and John Short separated in, I think it was, October of 1976. That's about five years before John Short met Diane. What was John Short telling Diane Lovejoy? *God, where were you five years ago?* In other words, 'Why couldn't I have met you after I left my first wife, *before I met Candy*.' "

He maintained that Diane remembered incorrectly where John wanted to take her for the weekend—Brizek believed that it was the Ocean Grove house rather than a place in the Hamptons that didn't exist—and that those plans were real. He rehashed the testimony from Will Lambert, Dennis King, and Dan Solowe—all of whom confirmed John's instant attraction to Diane. "Joseph Frank said that the defendant was all pumped up," Brizek related. "His ego was inflated by what he told Frank about Diane Lovejoy. There can be no question of the defendant's feelings for her. There can be no question that his head was turned, that he was prepared to do some rather strange things. Here you have a man, a married man with a child, and he's making plans to go away for the weekend, to abandon that wife and that child and spend the weekend with this new love interest. That's how powerful her effect upon him was."

Brizek next went on to describe how dreary life on Joralemon Street had become. The proof of it echoed in what John told Diane Lovejoy: "The defendant had so little feeling for his wife that he could make up a story about her being dead," Brizek said, feigning amazement.

"He was prepared to pretend for the night that his wife was murdered, and that caused him no discomfort. [The action] speaks volumes of his disenchantment with Candy. It shows his utter disdain and absence of any consideration for her, for their life together, for their relationship."

The words were a tour de force, designed to destroy John Short. After recalling the argument that had taken place in front of Betty and Joe, and emphasizing the rickety condition of the marriage, Brizek turned to the cross. For sheer physical impact, it was the strongest piece of evidence introduced. Flimsy and sloppily constructed, it had been an inexcusable way for Candy to be remembered. Whether or not John really was a master carpenter—which Caserta had insisted he was not—nobody would want a loved one's death to be marked with such a shabby memorial.

"It speaks clearly and powerfully," Brizek said of the rickety wooden slats. "It's as if the defendant had written in his diary how he truly felt for his wife. It's as though he had written in his diary that he had contempt for his wife and chose not to remember her or her memory. It's a testament, not to his love, but to his disenchantment, disdain, and absence of feeling for his wife Candy."

After reminding the jurors about the witnesses who had recalled seeing bruises on Candy, he tied all of the information together. "What you have here are the circumstantial facts presented by a number of witnesses," he explained. "You don't look at them individually. You put them together. You assemble that puzzle and you stand back. You can't help but reach one conclusion, and it's the incriminating conclusion. It's the conclusion that pointed the finger at John Short and nobody else as his wife's killer."

If Brizek's summation were a play, the curtain would have just come down on the close of the first act. Brizek would be bathing in applause prior to starting the second act with a discourse on the opportunity that Short had had to kill his wife. He discussed all of the fine points of the timing: how long the murder would have taken, how far Short would have had to drive from the mall to his parents' house, how he could have cleaned himself up and still made it to David Jones's house by nine o'clock. This chronology provided the nuts and bolts that held together the more speculative elements of his presentation. It was a brief, fairly dry listing of information that laid the groundwork for Brizek's finale, for his third act, for his reciting of the factors that he believed made it likely that John Short was the murderer.

But before that could begin, the judge called a recess for lunch. Brizek ate alone, nibbling on today's bran muffin while reviewing notes and tuning his mind to the ongoing performance. He spoke barely a word to anyone before returning to the courtroom, eagerly picking up where he left off.

Standing directly across from the jurors, Brizek began what resembled the final act of his American tragedy. It was certainly the most important part of his summation. It would bring together any disparate elements and provide a convincing overview of why John had to have been the killer.

He went through the testimonial highlights, recounting information given by Kevin Johnson (the bank vice-president to whom John inadvertently mentioned going with Candy to the mall on the night of her murder), Detective Jack Meurer (the police photographer who first saw John's keys beneath Candy's body), and Barbara Capalbo (who claimed to have witnessed the fight that preceded Candy's death).

He reminded the jury of the four witnesses who recognized the T-shirt-shaped key fob, and explained why it was important. "What is the significance of the fact that this is John Short's set of keys to Candy's car?" he asked the jury as well as himself. "Well, as I mentioned earlier, it places the defendant at the scene of the crime. But it does even more. It provides a reason for John Short to tell three lies to the Wayne police, three lies in a very short space [of time] during the interview that was video-taped on November 4, 1981."

Referring to the interrogation, the final meeting that took place between John and the Wayne detectives, Brizek ticked off a trio of instances in which the truth had been evaded: John's claim that the keys discovered beneath Candy had belonged to her, his maintaining that the T-shirt-shaped fob had always been on Candy's key ring, and a statement that they were the only set of keys for Candy's car. Reminding the jury that the keys found beneath Candy were duplicates, he made sure they understood that a flip-flop-shaped fob was attached to Candy's key ring along with the original set of keys.

Next Brizek turned to the blanket that had covered Candy's dead body. He refreshed the jurors' memories about Judy Chamberlain recognizing the blanket that had always been stored in the trunk. And, the reasoning went, if she had known it was in the trunk John would have as well. No stranger would think to cover his victim with a blanket that just might be in the trunk of a car.

Recounting other curious facts that pointed to John Short, Brizek spoke as if he had limitless pieces with which to construct his puzzle: the car had been moved from the area where Candy always parked; Candy had inexplicably changed her pattern of taking Jesse wherever she went and chose instead to leave the little girl with Betty Frank; John was known for wearing T-shirts—"It was part of his *uniform*," Brizek elaborated to the jury—and the man Barbara Capalbo had spotted was wearing a T-shirt. Most incriminating of all, perhaps, was the fact that Candy had not been robbed or raped. Her purse was open but credit cards and a few dollars remained in place, and nothing of value was stolen.

The jurors could easily ascend with Brizek to his next plateau of reason. "What is involved, then, if we don't have a robbery and rape?" the assistant prosecutor wanted to know, as he led the jurors through the gruesome details of the strangulation and stabbing. "We have a killer who intended to cause serious bodily injury to Candy. He purposely and knowingly strangled her to death. That he purposely and knowingly thrust a screwdriver-type object into her chest speaks volumes. It indicates the killer's frame of mind. This all points to the fact that the killer was emotionally involved with Candy. He was angry at her. He was filled with enough hate, contempt, and disdain to undergo the risk of committing this act without the motive of robbery or rape. *The killer knew her.*"

Ironically, there was also a tiny act of mercy attached to the killing, and that too pinned the defendant as the murderer. When Fred and John found Candy's body, specks of dirt covered her clothing and the pullover shirt was yanked up to her neck. Obviously she had been dragged into the wooded area that surrounded the mall—presumably to be abandoned—yet her killer had thought better of the act and decided to return Candy's body to the car. "Candy Short was the mother of John Short's daughter; he was not so callous as to let her remain in that dirt-covered area," Brizek said, pointing out that the murderer had eventually experienced feelings of guilt. "He took pains to see that she was properly attended to and disposed of. A stranger would not have done that. But the arrangements were made by Candy's killer in such a way so as not to cast suspicion on him. Arranging for someone or himself to 'discover the body in the car' would accomplish two things for the killer: Her body would be properly disposed of, and suspicion would be cast away [from him] as the killer."

As Brizek spoke, he increasingly lived up to the promise that had been made prior to his summation. Piece by piece, he put together the puzzle for the jurors, and a picture began to form. The picture, he believed, would finally be complete after the behavior of the defendant had been explored.

Brizek explained John's desire first to cancel his meeting with Jones, then to postpone it as far back as possible. He reminded them how long it took Short to drive to the meeting, and how familiar he supposedly had been with the area around Jones's house. "When he tells you in his statement to Detective Webster that it took him an hour and ten minutes, when he tells Will Lambert that it took him two hours, he's lying," stated Brizek. "He's trying to account for the time he can not account for. During that period of time he was killing his wife, arranging for the disposal of her body, driving down to his [parents'] house, washing up, changing his clothing, composing himself, and then driving to Jones's house."

In his recounting of the events that had taken place on the eve of Candy's death, Brizek increasingly personalized his references. He kept inserting John Short's name into the sentences, reiterating the fact that it was this man who had murdered his wife on the night of June 22, 1981. Like a masterful storyteller, Brizek wove the tale of what had gone on in the pitch-black parking lot. He explained it in such a way that the jurors immersed themselves in his words and got lost in the campfire drama: "John Short says, 'There's the car. Back there.' Mr. Austin looks in the rearview mirror. He can't see a thing. They swing the car around, but he still sees nothing. . . ."

A few minutes later, shaking his head in disbelief, Brizek confidentially recounted an exchange between Fred Austin and Pat Caserta. It had centered on how Fred was able to find the car after he'd called the police. The gist of Caserta's claim had been that if Fred was able to find it then, John could have found it the first time. Ever resourceful, Brizek took that bit of testimony and twisted it around, turned it against the man he hoped to convict. "Once you knew where the car was, you *could* find it," Brizek announced. "But that's just the point. *You had to know where the car was.* John Short knew where the car was because he put it there."

He reviewed testimony from expert witnesses who had reported on the parking lot's darkness, then reminded the jurors that John Short had basically destroyed the crime scene when he smashed open the passenger-side window. The man who saw him do it, Fred Austin, was badly maligned by Caserta's questioning, and Brizek now came to the witness's defense. Parroting what Austin had said on the stand, he pointed out that lucidity could hardly have been expected so soon after the discovery of his daughter's body.

Brizek also came to the defense of George Brejack. Brizek may have sensed that the jurors found the investigator a bit overbearing, and felt a need to play down his inherent abrasiveness. "Investigator Brejack's eighteen years of law enforcement experience serves him well," Brizek said, recalling how the investigator had asked Austin to meet him for breakfast at the Tick Tock Diner. "He knew he had a witness with something on his chest, a subject that he was reluctant to broach in front of his wife."

Cutting to the Willowbrook Mall, to Brejack and the Austins retracking the path that Fred and John had taken, Brizek insisted that Fred's version was the true version of what had happened that night in 1981. "The suggestion that Mr. Austin is fabricating this story, that he's a liar, that he's befuddled, is preposterous," said the assistant prosecutor. "You saw him testify. You were able to analyze his demeanor. He was frank, he was honest, he was straightforward." The person who had lied, Brizek added, was John Short.

As the assistant prosecutor wound up his summation, he turned to the case that had been presented by Pat Caserta and attempted to shake it at its foundation. He began with John's failure to personally approach the woman at the Belle Maid and ask her to vouch for his presence in the store. Then he dismissed the witnesses who claimed to have seen Candy's car near the mall in the late afternoon (any time period other than the hours after six-thirty, Brizek insisted, is irrelevant), and turned to the supposedly shady people who might have been potential suspects but were all repudiated by the State.

Before finishing, Brizek addressed an important point that had barely come up in the trial: the particulars of the charge. He saved this for the end, knowing that it would be important for the jurors to have it fresh in their minds when they made their decision. He explained that "knowing" and "purposeful" were the two requirements for charging one with murder in the state of New Jersey, adding that Candy had not been killed recklessly or in the heat of passion. "So it doesn't matter that the statute of limitations eliminates the lesser degrees of homicide," he said. "The only charge this evidence would support is a charge of purposeful and knowing murder, the charge which is set forth in the indictment."

He characterized Caserta's allegations that the State had piloted a corrupt investigation as "comments you would expect from one flailing about in the face of overwhelming evidence of guilt." As far as the corruption went, Brizek attacked the charge head-on. "If it is corruption to interview witnessses and discuss their testimony with them, and ready them for the surely unsettling task of testifying in court, then the State's corrupt. If it is corruption to have witnesses continue to reach into their memories, to rekindle long dormant thoughts, to conjure up long-ago events, to encourage them to think and to ponder and testify to their best recollection of the truth, then the State is corrupt."

Dismissing the other accusations brought forth by Caserta about the investigator and what seemed to be conveniently jogged memories, he allowed, "Knowing that Mr. Caserta could not have meant what he said, no offense could possibly be taken by the State."

For the final piece of his gruesome but convincing puzzle, Brizek turned to the cross and emoted disgust as he picked it up. "John Short had carpenters and craftsmen at his disposal," Brizek said piously. "He could have chosen to use his own skills as a craftsman to bless his wife's grave with a finely wrought marker of his own making. But he chose not to do that. What he chose to do instead was an insult to her memory."

Brizek maneuvered his way to the jury box and held the cross in his outstretched hands as if it were a baby's coffin. "He withheld from her the last thing, the only thing he had left to give her, and that is the benefit of his skills and resources as a builder. John Short did indeed keep the promise he made to his wife a few weeks before he killed her, the promise that Joseph and Betty Frank heard him make. But, what's more to the point, Candy has also kept the promise she made to him in return."

Brizek hesitated dramatically. If he had looked into the courtroom he would have noticed several of the women crying, but he didn't. Brizek focused every bit of his attention on the jurors, as he closed with a pair of final, strong sentences: "On this cross John Short wrote in some sort of black paint, 'Candice Carol Austin Short—1957 to 1981—Wife and Mother.' The only thing he left off was the word, 'Victim.' " Brizek gently laid the cross down in front of the jurors, leaving them with a strong, highly emotional physical memento of the murder.

The State rested, and later that evening so did Steve Brizek. For the first time in more than a month he slept long and sound, satisfied with the job he had just completed.

CHAPTER
23

Brizek had laid the cross down like a gauntlet in front of the jury box, practically daring those inside it to find John Short innocent. A pall fell over the twelve men and women as they confronted their overwhelming responsibility. The jurors would soon begin the grim business of deciding another man's fate, a job that everybody in the box dreaded completing.

Because Brizek finished his summation late in the day, they had one night in which to consider their responsibility, to mull over the things they had seen and heard during the last three weeks, to begin formulating opinions on the future of John Short. The glamour and attention that initially made this task seem appealing quickly evaporated as they were dismissed from the courtroom. The dozen jurors headed for their cars, retreating home to safe places where their decisions had less immediate impact upon the lives of others.

A day later, on Wednesday, February 8th, at nine o'clock in the morning, Judge Hull had a few thoughts to impart before the jurors began grappling with the evidence. Prior to telling the jurors that only a charge of guilty or not guilty of murder would be accepted, Hull gave them a lengthy explanation as to what would have to be present for the charge to stick. "In order for you to find the defendant guilty of murder, the State must first establish, beyond a reasonable doubt, that the killing of Candice Short was committed by the defendant and that it was done purposely or knowingly," he explained. "If the State has proved the essential elements of the offense beyond a reasonable doubt, the defendant must be found guilty of that offense regardless of his motive or lack of motive."

He defined the lesser charges for the jurors and reminded them that if they were to find Short guilty of those, he would go free due to the statute of limitations. After selecting Philip Cohen as the jury's foreman (he spent the trial in the number-one seat), the judge notified the jurors that they would have access to any tapes and transcripts they might need. At nine-forty Hull completed his charge by saying, "Will you please step back into the jury room? As soon as we gather up all of the exhibits, one of the officers will signal you to start deliberating."

The jurors solemnly departed, feeling a bit dazed by the task they were being asked to perform. They would go on to spend two full days deliberating, arguing over testimony, struggling to reach a decision.

At around ten-thirty A.M., when they began discussing the trial for the first time, there were many opinions as to exactly what had transpired in the parking lot of Willowbrook Mall on the night of June 22, 1981. In order to resolve certain issues, the jurors made written requests to see the videotape of John's interrogation and asked for read-backs of testimony made by Will Lambert, Diane Lovejoy, Barbara Capalbo, Fred Austin, and Kevin Johnson. During that first day of deliberation, however, only the first two read-backs were available.

Fresh from the courtroom, before hearing any of the testimony for a second time, the jurors casually discussed the issues, then voted on Short's guilt. Several of them could not say for certain that John Short had committed the murder. They voted against convicting him.

By Thursday morning, however, following a day of examining the fine points of the trial—including the defendant's refusal to testify on his own behalf—the jurors agreed on one thing: John Short had killed his wife. Still unresolved was the more complex and crucial issue of whether or not the act had been committed knowingly and purposely. Surprisingly, the factual discrepancies in the testimony of prosecution witnesses were easily overlooked by most of the jurors. They basically regarded the changes in testimony as minor revisions in recall that were inevitable considering the amount of time that had elapsed between the murder and the arrest.

Nevertheless, three people spent most of Thursday trying to convince the other jurors that John Short should not be found guilty of murder. "It was a moment of insanity," one of them argued. "He beat her and strangled her in a fit of rage, but he did not want Candy dead."

"Look at all the circumstantial evidence," maintained another juror who had already decided John was guilty. "It's not just one thing that points to Short. It's his behavior, the cross that he made for his wife's grave, the fact that he couldn't possibly have gotten lost in West Orange. And if he's innocent, why would he have lied about so many things?"

Rather than trying to answer the question, the jurors took another vote, and remained hung. Two women, both of whom found it impossible to enter a murder verdict, broke down and began crying. But they stuck to their beliefs and would not let the others sway them.

Deliberation proceeded that way until after the lunch break. Then, in the afternoon, a very clear-cut rationale emerged. "Yes," one juror explained, "it's possible that John and Candy engaged in an argument at Willowbrook. And maybe things *did* get out of control, John became more violent than he intended, and that's why he smashed Candy's head against the dashboard. But strangling her? I doubt if anybody can do that without meaning it. And what ultimately makes me find him guilty of murder is the fact that he took a screwdriver and pushed it through her chest. That's one thing you wouldn't do unless you definitely wanted the other person dead."

The logic was difficult to refute, and in the end nobody did. Late on Thursday afternoon, the jurors reached a unanimous decision. They could have passed the information on to Judge Hull and had their foreman read the verdict within minutes, but they thought better of it. All the jurors wanted one more night to think it over. Then, if they could still live with that decision on Friday, a final verdict would be tendered.

The next morning the jurors repeated the vote, and once again the decision was unanimous. Philip Cohen notified Judge Hull that they'd come to a decision, and the family members, reporters, and curious spectators were called back to the courtroom before the jury returned. Looking out at the assembled group, Hull said sternly, "Let me just go over a couple of ground rules before we take the verdict. Everyone who is here, waiting for the verdict, must remain seated until all of the jurors leave the courtroom and leave the fifth floor. If anybody can't abide by that request, please leave now."

Nobody made a move toward the door, and Hull continued, "The second request is that I do not expect an outcry from any spectators, regardless of whatever the verdict may be." He hesitated before calling to the bailiff: "Okay. Let's have the jury."

Looking the worse for wear, the jurors emerged from the cinder-blocked conference room and took their places in the jury box. The foreman was asked to read his verdict, and Cohen stood up. Speaking in a clear and confident voice, he said one word: "Guilty."

Despite Judge Hull's request, emotions were uncontainable. A victorious cheer rose from the section where the Austin family members sat. The two Short women cried with sorrow. Brejack cradled his head in his hands and he, too, burst into tears. His were tears of joy, tears of thankfulness, the tears that come from beating the odds. George Brejack experienced the long sought-after sensation of redemption. He got up, made his way to the prosecution's table, and hugged Steve Brizek. Right next to them, in the defense's area, Pat Caserta was silent; he felt that his client had been dealt an unfair hand, that the jurors had been swayed more by emotions than by the facts. John Short, for the first time during the entire trial, revealed the sorts of feelings that the jurors had been looking for. Hands folded in front of him on the counsel table, Short slowly lowered his head and cried out, "Oh, no! . . ." He sobbed softly and kept repeating, "I didn't do it! I didn't kill her! . . ."

Judge Hull banged the gavel for order and the court clerk polled the jury, requesting that its members stand up and state whether or not they agreed with the verdict. They all answered positively. Judge Hull then asked Brizek for his position regarding bail. Considering that the two hundred and fifty thousand dollars in existing bail had kept Short from taking off during the trial, Brizek left that decision up to the court. Hull decided to keep him on bail, leaving Short free to go home. Visibly trembling, he hastily exited the courtroom without saying a word to anybody.

Walking out of the courtroom, Short happened to see George Brejack and called him a "rotten bastard." A few minutes later, en route to his car, he encountered Joe Frank and stuck up his middle finger. Then Short slid behind the wheel and retreated to his room at the Howard Johnson's motel.

Going from the courthouse to his office, Steve Brizek was stopped by Helen Austin, who expressed concern for Jesse's well-being as long as John was on the street. The assistant prosecutor agreed with her and took steps to have the bail revoked. With Short's resigned cooperation, investigators retrieved him from the motel room and brought him back to court. Despite Caserta's objection, Hull granted Brizek's motion to revoke the bail. A guard then led a whimpering John Short off to the Passaic County Jail, where he would await his sentencing.

Before that, though, came the most touching moment of the trial. It happened in the courtroom, soon after Short had left. His mother Adele and Candy's mother, Helen, hugged each other and cried for the children that they had lost. Between the tears, Adele said, "I was really sorry for you."

When a reporter expressed surprise at the compassion that the two women had for one another, Helen looked up at him and said, "I always liked her. We share a granddaughter, you know." Mentioning Jesse reminded Helen of something else, and for some reason she felt compelled to share this with the reporter. "I still have to tell John's daughter. She doesn't know whether to love him or hate him, and I won't tell her either way."

With that Fred took Helen's arm, and the Austins left the courthouse. Reporters followed them into the street, wanting comments, but the couple didn't feel much like talking. Grateful to Brejack for solving the crime and ending their speculation, Helen and Fred Austin now wanted to get on with their lives and continue raising their granddaughter.

Between February 10th and March 31st friends and relatives of James, Adele, and John Short embarked on an intense letter-writing campaign. They requested that Judge Hull show leniency in the sentencing of John. Judy's ten-year-old son, Brant, wrote an impassioned plea in a grade-schooler's awkward print: "Now listen, Judge," it concluded, "he is a caring father, and I don't see how he would kill someone. I think he is inasent [sic]." Unbidden by anybody, Jesse also wrote something that pertained to her father. A school essay entitled "Jim's Mistake," it described a woman being murdered by her husband, though the names John and Candy did not appear in it. Both pieces of work, along with the letters, were emotionally stirring, yet they would all be ignored by Hull. He knew better than to assign much weight to such efforts.

He allowed both lawyers to plead for harsh and lenient sentences, and agreed to hear what the defendant himself had to say. Dressed in the same blue suit that he wore for most of the trial, John nervously approached the bench. He spoke in a small, trembling voice and already seemed to have been beaten down by the correctional system. "Well, to begin with, your Honor," he said, "it's the first time I've been through something like this, and it's quite overwhelming. With all I've been through in the past eight years, I still say I'm innocent. I did not kill my wife Candice. I do not know who did it, and I plan to appeal this. I think that if I had more experience with this type of courtroom setting and was less nervous, the trial would have been more in my favor."

John told the judge that he had been a good and responsible father to Jesse, that he had tried to do his best under adverse circumstances. He claimed to have had a good relationship with the Austins until Brejack got involved; then John brought James and Adele Short into the discussion. "My parents will probably not be alive by the time I get out of prison," John said, "and that's very hard for me to accept. Also, my children will grow up without me to guide them. It's hard to tell a five-year-old from behind a jailhouse window why you can't come home. And I can't imagine how these children are going to react to this as they get older.

"I had so many more things I got to say, but they've gone out of my mind completely. Please try to take these things into consideration, your Honor. Thank you."

After hearing everything that the defense attorney, defendant, and assistant prosecutor had to say, Judge Hull began his own speech, defining the terms of various sentences and offering his opinion that Fred Austin's testimony was the most damaging. "Ultimately, Mr. Austin was guided to the area by the defendant," Hull said, "and he came upon the car where his daughter's body was found. The defendant told him where the car was that could not be seen by anyone else, except the person who had put it in that position."

He pointed out the mitigating factor that John had basically led a law-abiding life before and after this incident, so he chose a relatively light sentence, considering the severity of the charge. "Mr. Short will be sentenced to the custody of the Commissioner of the Department of Corrections for a term of thirty years," decreed Hull. "He will be required to serve fifteen years of this sentence before being eligible for parole."

John Short nodded and told the judge that he understood this, before he was led away and returned to Trenton State Prison, where he was to continue serving his sentence.

Epilogue

Even as a pair of guards transported John Short to prison, he proclaimed his innocence. With that in mind, it's no surprise that he challenged the conviction that had been handed down in 1989. On Friday, July 13, 1991, three appeals court judges heard the plea of Short's public defender. The strategy of his appeal centered around the fact that seven years had elapsed between the time of the murder and the trial. Using a rationale that had already been unsuccessfully employed by Pat Caserta, the attorney argued that this had hampered Short's defense and accounted for the jury finding him guilty. While the State offered no explanation for the delay, the judges agreed that it had done nothing to substantially undermine the case for John Short's innocence. The thirty-year prison sentence was upheld, although supposedly John is now planning a Supreme Court appeal.

One person who found herself pleased to see him remaining in prison was Helen Austin, a woman whose life had been shattered by Candy's murder. At the time of the appeal, she was still recovering from yet another tragedy: In December of 1990, Fred Austin died of complications brought on by heart disease. Only sixty-six years old, Fred had gone through a decade of slow physical deterioration that seemed to have been triggered by the killing of his youngest daughter.

Twelve-year-old Jesse had assumed the role of a fourth child to Fred and Helen, as the Austins gained custody of her after John's arrest. She is an intelligent, exuberant girl who has followed in her Aunt Jeanne's footsteps by becoming a member of Belleville's cheerleading squad. Even as Jesse was establishing herself in the new community, however, additional uprooting was in the offing. Soon after Fred's death, Helen sold their house and left the town in which she had spent most of her life. Uncomfortable living alone in a place that was filled with so many bittersweet memories, she and Jesse moved into a vacation home that Jeanne and John Suarez own at the Jersey shore. Ironically, they do not live far from John Short's wife Judy.

John and Judy have remained married, and she continues to occupy the Ocean Grove home with her two biological children. Members of the Short family (including John) elected not to be interviewed for this book, so current details on them are sketchy. Most of John's old friends—people like Steve Gottlieb, Louie Derringer, and Will Lambert—have given up drinking and womanizing; they now have no contact with him. Jesse was brought to see John in jail at least one time (James and Adele Short, who currently live in a central New Jersey retirement community, took her) and the Austins were visibly upset about it.

Of the Wayne policemen, only Andrew Webster remains on the force (Billy McCann died of a heart attack, and Jim Wilson retired). He is still a patrol sergeant. Max Swathmore, Brejack's old nemesis from the Passaic County Prosecutor's Office, retired in 1990 and John Nativo replaced him as the chief.

Pat Caserta continues to practice law out of an office in downtown Paterson, New Jersey. He made the local papers on the afternoon of June 21, 1991, for representing a man accused of stabbing to death his infant son. For reasons that he refuses to divulge, Caserta played no part in mounting John Short's appeal.

As for George Brejack, he is still a member of the Major Crimes Unit at the Passaic County Prosecutor's

Office. The on-the-job respect that he had hoped to get by solving the Candy Short mystery continues to elude him, though his rank has been upgraded to lieutenant and the big cases still come his way. Having split up with Lisa Clarke, Brejack now devotes more time than ever to law enforcement. United by their success on the Candy Short murder, he and Steve Brizek have forged an ongoing partnership. Since John Short's conviction, they've worked together on several investigations. As of this writing, the two of them are attempting to solve a multiple murder in which a family of deaf mutes were brutally stabbed in Paterson.

Predictably, Brejack believes that he can piece it together.